MIDLOTHIAN PUBLIC LIBRARY

3 1614 00097 1656

W9-CNZ-690

MIDLOTHIAN
PUBLIC LIBRARY

Midlothian
Public Library

□ □ □

14701 S. Kenton Ave.
Midlothian, IL 60445

DEMCO

AMERICAN DISASTERS

EDITED BY STEVEN BIEL

AMERICAN DISASTERS

MIDLOTHIAN PUBLIC LIBRARY
14701 S. KENTON AVE.
MIDLOTHIAN, IL 60445

New York University Press • *New York and London*

NEW YORK UNIVERSITY PRESS
New York and London

© 2001 by New York University
All rights reserved

Library of Congress Cataloging-in-Publication Data
American disasters / edited by Steven Biel.
p. cm.
Includes index.
ISBN 0–8147–1345–9 (cloth : alk. paper)
ISBN 0–8147–1346–7 (pbk. : alk. paper)
1. Disasters—United States. 2. Disasters—Social aspects—
United States. 3. Disasters—United States—Psychological
aspects. 4. National characteristics, American.
5. United States—Social conditions. 6. United States—
History—Anecdotes. I. Biel, Stephen, 1960–
E179 .A494 2001
973—dc21   2001004145

New York University Press books are printed on acid-free paper,
and their binding materials are chosen for strength and durability.

Manufactured in the United States of America

10 9 8 7 6 5 4 3 2

Contents

Introduction

On the Titanic Research and Recovery Expedition and the Production of Disasters

Steven Biel

I SEEM TO recall having been at sea in August 1998, hovering around 41°43' north latitude, 49°56' west longitude (although I'll admit it all looked the same to me), with the Titanic Research and Recovery Expedition. I hesitate because later I watched the Discovery Channel's documentary on the expedition—originally broadcast live on August 16, 1998—and it bore only the most superficial resemblance to what I think I experienced. The fact that I didn't appear on the show partially explains my doubts; since TV was the ultimate purpose of the expedition, my nonappearance at least hints at my nonpresence. But I knew early on that I was a backup—a potential talking head whose head would talk only if the live feed from the bottom of the ocean failed. If the live feed from the top of the ocean had failed, too, there were potential talking heads standing by in a studio in Secaucus, New Jersey, to help fill the two hours.

In any event, our appearance, contingent on technological failure, would never have come across the airwaves as evidence of technological failure. And this, more than my nonappearance on television, is the reason for my existential uncertainty. The August 16 broadcast is an unambiguous story of technological triumph that runs counter to the murkier reality, if I may be so bold, that I could swear I lived through.

"Titanic Live"—rather a macabre name for a show originating from a graveyard—begins with the disaster's conventional "lesson": "Fifteen hundred lives were lost," intones the anchor, John Siegenthaler. "Gone,

I

too, was our boundless faith in the promise of technology." Meanwhile, a state-of-the-art computer recreation of the collision fills the screen, followed by high-resolution scenes of the wreck and the submersibles exploring and televising it. When correspondent Bob McKeown announces that "You are watching something that no one has ever seen before—the first live images from the bottom of the ocean, from the final resting place of history's most legendary ship, *Titanic*," we know that we are in for something other than a sustained critique of technological hubris. Even before Siegenthaler officially welcomes us to "an unprecedented event in television"—"history in the making"—correspondent Sara James has reminded us that "the images you are seeing are unprecedented." I quickly lose count of how often John, Bob, and Sara tell us that these images are "incredible," "remarkable," "amazing," "astonishing," "extraordinary," and "unforgettable." During the rare gaps between superlatives, the graphic "LIVE" appears in the top right corner, lest we momentarily forget the significance of the images filling the rest of the screen.

Any story of triumph requires a subplot of adversity, not only to create tension and excitement but to magnify the ultimate victory. To give credit where credit is due, bringing us these images has not been easy. "Right up to airtime almost," Bob confesses, "we were afraid we wouldn't be able to get these pictures in." This confession leads into a segment titled "City at Sea," which Bob introduces by declaring that the expedition "may be the most complex peacetime operation at sea in history." While it promises to yield an "astonishing amount of new information," it is also "very risky." Potential disasters loom everywhere. "With so many links in this intricate chain," observes Bob, "almost anything could happen." A pinprick in the thin skin of the submersible *Nautile* and the vessel and its crew will implode. In the days before the broadcast, tethers and fiber-optic cables get tangled. The seas get rough, and submersibles can't be launched. There is a power outage on the unmanned submersible *Magellan*. Midway through the show, John again invokes the *Titanic*'s "enduring lesson" of "the vulnerability of technology when pitted against the power of nature." Bob cites Murphy's Law—if it can go wrong, it will.

But can it? Will it? Bob mentions Murphy's Law only because the show is already scripted as a victory over Murphy's Law. Had I or, God forbid, the talking heads in Secaucus appeared, would the producers have shifted to an alternative script—one in which Bob, Sara, and John tell a story of how everything got screwed up?

The key moments in the show occur when Sara interviews Paul Matthias, two and a half miles below her in *Nautile*. "You're making broadcast history," she announces. "Do you feel the pressure?" Paul answers that he gets the pun: the pressure of doing a live interview from the bottom of the ocean equals the pressure of the ocean at that depth. (A flubbed interview, by implication, is as mortifying as being instantaneously crushed into a pellet.) Later, returning to Paul, Sara paraphrases Neil Armstrong: "It feels like one small step for man, one big dive for mankind." Really for television, though. The show is centrally about the making of *broadcast* history; all the technologies described in the course of the show exist to make possible the images on our screens.

The ability of television to keep producing "unprecedented" images becomes the vindication of technological progress that the *Titanic* supposedly called into doubt. And so, broadcast history redeems history. Broadcast history also absorbs history. Looking at the remains of the *Titanic*'s crow's nest, Bob locates "the beginning of the story that brought us here tonight." In other words, the *Titanic* sank so that eighty-six years later the Discovery Channel could air live images of the wreck. This reminds me of Steven Spielberg's Academy Award acceptance speech for *Schindler's List*, when he remembered the six million Holocaust victims who couldn't be watching tonight. (I realize that the analogy doesn't quite work. Spielberg didn't say that the Holocaust happened so that he could make an Oscar-winning movie about it; he merely suggested that its real tragedy was that the six million had to miss the broadcast.) It also reminds me of Don DeLillo's 1985 novel *White Noise*, in which the passengers of a plane that nearly crashes feel empty because their narrowly averted disaster doesn't warrant media coverage. "They went through all that for nothing?" a character wonders. Later, the victims of an "airborne toxic event" demand the media's validation of their suffering and terror:

> Don't they know it's real? Shouldn't the streets be crawling with cameramen and soundmen and reporters? Shouldn't we be yelling through the window at them, "Leave us alone, we've been through enough, get out of here with your vile instruments of intrusion." Do they have to have two hundred dead, rare disaster footage, before they

come flocking to a given site in their helicopters and network limos? What exactly has to happen before they stick microphones in our faces and hound us to the doorsteps of our homes, camping out on our lawns, creating the usual media circus? Haven't we earned the right to despise their idiot questions? . . . But we look around and see no response from the official organs of the media.[1]

Postmodern disasters, *White Noise* suggests, happen for the sake of television. If television doesn't show up, they aren't disasters, perhaps not even to their victims.

Despite DeLillo's terrifying scenario, disasters are not mere constructs, fictions, wholly self-referential media contrivances that ignore the reality of human pain in favor of the "reality" of exciting programming. Neither, however, are they extricable from language and other forms of representation. The essays in this book recognize that disasters generate meanings and that these meanings—embedded in culture—constitute an inseparable and important part of the disasters' histories. "Titanic Live" is now part of the history of the sinking of the *Titanic*. So, in a much more limited way, is my version of the Titanic Research and Recovery Expedition. So are countless other attempts over almost ninety years to remember and represent this disaster.

Because the essays in this book share a central concern with meanings and representations, they collectively raise questions about how we define disasters. What makes a disaster a disaster? (There are no chapters here about wars, which are the most devastating of all disasters, because somehow wars are perceived as a separate category of experience and a separate subject for study.) What are the differences between natural and technological disasters, and where do the lines people have drawn between them begin to erode? In *Ecology of Fear*, urban historian and theorist Mike Davis describes how "the social construction of 'natural' disaster is largely hidden from view by a way of thinking that simultaneously imposes false expectations on the environment and then explains the inevitable disappointments as proof of a malign and hostile nature." Given the ways in which "market-driven urbanization has transgressed environmental common sense," Davis argues, there is nothing "natural" about the massive devastation wrought by floods, fires, and earthquakes in southern California.[2] How do disasters fit into conceptions

of historical processes, of cause and effect, continuity and discontinuity, progress and decline? What are the consequences of the struggles to define, represent, give meaning to disasters? Why do some
explanations win out over others?

By definition, disasters are out of the ordinary, the antitheses of
everyday life. Scholars and students concerned with the slower, stead-
ier rhythms of people's past and present lives may be wise to avoid
them, just as people try to do as they live their lives. "One of the crucial
jobs of culture," the sociologist Kai Erikson observes, ". . . is to help people camouflage the actual risks of the world around them—to help
them edit reality in such a way that it seems manageable, to help them
edit it in such a way that the perils pressing in on all sides are screened
out of their line of vision as they go about their daily rounds."[3]

Yet, as the essays in *American Disasters* demonstrate, catastrophic
disturbances of routine actually tell us a great deal about the "normal"
workings of culture, society, and politics. When disasters strike, when
the extraordinary occurs, the response is quite often a poignant reasser-
tion of the familiar. The victims and witnesses of calamitous events
can't help but try to make sense of disasters in the terms available and
comfortable to them. Established patterns of language, belief, and behavior become a significant kind of reassurance in the face of disaster:
assertions of order and continuity against disorder and disruption. In
Chicago in 1977, the terrifying surprise of an elevated train falling from
the sky was transformed into a "normal" accident through the
metaphor of an airplane crash. "On some level," observes Andrew
Hazucha in "Chicago on the Brink," "those of us who live in the modern era of air transportation know that airplanes are *supposed* to fall out
of the sky; we have cultural rituals in place to prepare us for such an
event." In Boston a century earlier, *The Atlantic Monthly* described distant earthquakes, volcanic eruptions, and floods in ways that both
evoked and assuaged more immediate political and social concerns. As
Sheila Hones explains in "Distant Disasters, Local Fears," *The Atlantic's*
"controlling narrative voice" rhetorically reinforced its writers' and
readers' essentially benign conception of "a divinely ordered nature."

But if studying disasters allows us to observe these familiar patterns at moments of heightened danger, it also invites us to see that the
"normal" workings of culture, society, and politics are far from smooth.
Disasters evoke the defense of established ways precisely because they
so dramatically reveal the challenges to established ways. "The central

intellectual drama in the consideration of the nature of disorder," writes the historian Carl Smith, "is the struggle of the imagination to explain what is inexplicable, troubling, or threatening." Imagining disasters "involves the attempt to find the best way in which to absorb those things that challenge the sense of what is right and normal."[4] For some, however, the "right and normal" takes the form of "ought" rather than "is," and the imagining of disaster becomes a contest between the defenders of the established ways and those for whom the disaster lays bare the injustices, inequities, or inefficiencies rather than the beneficence of the status quo.

These essays explore the complex cultural resonances and effects of a variety of disasters in American history. Not all "greatest hits," the little-known or forgotten as well as the famous are represented here. Some take as their subject the impact of disasters on local cultures: the disruption and transformation of familiar patterns of community life. Others discuss the responses of professional communities and organizational cultures to disasters: the claims of expertise and authority in the management of the aftermath and the prevention of future calamities. And others investigate the reception and representation of disasters by broader interpretive communities: the cultural work performed by preachers, poets, novelists, journalists, publicists, illustrators, photographers.

American Disasters is arranged into four thematic parts. Ranging from the colonial period to the early twentieth century, "Capital" explores how disasters have shaped and been shaped by, disrupted and bolstered capitalist development, both materially and ideologically. Kevin Rozario opens "What Comes Down Must Go Up" with the odd figure of *Harper's Weekly* editor George Harvey calmly surveying the aftermath of the San Francisco earthquake in 1906 and confidently predicting "the brand-new splendor of the resuscitated capital." Harvey's almost jovial response to the disaster seems less astonishing in light of the concept of "creative destruction"—"the notion that modern capitalist systems require the continual obliteration of outmoded goods and structures to clear space and make way for new production and development."

"Faith" inquires into the relationships between disasters and belief, especially the American creed of progress, from the Gilded Age to the present. This creed, of course, is a central component of the ideology of capitalism. "A talent for seeing mangled bodies and burnt-out buildings as signs of progress," Rozario wryly notes, "was widely shared among Harvey's class." Spiritual and material progress often blend together in depictions of disasters as redemptive events. "Chicago, and the new urban order it represented, might be humbled in a way that showed that God and not man was the ultimate ruler of earthly destiny," Carl Smith writes of the response to the Great Chicago Fire, "but through it all the city revealed itself to be astonishingly resilient because of its material and human resources, because of its vital connection to a far-flung yet tightly bound social and economic system, and because this system evidently had the blessing of the same God that in his wisdom chose to afflict Chicago for the nation's own good." "Nothing ends here," said Ronald Reagan after the explosion of the space shuttle *Challenger* in 1986, as he launched what Ann Larabee describes as the effort "to reinstate a national faith in technological existence." Perhaps nothing marks a disaster as "American" more than this ability to transform death and destruction into good news.

"Community" moves from the national to the local and examines how particular professional, ethnic, urban, and suburban communities have responded to disasters. What often gets obscured, distorted, or lost in grand disaster narratives of renewal and progress are the voices and experiences of the actual victims. The images of oiled otters that Thomas A. Birkland and Regina G. Lawrence discuss in their essay on the *Exxon Valdez* oil spill may have aroused national public ire against corporate polluters, but the media paid much less attention to the effects of the disaster on Alaskan Native culture. "Subsistence is the way of life of the Native people," says an Alaska Native in Duane A. Gill and J. Steven Picou's "The Day the Water Died." "We all feel great pain. The oil spill affected our lives because we live off the ocean and it is a source of fellowship among our people. We live to gather and think of others and help them when they cannot help themselves. We want to teach the next generation to gather, hunt, and share. It is an art, an identity, a being."

In "Possibility," disasters galvanize alternative politics and inspire utopian visions that directly challenge the equation of capitalism and progress. Where in the *Titanic* disaster did feminists, African Americans, and labor radicals see possibilities for a more egalitarian future? "We might rest our whole cause upon what happened that night on the *Titanic*," a socialist insisted, while another asked, "Is this not the greatest evidence of the falsity of the claim that only the possibility of making money serves as an incentive to people, that that is human nature and cannot be altered?" Where in the 1982 crash of Air Florida Flight 90, asks Ralph James Savarese, might we catch a glimpse of alternatives to the social, economic, and political catastrophe of Reaganism?

The essays in *American Disasters* span many disciplines—American studies, political science, geography, history, literature, sociology, cultural studies. They draw on many different kinds of evidence, from government reports to science fiction novels, oral histories to movies, newspaper articles to engineering plans. All are solidly rooted in empirical research, though many combine that research with the insights of critical theory. They are refreshingly readable and free of jargon, as essays that deal with the riveting subject of disasters should be.

NOTES

1. Don DeLillo, *White Noise* (New York: Viking, 1985), 162.

2. Mike Davis, *Ecology of Fear: Los Angeles and the Imagination of Disaster* (New York: Metropolitan Books, 1998), 9.

3. Kai Erikson, *A New Species of Trouble: Explorations in Disaster, Trauma, and Community* (New York: W. W. Norton, 1994), 152.

4. Carl Smith, *Urban Disorder and the Shape of Belief: The Great Chicago Fire, the Haymarket Bomb, and the Model Town of Pullman* (Chicago: University of Chicago Press, 1995), 6-7. See also Alessa Johns's introduction to *Dreadful Visitations: Confronting Natural Catastrophe in the Age of Enlightenment*, ed. Alessa Johns (New York: Routledge, 1999), xx.

PART I

CAPITAL

I

"A Tempestuous Spirit Called Hurri Cano"

Hurricanes and Colonial Society in the British Greater Caribbean

Matthew Mulcahy

English colonizers of the New World expected to encounter a harsh and threatening physical environment. The deep, dark forests, the unexpectedly extreme climate, the unknown flora and fauna—all were perceived as menacing and potentially disruptive to the colonial project. But perhaps nothing was more alien or more threatening to colonists in the Caribbean and southern colonies than the hurricanes and tropical storms that regularly swept across the region, leveling cities and plantations, disrupting trade and commerce, and plunging society into general disarray. Hurricanes were an entirely new phenomenon for the English in the seventeenth century. Matthew Mulcahy's essay explores the early English encounter with hurricanes, analyzes the manner in which these storms shaped perceptions of the physical environment of the New World, considers the social and cultural adaptations colonists made to accommodate these seasonal threats, and examines the role of hurricanes in marking the "Greater Caribbean"—a region stretching from Barbados to Virginia—as exotic and distinct from the rest of British America.

RESIDENTS OF SOUTH CAROLINA cast nervous eyes to the sky above them on the night of September 4, 1686.[1] The weather had grown turbulent during the day, and as night fell, the clouds became increasingly "black and menacing." Colonists had heard tales from local Indians of great storms along the coast that had raised the ocean and rivers above the houses and trees where their new city, Charles Town, now stood. Many began to wonder if such a storm was now upon them, and more ominously, if they and their infant colony would survive it. Daybreak confirmed their worst fears as the dark clouds were transformed into "a hurricane wonderfully horrid and destructive." An anonymous survivor reported later to the Lords Proprietors in London that the storm rose in intensity throughout the day with "dismal, dreadful, and fatal consequences." The winds and rain raged with such fury that "Your Lordships cannot imagine the distracting horror that these united evils plunged us into." Ships were driven ashore and crushed into pieces, houses were blown down, and many colonists had not the "least cottage to secure us from the rigor of the rain." Corn that the day before had stood tall in the fields was beaten down and lay "rotting on the ground," and many feared the onset of famine. When it was all over, few signs of English settlement appeared to have survived, except as ruins. "The whole country seems to be one entire map of devastation," the correspondent informed the Proprietors. Trees and fences were blown down into "confused heaps," and cows and pigs were dispersed into the woods. Roads were impassable, "whereby all society and communication with our neighbors, one of the greatest comforts of our lives, is for many years rendered extraordinarily difficult." Whatever high hopes colonists had had for themselves and their settlement lay dashed among the ruins, and the colony faced "sad consequences . . . both at present and . . . for the future."[2]

Seventeenth-century English colonists migrating to South Carolina and other colonies in the "Greater Caribbean"—the plantation region extending from Barbados through Carolina—expected to encounter a harsh physical environment as they set about establishing permanent settlements. For colonists accustomed to England's temperate climate and its cleared and "settled" landscape, the New World appeared as a "hideous and desolate wilderness."[3] Colonists worried about the scalding sun and sweltering temperatures of the region and their effects on English bodies and, by extension, English culture and values. The multitude of insects that greeted them was at best bothersome and at worst deadly. The dark forests were, in their eyes, home to wild beasts and wild men, both of which threatened to overwhelm them. None, however, were prepared for the seasonal hurricanes and tropical storms that routinely swept across the region and literally shook the fragile foundations of colonial society. Nothing about the New World environment was more alien or threatening to colonists in the Greater Caribbean than hurricanes. Indeed, nothing better represented the "wilderness" of America for colonists in the region than these strange and ferocious storms. "What is most to be feared," wrote one observer "is a general conspiracy of all the Winds . . . which is called a Hurricane."[4] Edmund Burke argued that while heat and humidity were "unpleasant to the English constitution," hurricanes were "the most terrible calamity" colonists faced in the Greater Caribbean.[5] A later commentator believed hurricanes were "the most formidable enemy" and "the principle dread" of those who lived in the region.[6]

Modern historians have paid little attention to such sentiments. Fears of heat, of the wilderness, and of Native Americans have all been well documented by scholars, but few have considered the importance of hurricanes in shaping English perceptions and fears of the physical environment in this part of the New World.[7] Nor have they examined in detail the impact of such fears on the mentality of colonists or the development of colonial society in the Greater Caribbean. Hurricanes were a new experience for English colonists, but their presence quickly distinguished the colonies of the Greater Caribbean from others in British America and forced colonists to adapt in unique ways to the environment of the region. Hurricanes destroyed colonists' crops and commerce, leveled their cities and plantations, and plunged society into general disarray. The physical and economic losses wrought by the storms certainly were tremendous and of great concern to colonists anxious to establish profitable plantation enterprises. But hurricanes also raised larger, and deeply troubling, questions for colonists in South Carolina and elsewhere in the region: What kind of stable societies could be established in the face of such regular destructive forces? What caused these unfamiliar and terrifying storms? Were they signs from God, and if so, what did they mean? Could anything be done to lessen their impact? Such questions had no easy answers in the seventeenth and eighteenth centuries, but in asking them colonists' letters, diaries, and travel accounts reveal the extent to which hurricanes dominated the thoughts of those living in the Greater Caribbean and shaped the type of societies they established there.

ENCOUNTERING HURRICANES

Hurricanes were a uniquely American phenomenon and an unexpected one for English travelers to the New World in the seventeenth century.

Although Europe occasionally experienced storms of great intensity, they were not comparable in magnitude (or seasonal regularity) to the hurricanes that lashed the southern North American coast and the Caribbean basin.[8] Columbus was the first European to encounter a hurricane, and it was through him that the Arawak and Carib Indian word for the storms entered European vocabularies. Sailing off the coast of Hispaniola in June 1495, Columbus reported a "whirlwind" so strong that it pulled up entire trees by their roots and "beat down to the bottom of the sea three ships." The local Arawak Indians, Columbus noted, called "these tempests of the air . . . Furacanes."[9] Columbus's account was first translated into English in 1555, but knowledge of the word and the storms remained the province of a small elite. When passengers on the ship *Sea Venture* encountered a terrible storm off the coast of Bermuda in 1609, none knew to call the storm a hurricane. "For mine own part," passenger William Strachey wrote, "I have been in some stormes before, as well as upon the coast of Barbary and Algeere, in the Levant. . . . Yet all I had suffered together might not hold comparison to this."[10] Likewise, when William Shakespeare used Strachey's account of the storm and the passengers' travails on Bermuda as the basis for his final play, he did not call it *The Hurricane*, although the word was known to him. ("Hurricano" appears in two earlier plays, *King Lear* and *Troilus and Cressida*.[11]) He perhaps recognized that such a title would prove puzzling to the vast majority of his audience and chose *The Tempest* instead.

Colonists may have had no knowledge of the storms when they left England, but they quickly learned about the destructive power of hurricanes as they attempted to establish settlements throughout the Greater Caribbean. John Smith reported that less than nine months after colonists had landed at St. Christopher in 1624 and begun the laborious process of building houses and planting fields, a "hericano" struck and "blew it all away." Two years later a second storm again leveled the colony. According to Smith, the hurricane "blew downe all our houses, Tobacco and two Drums [were thrown] into the aire we know not wither . . . all our provisions thus lost, we were very miserable." Smith wrote that colonists were forced to scavenge in the "wilde woods" for food, and they struggled to survive until the next June when turtles came ashore, providing a welcome addition to their scanty diet.[12]

Smith's terse comments tell us little about how early colonists reacted to hurricanes. Details on the terror caused by the storms, however, came twelve years later when another tempest leveled St. Christopher in 1638. John Taylor, an English writer, heard about the strange storm in the West Indies from sailors on the London docks. He published a short pamphlet based on their stories entitled *New and Strange Newes from St. Christopher, of a tempestuous spirit which is called by the Indians a Hurri Cano*.[13] The hurricane did extensive damage, according to Taylor, killing seventy-five people and sinking five ships, "besides the harm it did to many Houses and goods." The winds were so strong that they carried men "into the Aire five or sixe foote high, as if they were no more but ragges." Panic-stricken colonists evacuated their houses,

> not daring to remaine in them for feare that they should be blowne down about their eaves; at which dangerous times they do creep for safety into holes, Caves, pits, Dens, and hollow places of the Earth, which are either naturall of themselves, or digged and framed by Art or laborious industry of man, which places are good harbours and defences against the Hurri-cano. They doe likewise tye or make fast Hamackoes or hanging Cabins unto two Trees . . . being hang'd above the ground six or seven foote, either with strong ropes or Iron Chaines; and so they swing two and againe like a Bell when it is rung, when this tempest is.

Some also followed the example of local Indians, who tied themselves to trees to keep from being blown away. Taylor depicted such a scene in a woodcut accompanying his text, providing the first illustration of a hurricane for English readers.

As colonization efforts expanded in the seventeenth century and new colonies were established or captured from the Spanish, reports of the storms and of the terror and damage wrought by them arrived from all the colonies throughout the region. The word "hurricane" was soon applied mistakenly to any violent storm of wind and rain. Accounts of "hurricanes" surfaced in England, New England, and even Holland.[14] Although hurricanes occasionally make their way up the Atlantic coast, and rarer still across the Atlantic, most of the storms described in these accounts were not actually hurricanes. Increase Mather, for example, wrote of "a formidable Hurricane, scarce bearing sixty yards in its breadth, and spending itself in about seven minutes of time," that hit Massachusetts in 1669.[15] Tornadoes, wind squalls, and simply violent storms often

FIGURE 1.1. Frontispiece to John Taylor's *New and Strange Newes from St. Christopher of a tempestuous Spirit, which is called by the Indians a Hurri-Cano*, depicting a 1638 hurricane on the island. This was the first illustration of this new phenomenon published in England. Courtesy of the Huntington Library.

were labeled hurricanes by observers who had heard of the storms but knew little about them.

Despite some confusion, most contemporaries quickly realized that the storms had definite geographic limits. Hurricanes were, according to Edmond Halley (he of comet fame), "peculiar to the Caribbean."[16] When a violent storm struck the Plymouth colony in August 1635, William Bradford described it as a "mighty storm of wind and rain as none ever living in these parts, either English or Indian, ever saw, being like . . . those hurricanes or typhoons that writers make mention of in the Indies."[17] European commentators explicitly discouraged facile comparisons between hurricanes and storms in Europe. Daniel Defoe assured his readers that although the "Great Storm" that hit England in 1703 was terrible and its destruction great, it was nothing compared to an actual hurricane. "In England we feel none of the hurricanes of Barbados and Jamaica," Defoe wrote.[18]

Although the storms were "peculiar to the Caribbean," the idea of the Caribbean in the colonial period extended beyond the region we think of today. Many contemporaries spoke of South Carolina as "Carolina in ye West Indies," and the presence of hurricanes was one reason they did so.[19] For the most part, in the eyes of contemporaries, the hurricane zone was limited geographically to this Greater Caribbean. Storms may occasionally have struck other parts of British America, but in no other region were hurricanes so regular a threat or so feared by colonists.

In addition to geographic limits, colonists also slowly discovered that hurricanes (and tropical storms more generally) were a seasonal problem. Writers in the first decades of colonization believed the storms could strike at any time. John Taylor wrote that it was "uncertaine" when a hurricane might hit, "for it hath no certaine or set times either yeares or dayes for the coming of it."[20] A 1655 pamphlet advised travelers to arrive in the region before August lest they encounter "the hurricanes, as they call them . . . that doe terribly infest the Atlantick and Indian Seas all winter long, from September to March."[21] Gradually, however, colonists learned that the storms had more limited seasonal boundaries. This information came from Carib Indians. Several colonists noted that the Caribs had the ability to forecast the onset of storms. "The Indians are so skilfull that they doe know two or three or fore dayes before hand the coming of it," Taylor observed. "They doe observe that just so many dayes as it will be before the Hurri-Cano doth come, so many circles will bee as it were fringed and gleaming about the Moone; as if it bee but one day before it come, then there will be but one Circle; if two Circles, then it will be two daies."[22] The Indians regularly warned colonists to beware of hurricanes in the late summer, and by the 1660s, colonists had learned enough to report that the storms were limited to "the monthes of July, August, or September: at other times there is no fear of it."[23] At some point this information was recorded in a local proverb: "June too soon, July stand by, August you must, September remember, October all over."[24]

The seasonality of the storms did little to assuage the terror they inspired, and colonists lived in constant fear throughout these months. Residents never knew if a late summer storm might simply blow over or turn into a terrible tempest. Any storm in August or September was often viewed as "the forerunner of a hurricane" and created panic among colonists.[25] Traveling through the Carolinas in 1765, John Bartram noted:

> I frequently heard ye women talk how fearfull thay was if A thunder gust arose, of ye wind tacking to ye Northeast and ye danger of

a hurricane, which I looked upon as a feminin weakness . . . sup-
posing thes grievous calamities came but once an age. But upon
making perticular enquiry of ye oldest inhabitants I was satisfied
that by their frequent grevious sufferings thay had Sufficient reason
for those anctious concerns.[26]

Colonists and travelers had various opinions about how often hurricanes struck. Most believed they could be expected once every seven
years; others thought they had become more frequent by the end of the
seventeenth century. But ultimately no one knew for certain, and there
were enough examples of frequent, even yearly, hurricanes to give all residents pause. Although individual colonies often went years without experiencing a hurricane or major tropical storm, hardly a year went by that
some colony in the region did not suffer tremendous devastation. Even
if they escaped, residents soon heard the bad news from elsewhere and
knew that it was only a matter of time before they too were hit.[27]

INTERPRETING HURRICANES

Increased knowledge about the geographical and seasonal limits of
hurricanes raised questions among colonists regarding the causes of the
storms. Early colonists in the region, like those throughout British
America, interpreted great and violent storms and other disasters as
"wonders." Wonders were, in David Hall's words, strange and unusual
events "betokening the presence of the supernatural."[28] The Protestant
deity was an activist one who could and did intervene in the affairs of
the world, causing comets to streak across the sky, earthquakes to rum-
ble underfoot, and storms to rage. These events were special providences by which God expressed his displeasure with the world and sig-
naled worse fates to come if repentance was not offered and reformation not undertaken. Although most had divine origins, some wonders
arose from the supernatural power of Satan, whom God allowed to interfere with sinners on earth. Always, however, "wonders evidenced
the will of God."[29]

Most early colonists agreed that hurricanes were wondrous events,
but a great deal of confusion existed at first about what message they
contained and for whom the message was intended. Were the storms
sent to punish and instruct colonists or the "barbarous" Caribs? For

many early colonists, the ability of the Caribs to forecast the storms be-
spoke some nefarious interaction with evil forces. As John Taylor noted,
"where God is least known and honoured, there the Devill hath the
most power and domination." Others agreed, writing that Caribs
knowledge of the storms and their patterns was evidence of "witch-
crafts" and "Councel with the Devil."[30] Some colonists, however, believed the storms were directed at colonists. Taylor, for example, noted
that if hurricanes had some links to the devil, they also fulfilled the
wishes of God and contained a message to colonists to begin the work
of converting the Indians to Christianity. Just as in the Old World God
had used slavery to bring heathens to "Christian Liberty," in the Greater
Caribbean hurricanes were his tool for proselytizing. "In the latest
Dayes of the World all are not civilized; there are yet many Heathens,
Indians, and barbarous Nations unconverted [and] Knowne Examples
in America, and in divirs Islands, adjacent, where this Huri Cano is frequent," Taylor wrote, and it was the colonists' duty to set about the
work of conversion.[31] Others saw the storms more directly as a sign
from God regarding their own sinful behavior. Virginians had no doubt
that a 1667 hurricane was a judgment from God, and one noted that the
storm would seem a minor event if colonists did not alter their ways:
"God doth not for every small sin send a great Judgment, but being like
a loving Father, First he admonisheth and warneth of our sins." The
hurricane was such a warning, and if sin persisted in Virginia, "He will
utterly destroy us."[32]

Belief in the divine origins of hurricanes continued throughout the
eighteenth century, and many continued to interpret the storms as
warnings or punishments for their sins. Sophia Hulme, a Quaker in
South Carolina, for example, informed residents that the 1752 hurricane
that devastated the colony was a "humbling visitation from the most
high God" and a clear "Mark of his displeasure against your transgressions."[33] Colonial governors in the Greater Caribbean likewise continued to call for days of fasting and thanksgiving after major hurricanes
throughout the eighteenth century. Proclamations announcing the fasts
declared the storms "punishments from God" and called upon
colonists to humble themselves and give thanks for their survival. Indeed, according to one observer, such days were the only true "religious" holidays observed in Jamaica.[34]

Nevertheless, beginning in the latter decades of the seventeenth
century some colonists began to question the supernatural origins of

the storms. If these storms were indeed the work of supernatural forces, several writers asked, why did they strike with such regularity during certain months of the year? And why did they only strike in this particular part of the world? Rather than coming from the hand of God with a message for colonists, these writers suggested, hurricanes derived from natural causes.

One of the earliest statements of this view came from a ship's captain named Langford who spent several years in the Caribbean in the 1650s. Langford argued that hurricanes were natural occurrences, and moreover, that the Caribs ability to forecast their onset had nothing to do with the devil and everything to do with their close observations of the natural world. Langford learned the "Signs or Prognosticks" by which the Caribs foretold hurricanes from a captured Indian slave. According to his informant, the storms struck only on the "Full, Change, or Quarters of the Moon." Prior to a storm, according to Langford, the following conditions were noticeable:

> That Day you will see the Skies very turbulent, the Sun more red than at other times, a great calm, and the Hills clear of Clouds or Foggs, over them, which in the high lands are seldom so. Likewise in the Hollows or Concaves of the Earth, or Wells, there will be a great Noise as if you were in a great Storm, and at the Night the Stars looking very big with Burrs about them and the North West Sky very black and foul, the Sea smelling Stronger than at other times, as usually It doth in great Storms; and sometimes that Day, for an Hour or two, the Wind blows very hard Westerly, out of his usual Course. On the Full of the Moon you have the same Signs, but a great Burr about the Moon, and many times about the Sun.[35]

Building from such information, Langford and others began a sustained inquiry into the natural "causes" of hurricanes. A number of theories were advanced over the next century. Most involved the effects of the sun. After the sun had reached its zenith and began a retreat southward during the late summer months, the argument went, the regular easterly trade winds in the region lessened. As this happened, the westerly winds, usually held in check "by the power of the Sun," increased, causing the winds to "Shuffl[e] from Point to Point." As the westerlies came into direct contact with the easterlies, a "Reverse or Rebounding back of the Wind" occurred, and in that rebounding hurricanes were born. Although the specifics of what caused the "rebounding" of the winds were debated, most writers agreed that the influence of the sun was of prime importance. Likewise, all commentators argued erroneously that hurricane winds came in from the west, off the North American continent.[36]

The increasing emphasis given to natural explanations for hurricanes was part of a larger movement away from belief in wonders that occurred in the second half of the seventeenth century, particularly (but not exclusively) among elites, in England and America. Historians have argued that a number of factors were responsible for this transition, including the rise of the "new science," increasing social and political conflict between Puritans and Anglicans (in which interpretation of wondrous events was a key battleground), and changing notions of gentility, knowledge, and refinement.[37] All of these factors influenced colonists in the Greater Caribbean and others elsewhere interested in hurricanes, but the emerging doctrines of the "new science" were perhaps most important. This new intellectual paradigm, with its emphasis on observation and experience rather than on classical texts as a means of understanding the natural world, found ready acceptance among many struggling to make sense of the new and terrifying storms in the Greater Caribbean. Writers like Langford, Ralph Bohun, and Pierre Charlevoix noted that their ideas about hurricanes were "back'd by experience" and close observation of the natural world.[38] Bohun stated that his theories on the storms were "not to be had in any Colleges or Books, but . . . fetched from both Indies."[39] Edmund Burke even celebrated the Caribs' knowledge of hurricanes and chastised European intellectuals who failed to appreciate the Indians' close observations of the workings of the natural world more generally.[40]

Such explanations did not deny the existence or importance of God. Instead, new scientists and their followers believed that God had created an orderly universe in which events such as hurricanes followed fixed patterns and processes discernible by humans. Revealing the logic and the mechanistic order of the natural world bore witness to the power and glory of God even if such interpretations deemphasized the idea that wonders had specific moral messages. Science, thus, did not triumph over religion, and rational and religious interpretations of hurricanes and other events often existed side by side in the thoughts and writings of even the most scientifically minded. Still, it is clear that as colonists and travelers to the region gained more experience with hurricanes and learned more about the signs connected to them, they increasingly stressed the natural rather than the divine origin of storms.[41]

Numerous theories regarding the natural causes of hurricanes were advanced during the seventeenth and eighteenth centuries—the most interesting involved melting snow from the North Pole—but ultimately none proved satisfactory and the natural causes of the storms remained a mystery.[42] In an extensive 1687 treatise on winds, Edmond Halley simply did not discuss hurricanes, arguing that "Their Violence is so unconceivable, and their other phenomenon so surprising that they merit well to be considered apart."[43] (Halley never got around to considering them.) One hundred years later, following dozens of reports and investigations, another writer concluded simply, "Their immediate cause seems to lie far beyond the limits of our circumscribed knowledge."[44]

HURRICANES AND COLONIAL SOCIETY

If the natural causes of hurricanes remained a mystery to colonists, the effects of the storms were abundantly clear. Major tempests swept across the region annually, destroying everything in their path. Fields which the day before had been filled with neat rows of valuable sugar cane lay torn and twisted, and "the necessities of life [we]re wasted and corrupted" in the aftermath.[45] "Ye whole face of nature in ye morning seem'd chang'd from a beautifull appearance of spring to ye depths of a winter," wrote one survivor of a 1712 storm in Jamaica.[46] The power of the winds awed colonists: they wrote in amazement of hundred-pound copper kettles (used in the production of sugar) being tossed about plantations as if they were small bowls, of huge trees being torn up by their roots, and of the strongest and most secure houses being crushed to pieces.[47]

Such widespread destruction was measured first in terms of economics. Colonists came to the Greater Caribbean in search of wealth, and hurricanes presented a major obstacle to its accumulation. Sugar and rice required extensive equipment and infrastructure to grow and process, which compounded colonists' losses. Not only did the storms deprive planters of an entire year's crop and its profits; the damage to mills, fields, dikes, and dams required costly investments to rebuild.[48] One South Carolina planter calculated his losses from the 1752 hurricane—in terms of lost crops, damage to buildings, and repair costs—at more than £20,000.[49] The Great Hurricane of 1780 in Barbados caused more than £1,000,000 in damage to property.[50] Colonists quickly recognized that their efforts to build sustainable and profitable enterprises were particularly vulnerable to the whims of nature. Daniel Parke, for example, accepted the governorship of the Leeward Islands in the early eighteenth century with high hopes of increasing his wealth and status. He constructed a new house on St. Christopher and rented a plantation, but a 1707 hurricane swept away his personal improvements and left him "much a poorer man than when I came."[51] Parke continued in his position, hoping to recoup his losses and fulfill his goal of increased wealth, but he did so with prayers "that we shall not have hurricanes every year."[52] Henry Laurens, a prominent South Carolina merchant and planter, repeatedly warned his correspondents that they should not begin calculating profits before the end of October. "For my own part, I never draw conclusions of the quantity of a Crop of Rice before Harvest is fairly over," he wrote. "A Hurricane in August or September and even so late as October in a backward Season, will spoil one half or two thirds of the whole quantity in a Field."[53] Surveying the damage from a hurricane in Jamaica, a later eighteenth-century commentator noted simply, "Property here is extremely precarious."[54]

Economic losses from the bad weather, of course, were not unique to the Greater Caribbean. Weather concerned residents everywhere in the overwhelmingly agricultural colonies of British North America. A severe storm, a drought, a plague of insects—all could spell economic ruin for farmers and planters in Massachusetts as readily as for those in Barbados. No other colonies, however, faced such routine threats not only to their economic well-being but to the basic infrastructure of society as those in the Greater Caribbean did from hurricanes. In addition to fields and agricultural equipment, hurricanes regularly destroyed houses, roads, docks, fences, and basic supplies. Such losses were calculated in monetary terms, to be sure, but this kind of destruction had larger cultural implications as well. Colonists came to the New World determined to "improve" and civilize the American "wilderness." As Jack Greene notes, "the language of improvement was ubiquitous in the early modern British world," and it had many meanings. In a narrow, economic sense improvement defined specific projects by which individuals or societies gathered wealth. More broadly, an "improved society" stood at the opposite end of the spectrum from a "barbaric" one; it was "settled, cultivated, and civilized" rather than "wild . . . irregular, rustic or crude."[55] Seventeenth- and eighteenth-century colonists had few romantic visions of the "untamed" frontier, and, with England as their model, they labored to improve the American environment by clearing forests, building farms, and planning towns. Hurricanes, however, swept away these measures of social progress and pushed colonists back into a Lockean state of nature. Colonists had "neither victuals to eat, dry cloathes to put on, or a house to shelter in," wrote Christopher Jeaffreson after a 1681 hurricane on St. Christopher.[56] The grandest planters were reduced for a time to living in the huts of slaves, and the "surface of the earth [was] left truly bared."[57] As one official commented following a major disaster, the hurricane "reduced those miserable people to their first principles."[58]

The destruction of houses and fences was especially troublesome for colonists. Not only were these structures visible manifestations of English improvements and culture; they were also the means by which the English claimed possession of New World lands. As Patricia Seed shows, English colonists, unlike the Spanish and French, did not plant flags or crosses nor engage in any ceremonies to declare their conquest of the New World. Instead, they built houses and fences. Such structures were markers of territory and provided "legal" title to lands (at least in their eyes). Fences were particularly important in this regard because they mapped the extent of colonial landholdings and denoted the boundary between civil society and wilderness (with all its terrifying connotations). Within these fences and other boundary markers, English "improvements" (especially planting crops) reinforced ideas of possession and ownership. Such ideas provided the ideological framework by which colonists throughout British America justified their conquest and dispossession of Native Americans.[59] The destruction wrought by hurricanes thus challenged the very foundations of the English colonial project in the region. As one distressed colonist wrote in 1689, "If a hurricane comes . . . , it puts us to begin the world anew."[60] Although many colonists had come to the New World with the hope of starting the world anew, none anticipated or wanted such regular opportunities to put their hopes into practice.

Hurricanes raised challenges to English possession in more direct ways as well. Improvements may have marked the colonies as English territory, but fortifications defended their boundaries. Hurricanes, however, routinely destroyed fortifications and military supplies, leaving the colonies vulnerable to attack from enemies foreign and domestic. Throughout much of the seventeenth and eighteenth centuries, England was at war with France, Spain, and different Native American groups, and the threat of invasion was a constant concern for colonial officials. Damage from hurricanes exacerbated the fear that England's enemies would take advantage of their weakened defenses and attack. South Carolina officials, for example, begged London officials for military aid in 1719. The colony's forts, having "been demolished by hurricanes," left them exposed to "continued incursions and depredations" by the Spanish and by Native American groups.[61]

In addition to outside threats, colonists were terrified that slaves would take advantage of the disorder and the breakdown of defenses to run away—or worse, to rebel. Such concerns intensified during the second half of the seventeenth century as sugar production and the slave trade expanded enormously. (A similar transition occurred in South Carolina following the introduction of rice in the early eighteenth century.)[62] By the eighteenth century, African slave majorities characterized all of the colonies in the Greater Caribbean, and slaves outnumbered whites eleven to one in some colonies. All of the colonies experienced slave rebellions on some scale and, as a result, placed great emphasis on social order and control. Colonists were thus understandably on edge in the aftermath of hurricanes.[63] Following a major storm in 1694, for example, the governor of Barbados, fearful that "the negroes should take advantage of the disorder to rise . . . ordered all the houses to put out lights and kept the constables on watch in the town."[64] The situation was particularly tense in 1675 when a hurricane struck Barbados a few weeks after a slave plot was uncovered. Terrified planters immediately petitioned the king, requesting aid to replace guns and powder that had been destroyed, while elected officials pleaded for "a supply of servants from Scotland to strengthen the island against the outrages of the negroes."[65]

There is no evidence that any foreign power ever mounted a challenge to the English in the aftermath of a hurricane, nor do slaves appear to have engaged in any activity other than looting. Nevertheless, colonists perceived both threats to be terrifyingly real amid the chaos wrought by the storms. Indeed, many colonists came to refer to hurricanes as "enemies." The storms in their eyes were as dangerous and destructive as invading Spanish and French forces or rebelling slaves would be, and the combination of the two was potentially devastating.[66]

Colonists hoped that their efforts to transform the American wilderness into a pastoral landscape would ease the threat from hurricanes. Contemporary theories held that extreme climates could be altered—temperatures moderated and winds and rains regulated—by clearing fields and establishing settlements.[67] Some writers believed this had happened in the Greater Caribbean. In his 1708 history of the British colonies, for example, John Oldmixon stated that the "dreadful . . . Hurricanes that us'd to threaten this Island [Barbados] with ruin, are not so frequent as formerly," which he attributed to the increasingly "settled" nature of the colony.[68] The appearance of the next major storm, however, quickly undermined such faith, and colonists were forced to accept that little could be done to diminish the frequency or intensity of hurricanes.

While they could do nothing to stop hurricanes, colonists did attempt to mitigate the damage wrought by the storms. In the aftermath of major storms, colonial legislatures passed laws requiring that new buildings be constructed with brick and stone in an effort to limit the destruction of houses and mills. These laws were rarely enforced, and it is questionable how great an impact they had in the seventeenth and eighteenth centuries. More important was the decision by many individual colonists to lower the height of their houses. After the initial years of settlement, colonists who could afford to do so began building large, four-story houses following English models. Such structures were not only poorly suited to the heat of the Greater Caribbean, they were particularly vulnerable to high winds, and most were routinely leveled by hurricanes and lesser tropical storms. For survivors, the experience of living through a hurricane pushed them to reduce the height of their buildings to one or two stories.[69] One colonial governor reported to London, "Hurri-canes . . . taught the people to build low," and travelers to the region regularly commented on the height of buildings.[70]

In addition, many colonists built specific "hurricane houses" in which to seek refuge when major tempests struck. Such structures varied in size and shape. In the West Indies during the seventeenth century, they tended to be low, long, and rectangular. They were often as large as the main dwelling house. Thomas Joseph, for example, a planter on St. Christopher, had a three-room house measuring 34 feet by 16 feet. His "hurry cano house" was 26 feet by 13 feet.[71] Al-

FIGURE 1.2. A conjectural drawing of a South Carolina storm tower. Storm towers, or hurricane houses, were built on plantations throughout the Greater Caribbean in the seventeenth and eighteenth centuries to provide shelter for slaves. Courtesy of the South Carolina Historical Society.

though the size and strength of the houses varied somewhat according to wealth, even small-scale planters with little capital had small shelters. Another St. Christopher resident, John Abbot, had a total estate valued at only £32, but it included a 12-foot-by-9-foot hurricane house worth £3.[72]

Hurricane houses do not appear to have been used in South Carolina until the latter decades of the eighteenth century. At that point many planters, particularly in the low-lying sea islands, began building "storm towers" to provide shelter for their slaves. The word "tower" is something of a misnomer; the brick structures were no more than twenty feet high, and unlike the West Indian structures, these were round, to better deflect the brunt of the wind's fury. The floor of the towers was actually several feet off the ground to prevent their sinking into the loose soils in the low-country delta.[73] The towers provided shelter for thousands of slaves and no doubt saved the lives of many in the late eighteenth and nineteenth centuries. Both the building styles and the hurricane houses contributed to the development of a distinct plantation landscape in the Greater Caribbean.

Besides architectural changes, colonists also tried to limit economic damage by regulating trade in and out of the region. Planters had no way of protecting their crops while they lay unharvested in the fields—there was no crop insurance of any kind in the seventeenth and eighteenth centuries and little in the way of organized public or private relief for agricultural losses—but they did adjust shipping schedules to avoid having cargo-laden vessels caught in a major storm. The governor of the Leeward Islands complained to London officials in 1671 that "he is abandoned by all shipping about the hurricane season."[74] Henry Laurens, a major slave-trader, specifically warned correspondents to stay away from Charleston in the late summer. "We would not choose [slaves] sent in the Hurricane season," he wrote to one, because the risk of loss was simply too great.[75] Ships that traveled in the region during the late summer faced higher insurance premiums from anxious investors.[76] Many that arrived unexpectedly were ordered away to safer ports, or in South Carolina, sent up the Cooper River, until after the hurricane season had passed.[77]

Such adaptations offered only minimal protection from the ravages of hurricanes, and all colonists in the region continued to face the prospect of widespread death and destruction from the storms. The threat from and impact of hurricanes had important consequences for the type of society that ultimately developed in the Greater Caribbean. First, the economic devastation wrought by the storms drove many settlers—particularly smaller planters and farmers in the sugar colonies—away from the region and to other colonies in British North America. In doing so, the hurricanes furthered the process of consolidating land ownership among a small group of wealthy planters who had access to the necessary capital to cover short-term losses and rebuilding costs. Following the 1675 hurricane, for example, the Governor of Barbados reported to London that many terrified residents were "resolved never to build again but to leave the island." Although many changed their minds and started to rebuild, a great many others, lacking resources, "can never be able to do it." Richard Dunn, employing a 1674 map and a 1680 census to gauge the effect of the hurricane on Barbados, concluded that dozens of the smaller planters and property holders listed on the map, but not in the census, had sold their lands to bigger planters and left the island.[78] A similar process appears following a 1731 hurricane in Barbados. "So great is our present desolation," Assembly leaders wrote following the storm, "that many of the poorer inhabitants, unable to rebuild their ruined houses, will be driven to quit the Island."[79] We lack specifics regarding the number of colonists who lost their lands, but Frank Wesley Pitman argues that throughout the colonial period the storms regularly forced smaller planters to sell off their lands. "The frequency with which they [hurricanes] are reported," Pitman wrote, "and the accounts of them indicate that every few years hundreds of weaker settlers were forced into bankruptcy and their estates amalgamated with those of the rich."[80]

The storms not only pushed smaller planters with few resources off the islands and furthered the process of land consolidation, but also pushed wealthy planters away from the colonies. Historians have long noted that absenteeism characterized the colonies of the West Indies and (to a lesser but still significant extent) South Carolina. The many rigors of the tropical climate led planters who could afford it to return to England or to settle in the northern colonies. Planters residing in England, for example, owned perhaps as much as 30 percent of the cultivated lands in Jamaica by the middle of the eighteenth century.[81] One consequence of this, some historians argue, was that the colonies of the Greater Caribbean—particularly the sugar islands—never developed the social infrastructure (families, schools, political institutions) common in northern colonies and were deprived of their best and brightest leaders. Other scholars suggest that such distinctions have been exaggerated and that the colonies in the region were fully developed settler societies.[82]

While the extent of the impact of absenteeism on colonial society is debatable, there is no doubt that the large number of absentees had *some* effect on the social and political development of the colonies in the region. Certainly, absenteeism distinguished the Greater Caribbean from other regions in British North America. The key point here is that hurricanes were a major factor contributing to the development of an absentee class of planters in the region. The experience of living through one hurricane convinced many planters that they did not want to stay in the region to experience another. Christopher Jeaffreson, for example, survived two harrowing back-to-back storms on St. Christopher in 1681. The hurricanes leveled his plantation, and Jeaffreson worked over the next several months to get his plantation in order. On the eve of the next year's hurricane season, however, he was safely on board a ship back to England.[83] Many others followed a similar path.

CONCLUSION

Hurricanes remained the "principle dread" of those with property in the Greater Caribbean throughout the seventeenth and eighteenth centuries. As one colonist wrote, hurricanes "threaten [a planter's] life and estate, and for that reason he trembles at the thought of [them]."[84] The fear of the storms, it should be emphasized, never disappeared in the Greater Caribbean, but by the middle of the eighteenth century a number of factors helped mitigate colonists' concerns. First, attention to building practices lessened the level of devastation caused by the storms. The impact of construction changes was minimal and major storms still caused tremendous damage, but such adaptations enabled some buildings to survive that might not have otherwise. By extension, as time passed and more colonists migrated to the region in search of wealth, the built environment had reached a point where no amount of devastation could completely destroy colonists' improvements. Second, the development of private—and, by the end of the eighteenth century, public—relief networks helped planters recover from major calamities. Beginning in the 1740s, private organizations in England and in the northern colonies provided supplies and money to colonists in the Greater Caribbean, which eased the economic burdens wrought by hurricanes. Such aid did not provide complete compensation, but again, even minimal aid was important to distraught colonists.[85]

Finally, colonists recognized that the storms had some positive environmental consequences. Many noted that rainfall, so central to successful agriculture, increased in years after major tempests. One observer wrote, "hurricanes . . . contribute to produce more plentiful crops, and to ripen the fruit of the earth."[86] Others thought the storms helped purify the air of the region.[87] Edward Long, a Jamaican planter and politician, believed hurricanes answered to "some wise, perhaps salutary purpose in the economy of nature," although he noted "they are the sort of medicines extremely rough in their operations."[88]

What compelled colonists to stay in so unstable a region, one subject to such violent fits of nature, one in which property was so precarious? The answer was simple: money. The same environment that produced hurricanes also allowed for the production of exotic staple crops that generated tremendous wealth for those who had the resources and fortitude to withstand the calamities that regularly tested both. If the colonies of the Greater Caribbean "were not troubled . . . by hurri-

canes," commented one observer in the 1740s, "the fertility and beauty
. . . would make [them] as desirable a situation for pleasure, as . . . for
profits, which in spite of these disadvantages, draw hither such a number of people."[89] Hurricanes did not stop the development of colonies
in the Greater Caribbean, but they did help shape the type of society
that developed there. And for colonists steeped in ideologies of improvement, the mangled fields and shattered buildings that littered the
landscape in the wake of these strange and violent storms provided potent reminders of the power of nature in the New World and the
fragility of human efforts to transform it.

NOTES

1. Thanks to Russell Menard, John Howe, and Steven Biel for their sug-
gestions. Earlier versions of this paper were presented at the Fourth Annual
Conference of the Omohundro Institute of Early American History and Culture,
Worcester, Massachusetts, in June 1997, and at the Early American History
Workshop at the University of Minnesota in January 1997. I am grateful for the
comments and criticisms of participants at the conference and the workshop.

2. "Paper to the Lords Proprietor," c. 1686, quoted in David Ludlum, *Early
American Hurricanes, 1492-1870* (Boston: American Meteorological Association,
1963), 41.

3. William Bradford, *Of Plymouth Plantation*, ed. Samuel Eliot Morrison,
vol. 1 (New York: Alfred A. Knopf, 1952), 155-56.

4. Charles de Rochefort, *The History of the Caribby-Islands*, trans. John
Davies (London, 1666), 143-44.

5. Edmund Burke, *An Account of European Settlements in America*, vol. 2.
(London, 1757), 93–94.

6. William Beckford, *A Descriptive Account of the Island of Jamaica* (London,
1790), 89.

7. See Roderick Nash, *Wilderness and the American Mind* (New Haven,
Conn.: Yale University Press, 1967); John Canup, *Out of the Wilderness: The Emergence of an American Identity in Colonial New England* (Middletown, Conn.: Wes-
leyan University Press, 1990); and Peter Carroll, *Puritanism and Wilderness: The
Intellectual Significance of the New England Frontier, 1629-1700* (New York: Columbia University Press, 1970). On the fear of Indians, see Jill Lepore, *In the
Name of War: King Philip's War and the Origins of American Identity* (New York: Alfred A. Knopf, 1998). Studies of the environment in the Greater Caribbean include: Karen Kupperman, "The Fear of Hot Climate in the Anglo-American
Colonial Experience," *William and Mary Quarterly* 41 (1984): 213-40, and "The

Puzzle of the American Climate in the Early Colonial Period," *American Historical Review* 87 (1982): 1262-89; Joyce Chaplin, "Climate and Southern Pessimism: The Natural History of an Idea," in *The South as an American Problem*, ed. Larry Griffin and Don Doyles (Athens: University of Georgia Press, 1995), 57-82.

8. The classic example is the Great Storm of 1703. For a contemporary account, see Daniel Defoe, *The Storm, or a Collection of the Most Remarkable Casualties and Disasters which Happen'd in the late Dreadful Tempest* (London, 1704); reprinted as *An Historical Account of the Great and Tremendous Storm which happened here on November 26, 1703* (London, 1769).

9. There is some debate about whether this particular storm was actually a hurricane. David Ludlum, author of the best modern compilation of hurricane accounts, suggests it was more likely a strong storm that formed a waterspout. The wind direction, lack of sea swells, and limited destruction all argue against it being a hurricane. See Ludlum, *Early American Hurricanes*. For the other position, see Samuel Eliot Morrison, *Admiral of the Ocean Sea: A Life of Christopher Columbus* (Boston: Little, Brown, 1942), vol. 2, 172-73.

10. William Strachey, "A True Reportory of the Wracke and Redemption of Sir Thomas Gates," in *The Elizabethan's America: A Collection of Early Reports by Englishmen on the New World*, ed. Louis Wright (London: E. Arnold, 1965), 188-94.

11. *Troilus and Cressida* (1602): "not the dreadful spout / Which shipman do the hurricano call" (V, ii, 171); *King Lear* (1605): "Blow, winds, and crack your cheeks! Rage! Blow! / You cataracts and hurricanoes" (III.ii.1-2). See S. K. Heninger, *A Handbook of Renaissance Meteorology, with Particular Reference to Elizabethan and Jacobean Literature* (Durham, N.C.: Duke University Press, 1960), 212. There is some literary debate about the sources for *The Tempest* and its relationship to the "discovery" of the New World, and some scholars maintain the play has no connection to Bermuda or Strachey's account. Peter Hulme outlines some of the major positions and presents a convincing argument that the play should be read in the "discursive milieux" of English colonialism, regardless of its specific sources. See Hulme, *Colonial Encounters: Europe and the Native Caribbean, 1492-1797* (London: Methuen, 1986), 89-95.

12. *The Complete Works of Captain John Smith, 1580-1632*, ed. Philip Barbour (Chapel Hill: University of North Carolina Press, 1986), vol. 3, 226-29.

13. John Taylor, *New and Strange Newes from St. Christopher, of a tempestuous spirit which is called by the Indians a Hurri Cano* in *Two Tracts*, ed. C. H. Wilkinson (Oxford, 1946). Wilkinson's book is almost as rare as the original document. The two known copies of the original are found at the Huntington Library in California and Worcester College Library, Oxford.

14. *A Relation of the Late Dreadful Tempest, or Hurricane that happened in Holland and Utrech* (London, 1674).

15. Increase Mather, *An Essay for the Recording of Illustrious Providences* (Boston, 1684; reprint, Delmar, N.Y.: Scholars' Facsimiles, 1977), 320.

16. Edmond Halley, "An Account of the Trade Winds, and Monsoons, observable in the seas between and near the Tropics," *Philosophical Transactions of the Royal Society* 16 (1686): 153–68.

17. Bradford, *Of Plymouth Plantation, 1620–1647*, 279-80.

18. Daniel Defoe, *An Historical Account*, 16–17n.

19. Quoted in Peter Wood, *Black Majority: Negroes in Colonial South Carolina from 1670 through the Stono Rebellion* (New York: Alfred A. Knopf, 1974), 33. On other connections and similarities between South Carolina and the West Indian colonies, see Jack Greene, "Colonial South Carolina and the Caribbean Connection," in his *Imperatives, Behaviors, and Identities: Essays in Early American Cultural History* (Charlottesville: University of Virginia Press, 1992), 68-86.

20. Taylor, *New and Strange Newes from St. Christophers.*

21. N.N., *America: or an Exact Description of the West Indies* (London, 1655), 47.

22. Taylor, *New and Strange Newes from St. Christophers.*

23. Rochefort, *History of the Caribby-Islands*, 143.

24. Quoted in Carl and Roberta Bridenbaugh, *No Peace Beyond the Line: The English in the Caribbean, 1624–1690* (New York: Oxford University Press, 1972), 186.

25. Major John Scott (Nevis) to Joseph Williamson, 16 July 1667, in *Calendar of State Papers, Colonial Series, America and West Indies* (London: Her Majesty's Stationery Office, 1860–), vol. 5, 483. Hereafter cited as *CSPC.*

26. John Bartram, "Diary of a Journey through the Carolinas, Georgia, and Florida, 1765-66," *Transactions of the American Philosophical Society* 33 (1942): 20.

27. Ralph Bohun noted that hurricanes had become major "subjects of our [English] Gazets; and scarce a year passes but we have Accounts from the American Plantations, of the Damages they have sustain'd by Hurricanes." Ralph Bohun, *A Discourse on the Origine and Properties of Wind, with An Historical Account of Hurricanes and other Tempestuous Winds* (Oxford, 1671), 295.

28. David Hall, *Worlds of Wonder, Days of Judgment: Popular Religious Belief in Early New England* (Cambridge: Harvard University Press, 1989), 71-72.

29. Hall, *Worlds of Wonder*, 72. In addition to Hall, see Keith Thomas, *Religion and the Decline of Magic* (New York: Scribner, 1971; reprint, London: Penguin, 1973); Lorraine Daston and Katherine Park, *Wonders and the Order of Nature, 1150-1750* (New York: Zone Books, 1998); and Jon Butler, *Awash in a Sea of Faith: Christianizing the America People* (Cambridge: Harvard University Press, 1990).

30. "Captain Langford's Observations of his own Experience upon Hurricanes, and their Prognosticks," *Philosophical Transactions of the Royal Society* 20 (1698): 407-16.

31. Taylor, *New and Strange Newes from St. Christophers.*

32. *Strange News from Virginia.*

33. Sophia Hulme, *An Epistle to the Inhabitants of South Carolina* (London, 1754), 5-6.

34. Acts of Jamaica, CO 139/8/102, Public Record Office, Kew; Charles Leslie, *A True and Exact History of Jamaica* (London, 1740), 307. For examples of eighteenth-century fast day sermons, see P. Touch, *A Thanksgiving Sermon, preached at St. Lucia, the Sunday after the Hurricane in October 1780, on board HMS Vengeance* (London, 1794). See also *A Form of Prayer to be Used on the Tenth of October* (Bridgetown, 1786). Both can be found at the John Carter Brown Library.

35. "Captain Langford's Observations," 407-16.

36. "Captain Langford's Observations," 407-16. Besides Langford, the following writers advanced theories regarding the natural causes of hurricanes: Bohun, *Origine and Properties of Wind*; Jonathan Atkins, *A Voyage to Guinea, Brasil, and the West Indies* (London, 1735), 237-38; Griffin Hughes, *The Natural History of Barbados* (London, 1750), 28-29; Dr. Peyssonnell, "Observations upon the Currents of the Sea, at the Antilles of America," *Philosophical Transactions of the Royal Society* 49 (1756): 624-30; Edward Long, *The History of Jamaica* (London, 1774), vol. 3, 620.

37. Thomas, *Religion and the Decline of Magic*, 767-800; Daston and Park, *Wonders and the Order of Nature*; Michael Winship, *Seers of God: Puritan Providentialism in the Restoration and Early Enlightenment* (Baltimore: Johns Hopkins University Press, 1996); Sara Errington, "The History of Wonders in Eighteenth-Century New England" (Ph.D. dissertation, Brown University, forthcoming). I want to thank Sara Errington for sharing with me her work in progress.

38. "Captain Langford's Observations," 407; Ralph Bohun, *Origine and Properties of Wind*, 2-5; P. Charlevoix, *A Voyage to North America . . . and a Description and Natural History of the Islands of the West Indies* (Dublin, 1766), 291-92.

39. Bohun, *Origine and Properties of Wind*, 2-5.

40. Burke, *European Settlements in America*, 94. Burke, it should be noted, essentially plagiarized Charlevoix's account of the New World.

41. The complex relationship between scientific and religious explanations for disasters in the eighteenth century is a central theme of several essays in *Dreadful Visitations: Confronting Natural Catastrophe in the Age of Enlightenment*, ed. Alessa Johns (New York: Routledge, 1999).

42. John Taylor, "Multum in Pravo or Parvum in Multo, Taylor's Historie of his Life and Travels in America," vol. 2 (1686), manuscript, Institute of Jamaica, Kingston, folio 316-17. This is not the same John Taylor that wrote the treatise on the St. Christopher hurricane.

43. Edmond Halley, "An Historical Account of the Trade Winds, and Monsoons, observable in the seas between and near the Tropicks," *Philosophical Transactions of the Royal Society* 16 (1686): 153-68.

44. Bryan Edwards, *The History of the British Colonies in the West Indies* (London, 1794), 9-10.

45. Antoine Biet, *Voyage de la France Equinoxiale en l'Isle de Cayenne* (Paris, 1664), 288 (my translation).

46. Governor Lord Hamilton to Council of Trade and Plantations, 10 October 1712, in *CSPC*, vol. 27, 61.

47. Charlevoix, *Voyage to North America,* 291.

48. For a discussion of the equipment used in sugar production, see Richard Dunn, *Sugar and Slaves: The Rise of the Planter Class in the British West Indies, 1624-1713* (New York: W. W. Norton, 1972), 189-190. For rice production, see Joyce Chaplin, *An Anxious Pursuit: Agricultural Innovation and Modernity in the Lower South, 1715-1830* (Chapel Hill: University of North Carolina Press, 1993), 227-76.

49. *South Carolina Gazette*, 10 October 1752.

50. Colonial Office Records, CO 28/60/181, British Public Record Office, Kew.

51. Governor Parke to Council of Trade and Plantations, 8 October 1707, *CSPC*, vol. 23, 558-59.

52. Governor Parke to Council of Trade and Plantations, 6 March 1708, *CSPC*, vol. 23, 689-90.

53. Laurens to Reynolds, Getly and Co., 21 September 1772, in *The Papers of Henry Laurens*, ed. George Rogers et al. (Columbia: University of South Carolina Press, 1980), 466.

54. Peter Marsden, *A Gentleman Lately Resident on a Plantation* (Newcastle, 1788), 44.

55. Jack Greene, "Changing Identity in the British West Indies in the Early Modern Period: Barbados as a Case Study," in Greene, *Imperatives, Behaviors, and Identities*, 13-67.

56. John Cordy Jeaffreson, ed., *A Young Squire of the Seventeenth Century: From the Papers of Christopher Jeaffreson* (London, 1878), 277.

57. Jeaffreson, *A Young Squire of the Seventeenth Century*, 277; An American, *American Husbandry: Containing an Account of the Soil, Climate, Production, and Agriculture of the British Colonies* (London, 1775), 114.

58. Governor William Lord Willoughby to the King, 11 February 1668, *CSPC*, vol. 5, 546.

59. Patricia Seed, *Ceremonies of Possession in the European Conquest of the New World, 1492-1640* (New York: Cambridge University Press, 1995), 16-40. For a discussion of the importance of fences, see also William Cronon, *Changes in the Land: Indians, Colonists, and the Ecology of New England* (New York: Hill and Wang, 1983), 55-81, 127-56. For another discussion of the symbolic importance of houses and other improvements to English colonists in the New World, see Lepore, *In the Name of War*, 79-83.

60. Edward Littleton, *The Groans of the Plantations* (London, 1689), 19.

61. Council and Assembly of South Carolina to Council of Trade and Plantations, 24 December 1719, in *CSPC*, vol. 31, 288.

62. On the transition to slavery in the Caribbean, see Dunn, *Sugar and Slaves*, 224-62; for South Carolina, see Wood, *Black Majority*, 35-62, 131-66.

63. Jack Greene, "Colonial South Carolina and the Caribbean Connection," in Greene, *Imperatives, Behaviors, and Identities*, 68-86.

64. Governor Russell to Lords of Trade and Plantations, 24 October 1694, in *CSPC*, vol. 14, 385.

65. Minutes of the Assembly of Barbados, 28-29 September 1675, in *CSPC*, vol. 9, 288; Petition of the Merchants and Planters in Barbados to the King, 11 May 1675, in *CSPC*, vol. 10, 83.

66. John Oldmixon, *The British Empire in America, Containing a History of the Discovery, Settlement, Progress, and Present State of all the British Colonies on the Continent and Islands of America* (London, 1708), vol. 2, 36, 203.

67. Karen Kupperman, "Climate and Mastery of the Wilderness in Seventeenth-Century New England," in *Seventeenth-Century New England*, ed. David Hall and David Grayson (Boston: Colonial Society of Massachusetts, 1984), 3-37.

68. Oldmixon, *British Empire in America*, vol. 2, 102. Griffin Hughes, writing somewhat later, agreed that hurricanes had become less frequent. Hughes, *Natural History of Barbados*, 29.

69. Oldmixon, *British Empire in America*, vol. 2, 38, 87. On English housing in the region, see Dunn, *Sugar and Slaves*, 287-94.

70. "Answers to the Inquiries sent to Colonel Stapleton, Governor of the Leeward Islands," 22 November 1676, in *CSPC*, vol. 9, 499.

71. The most detailed information on hurricane houses comes from a series of claims filed by planters on Nevis and St. Kitts in the aftermath of the French invasion in 1707. These claims give detailed accounts of the property lost during the invasion; many note the destruction of "hurricane houses." The Leeward Islands claims are found in three volumes housed in the British Public Record Office in Kew, Colonial Series, 243/2, vols. 1-3. Details on Thomas Joseph are in CO 243/2, vol. 2.

72. CO 243/2, vol. 3.

73. Elias Bull, "Storm Towers of the Santee Delta," *South Carolina Historical Magazine* 81 (1980): 95-105.

74. Sir Charles Wheler to Council for Foreign Plantations, 9 December 1671, in *CSPC*, vol. 7, 289. Ian Steele rightly notes that colonial governors had reason to exaggerate their isolation, since it gave them greater control over local affairs. Moreover there is evidence that the colonies were not as cut off as such statements may suggest. Shipping returns indicate that vessels cleared in and out of Greater Caribbean ports throughout the year. Nevertheless, there was a marked decrease in shipping activity during the hurricane months. See Steele, *The English Atlantic*,

1675-1740: An Exploration of Communication and Community (New York: Oxford University Press, 1986); Matthew Mulcahy, "Melancholy and Fatal Calamities: Natural Disasters and Colonial Society in the British Greater Caribbean, 1623-1781" (Ph.D. dissertation, University of Minnesota, 1999), 130-39.

75. Laurens to Smith and Clifton, 17 July 1755, in *The Papers of Henry Laurens*, ed. Philip Hamer et al. (Columbia: University of South Carolina Press, 1968), 295. See also Benjamin Mosely, *A Treatise of Tropical Diseases; and on the Climate of the West-Indies* (London, 1787), 8-9.

76. Ralph Davis, *The Rise of the English Shipping Industry in the Seventeenth and Eighteenth Centuries* (London: Macmillan, 1962), 318, 377; Richard Pares, *War and Trade in the West Indies, 1739-1763* (London: Frank Cass, 1936), 496-97.

77. See, for example, Governor Stapleton to Lords of Trade and Plantations, 8 August 1678, in *CSPC*, vol. 10, 281; Governor Hamilton (Antigua) to Mr. Popple, 10 September 1718, in *CSPC*, vol. 30, 349. For South Carolina, see Robert Pringle to Andrew Pringle, 7 September 1742, in *The Letterbook of Robert Pringle*, ed. Walter Edgar (Columbia: University of South Carolina Press, 1972), vol. 1, 407.

78. Dunn, *Sugar and Slaves*, 93-95. Peter Wood likewise speculated that the hurricane was one of several factors that pushed distraught Barbadians to emigrate to the newly established colony in South Carolina. Wood, *Black Majority*, 8-9. The Governor of Barbados complained that "land monopolized into so few hands" was a major problem as early as 1667. "Observations on the Island of Barbados," December 1667, in *CSPC*, vol. 5, 528-29.

79. Representation of the General Assembly of Barbados to the Council of Trade and Plantations, 27 August 1731, in *CSPC*, vol. 38, 242-45.

80. Frank Wesley Pitman, *The Development of the British West Indies, 1700-1763* (New Haven: Yale University Press, 1917), 91.

81. Jack Greene, "Colonial South Carolina and the Caribbean Connection," in Greene, *Imperatives, Behaviors, and Identities*, 80.

82. The most powerful case for the West Indies colonies as social failures during the seventeenth century is made in Bridenbaugh, *No Peace Beyond the Line*. Alan Karras likewise writes that he does "not believe that what could be called a creole society developed in the eighteenth century" in Jamaica. Karras, *Sojourners in the Sun: Scottish Migrants in Jamaica and the Chesapeake, 1740-1800* (Ithaca, N.Y.: Cornell University Press, 1992), 47, n. 4. The biggest supporter of the colonies as settler societies is Jack Greene, who makes his case most forcefully for Barbados in his essay "Changing Identity in the British West Indies in the Early Modern Era: Barbados as a Case Study," in Greene, *Imperatives, Behaviors, and Identities*, 13-67. Edward Brathwaite argues that a creole society did develop in Jamaica, but not until after the American Revolution. Brathwaite, *The Development of Creole Society in Jamaica, 1770-1820* (Oxford: Clarendon Press, 1971).

83. Jeaffreson, ed., *A Young Squire of the Seventeenth Century*, 274-80.

84. Leslie, *New and Exact History of Jamaica*, 40.

85. Mulcahy, "Melancholy and Fatal Calamities," 210-50.

86. Abbe Raynal, *A Philosophical and Political History of the Settlements and Trade of Europeans in the East and West Indies* (London, 1778), vol. 3, 254.

87. Lionel Chalmers, *An Account of the Weather and Diseases of South Carolina* (London, 1750), 10-11.

88. Edward Long, *History of Jamaica*, vol. 3, 619.

89. Charlevoix, *Voyage to North America*, 305.

2

"The Hungry Year"

1789 on the Northern Border of Revolutionary America

Alan Taylor

In 1789, hunger was so severe along the border between the United States and Canada that those who suffered described what they endured as a "famine." Yet, according to Alan Taylor, "American historians are wont to deny even the possibility of such an episode of widespread hunger in the nation's past." Taylor's essay remedies that denial by painstakingly reconstructing the experience of the "dearth," assessing its magnitude, investigating its causes, and charting the divergent American and Canadian attempts to relieve the suffering. Challenging the notion of "natural" disasters, Taylor contends "that the causes for the dearth of 1789 were a complex medley where social and cultural considerations loomed larger than the intervention of what we call 'nature.'"

IN THE SPRING and early summer of 1789, hunger became widespread on the northern borderland shared by Canada and the United States. Within the United States, the suffering was greatest in the newly settled upland districts in northeastern Pennsylvania, upstate New York, and western Vermont. In Canada, the hunger extended from Niagara on the west through the Province of Quebec and into the Maritimes. Although occasionally noted in local histories, the extent and significance of the dearth of 1789 has escaped the attention of national historians in the United States; no previous work has drawn together the many local episodes to reconstruct its sweep. Indeed, American historians are wont to deny even the possibility of such an episode of widespread hunger in their nation's past.

The contemporary sources often, yet vaguely, refer to deaths from starvation, but they never specify names and numbers. Usually the sources locate the purported deaths just over the horizon in some other locale. Because the hunger prevailed primarily in places without comprehensive vital records, the demographic consequences of the dearth remain murky. My best guess is that, although the suffering was widespread and severe, deaths were few. Consequently, the hunger is best called a "dearth" rather than a "famine" (which is characterized by a severely enhanced level of mortality). However, this is a distinction of contemporary social science that was not available to the sufferers of 1789, who often referred to their plight as a "famine."

In addition to documenting the extent and intensity of the dearth of 1789, this essay seeks its causes. Our commonplace view of "disasters" takes for granted the human presence in harm's way and characterizes disasters as "natural," as simply the uncontrollable—albeit lamentable—consequence of extreme swings in geophysical processes: storms, earthquakes, floods, and volcanoes. However, recent revisionist scholarship on contemporary disasters argues, in the words of Anthony Oliver-Smith, "that human groups and institutions play a far more active role in the creation of destructive agents and circumstances than is usually imagined or portrayed." Societies tend to place certain people, usually the poorest and most powerless, in dangerous circumstances; blaming "nature" for the consequent "disaster" serves to absolve the social order, reaffirming its claims to justice—especially if the rulers can provide palliatives to the victims. Following the lead of this revisionist scholarship, I argue that the causes for the dearth of 1789 were a complex medley where social and cultural considerations loomed larger than the intervention of what we call "nature."[1]

Nature did contribute to the dearth in two related forms: a wheat parasite, the Hessian fly, curtailed the wheat harvest of 1788 in parts of the borderland; and an unusually cold spring in 1789 was psychologically devastating. Both forms derived largely from a global cooling effected by volcanic dust in the upper atmosphere. But three social aspects intensified and extended the localized natural problems into a geographically broad crisis. First, market incentives drained provisions from the borderland at the worst possible time—in the fall and winter of 1788-1789. Second, during the following spring, poor and poorly informed settlers emigrated into the suffering districts, compounding the shortage of food (especially in northern Pennsylvania, upstate New

York, and western Vermont). Third, belated but alarmist reporting of the crisis by the press in June extended the alarm, raising grain prices and provoking speculative hoarding where there had previously been a "natural" surplus (primarily in southern and eastern New England).

As is often the case with dearths and famines, the crisis was primarily one of maldistribution of supply, rather than absolute shortfall in production. Only the inroads of the Hessian fly reduced farm production, and this was limited to one grain—wheat—and geographically confined to parts of Canada and New England. From that core region, the crisis became widespread through a process of exacerbation by the other four causes. Although essentially "natural," the cold spring did not so much reduce food supply as spread panic. By arousing fears that the crisis would be prolonged, the long, cold spring discouraged people who had grain from parting with it, hindering the movement of food that might have alleviated suffering in the few places with an absolute shortfall. The combined effects of external market, internal migration, and alarmist reporting did not reduce food production, but instead exported a surplus from an area in which especially vulnerable people were then concentrated.

Because disasters are conjunctions between the social and the natural, they offer richly documented occasions for assessing the social structures and norms of afflicted communities. During the dearth of 1789, inequalities in market power enabled people with the best information and a surplus of grain to reap windfall profits, at the expense of both those who needed the grain and those who lacked the information. Fundamentally, disasters both reveal and heighten a society's inequalities.

The dearth of 1789 is also politically telling because the suffering region was bisected by a newly established boundary between the American republic and the Canadian provinces of the British Empire. The contrasting responses, north and south, to the dearth reveal the differing public cultures established by the American Revolution and demarcated by the new border. Although both British North America and the United States were market-based societies, the larger public sector and more paternalistic ethos of the British Empire contrasted with the virtual absence of state action and public resources in the American republic. Indeed, the differing responses to the dearth furthered the cultural process by which the British colonial elite defined their identity against their understanding of the Americans as excessively commercial and socially callous.

EXTENT

In the spring and early summer of 1789 hunger reigned in the Indian villages and the many new settlements of the northeastern United States and in their counterparts across the border in British-held Canada. Throughout that vast northern borderland, settlers and visitors described a severe and occasionally deadly dearth of food for people and their livestock. In April 1789, land speculator and developer William Cooper returned to Cooperstown, his new settlement in central New York. He found that "there remained nor one pound of salt meat nor a single biscuit. . . . Judge of my feelings at this epoch, with two hundred families about me, and not a morsel of bread."[2]

To Cooper's immediate south, hunger prevailed in the new settlements along the Susquehanna valley of New York and northeastern Pennsylvania. Armed, hungry, and penniless settlers halted and plundered several boats transporting flour up and down the river. One merchant lost twenty bushels of flour. His friend reported, "The people . . . collected about him in arms & told him they would not starve, that they had not money to pay him but must have flour & would pay him when they were able." In normal times, the settlers obeyed the laws protecting private property. But during an emergency they claimed the right to seize food, promising eventual payment at pre-dearth prices. Apparently, such bread rioting was confined to the Upper Susquehanna because there the settlers were especially desperate and there they had access to cargoes of grain from elsewhere moving up and down the river. Most other hungry settlers lived too far from shipments of grain for rioting to have any effect.[3]

In mid-July, Samuel Preston led a party of surveyors up the Susquehanna to lay out a road along the New York-Pennsylvania border. Hungry settlers gathered and followed along, begging for food. On July 18, Preston assured them that he could not afford to part with his scant supplies. "But all these arguments had no effect . . . and I was obliged to dribble them out a little at a time, lest they should rise and take it all by violence, which considering the starving condition of the people, for very few of them had any kind of bread, I apprehended there was danger of." During the next three days, he encountered twenty more families "all in a starving condition for provision, many . . . weakened with starving, even past ability to labor or tend their corn." On July 31, he recorded in his journal, "The people's distress for provisions increased. Their importuning me increased also . . . I fully expected them to raise [up] and take all I had." Whenever Preston did spare them a little food, he observed, "I believe they were really very hungry by the way they eat."[4]

Conditions were even worse further north and west in the Genesee country of western New York. Indeed, many Genesee settlers fled eastward to the comparative plenty of the Susquehanna valley. In June 1789, Benjamin Young reported from Loyalsock Creek on the Upper Susquehanna:

> The people of the Genesee and Niagara Country are crouding in upon us every day, owing to the great scarsity of provisions, the most of them who have gone there lately are starving to death and it is shocking to humanity to hear of the number of families that are dying daily for want of sustenance. . . . The wild roots and herbs that the country affords, boiled & without salt, constitute the whole food of most of the unhappy people who have been decoyed there thro' the flattering account of the quality of the land.

During the summer, eastern newspapers printed and reprinted Young's letter as a warning to prospective settlers to stay home.[5]

Hunger also prevailed among the Indian villages of central and western New York. In February, the Onondaga sachem Kaightoten reported "that his nation were in great want of provisions." Bearing that news to New York's governor in Albany, the Onondaga emissary had to kill his horse for provisions en route. On June 1–3, the Oneida tribe assembled at Fort Schuyler, on the Upper Mohawk River, in hope of obtaining food from the visiting New York Commissioners of Indian Affairs. The sachem Good Peter explained, "We are so faint that we cannot speak to you, and our Women and Children are come likewise to see you and are very hungry and have no provisions at home." But the commissioners had little food to spare. Further west, at Canandaigua, in mid-July the land speculator Oliver Phelps had to feed hundreds of starving Cayuga, Onondaga, and Seneca Indians. His agent Judah Colt recalled:

> They came & went away hungry, notwithstanding upwards of 100 heads of Cattle was killed for them. Flour was not plenty. It was reported during the Treaty & I think [it] not unlikely that the flour of one barrel made up into bread sold for 100 Dollars worth in silver plates of various kind of Indian ornaments. Many horses died distempered

during the Treaty. The Indians fed on them freely & also the blood and entrails of all the Beef slaughtered.[6]

In the spring and summer of 1789, the Reverend Samuel Kirkland, a missionary among the Oneida Indians, recorded the hunger's grim inroads on his people and himself. In March, Kirkland reported that "the uncommon scarcity of provisions" prevailed "universally through the territory of the Six Nations, and down the Mohawk-River till we reach Albany." In late April, as the Indians exhausted their supply of corn, "Their pressing, importunate applications to me for relief are too much for the feelings of humanity to remain unmoved, even to the injury of one's property. They come with their intreaties and apply to me as their Father and only friend, who will compassionate them in their distresses; and I cannot turn a deaf ear to their cries." On June 25, an Indian father with five children pleaded to Kirkland, "We are very hungry and almost starved. . . . My family have not tasted any bread, or meat for many days; nothing but herbs and sometimes small fish. I am so weak I can't hoe any corn. I have been travelling all day among white people, but they can't give me any thing." Kirkland's own supplies ran low and he reduced himself to two and sometimes only one meal a day. In early July, he became bedridden with fatigue and dysentery for "want of suitable food."[7]

Hunger also prevailed eastward among the new towns in the hill country of the Upper Hudson valley and the New England interior. On May 13, 1789, Dr. Alexander Coventry went to the gristmill near Claverack, New York, for grain, but he could get only a single bushel of rye, "there being only two bushels in the mill." On the other side of the Massachusetts border in Lanesborough, a town in Berkshire County, Captain Daniel Brown gave away three hundred bushels of grain "and a very large quantity of potatoes" to the "poor families in the vicinity . . . and thereby saved them from distress, and perhaps death." Further north, on the New York shore of Lake Champlain, in early May a correspondent reported that "It is almost impossible to describe the extreme distress surrounding the people here. No bread or provision of any kind. The scene is truly painful. . . . Some have died, and many are sick. I was without bread fourteen days, and obliged to live on my seed potatoes."[8]

The hunger was also severe and widespread in the new settlements among the Green Mountains of Vermont. In May, the Reverend Nathan Perkins, a visiting missionary, grimly reported, "The year 1789 will be remembered by Vermont as a day of calamity and famine—dearness of truck & want of bread in all their dwellings. It is supposed by the most judicious & knowing that more than 1/4 part of the people will have neither bread nor meat for 8 weeks—and that some will starve." He noted, "Several women I saw had lived four or five days without any food, and had eight or ten Children starving around them—crying for bread & the poor women had wept till they looked like Ghosts."[9]

Similar reports of hunger extended from Nova Scotia in the Maritimes westward through the old French villages and towns along the St. Lawrence River to the newer settlements founded by Loyalist refugees around Lake Ontario. In June William Clark reported from Digby, Nova Scotia, "The Dearness of Provisions & Scarcity of many things, not to be had for money, the Poverty of the People, and apprehensions of an approaching famine, have induced Some Gentlemen to put forward a petition to his Majesty, praying [for] some immediate Relief, or Numbers of the people must actually Starve."[10]

Conditions were equally harsh in the province of Quebec, especially in the rural villages near Montreal. In early June, the executive council of Quebec collected grim testimony about the hunger. Witnesses calculated that the wheat harvest of 1788 was less than half that of the preceding year. William Grant testified "that there is not one bushel of wheat for sale within twenty miles" of his residence at Trois Rivières. After touring the rural parishes in the District of Montreal, John Blackwood reported in early June:

> The distresses of the generality of the inhabitants was inconceivable, numbers leaving their habitations and were begging about the Country to avoid starving. . . . Many of the Inhabitants even eat the carcases of every Dead animal they found, and that several had even killed their Horses for the sustenance of their families, and that many had little else to give their Children than broth of boiled peas [and] straw.

The merchant Alexander Cairns could not obtain a single bushel of wheat from his habitant debtors, in a district where he had previously collected six thousand bushels annually.[11]

In response to the worsening shortage of grain, the magistrates of Quebec and Montreal, the province's leading towns, steadily raised "the assize of bread," the regulated price for loaves of white and brown bread. Examined over time, the shifting assize reveals the pace and severity of the dearth. In Montreal in July 1788, before the dearth began, the prevailing four-pound loaf of white bread cost six pence, as did the six-pound loaf of brown (such a loaf was considered sufficient to feed most families for a day). That price rose during the fall as merchants and consumers recognized the short harvest. By December, the white loaf cost nine pence and the brown cost ten pence. During the winter and spring of 1789, the price soared as consumption exhausted the previous fall's grain crops. In July 1789, the price peaked at fourteen pence for white and sixteen pence for brown—more than twice the cost of the year before (see Tables 1 and 2 at the end of this essay). As a consequence, most of the town's inhabitants could no longer afford their daily bread. In April and May 1789 in Montreal a charitable subscription provided rations of bread, beef, and peas to "about Fourteen Hundred Persons daily." On June 1, Alexander Fraser of Montreal warned that the charitable fund "is nearly consumed and God only knows what those poor families will suffer when that is finished."[12]

The hunger also prevailed in the Loyalist settlements along the Upper St. Lawrence and around Kingston, on the eastern end of Lake Ontario, and Niagara on the west. In March, a Niagara settler reported that "cats, &c. have been substituted for beef." He was "doubtful how he and his neighbours will be able to spin out life until next harvest." At the end of May, the merchant John Richardson ascended the St. Lawrence from Montreal to Kingston. Writing to a correspondent in New York's Mohawk valley, Richardson reported, "The people in the new settlements are starving for provisions, and pouring in crowds to your quarter for a supply." In early June, Philip Stedman traveled to Quebec to testify before the provincial council that only twenty of the six hundred settler families at Niagara had eaten bread during the preceding three months. For want of grain and meat, most had been reduced to boiling and eating basswood bark. Passing east from Niagara bound for Quebec, Stedman found similar suffering in the settlements along the Upper St. Lawrence. At the end of June, Captain Joseph Bunbury of Kingston reported that most of the inhabitants had "not for many weeks past tasted any kind of meat, bread or biscuit."[13]

CAUSES

The contemporary sources say remarkably little about the causes of the apparently short harvest of 1788. It seems that only in Canada, and perhaps in pockets of northern New England and upstate New York, was there an absolute decline in the harvest. In 1804, the agricultural reformer Lord Selkirk visited Canada and investigated the dearth of 1789. He concluded that "The cause of the failure is not well understood. It was called a Blight—from not knowing what else to call it. Some ascribe it to remarkably heavy rains just before harvest." More particular was the Montreal merchant John William Woolsey, who testified in June 1789 that "The cause of the scarcity, as he understood [it], was the wet season of the last year and the destruction by the insect called the Hessian Fly." This explanation fits the December 1788 observation by Lord Dorchester, the governor general of British North America: "The last harvest of wheat appears to have been more defective than was at first apprehended, many of the ears being found empty at the thrashing." The tiny Hessian fly penetrates the wheat stalk to lay its eggs; the hatched larvae feed upon and consume the ear as it matures, leaving a hollow kernel. The damp, cool weather of the summer of 1788 favored the inroads of the Hessian fly on the growing wheat.[14]

But even in Canada, where the crop shortfall was greatest, the inroads of the Hessian fly were more than "natural" because farmers had pursued a market-oriented strategy that gambled their life's bread on the wheat crop that was the Hessian fly's special delight. Instead of pursuing a subsistence-first strategy of planting diversified grain crops that included barley and rye (which were more resistant to the Hessian fly), Canadian farmers dedicated most of their tillage to wheat. They did so first because the export market offered especially high prices for Canadian wheat in 1787 and 1788, and second because they did not anticipate the spread of the Hessian fly, a newly arrived European parasite that migrated northward from Long Island over the course of the 1780s. During the winter and spring of 1788, Canadian farmers had sold most of the previous fall's wheat harvest to merchants for export to England. During the summer of 1788, Quebec's merchants exported 200,358 bushels of wheat and 9,886 barrels of flour—food that would be sorely missed in a few months. Farmers and merchants felt secure in the exports, counting upon the promising harvest of 1788 to restock the granaries. Consequently, the devastation wrought by the Hessian fly on the 1788 wheat crop came as a very painful surprise. The damage only became manifest when the farmers began to thresh the September 1788 wheat harvest. Lord Dorchester later explained, "The number of sheaves gathered having promised . . . three times the quantity of grain

[that] they were found actually to contain at the thrashing . . . so that the real state of the country was unknown till the stock was nearly exhausted." With perfect hindsight, in September 1789 Captain Freeman of Quebec blamed the spring and early summer hunger on the governor general for "inconsiderately permitting, last autumn, too general an exportation." Had Canadians been less wedded to the export market and, consequently, less dedicated to wheat, the impact of the Hessian fly would have been less life-threatening.[15]

The especially cold and damp summer of 1788, which facilitated the Hessian fly's proliferation, derived from the relatively cold global climate and abnormal wind circulation patterns of the 1780s. Climate historians attribute the unusual global pattern to major volcanic explosions in Iceland and Japan in the spring and summer of 1783. The eruptions blew millions of tons of particulates into the upper atmosphere, reducing the amount of warming sunlight reaching the earth's surface. Because it took years for the dust to dissipate, the eruptions lowered global temperatures, curtailed growing seasons, disrupted regional wind patterns, and dislocated precipitation for the rest of the decade. The suffering was especially intense in Japan, where as many as a million peasants may have died from the volcano-induced famine of 1783-1784. The disruption of "normal" precipitation patterns also curtailed the 1785 grain harvest in the uplands of Mexico, producing famine conditions there in 1786.[16]

Northeastern North America and northwestern Europe felt the greatest climatic impact in 1788 and early 1789. Ordinarily relatively dry in summer, New England and Canada experienced unusual cold and heavy rains during the summer of 1788. Ordinarily cool and wet, England and France suffered through a hot and prolonged drought in the summer of 1788. Because farmers and grain merchants in northeastern North America and northwestern Europe had made their crop choices in anticipation of normal conditions, they suffered grievous disappointments in the abnormal conditions of 1788.

During the summer of 1788, England and especially France experienced an untimely inflow and unusual stagnation of torrid air from the Sahara to the south; hail storms followed in July, when the Atlantic provided a cold, damp front that collided with the "anti-cyclone from the Sahara." According to climate historian H. H. Lamb, 1788 was the driest year in 250 years of English record keeping. The summer drought withered, and then the hail stones battered the standing grain plants, producing a fall shortage of flour, escalating bread prices, and widespread rural anxiety. The winter of 1788-1789 proved unusually cold, and the spring of 1789 was especially late, delaying planting and arousing fears that the dearth would continue through the year. Because northeastern North America and northwestern Europe were linked by the transatlantic market, the greater harvest failure in the latter led to increased demands on the former, extending and deepening the hunger there.[17]

Political intervention, especially in France, magnified the market incentives for American merchants to export grains to Europe. Recognizing the crisis, on November 23, 1788, the French king and the Council of State offered unusual incentives for American imports: premiums of thirty sous per quintal of wheat and forty sous per quintal of flour imported between February 15 and June 30, 1789. In addition, the French exempted from the usual freight duties any American vessels bearing wheat or flour. In April 1789, the French doubled the bounties and extended them and the exemption on duties through August. In April, the British Parliament passed a bill permitting the importation of grain and flour from the United States—previously prohibited by law. Mercantile correspondence and newspaper reports carried the profitable news of the European demand and incentives to American seaport merchants, who scrambled to assemble cargoes of wheat for export. In 1789, France imported from the United States an unprecedented 140,959 barrels of flour; 3,664,176 bushels of wheat; 558,891 bushels of rye; and 520,262 bushels of barley. In May 1789, the Quebec merchant John William Woolsey traveled to New York City, hoping to purchase grain for importation into Canada. Finding little, he was "informed by the merchants there, that the country had been lately drained by great exportations."[18]

The urban merchant's windfall was the frontier settler's despair. Export of American grain from the older towns with surpluses deprived the frontier settlements of a reserve at the worst moment. In effect, frontier settlers in new communities with a grain shortfall found themselves losing out in the bidding for the grain surpluses in older farm districts. For example, during the 1780s the newer settlements in the uplands of central New York relied upon the wheat raised in the nearby but older farms in the warmer and more fertile Mohawk valley. William Cooper of Cooperstown (in upstate Otsego County) recalled, "In the winter preceding the summer of 1789, grain rose in Albany to a price before unknown. The demand swept the whole granaries of the Mohawk country. The number of beginners who depended upon it for their bread greatly aggravated the evil, and a famine ensued." Frontier settlers had not escaped into self-sufficient independence from a market society. On the contrary, the dearth of 1789 revealed the power and reach of the transatlantic market, and it demonstrated the dependence of frontier settlers on external food reserves.[19]

In 1788 and early 1789, a surge in settler migration to frontier communities in the uplands of New York, Vermont, and Pennsylvania concentrated poor families in the worst places at the worst time, when and where food was scarcest. The migrants, mistakenly counting on obtaining provisions from nearby farmers, brought too little food with them. To the settlers' dismay, in late spring 1789 they belatedly discovered that the farmers had already sold their surplus to merchants and were hard pressed to feed themselves. The mid- to late 1780s was a period of explosive frontier settlement as the return of peace unleashed the demand for new farms, a demand pent up during the long years of revolutionary war. For example, according to annual tax lists, in New York's Otsego country the number of families tripled from 64 in 1787 to 170 a year later. In April 1788 John Tunnecliff assured William Cooper, "Our Cunterey Grose Very fast. The Rode to the Butternutes is thro your Estate as thick setteled as Great Briton is in general. At the W[es]t side of Lake Otseager is still fuller." The prospects for further growth were promising because "several of your Tenance has Larg family of children which I Pray God to Bless With Helth and Sucksess." However, all those young, hungry mouths proved a liability a year later when the settlers ran out of food and even more newcomers arrived without sufficient provisions. At Cooperstown on May 7, 1789, William Cooper explained to his friend (and fellow land speculator) Henry Drinker, "The Vast Multitudes of People that Come Dayly to this Country have Causd a Scarcity of Provitions allmost to Famine and in the Genesee quite so . . . (Henry I have had 30 in a Day Seaking Lands of me but [who] Could not Look out much in the woods for want of Something to Subsist upon)."[20]

Just as the new settlers recognized their plight, the climate threatened an even bleaker future. In 1789, in northern North America the global cold regime produced a particularly long and cold winter. In some locales, the especially severe and snowy winter depleted the deer herds, to the detriment of human hunters. The deep snows hid the deer's usual sources of ground feed and encumbered their movements, rendering them an easier prey to wolves. A Canadian settler at the Bay of Quinte recalled the dispiriting consequences for human hunters: "The snow was unusually deep, so that the Deer fell an easy prey to their rapacious enemies, the wolves, who fattened on their destruction, whilst men were perishing from want. Nothing could be had in the woods."[21]

The prolonged winter cold delayed the spring, postponing the date when farmers could pasture their livestock and plant their grains. On April 30, 1789, Dr. Alexander Coventry of Claverack, Columbia County, New York, recorded in his diary, "Cold, cloudy, pretty calm; Blue Mountains covered with snow. This [is] a very backward season; wheat . . . does not seem to have grown any this spring. . . . Hoar frost yesterday morning, and cold for season." In early June a Vermont newspaper observed:

> The great want of that necessary article BREAD, it is feared . . . will be more severely felt the next season than it is the present, occasioned by the warm enlivening beams of the sun being withheld From us—for we can assure the public, that on ascending Mount Ayscutney, the 3d instant the snow was found from 12 to 25 inches in depth; and on the night of the 4th instant the frost was so severe in this place, as to congeal the water in a bucket to ice of a considerable thickness.

Similarly, on June 4, 1789, a correspondent from the Susquehanna valley of northern Pennsylvania reported, "The weather continues remarkably cold, and the season backward—the buds of many hickory trees not all expanded—frosts the three last nights—this morning ice as thick as window glass in the watering-trough in my yard."[22]

The late spring imperiled the settlers' cattle, who had exhausted their supply of winter hay and desperately needed new grass in their pastures. Many farmers were forced to slaughter cattle they had counted on as breeding and working stock. Livestock deaths deprived many north country families of the dairy cow that provided their milk and of the oxen they needed to plow their fields to plant a new crop. By debilitating (or killing) livestock and by delaying planting, the sustained spring frosts threatened to postpone the harvest of 1789. Given the short northern growing season in upland districts, the late planting raised the specter that the grain crops might not mature before the killing frosts of September. Consequently, the late spring and dying cattle took a psychological toll on settler morale. Already anxious over the short or overexported crop of 1788, many Americans and Canadians dreaded that the cold and late spring meant that worse was to come. The public alarm drove up prices and encouraged speculative hoarding, especially in June, when eastern newspapers spread the combined news of frontier hunger and the bleak prospects for the next harvest.[23]

Those news reports extended the dearth's reach south into the older and more eastern towns, which had not suffered from any significant shortfall in agricultural production. In southern New England, prosperous farmers and merchants began to hoard grain in anticipation of rising prices that would net them windfall profits. By reporting frontier hardships, editors had meant to help by discouraging further migration to the frontier and by encouraging relief efforts. Instead, the news spread the hunger as cupidity proved more compelling than empathy. In June, a newspaper writer in Vermont complained bitterly that "many persons of distinguished rank in life" had proved "the most officious and instrumental, in raising the price of grain to such an unreasonable height, as to render it utterly impossible for the sons of affliction to purchase, pleading in excuse *'That there is no way to determine the value of a bushel of wheat, only by what it will bring.'"* Although Stamford, Connecticut, was an old, coastal community far from the northern and upland origins of the dearth, by June that town's poorer inhabitants were suffering from hunger. On June 28, 1789, Ebenezer Dibble reported, "I never knew so great a cry for bread, and want of means to procure it."[24]

Some editors belatedly recognized their role in spreading the panic that exacerbated the dearth. As the publisher and editor of the *Worcester Spy,* Isaiah Thomas had played a key role in reporting the hunger. On June 18 he tried a different tack:

> The accounts lately published and circulated, respecting the scarcity of grain, appear to be greatly exaggerated. That there was not a sufficient supply in the British settlements is without a doubt true; and in consequence large quantities have been sold to the British subjects in America by the inhabitants of these States. A great handle we are assured has been made of this, by speculators and avaricious holders of grain, to enhance the price, but as the crops now look promising—the probability is that in a short time grain will be much more plenty and

cheaper than at present, and these canker worms to society [will] be disappointed in acquiring unjust gain.

In ensuing weeks, other newspapers from Portsmouth, New Hampshire to Philadelphia, Pennsylvania reprinted Isaiah Thomas's attempt to deflate the speculative bubble.[25]

Forsaking their earlier alarmism, in July and August the northeastern newspapers sought to allay public anxiety with reassuring reports that the new crops appeared especially promising, despite the late spring. A Vermont newspaper insisted (and other newspapers reprinted) that "The gloom is dispelled from the countenance of the industrious peasant, and the pleasing anticipation of plentiful harvests relieves the mind amidst the present scarcity." On July 9 the *New Hampshire Gazette* asserted, "The probability is, that within a short time, bread corn will be more plenty and cheaper than it has been the year past; and that the avaricious, oppressive monopolizers and holders of this stuff of life, will be obliged to eat it themselves, or sell it at a less price than they gave."[26]

In sum, in its full extent and at its deepest intensity in June and early July 1789, the dearth derived from the interplay of natural deviations from norms of temperature and precipitation with the social consequences of the transatlantic market. Even in Canada, social arrangements—primarily the export market that led merchants to demand payment in wheat from their farmer-creditors—compounded nature's assault on the expected harvest. Moreover, the dearth's southern and eastern extension into the new settlements of upstate New York, northern Pennsylvania, and western New England owed much to nature's unusually late spring of 1789. But that southern and eastern expansion primarily depended on the untimely and simultaneous escalations in grain exports to Europe and human imports into frontier settlements. Finally, the third extension of the dearth, south into the older towns of eastern New England, derived principally from the alarm and hoarding inspired by newspaper coverage.

RELIEF

Throughout spring and summer 1789, the starving settlers of the northern borderland had a threefold problem: they did not have enough to eat; they had little or no money to buy food; and there was little or no food to be bought in their vicinity. For immediate relief, the settlers had to hunt for and eat small animals and wild plants they had previously disdained as distasteful or paltry. Although unpleasant and laborious, this recourse to gathering had the advantages of being immediate and proximate: several wild plants produced edible fruits, nuts, or roots in June or July, well before the slower-growing domesticated plants the settlers cultivated in their new clearings. In May 1789, a resident of northern New York reported, "The common sustenance of the women and children has been tadpoles boiled in water, and pea straw which they swallowed till they began to swell in the glands of the throat." Niagara's settlers told a visitor that they survived by eating "strawberry leaves, beech leaves, flax seed dried, and ground in a coffee mill—catched the blood of a little pig—bled the almost famished cow and oxen. . . . The children leaped for joy at one robin being caught, out of which a whole pot of broth was made. They eat mustard, potato tops, sassafras root, and made tea of the tops. The relation was deeply affecting." Ironically, although their ultimate goal as settlers was to replace the diverse array of wild plants and animals with a narrower range of domesticated grasses, grains, and livestock, in the crisis of 1789 the settlers had to depend on the natural flora and fauna for their immediate survival.[27]

Wild leeks were an especially important emergency food because they matured early and abounded in the low, moist, shady grounds by creeks and hollows. In flush times settlers disdained its strong taste, but when dearth reigned, starvers could not be choosers. In central New York, William Cooper recalled:

> Many were reduced to such distress, as to live upon the roots of wild leeks; some more fortunate lived upon milk, whilst others supported nature by drinking a syrup made of maple sugar and water. The quantity of [wild] leeks they eat had such an effect upon their breath, that they could be smelled at many paces distance, and when they came together, it was like cattle that had pastured in a garlic field. A man of the name of Beets mistaking some poisonous herb for a leek, eat it, and died in consequence.

In search of the wild leek, some hungry settlers made hasty, fatal mistakes. Poisonous "muskrat root" (or "water hemlock"), which grew along stream banks, bore a dangerous resemblance to the edible wild leek. The root occasionally claimed the lives of unwary settlers after a few hours of intense torment. It may be that in 1789 more settlers died from eating poisonous plants than from starvation. In the vicinity of Niagara, the settlers learned to find edible and to avoid poisonous plants by following their rooting pigs into and through the woods.[28]

The annual spring run upstream by migratory fish species— alewife, shad, salmon, and herring—proved especially timely in 1789 for frontier settlers and Indians throughout the afflicted districts. In June, Lord Dorchester had no food to spare for the starving Indians dwelling at Buffalo Creek and Grand River, both near Niagara. Instead, he directed the local commander to loan two seine nets so that the Indians could more readily catch fish. In central New York, William Cooper's settlers wove twigs into a crude seine net to capture thousands of herring ascending the Susquehanna River. In subsequent decades millers would destroy these fish runs by damming the rivers for water power, but in 1789 most of the frontier rivers flowed unobstructed, providing essential relief to the starving settlers.[29]

Caught between the exhausted harvest of 1788 and the delayed crops of 1789, the suffering settlers and Indians watched their slowly maturing grain plants with desperate impatience. In late July and early August, many hastened the harvest by cutting some of their immature wheat for artificial ripening by drying in the sun or over a fire. After shelling the husks, they boiled the wheat to make an edible mush. On the Upper Susquehanna in early August, Samuel Preston reported that, as a result of their first substantial meal in weeks, "the distress and pain was very great, so when they came to eat boiled wheat it . . . [made] them exceedingly sick and raise[d] a high fever."[30]

Ultimate relief came at summer's end as hot weather combined with abundant rains to make for an abundant harvest. In August, Nathaniel Gorham reported, "A prospect of great crops of every kind—plenty of rain & a very hot season has brought forward the Indian Corn in a most surprising manner. The English harvest [i.e., rye and wheat] was very abundant." Despite their late start in the spring, the borderland farmers harvested good crops of grain in August and September. In October 1789, Captain Freeman of Quebec reported that "the abundant crops of this Season makes our Province the land of plenty." Farmers reaped a still better crop a year later. In July 1790, William Cooper celebrated his relief: "The Crops here away are much Better than hath been Ever known. My Settlment will have thousands of Bushells." In September 1790, the bread price in Montreal fell to six pence—the same price that had prevailed two years earlier, before the dearth (see Tables 1 and 3). In 1791, the traveler Patrick Campbell reported that the Canadian merchants complained of a glut of grain on hand.[31]

The good harvests of 1789 and 1790 indicate that the volcanic dust in the upper atmosphere had dissipated, permitting global temperatures, wind currents, and rainfall patterns to revert to normal. Complaints about the Hessian fly diminished. Because long and frigid winters inhibit or destroy the fly's larvae, the very late spring of 1789 may have been an unanticipated boon to the farmers. Although the spring frosts delayed the 1789 crop, they may ultimately have saved it. After 1789 some northern frontier districts occasionally suffered for want of food, but there was not another general dearth in the northern borderland until 1816, when another especially powerful volcanic eruption produced the notorious "year without a summer."[32]

THE STATE

On the American side of the border most settlers and Indians muddled through with little help from the state, but Canadian natives and newcomers benefited from a larger and more paternalistic government. On both sides of the border, the first recourse of governments was to impose an embargo on the export of grains. The authorities hoped to husband local supplies of grain and alleviate public panic. Vermont acted first. On March 7, the governor and council declared a one-month ban on the export of food produced within the state. On April 17, Lord Dorchester suspended all grain and flour exports from the Province of Quebec for a year. On May 28 and June 10, Connecticut and Rhode Island adopted temporary embargoes on grain raised within their states. On July 18, Nova Scotia's lieutenant governor and executive council struck a blow against Canadian solidarity by forbidding the re-export to Quebec of any grains obtained from the United States. Given that there was precious little grain available in the suffering regions, and that only at very high prices, the embargoes were at best mere palliatives to public anxiety. At worst, the embargoes were counterproductive, adding to the panic that induced those with surpluses to hoard rather than sell.[33]

British colonial officials simultaneously imposed an embargo on domestic grains and threw open their ports to foodstuffs imported from the United States. Previously the British Empire's mercantile regulations had banned such imports in order to protect and promote grain cultivation in Canada. But the failed harvest of 1788 compelled the governor general to suspend the restriction on American imports. By proclamations issued in January, April, and June, Lord Dorchester gradually widened the opening, initially limited to the Lake Champlain corridor, to include the Maritimes and the entire St. Lawrence valley. Clinging to mercantile principle, Dorchester continued to restrict the provision trade to boats and ships owned and navigated by British subjects. But on the provincial periphery, subordinate officers wisely tolerated food imports in American boats. An officer at Kingston explained that enforcing the restriction to British boats would have brought "fatal consequences to the distressed Inhabitants of Upper Canada."[34]

The opening to American imports provided far more relief than did the hollow embargo on the nonexistent domestic grains. Although foodstuffs were equally scarce in the border country of New York and Vermont, grains and flour abounded in the warmer climes farther south, especially in Virginia and Maryland, where the harvest of 1788 had been good. In the mid-Atlantic states during the summer of 1789, merchants assembled cargoes of grain and flour for shipment to the northern frontier and Canada. On July 20, in northern New York, a correspondent reported, "The number of waggons, laden with Indian corn, which, for about two months past, have passed Stillwater and Saratoga, for the [Great] Lakes and Canada, is almost incredible." He counted about one hundred wagons per day in late July. Even more American grain moved by ship to the port of Quebec on the St. Lawrence, where by July 30 the merchants had procured 2,092 barrels of American flour, compared to only 8 barrels imported from Great Britain. On July 28, the Quebec merchant Thomas Ashton Coffin reported that the importation "has afforded great relief & dissipated the gloom—a further considerable quantity is daily expected." Over the following week, another 3,169 barrels of American flour reached the port of Quebec. As a consequence of the American imports, the Montreal assize of white bread fell from fourteen pence per loaf in July to nine in August (see Table 2).[35]

In addition to adopting regulations to preclude food exports and to attract food imports, governments might have expended funds directly to purchase and deliver provisions to the hungry. In the United States, the new and feeble federal government could do nothing, and only one state—New York—provided public relief. Large parts of Pennsylvania, Vermont, Connecticut, Massachusetts, Rhode Island, and New Hampshire suffered from hunger, but their governments expended no funds for food relief.

Two special circumstances catalyzed New York's allocation of food aid. Of the northeastern states, New York had both the largest stock of public lands for sale and the largest population of Indians. In the short run, keeping the peace with the natives was essential to the state's long-run ambitions to sell, settle, and develop its immense interior. Throughout the 1780s, New York's leaders worked zealously to render the Indians dependent on modest annuities delivered in cash, food, and clothing in payment for title to most of their lands. The dearth of 1789 presented the state with an unanticipated crisis and a new opportunity. On the one hand, a failure to feed the Indians would undermine New York's power over them. The Indians were quick to remind the state's Indian commissioners that they had a responsibility to live up to their paternalistic pretenses. On June 3, when the commissioners neglected to provide anticipated food relief, the Oneida sachem Good Peter complained, "This is very strange and we are not accustomed to such treatment." On June 30, the Oneida sachems objected, "If hunger should kill us while so near our American Brothers, it would be a lamentable story indeed." On the other hand, by rescuing the Indians from the dearth, the state subsequently could claim an obligation from the Indians to make further land concessions.[36]

Moreover, as the northeastern state with the largest public domain for sale and settlement, New York especially needed to preserve the good reputation of its frontier lands. If settlers starved and fled, they would blacken that reputation, imperiling New York's ambitions to develop its hinterland rapidly and to rely on land sales, rather than taxes, for public revenue. In a July 6 speech to the state legislature, Governor George Clinton urged an appropriation to relieve the "distresses experienced by the failure of the last year's crops, particularly in the exterior settlements, and by the poorer class of people." On July 14, the New York state legislature appropriated £600 to buy corn in southern counties for distribution to the settlers and Indians in the state's four northern frontier counties.[37]

Given the extent of the crisis, the aid allocated by New York was late and paltry. The state sent 350 bushels to feed six Indian tribes who numbered at least 2,000. Given an average annual minimum consumption of 6 bushels per person, the food aid—if evenly distributed—would have lasted the total Indian population just eleven days. The appropriation probably purchased another 1,650 bushels for distribution among a settler population of about 45,000 in the four afflicted counties—the equivalent of three days' rations per person. Ostensibly the Indians received the aid as a gift, "as," in the words of Governor Clinton, "a testimony of our Friendship for you." Of course, they would pay dearly for it in future land concessions. The food advanced to the settlers was deemed a loan rather than a gift; recipients were supposed to pay for their share by January 1, 1790. The belated and stingy nature of this aid attests to the limited scope of the state in the American republic—and to the pervasive belief that problems should be coped with by individuals and locales.[38]

More New York Indians and settlers obtained relief by striking private deals with external merchants. Tired of waiting on the state legislature, the Mohican Indians of New Stockbridge (in central New York) sent emissaries to the merchants of Schenectady and Albany to contract for 150 bushels of Indian corn. Lacking cash, the Mohicans promised payment in October in ginseng root. During the 1780s, ginseng was a wild plant that abounded in the forests of central New York, and it was in great mercantile demand for profitable export to the Chinese market. The settlers in the hinterland of Whitestown, New York sent a delegation to Fort Plain in the Mohawk valley to plead with Isaac Paris, a merchant and miller, for relief. In return for promised ginseng, he diverted to them flour and meal that he could have exported via New York City to Europe. To honor their saving bargain with the merchant, the settlers named their town "Paris" in his honor. This attests to the cultural, social, and political power of the entrepreneur in the early American republic.[39]

In contrast to the United States, the public sector played a larger role in relieving hunger in Canada, especially in the settlements near the British army posts around the Great Lakes. Because the posts had stockpiled provisions for their garrisons, the commanders could loan food to starving settlers. In theory (and in normal years), the nearby Loyalist settlers were supposed to supply the British garrisons, but in 1789 the army had to feed the starving farmers of Upper Canada. The need and relief were both greatest at Niagara, where Lt. Col. Peter Hunter advanced barrels of pork, peas, and rice to the needy settlers as a loan to be repaid in their more prosperous future. In mid-June, the visiting merchant John Richardson reported, "The distresses of this settlement for provisions have been great, and had it not been for the humane assistance of Col. Hunter, and the uncommon plenty of fish, half the people must literally have starved." The Loyalist settlers around Kingston and Detroit (then occupied by the British) obtained similar but smaller loans from their local garrisons. Because neither the American state governments nor their new and impecunious federal government possessed any military posts on the northern frontier, American settlers could not turn to them for relief.[40]

Still greater public relief came to the Canadians in emergency cargoes of wheat, flour, and peas shipped to Quebec from England by the home government. The relief shipment reached Quebec in the early fall. By the end of November the shipments totaled 1,000 tons of flour, 23,000 bushels of wheat, and 24,000 bushels of peas. This publicly funded relief effort by the British dwarfed the paltry American response, which was limited to a single state. Although Quebec's population was less than half that of New York state, the former received about twenty-five times as much public relief thanks to the largesse of the British government.[41]

Although abundant, the aid was belated, arriving in Quebec in October and November, after the new harvest and American imports had abated the hunger. In late October, Judge Adam Mabane of Quebec observed:

> Several Vessels have arrived from England laden with Provisions as it seems the Ministry had been alarmed with the accounts of the Scarcity which prevailed here last May and June. The measure was certainly benevolent, but the Evil had ceased by the Supplies which had arrived from the American States and by the new Crop which has been very good and abundant.

In Montreal, the official price for a loaf of white bread had already fallen from fourteen pence in July to nine in August. The October arrival of the public relief had a more modest impact, lowering the white bread price to seven pence. However, by swelling food stocks and appeasing public anxiety, the public relief maintained bread prices at modest levels through the subsequent winter and spring (see Tables 2 and 3).[42]

BORDERS

From 1763 until the American Revolution, Canada and the Atlantic colonies belonged to the same British Empire. At the end of the American Revolutionary War, the peace treaty of 1783 established an artificial border between the new American republic and the British provinces of Canada. British leaders tried to give significance to the northern border by settling thousands of Loyalist refugees as frontier farmers and by imposing mercantile restrictions on the flow of commerce. The imperial officials hoped to strengthen the border defenses with a population alienated from the new American republic and capable of transforming the forest into productive farms that could feed the frontier's garrisons. The British government subsidized the Loyalist settlers with free land grants, two years of rations, winter wheat seed, farm tools, and the construction of public grist mills. Imperial officials also hoped to boost Canadian agricultural development by prohibiting the importation of grains, flour, and livestock from the United States. The officials anticipated that, in the short run Canada would become self-sufficient in foodstuffs, and that in the longer run Canada could replace the American republic as the primary provisioner of the British colonies in the West Indies.[43]

The dearth of 1789 threatened the British neomercantilist effort to distinguish and develop Canada. To save his starving settlers, the governor general had to rescind for a year the ban on American food imports that he had helped to design earlier in the decade. The influx of American grain and flour eased the hunger in Canada but underlined the agricultural superiority of the more temperate United States, discouraging British ambitions to develop Canada as the empire's bread basket.

On the other hand, the dearth of 1789 presented an opportunity for the British to demonstrate that they were committed to the well-being of their Canadian subjects and that their rule was preferable to that of the American republic. In the 1780s, British authorities in Canada chronically worried that the loyalty of the people, both Francophone and Anglophone, was weak and needed bolstering. It seemed clear that most of the French inhabitants were dangerously unreconciled to the British conquest and occupation of Quebec. And, despite their wartime sacrifices and sufferings, the Loyalists remained suspect because, as Americans, they seemed susceptible to the seditious contagion of republicanism. By delivering abundant food relief with a paternalistic flair, the British hoped to strengthen their weak hold over Canadian hearts and minds. In October 1789, Lord Grenville, the British secretary of state, explained to Lord Dorchester that the aid was supposed to have "the effect of impressing the minds of His Majesty's Subjects under your Lordship's Government with a just sense of His Majesty's paternal regard for the welfare of all his People." Grenville understood that imperial authority required occasional, conspicuous displays of paternalism.[44]

In 1791, the British rulers canceled the Canadians' debts for the food relief with a flourish intended to contrast the paternalism of their regime with the commercialism of the neighboring American republic. In 1791, Prince Edward toured Canada and announced, "My father is not a merchant to deal in bread and ask payment for food granted for the relief of his loyal subjects." The contrast with the commercialized American republic could not have been more pointed. In republican America, the bread merchants ruled (and the towns bore their names).[45]

By employing food relief as a performance of imperial theater, the British compensated for the dearth's economic demonstration that Canada was agriculturally marginal and recurrently dependent on American foodstuffs. In early 1789, the British had to suspend their mercantile regulations to enable their subjects to survive by trading with the Americans, undermining the British claims that their imperial framework was essential to Canadian prosperity. The renewed demonstration of the empire's economic vulnerability in North America rendered British authorities uneasy and helped to drive their rhetoric, which posited a sharp boundary in political culture between their own subjects and the American republicans to the south. Persistent economic interdependence obliged the British to invent a border primarily in the realm of political culture.[46]

Through the 1790s and into the early nineteenth century, the northern border gradually came to demarcate significantly different national identities and political values as the British Canadian elite defined themselves dialectically against their understanding of the United States as a greedy commercial republic that flattered the common folk but ignored or exploited the poor among them. The British colonists gave cultural meaning to the border as they constructed a paternalistic counter to the crass identity they constructed of the United States. Initially, the dearth of 1789 threatened to unravel the construction of an effective northern border, but the contrast of American and Canadian responses to the hunger was one important early step in the postrevolutionary partition of North America.[47]

The legacy of that partition endures in the contrasting historical memory (or amnesia) regarding the dearth of 1789 in Canada and the United States. Unknown in American historiography, the dearth does appear conspicuously in Canadian tradition and history, where "the hungry year" represents a great national ordeal successfully endured. In part, Canadians remember and Americans forget the dearth because it affected almost everyone in Canada but menaced a smaller proportion of the larger and more widely distributed population of the United States. But American historians also have not seen the dearth of 1789 because it so poorly fits our nation's master narrative of sustained growth, frontier opportunity, and widespread prosperity. Denial in historical memory echoes the denial of public assistance to most of the American hungry in 1789. In contrast, the dearth of 1789 better suits the Canadian pride in their patient and stoic endurance of a harsh climate.[48]

Table 1

The Montreal Assize of Bread, in Pence, 1788

Month	4 Lb. White Loaf	6 Lb. Brown Loaf
May 1788	5.5	5.5
June 1788	6.0	6.0
July 1788	6.0	6.0
August 1788	6.0	6.0
September 1788	6.5	6.5
October 1788	8.0	8.0
November 1788	8.0	8.0
December 1788	9.0	9.0

Sources: Quebec Gazette, 15 May, 12 June, 10 July, 7 August, 4 September, 9 October, and 4 December 1788; *Montreal Gazette*, 6 November and 4 December 1788.

Table 2

The Montreal Assize of Bread, in Pence, 1789

Month	4 Lb. White Loaf	6 Lb. Brown Loaf
January 1789	9.0	10.0
February 1789	9.0	10.0
March 1789	10.0	11.0
April 1789	12.5	14.0
May 1789	13.0	15.0
June 1789	13.0	15.0
July 1789	14.0	16.0
August 1789	9.0	10.0
September 1789	9.0	10.5
October 1789	7.0	7.5
November 1789	7.5	8.5
December 1789	7.5	8.5

Sources: Montreal Gazette, 4 January, 5 February, 5 March, 9 April, 7 May, 4 June, 9 July, 4 August, 7 September, 8 October, 12 November, and 10 December 1789.

Table 3

The Montreal Assize of Bread, in Pence, 1790

Month	4 Lb. White Loaf	6 Lb. Brown Loaf
January 1790	7.5	8.5
February 1790	7.0	8.0
March 1790	7.0	8.0
April 1790	7.0	8.0
May 1790	7.0	8.0
June 1790	7.0	8.0
July 1790	6.5	7.5
August 1790	6.5	7.5
September 1790	6.0	6.0

Sources: Montreal Gazette, 7 January, 4 February, 4 March, 8 April, 6 May, 10 June, 8 July, 5 August, and 8 September 1790.

NOTES

I am indebted to Jenny Franchot, Carla Hesse, Alessa Johns, Elizabeth Mancke, Ted Steinberg, and Chuck Walker for comments that helped me to improve this chapter. I am also grateful to Alessa for her vision, humor, persistence, and leadership, in organizing a conference on eighteenth-century disasters and in shepherding diverse essays through to publication. This chapter also benefited from the questions and suggestions posed by audiences at the Institute of Governmental Affairs and the Agriculture History Center at the University of California at Davis; the Organization of American Historians; the early American history seminar of the University of Minnesota; and the Library Company of Philadelphia.

1. Anthony Oliver-Smith, "Introduction: Disaster Context and Causation: An Overview of Changing Perspectives in Disaster Research," in *Natural Disasters and Cultural Responses,* ed. Anthony Oliver-Smith, Publication 36 of *Studies in Third World Societies* (1986), 1-34, quotation 8; Kenneth Hewitt, "The Idea of Calamity in a Technocratic Age," in *Interpretations of Calamity from the Viewpoint of Human Ecology,* ed. K. Hewitt (Boston: Allen & Unwin, 1983), 3-32.

2. William Cooper, *A Guide in the Wilderness; or, The History of the First Settlements in the Western Counties of New York, with Useful Instructions to Future Settlers* (Cooperstown: New York State Historical Association, 1986; reprint of Dublin, 1810), 15-16; James Fenimore Cooper, *The Pioneers; or, The Sources of the Susquehanna: A Descriptive Tale* (Albany: State University of New York Press, 1980; critical ed. of New York, 1823), 234; Levi Beardsley, *Reminiscences; Personal and Other Incidents; Early Settlement of Otsego County* (New York: Charles Vinten, 1852), 19-20.

3. Samuel Wallis, quoted in Peter Mancall, *Valley of Opportunity: Economic Culture along the Upper Susquehanna, 1700-1800* (Ithaca, N.Y.: Cornell University Press, 1991), 172; Benjamin Young to Benjamin Rush, 2 June 1789, Benjamin Rush Papers, Library Company of Philadelphia.

4. Samuel Preston, "Journey to Harmony," in *Samuel Preston, 1789-1989: From Buckingham to Buckingham,* ed. Patricia H. Christian (Equinunk, Pa.: Equinunk Historical Society, 1989), 78, 96, 103-7.

5. Benjamin Young to Benjamin Rush, 2 June 1789, Benjamin Rush Papers, vol. 32, 87, Library Company of Philadelphia. To discourage further migration to the frontier, Rush shared the letter with the newspapers; it reappeared in *Vermont Journal* (Windsor), 12 August 1789, and the *Royal Gazette* (Halifax), 25 August 1789.

6. Franklin B. Hough, ed., *Proceedings of the Commissioners of Indian Affairs Appointed by Law for the Extinguishment of Indian Titles in the State of New York,* 2 vols. (Albany: J. Munsell, 1861), 2: 313, 317-18; Oliver Phelps to Nathaniel Gorham, 14 July 1789, Phelps & Gorham Papers, Box 2, New York State Library, Albany; Judah Colt, "Diary," Ontario County Historical Society, Canandaigua, New York.

7. Walter Pilkington, ed., *The Journals of Samuel Kirkland, Eighteenth-Century Missionary to the Iroquois, Government Agent, Father of Hamilton College* (Clinton, N.Y.: Hamilton College Press, 1980), 160-68; Pomeroy Jones, *Annals and Recollections of Oneida County* (Rome, N.Y.: by the author, 1851), 176-77.

8. Alexander Coventry, *Memoirs of an Emigrant: The Journal of Alexander Coventry, M.D.,* 2 vols. (Albany, N.Y.: Albany Institute of History and Art, 1978), 2: 213; "Boston, June 22," *Independent Gazetteer* (Philadelphia), 1 July 1789 (Captain Brown); "Extract of a Letter from a Gentleman living on Lake Champlain . . . May 9," *New Hampshire Gazette* (Portsmouth), 2 July 1789. The latter also appeared in *New-York Journal,* 1 July 1789; *Independent Gazetteer* (Philadelphia), 19 July 1789. See also "Albany, June 15," *New-Jersey Journal,* 17 June 1789.

9. Nathan Perkins, *A Narrative of a Tour through the State of Vermont from April 27 to June 12, 1789* (Woodstock, Vt.: Woodstock Press, 1920), 21; Abby Maria Hemenway, ed., *The Vermont Historical Gazetteer: A Magazine Embracing a History of Each Town, Civil, Ecclesiastical, Biographical and Military*, 5 vols. (Burlington: State of Vermont, 1867), 1: 52, 313.

10. Nova Scotia Executive Council Minutes, 25 May 1789, Reel 95289, Public Archives of Nova Scotia, Halifax (PANS hereafter); William Clark to Rev. Samuel Peters, 23 June 1789, MG 1 (Rev. Samuel Peters Papers), Reel 10958, PANS.

11. Testimony of John Blackwell, William Grant, Thomas Coffin, William Cleghorn, David Barclay, Alexander Cairns, John Painter, Matthew Lymburner, John Lees, Isaac Todd, Robert Lester, John Young, George Alsopp, Joseph Crette, John Pagan, and George Miller, in Quebec Executive Council Minutes, 1-3 June 1789, MG 11, Colonial Office 42, vol. 66, Public Archives of Canada, Ottawa (PAC hereafter).

12. For the assize of bread, see the source notes to Tables 1-3. For the charitable relief, see *Montreal Gazette*, 11 June 1789; Alexander Fraser testimony, Quebec Executive Council Minutes, 1 June 1789, MG 11, Colonial Office 42, vol. 66, PAC.

13. "A Loyalist," *Montreal Gazette*, 5 March 1789; "Quebec, March 23," *Quebec Herald*, 13 April 1789 ("cats"); Alfred Leroy Burt, *The Old Province of Quebec* (Toronto: Ryerson Press, 1933), 378-81; John Richardson to John Porteous, 31 May 1789, in "The John Richardson Letters," ed. E. A. Cruikshank, Ontario Historical Society, *Papers and Records*, VI (Toronto: Champlain Society, 1905), 23; Philip Stedman testimony, 3 June 1789, Quebec Executive Council Minutes, MG 11, Colonial Office 42, vol. 66, PAC; Captain Joseph Bunbury to Captain Le Maistre, 30 June 1789, in *Kingston Before the War of 1812: A Collection of Documents*, ed. Richard Preston (Toronto: University of Toronto Press, 1959), 144. See also Joseph Forsyth to John Porteous, 1 July 1789; Rev. John Stuart to the Bishop of Nova Scotia, 19 July 1789; and Stuart to Rev. William White, 9 October 1789, in *Kingston Before the War*, 145, 146, 151; Edwin C. Guillet, *Early Life in Upper Canada* (Toronto: Ontario Publishing Co., 1963), 209-11.

14. Patrick C. T. White, ed., *Lord Selkirk's Diary 1803-1804: A Journal of His Travels in British North America and the Northeastern United States* (Toronto: Champlain Society, 1958), 179; John William Woolsey testimony, in Quebec Executive Council Report, 5 June 1789, enclosed in Lord Dorchester to Lord Sydney, 6 June 1789, MG 11, Colonial Office 42, vol. 64, PAC; Dorchester to Sydney, 8 December 1788, MG 11, Colonial Office 42, vol. 63, PAC. For the Hessian fly, see Timothy Dwight, *Travels in New England and New York*, 4 vols. (Cambridge: Harvard University Press, 1969; reprint of New Haven, 1821), 3: 210-11; Percy W. Bidwell and John I. Falconer, *History of Agriculture in the Northern United States, 1620-1860* (Washington, D.C.: The Carnegie Institute of Washington, 1925), 95-96; Louis B. Wright and Marion Tinling, eds., *Quebec to Carolina in 1785-1786: Being the Travel Diary and Observations of Robert*

Hunter, Jr., a Young Merchant of London (San Marino, Calif.: The Huntington Library, 1943), 150.

15. "Exports from the Province of Quebec in 1788," Miscellaneous Documents for 1788, MG 11, Colonial Office 42, vol. 66, PAC; Lord Dorchester to Lord Grenville, 30 September 1789, MG 11, Colonial Office 42, vol. 65, PAC; Captain Freeman to Sir Frederick Haldimand, 24 October 1789, MG 21, Haldimand Papers, Reel A-670, PAC.

16. H. H. Lamb, *Climate, History and the Modern World* (London: Methuen, 1982), 237; Anne Walthall, *Social Protest and Popular Culture in Eighteenth-Century Japan* (Tucson: University of Arizona Press, 1986), 126-34, 155-56; Conrad Totman, *Early Modern Japan* (Berkeley: University of California Press, 1993), 238-40; Arij Ouweneel, "Silent Drama in the Milpas: Changes in the Agro-Ecosystem of Anahuac during the 1780s and 1790s," in *Le Nouveau Monde/Mondes Nouveaux: L'Experience Americaine,* ed. Serge Gruzinski and Nathan Wachtel (Paris: Éditions Recherche sur les Civilisations: Éditions de l'École des Hautes Études en Sciences Sociales, 1996), 115-35. I am grateful to my colleague Arnold Bauer for alerting me to Ouweneel's essay.

17. H. H. Lamb, *Climate, History,* 238-39; Emmanuel Le Roy Ladurie, *Times of Feast, Times of Famine: A History of Climate since the Year 1000,* trans. Barbara Bray (London: Allen & Unwin, 1972), 72–75. For the operation of the wheat market, see Joyce O. Appleby, "The Changing Prospect of the Family Farm in the Early National Period," in *Working Papers from the Regional Economic History Research Center* (Wilmington, Del.: Hagley-Eleuthera Foundation, 1980), 1-25.

18. Thomas Jefferson to John Jay, 29 November 1788, in *The Papers of Thomas Jefferson,* ed. Julian P. Boyd (Princeton, N.J.: Princeton University Press, 1958), 14: 304-6; Jefferson, "Grain and Flour Imported from the United States of America into the Ports of France, in the Year 1789, from an Official Statement," in *Papers of Thomas Jefferson,* 19: 232; "Extract of a Letter dated Paris, 29 Nov. 1788, from the Honorable Mr. Jefferson to Mr. Jay," *New-York Journal,* 19 February 1789; *New-Jersey Journal* (Elizabeth Town), 25 February 1789; "London, April 22," *Cumberland Gazette* (Portland, Maine), 10 July 1789; testimony of John William Woolsey, in Quebec Executive Council Report, 5 June 1789, MG 11, Colonial Office 42, vol. 64, PAC.

19. William Cooper to Henry Drinker, 7 May 1789, Henry Drinker Papers, Correspondence Box 1741-1792, Historical Society of Pennsylvania (HSP hereafter), Philadelphia; Cooper, *Guide in the Wilderness,* 15 (quotation); Moses De Witt, Journal, 1 June 1789, De Witt Family Papers, Box 6, Syracuse University Library Special Collections, Syracuse, New York.

20. Josiah Priest, *Stories of Early Settlers in the Wilderness; Embracing the Life of Mrs. Priest, Late of Otsego County N.Y.* (Albany, N.Y.: J. Munsell, 1837), 28; Tax Lists for Old England District (Otsego), Montgomery County, 1787, in New York State Treasurers Records, Assessment Lists (1722-1788), box 2, folder 62,

New York State Archives, Albany; Tax List for Old England District, Montgomery County, 1788, in Gerrit Y. Lansing Papers, box 1, folder 12, New York State Library, Albany; John Tunnecliff to William Cooper, 14 April 1788, William Cooper Papers, Hartwick College Archives; William Cooper to Henry Drinker, 7 May 1789, Henry Drinker Papers, Correspondence Box 1741-1792, HSP. For the postwar surge of frontier settlement see Douglas S. Robertson, ed., *An Englishman in America, 1785, Being the Diary of Joseph Hadfield* (Toronto: Hunter-Rose Co., 1973), 26-27; Alan Taylor, *William Cooper's Town: Power and Persuasion on the Frontier of the Early American Republic* (New York: Alfred A. Knopf, 1995), 90-92.

21. Henry Ruttan, "Reminiscences," in *Loyalist Narratives from Upper Canada*, ed. James J. Talman (Toronto: Champlain Society, 1946), 300.

22. Coventry, *Memoirs*, 1: 213; "Windsor," *Vermont Journal* (Windsor), 8 June 1789; "New-York, June 15," *Independent Gazetteer* (Philadelphia), 17 June 1789. See also "Extract of a Letter from Quebec, date May 5," *New-Jersey Journal* (Elizabeth Town), 17 June 1789.

23. *Vermont Gazette* (Bennington), 8 June 1789; "Keene," *New- Hampshire Gazette* (Portsmouth), 11 June 1789; "Windsor," *Vermont Journal* (Windsor), 8 June 1789. For the loss of cattle in Upper Canada, see Patrick Campbell, *Travels in the Interior Inhabited Parts of North America in the Years 1791 and 1792*, ed. H. H. Langton (Toronto: Champlain Society, 1937), 155.

24. *Vermont Gazette* (Bennington), 8 June 1789; *Vermont Journal* (Windsor), 29 June 1789; *New-Jersey Journal* (Elizabeth Town), 17 June 1789; "Albany, June 15," *New-Hampshire Gazette* (Portsmouth), 9 July 1789; Ebenezer Dibble to Rev. Samuel Peters, 28 June 1789, Peters Papers, Reel 10958, PANS.

25. *Worcester Spy*, 18 June 1789; *New-Hampshire Gazette* (Portsmouth), 25 June 1789; *Independent Gazetteer* (Philadelphia), 26 June 1789.

26. *New-York Journal*, 25 June 1789; "Bennington," *Vermont Gazette* (Bennington), 6 July 1789; "Bennington, June 29," *Independent Gazetteer*, 27 July 1789; *New-Hampshire Gazette* (Portsmouth), 9 July 1789; *Connecticut Courant* (Hartford), 17 August 1789.

27. "Extract of a Letter from a Gentleman living on Lake Champlain . . . May 9," *New-Hampshire Gazette*, 2 July 1789; Jacob Lindley quoted in Robert Leslie Jones, *History of Agriculture in Ontario, 1613-1880* (Toronto: University of Toronto Press, 1946), 17-18; Guillet, *Early Life in Upper Canada*, 210; Rev. Amos D. Gridley, *History of the Town of Kirkland, New York* (New York: Hurd & Houghton, 1874), 32.

28. Gridley, *History of Kirkland*, 32; Cooper, *Guide in the Wilderness*, 16; *Otsego Herald*, 12 May 1796, 20 July 1815; Guillet, *Early Life in Upper Canada*, 210, 213.

29. Lord Dorchester to Sir John Johnson, 22 June 1789, RG 10, Indian Affairs, Reel C-1224, vol. 15, 363, PAC; Hemenway, *Vermont Historical Gazetteer*, 1: 52; Gridley, *History of Kirkland*, 32; Thompson, *Thorold Township*, 27; Cooper, *Guide in the Wilderness*, 16.

30. Hemenway, *Vermont Historical Gazetteer,* 1: 52; Guillet, *Early Life in Upper Canada,* 211; Thompson, *Thorold Township,* 28; Preston, "Journey to Harmony," 107-10.

31. Nathaniel Gorham to Oliver Phelps, 15 August 1789, Phelps & Gorham Papers, Box 17, New York State Library (Albany); Captain Freeman to Sir Frederick Haldimand, 24 October 1789, MG 21, Haldimand Papers, Reel A-670, PAC; Preston, "Journey to Harmony," 107-10; William Cooper to Henry Drinker, 21 July 1790 and 20 September 1791, Henry Drinker Papers, Correspondence Box 1741-1792, HSP; *Montreal Gazette,* 8 September 1790; Jones, *History of Agriculture in Ontario,* 25.

32. The settlements in Maine suffered more severely from hunger in 1790 than in 1789. See Alan Taylor, *Liberty Men and Great Proprietors: The Revolutionary Settlement on the Maine Frontier, 1760-1820* (Chapel Hill: University of North Carolina Press, 1990), 70. For the crisis of 1816, see Post, *The Last Great Subsistence Crisis.*

33. Eliakim P. Walton, ed., *Records of the Governor and Council of the State of Vermont,* 8 vols. (Montpelier: State of Vermont, 1873-80), 3: 181-82; "An Ordinance," *Vermont Journal* (Windsor), 16 March 1789; "An Ordinance, Chap. IX," *Montreal Gazette,* 27 May 1790; *New-Hampshire Gazette* (Portsmouth), 4 and 18 June 1789; *Independent Gazetteer* (Philadelphia), 16 July 1789; Samuel Huntington, *A Proclamation . . .* (Hartford: State of Connecticut, 1789, Evans #45457); Nova Scotia Executive Council Minutes, 18 July 1789, RG 1, reel 15289, vol. 190, PANS.

34. Gerald S. Graham, *British Policy and Canada, 1774-1791: A Study in Eighteenth-Century Trade Policy* (Westport, Conn.: Greenwood Press, 1974; reprint of London, 1930), 63-65, 70-71; "Quebec, January 29," *Montreal Gazette,* 5 February 1789; "Proclamation," *Montreal Gazette,* 9 April 1789; *Royal Gazette* (Halifax), 26 May 1789; "Secretary's Office—Quebec, 6th June 1789," *Montreal Gazette,* 18 June 1789; Captain Joseph Bunbury to Captain Le Maistre, 30 June 1789, *Kingston Before the War of 1812,* 144-45. For lax enforcement on Lake Ontario, see also John Richardson to John Porteous, 14 June 1789, "John Richardson Letters," 24.

35 "Albany, July 20," *New-Jersey Journal* (Elizabeth Town), 29 July 1789; "Quebec, August 6," *New York Journal,* 27 August 1789; Thomas Ashton Coffin to Mrs. Coffin, 28 July 1789, Coffin Papers, vol. 3, Massachusetts Historical Society. Apparently the Quebec customs house records no longer survive for the period 1786-1792. See Gilles Paquet and Jean-Pierre Wallot, "International Circumstances of Lower Canada, 1786-1810: Prolegomenon," *Canadian Historical Review* 53 (1972): 384.

36. Good Peter's speech, 3 June, and the Oneida letter to the commissioners, 30 June 1789, in *Proceedings of the Commissioners,* 2: 317, 328. For New York's land and Indian policies, see Barbara Graymont, *The Iroquois in the American Revolution* (Syracuse, N.Y.: Syracuse University Press, 1972), 259-91; Anthony F. C. Wallace, *The Death and Rebirth of the Seneca* (New York: Alfred A. Knopf, 1970),

150-83; Alfred F. Young, *The Democratic Republicans of New York: The Origins, 1763-1797* (Chapel Hill: University of North Carolina Press, 1967), 232-43, 267-70.

37. New York (State), *Journal of the Assembly . . . Thirteenth Session* (New York: State of New York, 1790, Evans #22009), 4 (Clinton speech), 19-20 (legislation); Gov. Clinton to the Oneida Indians, 14 July 1789, in *Proceedings of the Commissioners*, 2: 333.

38. New York (State), *Journal of the Assembly . . . Thirteenth Session*, 19-20; Gov. Clinton to the Oneida Indians, 14 July 1789, and Meeting of the Commissioners, 15 July 1789, in *Proceedings of the Commissioners*, 2: 333. At the 1789 price in Albany of six shillings per bushel, £600 would have procured two thousand bushels of corn. For the price of corn in 1789, see [William Cooper], "Extract of a Letter from Cooper's Town (Otsego Lake), dated 7 May 1789," *New-York Journal*, 2 July 1789. For thirty bushels a year as the subsistence level for a family of five, see Bettye Hobbs Pruitt, "Self-Sufficiency and the Agricultural Economy of Eighteenth-Century Massachusetts," *William and Mary Quarterly* 3d ser., 41 (summer 1984): 344-46.

39. Certificate by the Sachems and Councillors of the Muhheaconnuk Nation, 1 July 1989, Ayer Manuscript #836, Newberry Library, Chicago. I am grateful to Karim Tiro for alerting me to this document. Henry C. Rogers, *History of the Town of Paris and the Valley of the Sauquoit* (Utica, N.Y.: Utica Printing Co., 1881), 21.

40. Lt. Col. Peter Hunter to James Farquharson, 12 February 1789, Wolford Simcoe Transcripts, MG 23 H I 1, series 3, vol. 1, 260, PAC; John Richardson to John Porteous, 14 June 1789, in "Richardson Letters," 24; John Smith et al., petition, in *The Correspondence of Lieut. Governor John Graves Simcoe, with Allied Documents Relating to His Administration of the Government of Upper Canada*, ed. E. A. Cruikshank, 5 vols. (Toronto: Ontario Historical Society, 1923-31), 4: 359; W. H. Siebert, "The Loyalists and the Six Nation Indians in the Niagara Peninsular," Royal Society of Canada, *Transactions* 3d ser., 9 (1915-16): 102.

41. Burt, *The Old Province of Quebec*, 381; Thompson, *Thorold Township*, 28-29; *Quebec Herald*, 5 October 1789.

42. Burt, *Old Province of Quebec*, 381; Thompson, *Thorold Township*, 28-29; *Quebec Herald*, 5 October 1789; "Memorial and Petition," *Montreal Gazette*, 19 November 1789; Adam Mabane to Sir Frederick Haldimand, MG 21, Haldimand Papers, Reel A-670, PAC. For the monthly assize of bread, see source notes to Tables 1-3.

43. Jones, *History of Agriculture in Ontario*, 17-24; Graham, *British Policy and Canada*, 56-71; Harlow, *Founding of the Second British Empire*, 2: 609-15; John E. Crowley, *The Privileges of Independence* (Baltimore: Johns Hopkins University Press, 1993), 73-74.

44. Lord Grenville to Lord Dorchester, 20 October 1789, MG 11, Colonial Office 42, vol. 65, PAC.

45. Prince Edward, quoted in Guillet, *Early Life in Upper Canada,* 213.

46. This paragraph is indebted to helpful comments by Carla Hesse on an earlier version of this essay delivered as a paper in January 1998 at the annual meeting of the Organization of American Historians.

47. For the dialectical creation of meaningful borders, see Peter Sahlins, *Boundaries: The Making of France and Spain in the Pyrenees* (Berkeley: University of California Press, 1989), 267-78.

48. For the Canadian tradition, see Burt, *The Old Province of Quebec,* 377-81; Guillet, *Early Life in Upper Canada,* 209-13; Jones, *History of Agriculture in Ontario,* 17. For American historians who minimize the existence of hunger in eighteenth-century America, see Jack P. Greene, *Pursuits of Happiness: The Social Development of Early Modern British Colonies and the Formation of American Culture* (Chapel Hill: University of North Carolina Press, 1988), 72-74, 91-92, 136-37; Jackson Turner Main, *Society and Economy in Colonial Connecticut* (Princeton, N.J.: Princeton University Press, 1985), 149-51, 377-78; G. B. Warden, "Inequality and Instability in Eighteenth-Century Boston: A Reappraisal," *Journal of Interdisciplinary History* 6 (1975-1976): 585-620; Gordon S. Wood, *The Radicalism of the American Revolution* (New York: Alfred A. Knopf, 1992), 122. Wood insists, "Although by the mid-eighteenth century the numbers of poor were increasing in the urban ports of Boston, New York, and Philadelphia, there was not, Americans realized, 'the least danger of starving amongst us.'"

3

What Comes Down Must Go Up

Why Disasters Have Been Good for American Capitalism

Kevin Rozario

Why did some Americans in the late nineteenth and early twentieth centuries have a "talent for seeing mangled bodies and burnt-out buildings" as "blessings"? Kevin Rozario examines how disaster narratives (especially narratives about the San Francisco earthquake of 1906) spoke to the needs and social interests of middle- and upper-class Americans during the Gilded Age and the Progressive Era. These narratives became self-fulfilling prophesies, inspiring a faith in betterment; generating the energy, will, and capital commitment that made material reconstruction viable; and converting catastrophes into agents of moral and material "progress." The reigning conception of capitalism as a process of "creative destruction," Rozario explains, allows us to understand "disasters as events that transform space in ways that promote economic expansion and present (some) investors and businesses with opportunities for the accumulation of capital."

GEORGE HARVEY, the editor of *Harper's Weekly,* was strangely unshaken by the San Francisco earthquake and fire of April 1906.[1] Confronted by news reports of one of the greatest calamities in American history, his response was to sit down and write a "comment" on the inevitable future splendors of San Francisco. The Californian city was in ruins. Nearly five acres of stores, offices, factories, hotels, and homes had been destroyed, and many hundreds of people were dead, but Harvey's attention was captured by the new and improved city he foresaw emerging from the rubble. In just five years' time, he predicted, his countrymen would stand in awe before "the brand-new splendor of the resuscitated capital."[2]

A talent for seeing mangled bodies and burnt-out buildings as signs of progress was widely shared among Harvey's class. Many professionals and businessmen agreed that this "so-called catastrophe" was more a boon than a misfortune. Time only confirmed this happy assessment. As one spokesman for real estate interests observed three months after the earthquake, it was still a "commonplace" to maintain that the destruction of San Francisco was "a blessing in disguise." "Instinctively," he declared, "we feel that the heavy hand of fate which has so ruthlessly fallen on us has fallen for our good, if not for our comfort."[3] Why should so many merchants, industrialists, and entrepreneurs have viewed the San Francisco disaster as an opportunity for urban development rather than as an obstacle to growth? How do we explain this startling determination to overlook the appalling wreckage and to focus instead on the promise of reconstruction?

The tendency of middle- and upper-class Americans to regard disasters as "blessings" can be traced back to the endeavors of early American religious leaders to emphasize the corrective uses of "providential" afflictions. This religious genealogy is significant. Even in the twentieth century, American expectations about the benefits of destruction continue to rest as much upon faith, or at least habit, as upon rational calculation. My main concern here, however, is to explain how and why so many modern Americans came to view disasters as sources of economic growth and as agents of progress. I believe a hint of an answer can be found in the unintentional double meaning of George Harvey's phrase "resuscitated capital," which can be read not only as a reference to the soon-to-be-restored capital city, but also as an allusion to the revitalizing role of the calamity for American capitalism.

In recent years, economists, urban historians, and geographers have written extensively about the "geography of capital" and the "production of space," seeking to explain how capitalist economies shape built environments. Surely the most compelling concept to emerge from this scholarship is that of "creative destruction," the notion that modern capitalist systems require the continual obliteration of outmoded goods and structures to clear space and make way for new production and development. Creative destruction (according to powerful apologists like Federal Reserve Chairman Alan Greenspan and persistent critics like *Nation* correspondent William Greider) is the dialectic that keeps the wheels of industry turning.[4] Traditionally, economists have deployed this concept to explain entrepreneurial innovation, industrial restructuring, and planned obsolescence, but more recently scholars have begun to appreciate the role of creative destruction in shaping and reshaping modern urban environments.[5] If capitalism does depend for its survival on the endless ruin and renewal of physical structures, this is surely a matter of interest for those of us who seek to understand modern ways of imagining and managing disasters.

Within this framework, we can begin to appreciate natural disasters as events that transform space in ways that promote economic expansion and present (some) investors and businesses with opportunities for the accumulation of capital. Indeed, we can begin to understand why so many social thinkers have turned to calamities in search of metaphors to convey the destructive and reconstructive logics of modern capitalism. In his dazzling critical account of modernity, *All that Is Solid Melts into Air*, political theorist Marshall Berman was much taken by the saturation of Karl Marx's writings with calamitous images: the endless parade across his pages of "abysses, earthquakes, volcanic eruptions, crushing gravitational force." Berman speculated that Marx deployed these analogies to compel his readers to "feel" the dizzying, crashing power of a transformative modernity, but these were also surely the most compelling images available for conveying the dynamic and propulsive qualities of modern capitalism and, in particular, the embroilment of its creative and destructive forces.[6]

So deeply ingrained has the link between disaster and development become that even those who have fought most vigorously to contain the ravages of capital have tended to view further destruction as the necessary precondition for healing modernity's harms. Thus could Lewis Mumford fear that the bombing blitzes of World War II would prove *insufficient* to flatten the grimy cities of Europe to the extent necessary to transform modern urban sites from "dreary infernos" into "life-centered environments." "There is a sense," he wrote in 1942, "in which the demolition that is taking place through the war has not yet gone far enough. . . . We must . . . continue to do, in a more deliberate and rational fashion, what the bombs have done by brutal hit-or-miss, if we are to have space enough to live in and produce the proper means of living."[7] By the middle of the twentieth century, even Mumford, the ardent and humane critic of capitalism, was convinced that (controlled) destruction was a good thing, that responsible planners had to become destroyers before they could build a better world.

In the following pages, I analyze the origins and intricacies of this outlook. To explore the complex and sometimes surprising relations between disaster, capitalism, and urban development, I devote most of this essay to an investigation of responses to the San Francisco earthquake and fire of 1906, still the most destructive urban disaster in American history. As we shall see, this event can teach us an extraordinary amount about our culture of disaster.

But let us begin at, or near, the beginning. How did Americans learn to view calamities as opportunities? For an answer we have to look back to the colonial period. In 1727, an earthquake ripped through New England. Most inhabitants were understandably upset by this fearsome "affliction," but a surprising number were rhapsodic. The prominent Boston clergyman Cotton Mather, for example, gushed, "O Wonderful! O Wonderful! Our GOD instead of sending *earthquakes* to destroy us as He justly might, He sends them to fetch us home unto Himself, and to do us the greatest Good in the World!"[8] What exactly was this good that God intended? It is commonly known that the early settlers interpreted fires and storms and earthquakes as divine punishments for the sins and transgressions of a covenanted community. But there was a twist in this theology that enabled ministers to recast calamities as blessings: the supposition that God sent disasters to recall his chosen people to the path of righteousness.

Significantly, Puritans claimed to be especially gladdened by the fact that disasters destroyed property—reminding communities of the transience of worldly goods, freeing them from the distractions of material possessions, and refocusing their thoughts on the one thing that really mattered: salvation. Disasters, then, were blessings because they assisted colonists along the path to God's kingdom, inspiring moral and spiritual reformation, and promising them a final *transcendence* of space and time. Or so official sermons proclaimed. In truth, Puritans often found it easier to assert than to feel the blessings of destruction. When a fire razed the North End of Boston in 1676, the prominent minister Increase Mather claimed vindication for his repeated warnings that the "inordinate Affection to the World" of his congregation foredoomed them to an awful calamity.[9] In his private correspondence, however, he allowed his own regrets to surface, admitting his deep distress at the loss of his own home and the incineration of his furniture, clothes, and winter provisions. He was hopeful that the wealth of the community would be restored as soon as he and his neighbors had repented of their sins and abandoned their lustful pursuit of worldly goods and pleasures.[10]

What Mather, like other pious settlers, was unable to fathom was that calamities could actually promote economic prosperity. From the beginning of the European settlement of America, the impulse to transcend the physical world had coexisted uneasily with countervailing religious and political injunctions to tame the wilderness and, in New England at least, to construct the sort of orderly towns that manifested and made possible a proper devotion to God. It was thus both a civic and a religious duty to rebuild homes and cities as well and as solidly as possible in the wake of calamities. This injunction was not always easy to realize. In the days before fire insurance, dependable relief, and easy credit, it often took years for householders and communities to recover from the devastations of arson, wars, or natural disasters. On occasion, however, unexpected destruction spurred rudimentary adventures in urban renewal. After the 1676 fire, for example, Boston authorities seized the opportunity presented by the destruction to widen downtown streets—an action designed to rationalize space, but one that also helped to speed up the flow of traffic and stimulate business in the expanding and commercializing port city.[11]

If disasters played an important role in the (re)shaping of urban space throughout the colonial period, they also sometimes facilitated the accumulation of profits, and not just for profiteers but also for respectable entrepreneurs. Because ministers were so skillful at exploiting the fears stirred up by calamities to bully congregations into cultivating virtuous habits of self-discipline and hard work, disasters could (in classic Weberian fashion) boost productivity and economic development. Indeed, as literary critic Sacvan Bercovitch has shown, endless disaster sermons or "jeremiads" eventually persuaded colonists that crises and misfortunes were necessary and welcome catalysts for a distinctively American brand of "progress" that was measured in terms of personal betterment and social improvement.[12] Reassuring experiences of recovery gave credence to these improbable assertions, and over time Americans learned to treat disasters as both religious *and* economic blessings. By 1871, it seemed the most natural thing in the world for Henry Ward Beecher, the nation's most prominent clergyman, to declare that the United States could not afford to do without the great Chicago fire. He was hardly alone in his conviction that disasters were part of an essentially comforting divine plan, apparent afflictions that were actually sent to promote spiritual, moral, and material progress.[13]

Although faith in the blessings of disaster was already widespread by the end of the colonial period, speedy recovery from calamities could not be taken for granted until the spread of communications systems, credit networks, insurance companies, and all the other apparatus of industrialization in the nineteenth century. As Progressive reformers wryly pointed out at the end of the century, this resilience was just as well because one city after another was being devastated by conflagrations brought about by unregulated economic and urban growth in the era of competitive capitalism. Still, although cities might fall, they never just died. By 1906, *Harper's* editor George Harvey had seen Chicago, Boston, Charleston, Galveston, and Baltimore all bounce back after being "laid waste by conflagrations, earthquakes, or tidal waves" over the previous thirty-five years.[14] When the San Francisco earthquake struck, he had been well conditioned to treat calamities as economic opportunities. He was confident that Americans would invest whatever labor and capital was necessary to build a better city over the ruins of San Francisco. No less a force than the logic of capitalism demanded the creation of a magnificent new city in the Bay Area. But what was this logic? And how exactly did it shape responses to calamity in the age of industry?

As early as 1848, John Stuart Mill spelled out the uses of disasters for industrial economies in his influential *Principles of Political Economy.* Mill argued that in a free market system in which capital was constantly being consumed and reproduced, there was "nothing at all wonderful" about "the great rapidity with which countries recover from a state of devastation; the disappearance, in a short time, of all traces of the mischief done by earthquakes, floods, hurricanes, and the ravages of war." As long as the population remained productive, and as long as infrastructure was not completely destroyed, then "rapid repair" was always likely.[15] In fact, Mill expected disasters to produce long-term benefits by obliterating old stock and encouraging manufacturers to introduce new efficiencies into their production processes, adopting better technologies and building more efficient plants.

Mill did not discuss the New York fire of 1835, but few events corroborated his theory more amply. On December 16, during the coldest night in half a century, a warehouse in downtown Manhattan burst into flames. The fire spread quickly through the narrow and congested streets of the business district, destroying seventeen city blocks and burning so brightly that the glare was visible as far away as Philadelphia and New Haven.[16] Although religious leaders made familiar noises about the benevolent disciplining effects of providence, businessmen were not yet conditioned to see *economic* opportunity in the ruins. The *New York Herald* reported the grim conviction of prominent merchants that the development of their city would be put back by at least twenty years. For its part, the newspaper forecast hard times ahead, warning readers that "The destruction of seventeen millions of property cannot pass away as a summer cloud."[17] But pass away it did. Or at least seemed to do.

By the first anniversary of the fire, five hundred new and more splendid buildings had risen from the ruins, streets had been widened, a solution to chronic downtown pollution and water shortages was in sight, and business was better than ever. Many merchants actually emerged wealthier from the calamity than they had been on its eve. A building boom quickly and dramatically raised rents in the burned-out district. One proprietor, returning from Europe under the impression that he had been ruined by the destruction of his properties, discovered instead that he had become a very rich man.[18] Just two months after the fire, twenty empty lots were sold for $765,000; before the conflagration, the property had been worth just $93,000. Philip Hone, businessman, socialite, former mayor, and prominent member of the relief committee, marveled to see these lots command "the most enormous prices, greater than they would have brought before the fire, when covered with valuable buildings."[19] To be sure, the benefits of inflation were not shared by all. Despite the construction boom, most working people suffered a net decline in real wages as rising rents and food prices outpaced modest gains in earnings. But one thing seemed undeniable: the disaster had spurred business activity and economic growth. How had this happened?

In 1835, New York City was still enjoying the wave of economic expansion that had been stimulated by the opening of the Erie Canal ten years before, and businesses were generally prosperous enough to absorb the costs of the conflagration. More importantly, living in the nation's financial center, well-connected New Yorkers enjoyed singular access to international capital, as well as to the abundant credit made available by the expansion of state and "wildcat" banks in the aftermath of President Andrew Jackson's successful campaign to terminate the

WHAT COMES DOWN MUST GO UP   79

Bank of the United States' monopoly over the money supply. The tide of speculation that washed over these years indicates a broad faith in the expansive potential of the American economy. With abundant credit available, there was every indication that the business district was going to be swiftly restored (and even modernized with improved streets and services), and few merchants hesitated to rebuild their downtown enterprises.

In such an economy, even if entrepreneurs and financiers were not yet fully aware of the fact, calamities presented opportunities for capital accumulation. New York was already renewing itself every few years, with city blocks being demolished and rebuilt with astounding frequency. In many respects, the great fire simply accelerated the process by which obsolete buildings were replaced with more up-to-date structures. In 1845, Philip Hone reflected ruefully on this phenomenon. "Overturn, overturn, overturn!" he pronounced, "is the maxim of New York. The very bones of our ancestors are not permitted to lie quiet a quarter of a century, and one generation of men seem studious to remove all relics of those which preceded them."[20] Hone, who had managed to sell his downtown home in the aftermath of the conflagration for a staggering profit, was a beneficiary of this turbulent state of affairs, but he never fully came to terms with the emotional costs of living in a city devoted to the constant erasure of the past. As we shall see, this discomfort was itself one of the most profound effects of the transformative forces of modernity and an intimation of struggles to come that would pit sentimental local attachments against the interests of capital across the nineteenth and twentieth centuries.

For now, to make sense of the rhythms of ruin and renewal, Hone turned, like many compatriots of his class, to the comforting axioms of Harriet Martineau, the celebrated British writer he met while she was visiting the United States in the spring of 1836. She had been greatly interested in the fire, noting with some admiration, "It seems now as if the commercial credit of New York could stand any shock" short of a cataclysm like the earthquake that had obliterated Lisbon in 1755. This was evidence enough of the capability of an expansive economy to overcome any obstacles to growth, though Martineau did admit to some uneasiness about the long-term effects of the game of "wild speculation" that seemed to preoccupy so many Americans in this period.[21] Her misgivings proved well-founded. The correction, when it came in 1837, precipitated a devastating financial panic that tipped the country into a

severe recession. There was a stunning lesson here: in an advanced capitalist economy, paper transactions could present more of a threat to
prosperity than a fire or an earthquake.[22] What sort of a world was it
where natural disasters could produce prosperity while a contraction of
credit could bring the economic activity of a nation to a virtual halt? In
short, a world that was coming to be dominated by industrial and finance capitalism.

The material benefits of destruction would not be widely appreciated until Western economies entered their abundance stage at the end
of the nineteenth century, producing many more products than consumers needed or thought they wanted. At this point, disasters became
blessings because they approximated and amplified those dynamic
forces that inspired Austrian economist Joseph Schumpeter to compare
modern capitalism to a "gale of creative destruction."[23] A century after
Mill, Schumpeter made the case that destruction was a necessary and
desirable agent of invention and renewal in an expansive economy. He
celebrated the bold and unceasing innovations of entrepreneurs that
ensured the constant outdating of old commodities and their replacement by new ones. Schumpeter was concerned with changes over time
rather than changes across space and would surely have balked at the
idea that it was a good thing to tear down and rebuild *cities* with any
great frequency. According to a growing number of recent geographers,
however, this latter phenomenon has been absolutely essential for the
survival of capitalism.

Putting a Marxian spin on creative destruction, scholars like David
Harvey, Neil Smith, and Edward Soja have insisted that modern capitalism thrives on the constant reshaping of urban space—to the point,
we must presume, where calamities can be good for business. They base
this conclusion on analyses of the process Marx described as the "epic
of overproduction"—the tendency of capitalists to glut successful markets, drive down prices, and thereby provoke business failures and re-
cessions.[24] Apologists and critics disagree about whether capitalist systems move through boom and bust cycles toward increasing economic
strength or toward ultimate collapse, but they do share an appreciation
for the role of crises in restructuring and restoring health and efficiency
(however temporarily) to the economy.

According to Marx, one of the most valuable functions of a crisis
was to ensure the "enforced destruction of a mass of productive
forces."[25] If we substitute "calamity" for "crisis," we end up with a sen-

timent that sounds remarkably like Cotton Mather's old claim that disasters are good because they destroy property—but for modern economists, of course, the destruction of goods is valuable not as an inspiration for spiritual reformation but as a foundation for economic production and expansion. We have moved decisively here from transcendence to the conquest of space. But how exactly does capitalism change the land, and what is the value of destruction? According to David Harvey, capitalism requires the constant, if uneven, development of physical environments for its survival. In the nineteenth century, the key to economic growth was urbanization. New metropoles like Chicago boosted output and productivity by enabling economies of scale, by massing work forces near to factories, and by clustering consumers into conveniently large markets, speeding up the production, distribution, and exchange of goods and services. In the twentieth century, however, cities have also put up increasing obstacles to the accumulation of capital by concentrating and intensifying social conflicts, becoming congested and dangerous, and freezing capital in obsolete structures.[26] This obsolescence, it should be pointed out, has little to do with the suitability of buildings as living or working environments and everything to do with capital flows and profit margins.

In a financial capitalist system of the sort increasingly predominant in the twentieth and twenty-first centuries, profits are increased by the circulation of capital; the more capital circulates, the more possibilities there are for profits. (We are witnessing this mobility of capital on a global scale today as multinational corporations and investment firms move money, people, and resources across the planet in search of marginal advantage.) In such a system, urban developments offer investment opportunities, but infrastructure also tends to tie capital down. One of the primary benefits of a calamity is that it destroys urban environments and thereby liberates and recycles capital that has "ossified" in fixed structures, thus clearing space for new development and opening up new investment opportunities.[27] Of course, particular owners rarely welcome this destruction. After all, they have little incentive to demolish and rebuild their own buildings, and in fact, unless they have unusually good insurance coverage, they can rarely afford to do so until their initial property investments have paid off.[28] The beauty of disasters is that they render irrelevant any objections to renewal from individual property owners. And so it is that disasters are good for capitalism, if not for all capitalists. In such a system, as political theorist Marshall Berman contends provocatively, "Our lives are controlled by a ruling class with vested interests not merely in change but in crisis and chaos," and catastrophes become "lucrative opportunities for redevelopment and renewal."[29]

Theories of creative destruction can help us to understand not only why capitalism promotes the constant and dramatic reshaping of modern urban space, but also why good bourgeois men like George Harvey might welcome the San Francisco earthquake as an investment opportunity. After all, he was not just an influential editor, he had also played a small but important role in implanting modern financial institutions in the United States during his tenure as State Commissioner of Banking and Insurance in New Jersey in the 1880s. Although a vigorous critic of monopolies, he was a personal friend of J. P. Morgan and crony enough to big business to campaign, only half-jokingly, for a "holiday for capital" to complement the existing Labor Day.[30] He was certainly familiar enough with the workings of a credit economy to appreciate that the 1906 calamity presented a "promising investment" for capitalists and financiers who were on the lookout, in this time of low interest rates and high market confidence, for new ventures and risks.[31]

As one might expect, of course, the notion that disasters were good for the economy was hardly uncontested in 1906. The editor of the *New York Times*, in fact, was exasperated by the "absurdity" of the idea that a great fire "was an actual advantage." Although the Baltimore fire of 1904 had stimulated construction and provided that city with a "clean slate" for improvements, it had done so at "somebody's cost." Failing to grasp the principle of productive expenditures, the editor adamantly resisted the idea that debt-financed development increased the wealth of the nation. "Destruction of capital," he concluded unequivocally, "is never beneficial, not even in a successful war."[32] The insurance companies that found themselves suddenly liable for more than $200,000,000 worth of claims in San Francisco had narrow reasons for agreeing, as did corporations with extensive local interests such as the United Railroads or the Southern Pacific, both of which saw their stocks fall significantly when news of the conflagration reached New York. Indeed, investors as a group were distinctly unnerved by the calamity. Even as financiers, stockbrokers, and industrialists gathered in their clubs to pledge tens of thousands of dollars in donations for the Bay City, misgivings about the larger implications of the disaster precipitated a "heavy selling" of stocks on Wall Street.[33]

The collapse, however, was never likely to be more than momentary in the bullish market of 1906, and within three days stocks were moving upward again.[34] One writer, struck by this turnaround, decided to research previous "catastrophe markets" and discovered, to his surprise, that rapid recovery of stock prices after a major disaster was the rule rather than the exception.[35] San Francisco itself soon began to look like a promising field of investment. Eastern financiers and firms loaned significant sums to the Bay City, and the federal government had to import $45,000,000 in gold from Europe to cover the drain on bank holdings as firms withdrew deposits to pay insurance claims and construction costs. This expansion of the money supply made possible a tremendous upsurge in business activity in San Francisco, doubling employment in the building trades and dramatically increasing banks' clearings in the Bay Area, though it may also have fueled the national speculation frenzy that would lead to the "rich man's panic" in early 1907.[36]

Although some prospective investors were concerned about future earthquakes, there was general agreement that San Francisco would recover because it was a "natural metropolis," destined for a glorious future by virtue of its location on a harbor and its possession of a large hinterland. It was these "natural advantages" rather than "artificial enhancement by investment," according to the editor of the *Times*, that guaranteed the recuperation of the Bay City. More sophisticated observers recognized that it was a combination of geography and artificial enhancements (railroad connections, credit flows, trade networks, etc.) that ensured the city's continued prosperity.[37] As a writer for *Collier's* pointed out, San Francisco's resources were by no means "confined to the little blackened tip of land by the Golden Gate." On the contrary, this plot of land was "the focal point at which her streams of wealth converge." "San Francisco capital," in fact, was "breeding revenue all the way up and down the Pacific, from Panama to Alaska, and across from the Rocky Mountains to China."[38] San Francisco, then, was bound to be restored, but what was the new metropolis going to look like? And whose interests were going to be served and sacrificed by the reconstruction of the city?

If some outside investors can be said to have had a stake in the constant ruin and renewal of cities like San Francisco, merchants and manufacturers recognized that they required *more* substantial cities (with fixed assets like railroad lines and stations, factories, offices, parks, and stores) to facilitate the production and distribution of their goods and services, to boost the purchasing power of consumers, and to promote the social peace they believed was necessary for the orderly conduct of business. These individuals seized upon the disaster as an opportunity to build a more, not less, permanent city. They wished to harness and control rather than unleash the forces of creative destruction, and they were driven as much by sentimental as by economic motives.

One of the defining characteristics of modern (and postmodern) history is the resistance to creative destruction of those classes that have benefited most from it. Many powerful and wealthy residents of turn-of-the-century San Francisco were eager to contain the disintegrative forces of capitalism, to bring an end to the constant mutation of their living and working spaces. A combination of disgust at the chaotic physical and social evolution of their city and a sense of alarm provoked by the deep recession of the 1890s had induced a group of influential citizens to form an Association for the Improvement and Adornment of San Francisco in 1904. These progressive-minded industrialists, merchants, and professionals were determined to bring an end to unregulated development, to build a beautiful city that blended artistic form and efficient function. Accordingly, they commissioned Daniel Burnham, chief architect of the neoclassical "White City" at the 1893 Chicago World's Fair, to draw up plans for a more permanent city, a pleasing and orderly city of boulevards and parks and monuments. In the words of Hubert Howe Bancroft, the new city was going to be "modern and up to date, with some widened streets and winding boulevards, gardens hanging to the hillside, parks with lakes and cascades, reservoirs of sea water on every hilltop; public work and public service, street cars and lighting being of the best."[39]

In effect, Progressives wished to achieve in San Francisco the sort of improvements that Baron Haussmann had famously accomplished in his rebuilding of Paris fifty years before during the reign of Napoleon III, an enterprise that had inspired contemporaries to apply the phrase "creative destruction" to modern development for the first time.[40] Burnham, like most of the Improvement Association leaders, was an enthusiastic admirer of Haussmann's work, so it is worth briefly reminding ourselves of the Baron's contribution to urban planning. Essentially, Haussmann transformed Paris in the 1850s and 1860s from a medieval city of nooks and crannies into a modern metropolis of grand avenues and stately buildings. His genius was to harness the forces of creative destruction for the purposes of the imperial state. He relished his role as wrecker, actually using cannons to demolish entire neighborhoods so that he could cut his trademark boulevards across the old city. He was, in his own words, an "artist of demolition," destroying so that he might create.[41] But he also saw himself as an agent of order, attempting to bring an end to chaos by constructing a rational, efficient, and more durable urban environment. Few would deny that Haussmann's endeavors reflected a sincere determination to save the city from an urban crisis brought about by population growth, overcrowding, and inadequate public services. His magnificent water supply and sewerage system, in particular, led to significant improvements in the health of the city, helping to ensure, for example, that the horrifying cholera epidemics that had gripped Paris in 1832 and 1849 would become a thing of the past.

But Haussmann also sought stability and control over the city and particularly over what he viewed as its unruly working class. Part of his plan was to provide employment in order to appease the "rabble," and many thousands did indeed find work on his projects. At the same time, however, he also tore down slums and wiped out many vibrant working-class districts, replacing them with bourgeois neighborhoods. This early exercise in gentrification saw most of the working poor retreating to the cheaper edges of the city as downtown rents escalated. Haussmann himself was fully aware that urban design was a political weapon, and although he was personally more interested in aesthetic, health, and commercial matters, he knew that his beautiful boulevards would make it easier for the Napoleonic regime to impose its authority on the city, facilitating not just the flow of goods and services, but the flow of troops to quell disturbances, making it harder for mobs to riot or to put up barricades.[42] In other words, although Haussmann the artist of demolition was fully prepared to use creative destruction to build a better city, he was also trying to tame some of the annihilating forces of capitalism, seeking to discipline the working class as well as to place limits on profit-driven development.

Progressives in San Francisco hoped to achieve the same effect with the Burnham Plan: a more rational and efficient city that would facilitate the conduct of business, elevate the moral character of the inhabitants, and bring an end to chronic instability and conflict.[43] Obstacles to their scheme, however, were forbidding. The legal machinery for condemning and improving property was cumbersome, and the cost of demolition and construction promised to be so high that even Burnham thought his plan would take fifty years to implement. "And then," as Californian author Gertrude Atherton put it, "Nature stepped in."[44] In the words of one leading citizen, blending religion and real estate in a now conventional way, the calamity was "almost like a visitation of Providence to give complete scope and liberty to the Burnham plan for rebuilding the city."[45] Disasters had been appreciated before. French Emperor Napoleon III had envied the English for the great fire that had incinerated grubby medieval London in 1666, and he had essentially ordered Haussmann to reproduce, in a controlled fashion, the conditions of a conflagration in Paris.[46] He deliberately exploited the prestige of the throne to shelter the Baron from any constitutional or democratic checks that threatened to hinder his mandate to destroy by decree.

Lacking the imperial authority to tear San Francisco down, local Progressives seized on the disaster as their best chance for urban improvement. Freshly printed copies of the Plan for San Francisco had been delivered to City Hall just hours before the earthquake struck, and reformers moved quickly to seize this opportunity. For a brief moment it looked as if Burnham's design would reshape the new city. After all, who could find fault with clean streets, convenient throughways, parks, improved municipal services, and attractive and sturdy buildings? Despite the endorsement of some of the most powerful men in the country, however, the plan never made it off the drawing board. What went wrong? Why was this American city unable to replicate Haussmann's model of urban design and development? A good part of the responsibility rests with the contradictory priorities and goals of the reformers themselves.

Burnham and his supporters were deeply committed not only to beautification but to economic expansion. The architect Louis Sullivan was not always Burnham's most sympathetic critic, but he was on the money when he wrote about his rival's "intense commercialism."[47] At every turn, proponents of adornment insisted on the increased tourist revenues and commercial profits that were sure to be generated by planned cities. Just look, they said, at what Haussmann's monuments and boulevards had done for earnings in Paris.[48] Former city engineer Marsden Manson produced the numbers. In a report recommending the immediate widening and extension of key streets in San Francisco, he calculated that improvements costing as little as $7,821,580 would add $75,000,000 to the value of city property within a decade.[49] Improvement, it seemed, paid. But there was a contradiction here between the pursuit of profits and the quest for a city design that would endure, in Burnham's words, "for all time to come."[50]

The economic arrangements reformers made to promote commercial activity in San Francisco inevitably undermined their efforts to control urban development. In an expansive economy, especially one marked by overaccumulation, planned obsolescence, and constant technological innovation, there would always be pressure to build new and changing urban structures: factories, railroads, stores, restaurants. Highway construction alone would lead to demand for new bridges, parking lots, service stations, and bus depots. Moreover, rising downtown ground rents would introduce irresistible incentives for the construction of skyscrapers as well as transit systems and suburban developments for overflow populations. Finally, there was always bound to be pressure on downtown commercial and professional interests to gain an edge on competitors by building more distinctive and prestigious show stores, office blocks, and business districts. Burnham should have known this. After all, in the 1890s his own company designed and built the first of the skyscrapers that would by the 1920s come to overshadow San Francisco's downtown monuments, parks, and thoroughfares.[51]

Progressives tended to view the city as a stage upon which life and economics were performed, but space cannot be permanently fixed in a dynamic capitalist system. Walter Benjamin once wrote that "In the convulsions of the commodity economy we begin to recognize the monuments of the bourgeoisie as ruins even before they have crumbled."[52] What he meant to suggest by this cryptic remark was that fixed structures could never be ends in themselves in a capitalist economy. The imperial city envisioned by Daniel Burnham as a physical manifestation of modern progress always threatened to stand in the way of the flow of capital, presenting an obstacle to continuing downtown commercial development. Hence the opposition to monumentalism of so many of San Francisco's businesses.

The conservative *Chronicle* mobilized resistance to the Burnham Plan, insisting that the best guide to reconstruction was the "plain, common-sense of our best business men."[53] And most of these businessmen were "rapid reconstructionists," keen to throw up new warehouses, factories, and offices as quickly as possible in order to get back to trading and making money. It soon became clear that these men would be able to raise the money necessary to rebuild by drawing on savings, insurance claims, bank loans, and eastern capital.[54] In retrospect, it is clear that these impatient men were more in tune with the logic of creative destruction than were the luminaries of the Improvement Association. Indeed, it is hard to avoid the conclusion that the impulse to beautification and order was an anxious and nostalgic reaction on the part of a corporate class to the disintegrative forces of capitalism, even though reformers surely deserve credit for their sincere ambition "to make San Francisco a more agreeable city in which to live."[55] It would be tempting to view the labors of Progressive planners as a worthy instance of the mobilization of local interests against the ravages of "placeless" capital but for two things.[56] First, a point we shall return to momentarily, they actually did more than any other group to increase the presence and power of outside capital. Second, their reforms tended to be insensitive to the desires and needs of less advantaged citizens, proposing initiatives that stood to damage and displace many ordinary San Franciscans.

The entrepreneurs and downtown shopkeepers who opposed urban planning found unlikely allies among those of the city's working people likely to be harmed by the Burnham Plan. Their hostility would not have been so surprising to reformers if they had paid more attention to the outraged response of ordinary citizens to Haussmann's rebuilding of Paris. One of the Prefect's most important acts was to remove obstacles to the circulation of capital through the French economy. In order to fund his gargantuan projects, he had discarded old bourgeois pieties about living within one's means and built on credit, gambling on unending economic expansion (and increasing tax revenues) to pay off the debts he incurred. In so doing, he promoted a cycle of deficit financing, speculation, forced economic growth, and capital instability that has since become a trademark of the global economy.[57] Many Parisian property owners and investors grew rich, but laboring people did not fare as well. Although the great rebuilding added significantly to the city's housing stock, it paradoxically contributed to a worsening housing crisis by dramatically increasing downtown property values. Just as hundreds of thousands of rural migrants were pouring into Paris in search of work, landlords took advantage of improvements, and of a growing pool of bourgeois tenants (civil servants, professionals, and white-collar workers who enjoyed rising incomes during the Second Empire), to raise rents. Most poorer residents, as we have seen, were driven from their former homes into outlying districts far from their places of work. Those who stayed were sealed into slums quite as bad as those that had existed before the renovations.[58] Haussmann's policies only intensified the problem. Although he had been willing to regulate the size and appearance of the building fronts that looked out onto his new boulevards, he was unwilling to interfere in what he viewed as the private housing market, and he resisted appeals for rent controls or quality housing statutes. Huge profits for landlords went hand in hand with deteriorating housing conditions for the working population.

Haussmann was wont to contend that his improvements offered something for all classes of society: "Foreigners and provincials would be attracted to the fine new city, would flock there to spend their money and would pay the expense of the new buildings. The shops would reap a harvest, the bourgeoisie would invest their money in the ground rents of the new streets, and the working classes would have full time employment; everyone would prosper."[59] But many did not prosper. Even Robert Moses, the American developer who would be reviled by many critics for destroying urban neighborhoods as he thrust great roadways through the heart of New York City in the mid-twentieth century, was troubled by the prefect of Paris's tendency "to neglect the lower middle class and the poor."[60] The economic forces Haussmann unleashed and the resentments they inspired exploded in 1871 when the laboring people of Paris took over the city and established the Commune. More destruction would follow. The communards themselves set fire to the city as they fled before murderous Versailles soldiers during the May massacres, though in this case Karl Marx, for one, was sympathetic, contrasting the "vandalism of defense in despair" to the more destructive "vandalism of Haussmann, razing Paris to make place for the Paris of the sightseer."[61]

The important point here is that "improvement" or "beautification" was bitterly contested in France, that there were winners and losers, and that rebuilding programs helped to determine who prospered and who languished. Similar conflicts plagued the reconstruction of San Francisco, but whereas Haussmann could ignore opposition, building by edict, such an option was not available to officials in the Californian city. The Progressives who lobbied for adornment could be quite as contemptuous of democracy as the Prefect of Paris. A correspondent for *Collier's* gave voice to the frustrations of many wealthy Americans, fantasizing about establishing "an enlightened despotism" to ensure that reconstruction was dictated by the public interest rather than the individual search for the "quick profit." San Francisco, however, had unusually strong democratic traditions and a municipal council that depended on working-class votes for its survival.[62]

From the beginning, this constituency mobilized against those parts of the Burnham Plan that threatened to drive ordinary families from their homes. The demands of reformers to ban wooden structures from downtown promised to produce a more fireproof and attractive city center, but few working people could afford to build brick houses.[63] In this case, market logics (and a political voice) protected the interests of working-class householders much more effectively than did the deeds of civic-minded reformers.[64] Labor mobilized against the new building regulations, and the municipal authorities abandoned proposals to extend the city's fire limits. Progressives themselves lost interest in the political reforms that might have made the Burnham Plan possible when it dawned on them that an amendment to the state constitution allowing San Francisco to widen streets over the objections of property holders would place expansive new powers in the hands of politicians beholden to working-class constituents. Fearing that urban planning might become the thin end of a socialist wedge, reformers surrendered their imperial ambitions.[65]

In the end, George Harvey of *Harper's* was correct in his prediction: investors and insurance companies poured enough money into San Francisco to ensure that the city was rebuilt in less than five years. But while there were several improvements in design and structure, these owed more to the ambitions and whims of individual entrepreneurs, and to a pool of talented architects who had flocked to the city to exploit the sudden demand for their services, than to any Haussmannic planning.[66] The old street layout was little changed, and there was not even sufficient will to pass a bond issue for a new city hall until 1912, when prominent citizens were suddenly faced with the task of turning their city into a site impressive enough to host the impending 1915 Panama-Pacific International Exposition. Seeing immense potential for growth in the opening of the Panama Canal and eager to promote San Francisco as a city of global importance, residents finally voted to fund the construction of a monumental Beaux Arts civic center, one of the final achievements of the beautification movement. Still, Progressives could hardly claim to have to imposed a rational design on San Francisco.

One of the sources of their undoing, reformers believed, was the callous behavior of eastern corporations that seemed determined to put short-term profits ahead of responsible development. At the time of the earthquake, for example, United Railroads, a New York–financed company, was lobbying vigorously to defeat proposals that would have required it to house electrical lines for its trolley cars in expensive underground conduits, rather than in cheaper and unsightly overhead wires. For members of the Improvement and Adornment Association this was proof of the folly of leaving development to "foreign interests," to brokers and bankers in Wall Street and Europe who cared nothing for actual living conditions in San Francisco.[67] Only if development was left to the community-minded citizens of the Bay City, reformers reasoned, would it be possible to build a city that expedited the pursuit of commerce without sacrificing quality of life.

Hence the eagerness with which influential local reformers sought to control all money raised to finance the rebuilding. As a first step, they dispatched Senator Francis Newlands to Washington to try to arrange a loan from the federal government. When this failed, Newlands and other San Franciscan businessmen approached New York investors directly hoping to secure an advance of $100 million with which to implement the Burnham Plan.[68] This initiative also foundered, and it soon became clear that reconstruction was to be funded by private capital, acquired by businesses on a case-by-case basis. At first, individual companies would have to rely on the forbearance of suppliers. The merchant proprietor of Livingston Brothers, for one, later recorded that his business could not have survived without the willingness of Marshall Field and Company of Chicago to waive "the usual 60 day credit term."[69] Over the long haul, money was indispensable and fortunately it arrived in abundance. Ultimately, about half of the costs of construction (about $200 million) were covered by fire insurance, $115 million of which reached businesses and householders within six months of the earthquake. Relief donations and federal contributions covered a further 2 percent of costs; the rest of the money came from private savings and borrowings.[70]

When it became clear that they would not have a vast reconstruction fund at their disposal, reformers turned their attention to raising eastern capital for their private enterprises. James Duval Phelan, banker, property owner, former mayor, and president of the Improvement Association, lobbied to change provisions in the California Constitution that had hitherto given preferential mortgage terms to residents of the state and had thus deterred outside investment. Similarly, he and his allies secured the repeal of special taxes on the stocks and bonds of non-Californian corporations.[71] As so often in the twentieth century, the imperatives of development encouraged local leaders to try to entice outside investment by dismantling obstacles to the movement of capital. Their unintended legacy was to increase the influence of financiers over development patterns in a city once proud of its independence from eastern investors.[72] A city, according to William Issel and Robert Cherny, that had "enjoyed economic autonomy" to an extent surpassed only by New York City at the end of the nineteenth century would find itself increasingly subject to national and international capital flows that accelerated the very cycles of ruin and renewal Progressives abhorred.[73] And when they did have an opportunity to serve the local population they recoiled.

The merchants, professionals, and industrialists of the Improvement Association were willing to use the power of the state to promote private enterprise and to build the infrastructure they believed was necessary for the effective prosecution of commerce, but they remained profoundly uncomfortable with any intervention that threatened to distort what they viewed as a "free" market in wages or rents. Like Haussmann, in fact, their greatest failure lay in their inadequate response to housing problems. In the conditions that prevailed after the disaster, with a drastically reduced housing stock, market forces offered a strong economic incentive to landlords to supply overpriced and undermaintained accommodations for the refugees. The unburned Western Addition began its transformation from a comfortable middle-class district into a "blighted area" as property owners turned homes into lodging houses, cramming tenants into every available room and basement, and rented space to workshops, stores, and even dangerous industries. "Every condition that would make a modern city planner shudder," one historian later lamented, "was soon to be found in exaggerated form: indiscriminate mixture of land uses, excessive density of population, substandard housing, traffic congestion."[74]

And these middle-class tenants were the lucky ones. The destruction of some 55 percent of the city's housing stock hit blue-collar workers and their families especially hard. One of the unexpected effects of the calamity was to speed up the deindustrialization of the city, as manufacturing firms moved out to the suburbs or across the bay to Oakland in search of cheaper ground rents, surrendering the city center to banks, insurance companies, and other financial institutions. Many working people thus lost not only their jobs, but their homes too as the financial district expanded by about 44 percent in the aftermath of the fire, taking over sites that had formerly been occupied by low-income housing.[75] Poorer families were left in a precarious position.

The prominent charity worker Edward T. Devine, head of the American Red Cross operation to aid San Francisco, lobbied vigorously to release relief funds for the construction of simple but good quality housing that could be made available cheaply to working-class families. As he pointed out, and as was plain to see, the private sector was simply unable to supply the needs of working-class refugees for affordable shelter in the aftermath of the conflagration. Eight thousand houses were built in the year and a half following the calamity, but these were almost all taken by middle-class residents. Sadly, several months after the calamity, Devine had to report that a "golden opportunity" had been missed to spend aid surpluses on decent homes for "the working men of the community." The reason: the local business leaders responsible for the distribution of relief funds could not bring themselves to interfere with the private property market. Instead, they paid for the erection of "temporary" and often unsanitary shacks that became, as Devine predicted, lasting scars on the San Francisco landscape.[76]

Meanwhile, San Francisco began its evolution from a manufacturing center into an increasingly important financial center; by 1975, it would be home to the second largest concentration of international banks and financial institutions in the country, after New York City. It was these institutions that would push through plans to renew (or "Manhattanize") downtown San Francisco in the years after World War II, throwing up huge structures of steel, concrete, and glass, and producing finally the sort of imposing skyline that businessmen believed was worthy of this capital of capital. All this redevelopment accelerated the obliteration of low-income accommodation (guaranteeing that the city would suffer the highest housing prices in the country), while ensuring the disappearance of open spaces and the intensification of downtown congestion.[77]

Market forces, however, would not rule unopposed in the Bay City. If Improvement Association leaders failed to follow through on their ambition to impose limits on capital, activist communities throughout the twentieth century would enjoy considerable success resisting highway developments or building projects that threatened to destroy the neighborhood character of their city.[78] Such resistance to mobile capital, however, has not been without costs and may partly explain the increasing shift of money, people, and industries from the Bay City to more "flexible," development-driven Los Angeles in the years since 1906.[79] The legacy of the disaster was thus an ambiguous one, revealing the crucial influence of capitalist logics in restoring a devastated metropolis and promoting business interests at the expense of the poor, but also bringing to the surface profound and enduring discontents with the destructive aspects of capitalist development that would spur ongoing resistance to the relentless remaking of San Francisco to suit the needs of business.

The story of San Francisco's reconstruction substantiates the growing critical consensus that there has always been a vital spatial dimension to capitalist development and that some of the most urgent social conflicts of the twentieth century have been organized around concerns of space and place. The logic of creative destruction, in particular, helps to explain why so many well-positioned Americans at the turn of the century expected conflagrations to produce material benefits, even if those benefits were not shared by all.

In many respects, things have changed little since 1906. As the *Wall Street Journal* recently reported, calamities continue to generate economic gains that outweigh losses. "Afterward, retail sales soar as ruined goods are repaired or replaced, and construction is fueled by an influx of insurance money and federal disaster relief. Moreover, insured homeowners and businesses, already facing insurance-financed repairs, often seize the occasion to improve their properties." From 1989's Hurricane Hugo to the earthquake that shook Northridge, Los Angeles, in 1994, the effects have been the same. According to Steve Cochrane of Dismal Sciences, Inc., natural disasters invariably generate "a rapid rise in employment and income." And yet, calamities still ruin many individuals, and even those people who profit "would rather not face the risk."[80] A financial windfall rarely compensates for the loss of treasured possessions or for the stresses of renovation.

In the world made by late capitalism, disasters continue to mimic (and perhaps even burlesque) the destructive forces of capitalism, breeding a nostalgic preoccupation with order, permanence, and continuity, even as they promote economic growth and the expectation that ruin leads to renewal and improvement. But if calamities enable progress, "progress" itself often seems only to increase human vulnerability to increasingly severe calamities.[81] Nowhere has creative destruction contributed more to the shape of economic and urban development than in San Francisco's southern neighbor and rival, Los Angeles, and nowhere, significantly, have disasters become such a persistent presence.

Until recently, as Mike Davis points out in *Ecology of Fear,* few have appreciated the costs of radically transforming the landscape according to the whims of capital. Viewing disasters as opportunities for development and exhibiting a reckless disregard for environmental limits, Americans have too often failed to heed the warnings that calamities bring. As a result, there have never been enough checks on unregulated, ecologically irresponsible construction: "Historic wildfire corridors have been turned into view-lot suburbs, wetland liquefaction zones into marinas, and floodplains into industrial districts and housing tracts." Meanwhile, Californians have continued to build homes, highways, and even nuclear power plants over fault lines. "As a result," as Davis concludes, "Southern California has reaped flood, fire, and earthquake tragedies that were as avoidable as the beating of Rodney King and the ensuing explosion in the streets."[82]

At the dawn of the twenty-first century, calamities (social and natural) are becoming such regular features of southern Californian and American life that old optimisms about the benefits of disaster are finally wearing thin.[83] Faith in progress seems to be waning, and as a result Americans increasingly view disasters as threats rather than as blessings, or at best as spectacles without moral or meaning. There is little sign, however, that we will see an end to the constant transformation of urban space any time soon. Many businessmen and financiers continue to follow the lead of Alan Greenspan, who speaks warmly of creative destruction as the engine of an ever-innovating and expanding American economy, though there are also critics aplenty who insist that unending growth is an environmentally unsustainable option that may well produce a calamity that finally buries rather than invigorates capitalism.[84]

Destruction has enabled capitalist development. Over the last century and more, it has facilitated extraordinary economic expansion and invention, affirming many Americans in their longstanding conviction that calamities are blessings. The benefits, however, have not been spread equally, and we all have to find a way to live with and under a capitalist system that must constantly destroy to create, and at times seems to create solely in order to destroy. Whether this chaos and flux will in the twenty-first century enrich and liberate more people than it impoverishes, only time (and space) will tell.

NOTES

1. I would like to thank Todd De Pastino, Ambreen Hai, and Lane Witt for their invaluable contributions (intellectual and editorial) to this essay. I am also grateful to Steven Biel and Dan Horowitz for comments, suggestions, and guidance.

2. George Harvey, "Comment," *Harper's Weekly*, 5 May 1906, 616.

3. J. S. Cahill, "The So-Called Catastrophe," *American Builders Review* 4, no. 1 (July 1906): 177.

4. See, for example, William Greider, *One World, Ready or Not: The Manic Logic of Global Capitalism* (New York: Simon and Schuster, 1997).

5. One elegant recent work of urban history absorbs this key concept into its very title: Max Page, *The Creative Destruction of Manhattan, 1900-1940* (Chicago: University of Chicago Press, 1999).

6. Marshall Berman, *All that Is Solid Melts into Air: The Experience of Modernity* (New York: Penguin, 1988), 19.

7. Lewis Mumford, *City Development: Studies in Renewal and Development* (New York: Harcourt, Brace, 1946), 191, 160, 157.

8. Cotton Mather, "BOANERGES. A Short Essay to Preserve and Strengthen the Good Impressions Produced by Earthquakes. Boston, 1727," in *Days of Humiliation, Times of Affliction* (Gainesville, Fla.: Scholars' Facsimiles and Reprints, 1970), 366.

9. Increase Mather, "An Earnest Exhortation to the Inhabitants of New England," in *Departing Glory: Eight Jeremiads by Increase Mather,* ed. Lee Scheninger (Delmar, N.Y.: Scholars' Facsimiles and Reprints, 1986), 15.

10. Increase Mather, letter to John Cotton, Boston, 13 December 1676, Manuscripts Collection, Mather Papers, American Antiquarian Society, and *Diary by Increase Mather, March 1675-December 1676,* ed. Samuel A. Green (Cambridge, Mass.: John Wilson and Son, 1900), 39.

11. See Charles C. Smith, "Boston and the Colony," and Edward L. Bynner, "Topography and Landmarks of the Provincial Period," in *The Memorial History of Boston,* ed. Justin Winsor (Boston: James R. Osgood, 1880), 1: 230-31, 2: 493.

12. Sacvan Bercovitch, *The American Jeremiad* (Madison: University of Wisconsin Press, 1978), 23.

13. Elias Colbert and Everett Chamberlin, *Chicago and the Great Conflagration* (1871; New York: Viking Press, 1971), 445.

14. George Harvey, "Comment," *Harper's Weekly*, 5 May 1906, 616.

15. John Stuart Mill, *Principles of Political Economy with Some of Their Applications to Social Philosophy,* in *Collected Works of John Stuart Mill* (Toronto: Routledge & Kegan Paul, 1965), 74-75.

16. Edwin G. Burrows and Mike Wallace, *Gotham: A History of New York City to 1898* (New York: Oxford University Press, 1999), 596-601.

17. "The Conflagration," *New York Herald,* 19 December 1835.

18. Harriet Martineau, *Society in America* (New York: Saunders and Otley, 1837), 2: 74.

19. *The Diary of Philip Hone, 1828-1851,* ed. Allan Nevins (New York: Dodd, Mead, and Co., 1927), 199-201.

20. *Diary of Philip Hone,* 2: 730.

21. Martineau, *Society in America,* 2: 74-75.

22. In fact, commentators borrowed from discourses of natural disaster to understand the logic of economic misfortune. Indeed, as Ann Fabian argues, weather metaphors may have helped to naturalize capitalism at moments of crisis, encouraging people to accept panics, like disasters, as blessings, as agents of ultimate order and well-being. "Speculation on Distress: The Popular Discourse of the Panics of 1837 and 1857," *Yale Journal of Criticism* 3, no. 1 (1989): 132-38.

23. Joseph A. Schumpeter, *Capitalism, Socialism, and Democracy* (New York: Harper, 1950), 83, 82.

24. Karl Marx and Friedrich Engels, *The Communist Manifesto* (New York: Bantam Books, 1992), 24.

25. Marx and Engels, *Communist Manifesto,* 25.

26. David Harvey, *The Urban Experience* (Baltimore: Johns Hopkins University Press, 1989), 33.

27. See Neil Smith, *Uneven Development: Nature, Capital and the Production of Space* (Cambridge, Mass.: Basil Blackwell, 1990), 124-30.

28. Neil Smith, *The New Urban Frontier: Gentrification and the Revanchist City* (New York: Routledge, 1996), 83-84. It has never been easy for property owners, singly or collectively, to tear down and replace existing structures or neighborhoods. As Christine Meisner Rosen shows in her comprehensive account of the politics and economics of reconstruction after the Chicago fire of 1871, the Boston fire of 1872, and the Baltimore fire of 1904, even the most concerted efforts to improve districts and buildings were hindered by "frictions" (the durability of urban buildings, the high costs of demolition and rebuilding, technological limitations,

political weaknesses, market and tax disincentives to improvements, etc.). Frustration with these obstacles to renewal helps to explain why so many business people were so enthusiastic about fires that promised to burn away some of these obstacles to change; the persistence of these frictions helps to explain why ambitious plans for reconstruction were so hard to accomplish. Rosen, *The Limits of Power: Great Fires and the Process of City Growth in America* (New York: Cambridge University Press, 1986).

29. Berman, *All that Is Solid Melts into Air*, 95.

30. Willis Fletcher Johnson, *George Harvey: A Passionate Patriot* (Boston: Houghton Mifflin, 1929), 32-33. As editor of both *Harper's Weekly* and the *North American Review*, Harvey was one of the most influential opinion makers of his day. "A Holiday for Capital" is reprinted in his book *Women, Etc.: Some Leaves from An Editor's Diary* (New York: Harper and Brothers, 1908), 139-43.

31. George Harvey, "San Francisco," *Harper's Weekly*, 5 May 1906, 619. It is also possible, however, that extraordinarily high returns in the stock markets in 1906 may have discouraged some financiers from investing in Californian real estate and infrastructures. John Moody, *The Masters of Capital: A Chronicle of Wall Street* (New Haven, Conn.: Yale University Press, 1919), 134-35.

32. "San Francisco Will Be Restored," *New York Times*, 20 April 1906.

33. "Heavy Sales of Stock," *New York Times*, 20 April 1906, 7.

34. Henry Clews, *Fifty Years in Wall Street* (New York: Irving, 1915), 783.

35. "Catastrophe Markets," *New York Times*, 23 April 1906, 14.

36. Clews, *Fifty Years in Wall Street*, 783-85.

37. For an exemplary analysis of the geography of capital and the development of another western metropolis, see William Cronon, *Nature's Metropolis: Chicago and the Great West* (New York: W. W. Norton, 1991), 263-309.

38. "Looking Ahead at San Francisco," *Collier's*, 12 May 1906, 24. For a similar argument, see William H. Mills, "Influences that Insure the Recovery of San Francisco," *California State Board of Trade Bulletin* 15 (1906).

39. Hubert Howe Bancroft, *Some Cities and San Francisco and Resurgam* (New York: Bancroft Company, 1907), 61-62.

40. David Harvey offers a brilliant technical analysis of "creative destruction" in imperial Paris in *Consciousness and the Urban Experience: Studies in the History and Theory of Capitalist Urbanization* (Baltimore: Johns Hopkins University Press, 1985), 63-220.

41. J. M. Chapman and Brian Chapman, *The Life and Times of Baron Haussmann: Paris in the Second Empire* (London: Weidenfeld and Nicolson, 1957), 209.

42. Richard Sennett, *The Uses of Disorder: Personal Identity and City Life* (New York: Alfred A. Knopf, 1970), 88-90.

43. On links between urban planning and the quest for moral order and social control, see Paul Boyer, *Urban Masses and Moral Order in America, 1820-1920* (Cambridge: Harvard University Press, 1978) and M. Christine Boyer, *Dreaming*

the Rational City: The Myth of American City Planning (Cambridge, Mass.: MIT Press, 1983).

44. Gertrude Atherton, "San Francisco's Tragic Dawn," *Harper's Weekly,* 12 May 1906, 660.

45. "What the Disaster Means to Oregon," *Oregon Mining Journal* 22, no. 1 (28 April 1906): 17.

46. Chapman, *Life and Times of Baron Haussmann,* 90.

47. Louis Sullivan, *Autobiography of an Idea* (New York: American Institute of Architects, 1926), 314.

48. See, for example, Daniel Burnham, "Presentation to the Merchant's Association, April 13, 1897," in Charles Moore, *Daniel Hudson Burnham, Architect, Planner of Cities* (Boston: Houghton Mifflin, 1921), 2: 102.

49. Marsden Manson, *Report of Marsden Manson to the Mayor and Committee on Reconstruction on those Portions of the Burnham Plans Which Meet Our Commercial Necessities and An Estimate of the Cost of the Same* (October 1906).

50. Burnham and Bennett, *Report on a Plan for San Francisco,* 35.

51. Mel Scott, *The San Francisco Bay Area: A Metropolis in Perspective* (Berkeley: University of California Press, 1959), 79-80.

52. Walter Benjamin, "Paris, Capital of the Nineteenth Century," in *Reflections: Essays, Aphorisms, Autobiographical Writings,* trans. Edmund Jephcott (New York: Schocken Books, 1978), 162.

53. "Proposed Street Changes," *San Francisco Chronicle,* 27 April 1906, 4.

54. A. P. Giannini was one banker who saw tremendous opportunity in the disaster, even though his own banking house was burned to the ground. Seizing the chance to increase business at a time when ordinary citizens were desperate for loans and for a safe place to keep their money, he doubled the deposits and transactions of his bank in the summer after the calamity and was easily able to afford the move to an impressive new nine-story headquarters in the new downtown financial district. This was a crucial moment in the transformation of his small neighborhood institution into the world's largest bank by the 1940s. Gerald D. Nash, *A. P. Giannini and the Bank of America* (Norman: University of Oklahoma Press, 1992), ix, 30-36; Felice A. Bondadio, *A. P. Giannini: Banker of America* (Berkeley: University of California Press, 1994), 32-37. As Marquis James and Bessie Rowland James point out, all San Francisco banks increased their business in 1906 during the reconstruction months. James and James, *Biography of a Bank: The Story of the Bank of America* (New York: Harper and Brothers, 1954), 31.

55. Daniel Hudson Burnham and Edward H. Bennett, *Report on a Plan for San Francisco* (San Francisco: City of San Francisco, 1905), 7.

56. On the "placeless power" of capital, see Allan Pred and Michael John Watts, *Reworking Modernity: Capitalism and Its Symbolic Discontents* (New Brunswick, N.J.: Rutgers University Press, 1992), 11-12.

57. For two fine accounts of the complex financial politics of the rebuilding of Paris that pay attention to the revolution of the national credit system, see David P. Jordan, *Transforming Paris: The Life and Labors of Baron Haussmann* (New York: Free Press, 1995), 227-45; and Harvey, *Consciousness and the Urban Experience*, 76-82, 97-98.

58. Lewis Mumford's observations on the contradictions of imperial planning are as trenchant today as they were when he composed them seventy-five years ago: "Historically, the imperial monument and the slum-tenement go hand in hand. The same process that creates an unearned increment for the landlords who possess favored sites, contributes a generous quota—which might be called the unearned excrement—of depression, overcrowding, and bad living, in the dormitory districts of the city. This had happened in imperial Rome; it had happened again in Paris under Napoleon III, where Haussmann's sweeping reconstructions created new slums in the districts behind the grand avenues, quite as bad, if far less obvious, as those that had been cleared away; and it happened once again in our American cities." Mumford, *Sticks and Stones: A Study of American Architecture and Civilization* (New York: Boni and Liveright, 1924), 143.

59. Quoted in Robert Moses, "What Happened to Haussmann," *Architectural Forum* 77 (July 1942): 61.

60. Moses, "What Happened to Haussmann," 6. In his absorbing biography, Robert A. Caro recalls the violent imagery deployed by Moses to justify the immense destruction that accompanied his developments: "You can't make an omelet without breaking eggs," or "when you operate in an overbuilt metropolis, you have to hack your way with a meat ax." Caro, *The Power Broker: Robert Moses and the Fall of New York* (New York: Alfred A. Knopf, 1974), 849.

61. Karl Marx, *The Civil War in France* (New York: International Publishers, 1933), 59-60.

62. *Collier's,* 12 May 1906, 6. Michael Kazin's history of the Building Trades Council emphasizes the extraordinary social, economic, and political influence of construction tradesmen in the 1900s and 1910s but complicates the characterization of San Francisco as a "labor city" in *Barons of Labor: The San Francisco Building Trades and Union Power in the Progressive Era* (Urbana: University of Illinois Press, 1987).

63. Oscar Lewis, *San Francisco: Mission to Metropolis* (San Diego: Howell-North, 1980), 203.

64. When working people stood to benefit financially from beautification projects such as the new civic center of the 1910s, they were much more supportive. Kazin, *Barons of Labor*, 87.

65. Judd Kahn, *Imperial San Francisco: Politics and Planning in an American City, 1897-1906* (Lincoln: University of Nebraska Press, 1979), 184-99, 212.

66. A. C. David, "The New San Francisco," *Architectural Record* 31, no. 1 (January 1912): 3-26; Richard Longstreth, *On the Edges of the World: Four Architects in San Francisco at the Turn of the Century* (Cambridge, Mass.: MIT Press, 1983), 297-98.

67. Kahn, *Imperial San Francisco*, 111-27.

68. For details of both initiatives, see *United States Senate Congressional Record*, 2 May 1906, 6244-48.

69. Edward Livingston, *A Personal History of the San Francisco Earthquake and Fire* (San Francisco, 1941), 29.

70. Christopher Morris Douty, *The Economics of Localized Disaster: The 1906 San Francisco Catastrophe* (New York: Arno Press, 1977), 198, 307; J. Eugene Haas, Robert W. Kates, and Martyn J. Bowden, eds., *Reconstruction Following Disaster* (Cambridge, Mass.: MIT Press, 1977), 6.

71. James D. Phelan, "The Regeneration of San Francisco," *The Independent*, 20 June 1907, 1449. For revealing glimpses into the efforts of private business enterprises to raise loans through contacts in New York City, see James Duval Phelan, Correspondence and Papers, Box 1, Bancroft Library, University of California, Berkeley.

72. William G. Robbins, *Colony and Empire: The Capitalist Transformation of the American West* (Lawrence: University of Kansas Press, 1994), 166.

73. William Issel and Robert W. Cheney, *San Francisco, 1865-1932: Politics, Power, and Urban Development* (Berkeley: University of California Press, 1986), 203.

74. Scott, *The San Francisco Bay Area*, 111.

75. Haas, Kates, and Bowden, *Reconstruction Following Disaster*, 75, 94.

76. Edward T. Devine, "The Housing Problem in San Francisco," *Political Science Quarterly* 21 (1906): 596-608.

77. See Chester Hartmann, *The Transformation of San Francisco* (Totowa, N.J.: Rowman and Allanheld, 1984).

78. Issel and Cheney, *San Francisco, 1865-1932*, 215-16. See also Stephen J. McGovern, *The Politics of Downtown Development: Dynamic Political Cultures in San Francisco and Washington, DC* (Lexington: University Press of Kentucky, 1998).

79. This statement needs qualifying. Although imperatives of profit and market-driven development played a more prominent role in shaping Los Angeles than they did in shaping San Francisco, it is important not to forget the southern city's "long history of formal planning." The expansion of Los Angeles is inconceivable in the absence of massive (often federally supported) regional planning projects such as the building of the harbor, the aqueduct system, and the vast freeway system. An activist, or "progressive," city council began work on the diversion of potable water from the Owens Valley to Los Angeles in the year of the San Francisco earthquake. Michael Dear, "In The City,

Time Becomes Visible: Intentionality and Urbanism in Los Angeles, 1781-1991," in *The City: Los Angeles and Urban Theory at the End of the Twentieth Century,* ed. Allan J. Scott and Edward W. Soja (Berkeley: University of California Press, 1996), 76-105.

80. "'Anthill' Economics: How Natural Disasters Can Change the Course of a Region's Growth," *Wall Street Journal,* 5 October 1999, 1.

81. According to Hervé Kempf, the beneficial economic impact of disasters may be discouraging the developed world from leading the "fight against climate change," although global warming is patently increasing the number and intensity of floods and hurricanes around the world. The repercussions, as he points out, are likely to be especially "appalling" for developing countries that lack the infrastructure or economic resiliency to cope with disasters. As a case in point, he cites the 20,000 deaths resulting from the Venezuelan floods of November 1999. "Every Catastrophe has a Silver Lining," *Guardian Weekly,* 20-26 January 2000, 30.

82. Mike Davis, *Ecology of Fear: Los Angeles and the Imagination of Disaster* (New York: Metropolitan Books, 1998), 7-9.

83. William Cronon, "Introduction: In Search of Nature," in *Uncommon Ground: Toward Reinventing Nature* (New York: W. W. Norton, 1995), 29-32.

84. Upon opening the "Testimony and Speeches" file at the official federal reserve Web site in April 2000, I found twenty-five references to "creative destruction," most made by Greenspan in speeches celebrating what he views as the remarkable efficiency with which investment markets shift capital toward innovative technologies like the Internet, technologies that are presumed to be catapulting the world into a new and sustained season of economic expansion (see www.federalreserve.gov). At the same time, an increasing number of economists are beginning to prophesy economic or environmental doom ahead for a world trapped in a debt economy, a world "enslaved" by a financial capitalist system that requires ceaseless expansion for its survival, regardless of the consequences for an already strained environment. Taking his theme from a literal, if slightly misleading, translation of the word "mort-gage," Michael Rowbotham, for example, writes vividly about a planet caught in "the grip of death." Rowbotham, *The Grip of Death: A Study of Modern Money, Debt Slavery and Destructive Economics* (Charlbury, U.K.: Jon Carpenter, 1998).

4

Smoke and Mirrors

The San Francisco Earthquake and Seismic Denial

Ted Steinberg

In response to the massive national and international coverage of the San Francisco earthquake—nearly a hundred popular books were published in 1906 alone—local and state officials and business elites engaged in a concerted attempt to describe the disaster as a fire rather than an earthquake. If San Francisco came to be seen as a uniquely dangerous place, these leaders feared, commercial investment and population growth would be threatened. And so, Ted Steinberg argues, they engaged in "seismic denial," blaming most of the damage on the fire rather than the earthquake and fostering a vision of the calamity consistent with continued growth and development. Even today, those "seeking to boost land development in the San Francisco area have tended to revive the conspiracy of seismic silence when it has suited them."

THE 1906 SAN FRANCISCO earthquake is arguably the calamity that defines calamity in the popular imagination. It is the Big One that lurks in the back of our minds. As the geographer Kenneth Hewitt has put it, the turn-of-the-century disaster has come to be seen through a process of "historical-geographical compression" as an icon representing the entire seismic risk problem "even as many other disasters occur and are forgotten."[1]

Mircea Eliade has talked about the ahistorical quality of popular memory, "the inability of collective memory to retain historical events . . . except insofar as it transforms them into archetypes."[2] The 1906 San Francisco calamity stands out as one such archetype. It

exists in an interpretive void of sorts. On the one hand, it is canon-
ized as the natural disaster to end all natural disasters; on the other,
its meaning rarely transcends the realm of caricature and myth. A
search of some 38 million records catalogued by U.S. libraries uncov-
ers 572 citations under the subject. Its closest competitor in terms of
the sheer volume of written, photographic, and map material is the
Johnstown Flood of 1889, which generated only a quarter as many
items (146 to be exact). Meanwhile, within San Francisco itself the
disaster continues to serve as a key memory marker in the city's collective unconscious.

But for all the talk of 1906 representing the very epitome of bigness,
the event is, when put in context, hardly the most sizable earthquake on
record. That distinction goes to a 1960 Chilean shaker (M 9.5[3]), a full 350
times more powerful in terms of seismic energy.[4] Moreover, the notorious San Francisco shaker, for all that has been said about it, for all the
tremendous attention lavished on this one slip of the earth, has hardly
had the effect on development and building in the city that one would
expect. In this sense, the disaster has both tremendous meaning and no
meaning at all—at least, no meaning in terms of its impact on reducing
seismic risk throughout the Bay Area.

FIRE

The battle over the meaning of the San Francisco disaster began even before the smoke had cleared. That struggle pitted those seeking to capi-
talize on the disaster's entertainment value against California's business
class, which expressed deep reservations about the adverse impact all the
publicity might have on the city's commercial prospects. Less than one
week after the disaster, the *New York Times* reported the preparation of a
hundred "distinct and separate books telling the complete story of the
San Francisco earthquake and fire."[5] In fact, at least eighty-two popular
accounts of the calamity, often lavishly illustrated, were published in
1906 alone—an extraordinary commemorative outpouring. And that
number does not include the many newspaper and magazine accounts
republished in book form. Nor, of course, does it include the huge number of separate photographs and postcards that circulated throughout
the country. "Ever since the disaster of April 18 the cooler members of the
community have looked askance at the wide dissemination of photo-

graphic views of San Francisco 'after the earthquake and fire,'" observed an editorial in the *San Francisco Call*. The paper, owned by John Spreckels, one of California's most prominent capitalists, objected to all the publicity. "Are we not damaging the city by every one of these views we send away?" The editorial continued: "The whole world is familiar with our calamity, but is it necessary to harp on the subject after it is all over? Why not forget it as soon as possible. . . . If we want to frighten people away from us this is about as good a way as any other."[6]

Calamity was big business in turn-of-the-century America and obviously many publishers saw the disaster as a potential source of profit. But for most of San Francisco's business class, the disaster was not something they chose to advertise. At the time of the earthquake, the city led the West in trade and manufacturing and was fast becoming a major financial center as well. As far as the business class was concerned, the jolt could not be allowed to impede San Francisco's commercial future. William Humphrey, president of the Tidewater Oil Company, noted that the calamity seemed to inspire "wonderful fraternalism" among the city's commercial leaders. "Everyone was in the same boat, so we forgot all else and pulled as a team."[7] And at nothing did they work harder than shaping the way the calamity would be understood. There were high stakes involved in how one interpreted the disaster.

The 1906 earthquake (M 7.7) occurred along the San Andreas fault (the most visible strike-slip fault in the world) and resulted in a rupture of the earth's surface that extended more than 250 miles. Although felt as far south as Los Angeles, as far north as southern Oregon, and as far east as central Nevada, the earthquake is still commonly understood as exclusively a San Francisco calamity. In fact, however, the jolt caused extensive damage throughout northern California.[8]

The shock occurred a little after 5 A.M. and lasted about one minute. Subsequently, fires erupted in San Francisco as electrical wires were severed and gas mains exploded. The fires burned for three days over an area of almost five square miles. Unable to stem the blaze because underground water mains had been damaged in the seismic jolt, the fire department stood by as more than 28,000 commercial and residential buildings succumbed to the flames. Annihilated were the business district, vast parts of the factory and entertainment areas, and the major hotels and restaurants, as well as nearly all of the city's most important buildings.[9] Exactly how many people died remains unclear, as we will see, but three thousand is by no means far-fetched.

The 1906 quake was, of course, not the first to rock the San Francisco area. Geologists have found signs that a shock of comparable magnitude occurred sometime in the mid-seventeenth century.[10] Much more concrete evidence is available of a major jolt in 1838 along the San Andreas fault; but this disturbance caused little damage because San Francisco was then just a tiny hamlet. Thirty years later, with the population of the city nearing 150,000, another M 6.8 shock took place, this time along the Hayward fault—which runs roughly sixty-five miles, from east of San Jose to San Pablo Bay—although only about thirty people died.[11] Indeed, in the fifty years prior to the 1906 event, temblors ranging from M 6 to M 7 happened one or more times each decade in the Bay Area.[12]

The 1868 disturbance, in particular, stands out for the damage it caused on so-called "made ground." In the 1850s, in the midst of the Gold Rush, Yerba Buena Cove was filled in and incorporated into San Francisco's business district. This 200-acre area experienced the brunt of the destruction when its unconsolidated soil took on the properties of quicksand, a process now known as liquefaction.[13] Although the science behind liquefaction was unknown in the 1860s, the damage to buildings on landfill was readily apparent and newspapers took note. The attention, however, had no real impact on future development in the city.[14]

The 1868 earthquake is also notable for spawning one of the more mysterious episodes in the annals of disaster. Soon after the calamity, George Gordon, a San Francisco real estate developer, urged the city's chamber of commerce to form a committee to study how to build earthquake-resistant structures. But curiously, the committee's work was never made public. George Davidson, a scientist and committee member, later claimed that Gordon himself sabotaged the group's efforts. As he wrote in 1908, "The report was carefully prepared but Mr. Gordon declared that it would ruin the commercial prospects of San Francisco to admit the large amount of damage and the cost thereof."[15] The committee, explained Davidson, had estimated $1.5 million in damage—five times the amount that Gordon and his business associates had made public in their telegraph messages to eastern capitalists. Exactly what Gordon's motives were remain unclear, though this may not have been the only such effort to divert attention away from northern California's seismic problem. "The prevailing tone in that region, at present," wrote geologist Josiah Whitney in 1869, "is that of assumed indifference to the dangers of earthquake calamities."[16]

Indeed, to hear the commercial community tell it in 1906, one would scarcely even imagine that San Francisco had a seismic history. Marion Scheitlin, who covered the disaster for the *Chicago Record-Herald*, wrote that "one hears the dual disaster referred to most as 'the fire.' Every effort is being made to induce capital to come to the city, and it is acknowledged here that capital is more chary of earthquake than of fire." Steps could be taken to minimize the risk of fires; but not so with earthquakes. This, Scheitlin observed, made capitalists wary of investing in seismically active locales. Realizing the threat seismic activity posed to the city's commercial future, "the men who are devoting their time to the restoration of confidence and the rehabilitation of the city, are very certain to minimize the disastrous effects of the earthquake. The expression is heard constantly: 'There would have been but little damage had not the fire started.'"[17]

It was as if San Francisco had become one large theater filled with sociopaths all yelling fire. No organization was more dedicated to stoking the fire-oriented view of the disaster than the Southern Pacific Company—the dominant economic force in California at the time. Railroads were notorious in the West for their promotional activities, and when the 1906 calamity struck every effort was brought to bear in one of the great disinformation campaigns of turn-of-the-century America. James Horsburgh Jr., general passenger agent for the Southern Pacific railroad, explained that the company had no intention of "advertising the earthquake" when "the real calamity in San Francisco was undoubtedly the fire."[18] In a promotional tract titled *San Francisco Imperishable*, the company observed that the earthquake seemed to appeal to "the imaginative and emotional." However, "the main mission of this message from the Southern Pacific Company is . . . most emphatically, that the destruction was due to fire and not to earthquake."[19] In fact, the 1906 shaker was powerful enough to damage 95 percent of the chimneys in San Francisco.[20] Listening to the Southern Pacific, one would never believe that what had actually occurred was a jolt measuring M 7.7, among the most powerful in the history of North America.[21]

The Southern Pacific was hardly alone in seeing fire as the main cause of the calamity. It had support from the business class throughout California, from the governor on down. Eager to show that the disaster had not been allowed to get in the way of business, Governor George Pardee observed that he had declared only forty-one legal holidays. This figure compared favorably, he pointed out, with the seventy-four such holidays declared after the Baltimore fire, "which occasioned much less damage." "The earthquake," he continued, "severe and destructive as it was, did not do, as has been so wildly heralded, much damage, in comparison with the following fire. . . . It was the fire, and not the earthquake, that laid half of San Francisco low."[22] Lining up behind the governor was the secretary of the California State Board of Trade, Arthur Briggs, who reported that San Francisco "has been destroyed by fire. . . . The earthquake damage relatively was inconsiderable."[23] And one could certainly count on the California Promotion Committee to fan the flames. Set up to lure people to the state, the committee issued this statement intended for audiences in the East: "The earthquake did some damage to poorly constructed buildings. . . . The disastrous effects of the fire were appalling."[24]

The city's newspapers, which were effectively an instrument of the social order, also fell into line in an attempt to downplay and normalize the calamity. The *Chronicle* constantly reminded readers that the city must be rebuilt and that earthquakes must not get in the way. "A few have been heard to express alarm lest the fact that the fire was preceded by an earthquake might retard the growth of the city," editorialized the paper. But the quake would have no real effect whatsoever, the paper continued. "Except while the earth actually trembles, and for a short time thereafter, nobody cares anything about earthquakes. . . . The earthquake in this city is of no consequence, except for the distress resulting to those present in the city at the time, who will speedily forget it."[25] The *Bulletin* told its readers that more people died each summer in large eastern cities from sunstroke than lost their lives from the earthquake.

> Familiar dangers lose most of their horror. If we had a severe earthquake every year or two in San Francisco we should think as little of earthquakes as people in Kansas think of cyclones. But because this earthquake was unique, because it was a calamity of a kind which had not happened before in California, people think and talk as if it were far more terrible than flood or pestilence, fire, wind or sun.[26]

In terms of the damage caused, the 1906 disturbance was certainly unique. But this effort at presenting the disaster as a freak occurrence was ultimately little more than an attempt to rationalize continued development by discounting the region's seismic past.

The award for the most shameless attempt to pass the disaster off as no more than a fire goes to the San Francisco Real Estate Board. Just a week after the shaker, the board met to discuss the calamity. "It was agreed," explained a report on their meeting, "that the calamity should be spoken of as 'the great fire,' and not as 'the great earthquake.'"[27]

Among individual members of the business class, probably the most spirited seismic denial came from Senator Francis Newlands (D-Nevada). Newlands—whose San Francisco real estate sustained severe damage in the jolt—played a critical role in securing more than $2 million in federal aid for the city. A patron of the Southern Pacific, Newlands was well known for this obsession with developing the West. So it is perhaps unsurprising to find him supporting a vision of the calamity consistent with continued growth in a city where he had a major financial stake. According to his account, what the city had on its hands here was a natural disaster, not an act of God. As he put it, "the forces of nature seized this great city and shook it like a rat in a trap. Nature itself contemplated no serious harm; it simply demonstrated its force by shaking the earth a little." Newlands believed the jolt caused only 3 percent of the destruction, though how he arrived at that figure is unclear; 20 percent is now the accepted number. "Earthquakes mean nothing," explained the senator. "A little shake in the earth's crust, resulting in a crack here and there of a few inches, constitute no real source of danger. The destructive element here was the fire."[28]

In focusing on the fire, however, Newlands and his fellow pyromaniacs were doing more than simply explaining the cause of their troubles. They were also protecting the prevailing social order by obscuring the true risk of earthquakes; that way, they hoped, capital would not be frightened from investing further in the city. On the one hand, the business class was selecting among dangers, making a political decision about what San Franciscans should and should not fear—fire versus earthquake. On the other hand, it was seeking to depoliticize the calamity, to drain it of meaning, to encourage people to forget the disaster in the hopes of hiding the explicitly political nature of the act of interpreting it as a fire.[29]

EARTHQUAKE COUNTRY

More than any other group, the scientific community spoke out against these attempts to interpret the earthquake away. In 1909, writing in *Sci-*

ence, the eminent geologist Grove Karl Gilbert observed, "It is feared that if the ground of California has a reputation for instability, the flow of immigration will be checked, capital will go elsewhere, and business activity will be impaired."[30] Some years later, John Branner of Stanford lamented the paucity of information on the 1906 calamity. He attributed this lack of knowledge to the commercial community's "deliberate suppression of news about earthquakes." As he explained,

> Shortly after the earthquake of April 1906 there was a general disposition that almost amounted to concerted action for the purpose of suppressing all mention of that catastrophe. When efforts were made by a few geologists to interest people and enterprises in the collection of information in regard to it, we were advised and even urged over and over again to gather no such information, and above all not to publish it. "Forget it," "the less said, the sooner mended," and "there hasn't been any earthquake" were the sentiments we heard on all sides.[31]

Branner's colleague, Andrew Lawson, the man who named the San Andreas fault, also commented on the widespread efforts to soft-pedal earthquake risk. "The commercial spirit of the people fears any discussion of earthquakes for the same reason as it taboos any mention of an occurrence of the plague in the city of San Francisco. It believes that such discussion will advertise California as an earthquake region and so hurt business."[32] But at this point at least, Lawson and his colleagues were helpless before the tectonic act of denial that rippled out across northern California's political landscape.

Just three days after the 1906 jolt, Governor Pardee appointed a scientific commission, including Gilbert, Branner, and Lawson, to investigate the effects of the seismic shock.[33] Pardee appointed the committee, but that was all he did; he offered the commission no money to conduct its work. In the end, the group had to turn to a private source, the Carnegie Institution of Washington, for the funds to publish its two-volume report in 1908 documenting in detail the calamitous effects of the earthquake.[34]

Apart from the publishers and the scientific community, only one other group seemed interested in taking the earthquake seriously: the people who were going to have to foot the bill, namely the insurance industry. Once the fires had been put out, a small army of insurance adjusters converged on the city. They faced one main problem: to distinguish between losses caused by the earthquake exclusively—not covered under the standard insurance contract—and those resulting from fire, which the companies would pay for.[35] Obviously, most policyholders were screaming fire because they had a vested financial stake in seeing the destruction this way. Five weeks after the initial shock, an article in *Insurance Field* reported: "Among the people with losses to adjust, the fact that there was an earthquake has been forgotten. In fact it is now tacitly understood that there never was any earthquake, and that the whole trouble was the fire."[36]

The product of what might be called the "insurance parallax"— where "truth" followed economic interest all too closely—the fire-oriented view, of course, scarcely helped the insurers' bottom line. Indeed, the pressures of land speculation in San Francisco (combined with the threat quakes posed to such activity) proved so unrelenting that even some insurance people themselves felt compelled to downplay the area's seismic risk. The *Coast Review*, a San Francisco insurance periodical, responded to fears voiced about California's seismic past in the eastern press by asserting that "California is not an earthquake country and never has been." Noting that earthquakes had occurred in Charleston and near St. Louis, the publication identified the stretch from the eastern seaboard north to the Great Lakes and west as far as Kansas as "the real earthquake country."[37] Placed in context, this claim is not quite as absurd as it might sound. With the 1886 Charleston earthquake calamity (M 7.0) only a generation old and California's status as the site of the vast majority of U.S. earthquakes not yet common knowledge, one could at least argue that the Golden State had no unique seismic problem. Seeing the destruction as emanating mainly from fire and not earthquake was thus an overdetermined conclusion that wound up costing insurance companies around the world a great deal of money. Frederick Hoffman, a statistician and insurance expert, wrote some years after the calamity that companies were "forced repeatedly to make payments which were not justified, as word was passed 'not to talk about an earthquake but about a terrible conflagration.'"[38]

California, to be sure, may rightly be judged earthquake country today, but this was not some predestined outcome. The Californization of seismic risk was manufactured—the product of western expansion and land development in league with twentieth-century scientific knowledge about the relative high seismicity of the state. Nonetheless, it is striking how, in San Francisco at least, attempts to shed this emerging image and deny the region's seismic hazard wound up having some very sorry consequences. After the 1906 earthquake, a local committee of the American Society of Civil Engineers urged the city to strengthen its building code.[39] In the summer following the calamity, the city followed suit and passed a new law requiring that buildings be constructed to withstand a wind force of thirty pounds per square foot. Predictably, the new law did not mention earthquakes by name. The section dealing with seismic stresses is titled "Wind Bracing," and one imagines the language here was chosen deliberately.[40] In any case, only three years later, the standard for wind bracing fell by one-third, to twenty pounds.[41] And by 1921 the standard originally recommended by the engineers had been cut in half, to just fifteen.[42] This downward trend led the seismologist Bailey Willis to write in 1924 that San Franciscans "have reason to anticipate the next earthquake with apprehension, for they have allowed the conditions favorable to an otherwise avoidable disaster to grow up in their midst." Willis lamented the "unsafe building conditions," which he claimed were "well known to architects, engineers, and other intelligent citizens."[43] The eminent civil engineer John Freeman, present in San Francisco on the twentieth anniversary of the 1906 calamity, also observed buildings that were being constructed "in the cheapest manner possible." City officials in San Francisco and throughout California, Freeman remarked, "appeared strangely lenient toward the speculative builder."[44]

Such lenience stemmed directly from the conspiracy of seismic silence that remained a major preoccupation of San Francisco's business community well into the 1920s. In 1925, an earthquake in Santa Barbara (M 6.3, surface wave, not moment magnitude), several hundred miles south of San Francisco, killed twelve and destroyed many brick and concrete buildings in the city's business district.[45] Boosters flew into action seeking to keep the disaster from sullying California's image as a safe haven for business. California, Inc., an organization based in San Francisco and set up to promote development in the state, pressured newsreel companies not to harp on the devastation. The group also met shortly after the disaster with booster organizations throughout California, including the San Francisco and Los Angeles chambers of commerce. Together they agreed among themselves to minimize the actual destruction and not to seek relief contributions from outside the state. Predictably, donations to Santa Barbara's relief effort failed to materialize. The California Development Association, charged with soliciting contributions from within the state, reached just half its fundraising goal.[46]

There were, however, some signs in California of a willingness to deal openly with the state's seismic risks. Unlike the 1906 calamity, no fire followed this jolt, a fact that highlighted the destructive nature of the seismic shock. Several months after the disaster, the Commonwealth Club of California, a group made up of businessmen and professionals, formally recognized the threat earthquakes posed to the northern part of the state. The group called on San Francisco, in particular, to revise its building code accordingly.[47]

As long as earthquakes were a fictional threat in California, insurance to protect against such phenomena was a hard sell. But after the Santa Barbara calamity, which caused losses valued at roughly nine times more than the $600,000 paid out by insurance companies, earthquake insurance suddenly came into fashion.[48] The increase in earthquake coverage was actually fueled by a spate of lesser-known seismic disturbances in 1925, including a severe jolt (M 6.6) that struck east of Helena, Montana, just two days before the Santa Barbara calamity. Earlier in the same year, the East Coast was shaken by an earthquake (M 6.2, surface wave) centered in Canada's Charlevoix-Kamouraska region. The tremors spread out over roughly two million square miles, extending from eastern Canada as far south as Virginia and as far west as the Mississippi River. More people probably experienced this shock—it was felt in such cities as New York and Boston—than any other seismic event up until that time.[49] The country seemed in the midst of what one observer writing in the *Independent* called an "earthquake crisis"—an observation suggesting that the equation of earthquakes with California alone had yet to solidify.[50]

In response to nationwide seismic activity, many Americans rushed out to see their brokers. Earthquake insurance had existed since 1916, but as late as 1924 premiums totaled only a little over $200,000. The following year, stimulated by the various temblors that rocked the nation, premium income skyrocketed to more than $2 million. Most of that increase in coverage, however, was on property based in California.[51] Thousands of Californians were putting up their own hard-earned money to protect themselves against a risk the business class had once said did not exist.

The reasons for this shift toward a more open recognition of earthquakes, especially on the part of California's business class, are difficult to pinpoint. Obviously, the disasters themselves and the ability to single out seismic activity alone—without the complication of fire—proved very important. It was also clear that the policy of denial did not always make good economic sense, and worse, could actually impede attempts to right society after disaster. Authorities in U.S. cities had since the late nineteenth century encouraged people to remain calm in the face of calamity in order to get on with the business of restoring economic life and property values to their predisaster state. But denying the possibility of calamity could thwart this goal by leaving people unprepared, creating a context for panic to occur, a point made by one Los Angeles insurance executive in 1925.[52] In addition, by the 1920s, California was more populous and richer than ever before. Between 1900 and 1920 San Francisco's population increased from 343,000 to 507,000, while the assessed value of property nearly doubled, rising from $413 million to $820 million.[53] It was clearly self-defeating, if not foolhardy and bad business, to fail to protect such vast amounts of wealth and people against a risk that clearly existed. Perhaps the crude attempts at denying seismic risk were wearing thin by the 1920s, as publicists moved away from such direct attempts to influence behavior toward a more indirect and nuanced psychological approach that preyed on people's unconscious yearnings.[54]

Then in 1933 an earthquake (M 6.3) rocked southern California along the Newport-Inglewood fault—yet another temblor that helped firm up California's status as the nation's earthquake capital. "An earthquake may be legally described as an act of God," intoned the *New Republic*, noting the 116 lives claimed in the disturbance. But those who died were hardly the victims of "God's will," the magazine continued, calling the nation's attention to the political economy of risk in California. "It is not too much to say that many of them, if not all, were murdered—murdered by the cupidity of California business men."[55]

Most of the damage was centered in Long Beach. Again, as in Santa Barbara, no sweeping fires erupted. Again, there was no denying that an earthquake, and only an earthquake, caused the destruction. Forty million dollars in damage resulted, with school buildings faring especially poorly. With the country in the midst of the Great Depression, the state's boosters could not afford to minimize publicity about the calamity by limiting their fundraising appeal to California alone, the strategy they had used back in 1925. Indeed, this time the state turned to the U.S. government for help. Five million dollars in federal relief eventually flowed into the state, but in return for this money, California's leaders were forced to concede the obvious: that a disaster of significant magnitude had in fact occurred.[56]

The earthquake was also notable in another respect. It led to the first major legislative initiative in California that recognized the region's seismic problem. Outrage over all the schools damaged (classes were out when the jolt hit) in part moved the legislature to action. The result was the Field Act of 1933, imposing seismic safety standards on school buildings. It was soon followed by the Riley Act, which applied similar earthquake-resistant criteria to all new buildings. According to historian Carl-Henry Geschwind, this new era of seismic enlightenment dawned when seismologists and engineers—motivated by a Progressive Era concern with using natural resources efficiently—marshaled enough scientific data and financial reserves (secured from businessmen, including some in San Francisco) to convince the state's leaders that economic development depended on open recognition of the earthquake risk.[57]

In 1936, on the thirtieth anniversary of the temblor, the Fireman's Fund, which nearly went under in the calamity, published a report surveying three decades of seismic denial. "The lessons of 1906 were speedily forgotten," the report observed. "Public apathy, an aversion to admitting that earthquakes occur in California, and the desire of building construction speculators to build for profit, combined gradually to prevail over the counsel of engineers." San Francisco's building code was weakened. The standard for wind bracing was reduced. Floor loads were cut. "Happily, this is now becoming history, although it required another major catastrophe—southern California's earthquake of 1933—to awaken the public once more to the necessity for taking steps for its own protection."[58] If nothing else, the seismic events of 1925 and 1933 seemed to prove that California was earthquake country after all.

Now, finally, the scene was set for the 1906 earthquake to go Hollywood. It is no accident that only after California's business class ended its seismic denial did Metro-Goldwyn-Mayer decide to cash in on what has become one of the most famous temblors in history. MGM's *San Francisco*, which opened in 1936, starred Clark Gable, Jeanette MacDonald, and Spencer Tracy. Reviewers took note of the fairly pedestrian plot (centered on a love triangle) and then gushed over the terrifying earthquake scene that capped off the film. *Esquire* wrote: "You actually feel the ground splitting under your seat."[59] "An earthquake in the real Metro-Goldwyn-Mayer manner," observed *Time*, "it lasts for 20 minutes on the screen and in all respects except casualties no doubt betters its original of 30 years ago."[60] According to the *New York Times*, the earthquake scenes were so downright frightening that the actors themselves "frequently and involuntarily rushed from the sets or sought shelter outside the main stages."[61] Imagine a movie about the 1906 earthquake that "betters" (*Time*)—that is, was worse than—the real thing, a movie made by Californians themselves, no less.

The irony here was not lost on one of Hollywood's most famous film critics, Rob Wagner. So impressed by the magnitude of the faux disaster that he "looked for the nearest EXIT," Wagner wrote that his first reaction was, "What will . . . the California Chamber of Commerce say?" As he continued, "Here I've been telling Outlanders that our California earthquakes are a joke, that we use 'em to rock the babies to sleep, that in San Francisco it was the Fire. And now along comes MGM and not only rocks the publicity boat but capsizes it."[62] California's worst-kept secret was out of the bag for good, or so it seemed.

The Californization of earthquake risk took yet another giant step forward in 1938. A map prepared by the chief geologist of California's Division of Mines showed for the first time on a state-issued document all known geologic faults. Although the Seismological Society of America had issued its own statewide fault map in 1923—a major achievement in itself—this was the first time a government mapping effort had seen fit to include information of seismic importance. The 1938 map superseded a 1916 map published by the California State Mining Bureau that had failed to include any delineation of faults whatsoever—omitting even the San Andreas—and this even though such geologic knowledge was available as early as 1910 in the atlas accompanying the state earthquake commission's investigation of the 1906 calamity.[63]

Seismic enlightenment was hardly a direct march onward and upward, however. Real estate interests and others seeking to boost land development in the San Francisco area have tended to revive the conspiracy of seismic silence when it has suited them. Beginning in the mid-1950s and continuing on through the next decade, as the Bay Area experienced explosive growth in the demand for housing, seismic risks were again actively denied in the rush to increase real estate prospects. Writing in 1964 for the *Nation*, David Cort observed that

> the very word, earthquake, is taboo in California. This prudery does not prevail in other earthquake areas, but California's tone is set by the realtors, as well as the undertakers. Earthquake talk lowers real estate values and raises insurance rates. The old joke about the "San Francisco Fire of 1906" is familiar, but it is no joke.[64]

No joke indeed, as events in Redwood Shores in the 1960s were to prove. Located on the San Francisco peninsula, Redwood Shores was once marsh and mud before dikes were used to reclaim it. In 1963, Redwood City, in search of additional tax revenues, joined with a salt company interested in making use of thousands of acres of evaporation ponds to announce plans for a major housing development. Situated just five miles from the San Andreas and fourteen miles from the Hayward fault, the site consisted of soil that some believed posed a major seismic hazard. The city, however, thought otherwise. It hired a well-known scientific consulting company that reported nothing terribly unique about the Redwood Shores site, nothing that made it any more seismically hazardous than parts of San Francisco itself— nothing, in short, to cause anyone to think twice about building on the mud.[65] Enter G. Brent Dalrymple and Marvin Lamphere of the U.S. Geological Survey. The two voiced serious concerns before a California legislative committee about the idea of building a new real estate development on landfill, citing evidence going back to 1865 showing that such land is generally more prone to seismic stress than terra firma. Although testifying unofficially as private citizens, the two geologists were chastised by their superiors in Washington and told not to answer any further questions. That happened after George McQueen, a public relations man for the real estate interests, and J. Arthur Younger of San Mateo, the district's congressman, put pressure on Geological Survey officials not to let seismic safety stand in the way of development.[66] Later, Congress—involved because the federal government was offering mortgage guarantees for the project—briefly blocked the progress of the venture, citing concern for seismic safety, but eventually caved in and allowed the building to proceed.[67] Despite evidence that landfill posed seismic hazards, including reports after the 1906 earthquake that buildings on "made ground" fared especially poorly, not to mention firm scientific evidence dating from the 1960s on liquefaction, the developers of Redwood Shores rushed feet first into the mud.

THE CROWDING OUT EFFECT

All the attention lavished on the 1906 calamity, the San Andreas fault, and California more generally has tended to crowd out any recognition of seismic hazards elsewhere in the West. Thus Salt Lake City is rarely mentioned as a potential seismic flash point when, in fact, the Wasatch fault runs straight through its heart.[68] Roughly 75 percent of the population of Utah lives near the fault, which has generated M 7.5 earthquakes in the past. California may well be rightly considered "earthquake country," since the state accounts for the vast majority of U.S. seismic activity.[69] But one must make a distinction between the risk of earthquakes and the risk of *disaster*, a distinction that is often conflated. Indeed, the tendency to collapse that division cuts to the very core, epistemologically speaking, of the natural disaster concept. And of course blurring the boundary between natural and human actions obscures the social and economic forces responsible for calamity in the first place.

The mythic status of 1906 and the San Andreas—the most famous fault system in the world—has also diverted attention from other immediate seismic threats in the Bay Area itself. This is not to say that the focus on the San Andreas has not led to progress. One of the most important scientific insights concerning earthquakes—the elastic rebound theory, still valid today—resulted from the intense study of the 1906 shaker.[70] But the obsessive concern with the San Andreas has caused many to overlook the threat posed, say, by the Hayward fault, which, surprisingly, is as close to the center of San Francisco as its better known counterpart.[71] The Hayward fault was last active in a destructive way back in 1868—an event that is now largely forgotten, and not by accident, as we have seen. Moreover, it hardly helped matters, as Karl Steinbrugge noted in the 1960s, that the threat of legal action on the part of property owners "reportedly kept some geologists . . . familiar with the location of the Hayward fault from publishing their knowledge in detail."[72] As a result, development prior to 1972 (when the

Alquist-Priolo Act made seismically irresponsible building illegal) saw the siting of many structures on active traces of the Hayward zone.[73] "The way many hospitals and schools were built around here, you'd think they used the fault as a guide for where to place those buildings," said Lloyd Cluff, who in the 1970s served as an advisor to the California legislature on seismic matters.[74]

A study done in 1987 showed that an M 7.5 disturbance on the Hayward fault would cause 1,500 to 4,500 deaths in the Bay Area.[75] Yet the fault itself is far from the consciousness of many who live near it, as a recent study has shown. Residents of Santa Clara County, interviewed soon after the 1989 Loma Prieta earthquake, were asked to identify the active fault closest to them. Just 21 percent of those living near the Hayward were able to name it correctly. Even more shockingly, 57 percent of those interviewed misperceived the San Andreas as being closer and thus a more significant threat.[76] Such is the power of the world's best known fault system.

PYROTECHNICS

To this day, how many people died in the 1906 disaster remains unclear. And one cannot help but wonder whether a connection exists between the way the calamity was domesticated in an attempt to avoid undermining the city's commercial prospects and the failure to reckon fully with the death toll. Major General Adolphus Greeley, who commanded the Pacific Division of the Army, called in to restore order after the jolt, reported 498 deaths. The city's Subcommittee on Statistics, meanwhile, relying on the coroner's office for its information, offered a figure of 674 confirmed dead or missing.[77] Yet Gladys Hansen, the disaster's foremost social historian, disputes both figures as far too low. In the early 1960s, while working as the City of San Francisco's archivist, Hansen fielded phone calls from people looking for information on relatives killed during the calamity. In answering such queries it dawned on her that the number of inquiries far surpassed the officially reported death figures. In a city with a population in excess of 400,000 struck by a monumental catastrophe, 500 to 700 dead seemed like an awfully small number. She pointed out further that Chinatown was obliterated in the calamity and yet just twelve Asian names appeared on the subcommittee's official death list. Embarking on a detailed examination of the issue, Hansen compiled a database of confirmed deaths—names verified as dead from more than one source. That list now stands at 3,000, but Hansen cautions that even this figure is probably far too conservative, predicting a final death tally of over 5,000.[78] For all the attention lavished on the San Francisco disaster, it is remarkable how the pyrotechnics of property destruction have eclipsed the truly deadly story here.

Perhaps not surprisingly, it was the transient and working poor, many of whom lived in hotels in the area south of Market Street, who suffered most in the disaster. The hotels were built on an area of landfill that was once the old Mission Bay Swamp. When the earthquake struck, a violent chain reaction ensued, as the jolt caused the hotels to collapse like dominos.[79]

In 1989 when the Loma Prieta (M 7.2) earthquake struck the San Francisco Bay Area, the dangers of building on landfill were again amply demonstrated in the heavy damage sustained by the Marina district. Although less powerful than the 1906 earthquake, the temblor managed nevertheless to cause buildings to collapse and water and gas mains to rupture. The Marina was once a giant lagoon before city fathers filled it in with, among other things, the burnt ruins left by the 1906 disaster (dumped to make way for the Panama-Pacific International Exposition of 1915). Now the interred past came back to haunt residents of this tony neighborhood.[80]

The media focused obsessively on the Marina, showing residents in Docksiders hauling their belongings about in plastic trash bags. But in truth, the worst hit area in the city was precisely the same one flattened in 1906: the South of Market area that was home to skid row. The Loma Prieta earthquake reduced to rubble 4,700 units of multifamily housing in the city, precipitating a major housing crisis among the poor. To this day, less than half of the affordable rental housing destroyed in the Bay Area has been replaced.[81]

When the Loma Prieta quake hit, San Francisco had yet to pass an ordinance to deal with the city's roughly 2,000 unreinforced masonry buildings. Some 800 of these vulnerable buildings housed approximately 25,000 residents of the city's low-end rental market in Chinatown and other poor sections. Yet unlike the 1906 calamity, which seismic expert Karl Steinbrugge notes did not lead to "any long lasting improvements in earthquake resistive construction," the 1989 jolt moved the city to act on the unreinforced building issue, something it had been considering since as far back as the 1970s.[82] In

1992, the city's voters passed a ballot initiative creating a $350 million loan program requiring owners to retrofit their buildings no later than 2006. Today many owners are still dragging their feet waiting to see if the city is serious about enforcing the ordinance. Meanwhile, architect Michael Johnstone wonders why the city has given landlords such a long time to comply. Building owners have long expressed concern that the high cost of retrofitting would ultimately wind up forcing out tenants who can't afford higher rents. But Johnstone is skeptical. "The idea of not inconveniencing someone—but allowing them to be killed, well, things seem upside down."[83]

In fact, there was nothing illogical here, at least not by the reigning standards of our economic order. Such thinking simply reflected the monetary calculus that informed the city's retrofitting program. Calculating that $835 million worth of structural redesign would save 415 lives (given an M 7.0 earthquake on the Hayward fault), and $335 million only 235 lives, the city chose the cheaper route. "You can't make a perfectly safe world. You always have to balance costs into whatever level of safety you make," said Kathleen Harrington, president of a property-owners' group that supported the city's retrofitting initiative.[84] All this may well be true. But it overlooks the ultimate question: whose lives are we talking about here? Clearly, some lives are worth more than others. Given the demographic makeup of the areas containing the suspect buildings, it seems almost certain that it will be the poor and people of color who will suffer the most in the coming earthquake. These are the people then who are truly at risk—unsurprisingly, the same people who were buried in 1906, people who never made it into the official death lists, people who have largely disappeared from the collective social memory.

Unable to embrace fully the meaning of the 1906 calamity, except as an archetype, unable to see the underlying political economy of risk that explains who lives and who dies when the earth shakes, northern California's real estate cartel is content to mortgage the future of the region's dispossessed. In this sense, the San Francisco Fire still smolders.

NOTES

1. Kenneth Hewitt, ed., *Interpretations of Calamity: From the Viewpoint of Human Ecology* (Boston: Allen and Unwin, 1983), 11-12.

2. Mircea Eliade, *The Myth of the Eternal Return; or, Cosmos and History,* trans. Willard R. Trask (Princeton, N.J.: Princeton University Press, 1954), 46.

3. The Richter scale for measuring earthquake magnitude was developed in 1935. However, in the 1980s, seismologists turned instead to a more descriptive way of measuring the size of earthquakes called "seismic moment." Moment magnitude (M) takes into account area, fault offset, and the rigidity of the rupturing rocks. Unless indicated otherwise, all figures for earthquakes are based on the moment magnitude scale.

4. Paul Segall, "New Insights into Old Earthquakes," *Nature,* 10 July 1997, 122.

5. "100 Disaster Books," *New York Times,* 24 April 1906.

6. "Pernicious Advertising," *San Francisco Call,* 20 May 1906.

7. Quoted in William Issel and Robert W. Cherny, *San Francisco, 1865-1932: Politics, Power, and Urban Development* (Berkeley: University of California Press, 1986), 39; for more on the economic history of the city, see pp. 23-52.

8. Santa Rosa, for example, was virtually leveled. See Robert L. Iacopi, *Earthquake Country,* 4th ed. (Tucson, Ariz.: Fisher Books, 1996), 96; Robert E. Wallace, ed., *San Andreas Fault System, California,* U.S. Geological Survey professional paper 1515 (Washington: Government Printing Office, 1990), v, 159; Dennis R. Dean, "The San Francisco Earthquake of 1906," *Annals of Science* 50 (1993): 510.

9. Figures are from *San Francisco Relief Survey: The Organization and Methods of Relief Used After the Earthquake and Fire of April 18, 1906,* from studies compiled by Charles J. O'Connor et al. (New York: Survey Associates, 1913), 4. See also Judd Kahn, *Imperial San Francisco: Politics and Planning in an American City, 1897-1906* (Lincoln: University of Nebraska Press, 1979), 130.

10. See "Historical Clues from the San Andreas," *Science News,* 2 November 1991, 286.

11. See Jerry L. Coffman, Carl A. von Hake, and Carl W. Stover, eds., *Earthquake History of the United States* (Boulder, Colo.: Department of Commerce, National Oceanic and Atmospheric Administration and Department of the Interior, Geological Survey, 1982), 138; and T. A. Heppenheimer, *The Coming Quake: Science and Trembling on the California Earthquake Frontier* (New York: Times Books, 1988), 76.

12. John McPhee, *Assembling California* (New York: Farrar, Straus, and Giroux, 1993), 279. There were also thirty-seven other notable earthquakes in the Bay Area and adjoining counties in the century before 1906—many of them reported in the California press. This statistic is derived from Fig. 1 in Karl V. Steinbrugge, *Earthquake Hazard in the San Francisco Bay Area: A Continuing Problem in Public Policy* (Berkeley: Institute of Governmental Studies, University of California, 1968), 6.

13. Charles Wollenberg, "Life on the Seismic Frontier: The Great San Francisco Earthquake," *California History* 71 (Winter 1992/1993): 498.

14. It was not until the 1960s that the science behind liquefaction was properly understood. See Steinbrugge, *Earthquake Hazard,* 26.

15. The quoted material is from a letter Davidson sent to the Seismological Society of America in 1908. The letter is reprinted in William H. Prescott, "Circumstances Surrounding the Preparation and Suppression of a Report on the 1868 California Earthquake," *Bulletin of the Seismological Society of America* 72 (1982): 2392. For biographical information on Gordon and Davidson, see Albert Shumate, *The California of George Gordon and the 1849 Sea Voyages of His California Association* (Glendale, Calif.: Arthur H. Clark, 1976); and Oscar Lewis, *George Davidson: A Pioneer West Coast Scientist* (Berkeley: University of California Press, 1954).

16. J. D. Whitney, "Earthquakes," *North American Review* 108 (1869): 609.

17. Marion G. Scheitlin, "Minimizing Effects of Earthquake in Frisco," *Insurance Field,* 3 May 1906, 17.

18. Quoted in Gladys Hansen and Emmet Condon, *Denial of Disaster: The Untold Story and Photographs of the San Francisco Earthquake and Fire of 1906* (San Francisco: Robert A. Cameron, 1989), 109.

19. Southern Pacific Company, *San Francisco Imperishable* (San Francisco: Southern Pacific Company, 1906), unpaginated.

20. This figure is from a report on the quake by the War Department. See Hansen and Condon, *Denial of Disaster,* 39.

21. Not surprisingly, there are very few close-up shots among the illustrations of the calamity in *Sunset Magazine*—established to promote business and tourism in California. Most of the images show the city and its buildings from a distance. See, for example, Charles Aiken, "San Francisco's Plight and Prospect," *Sunset Magazine,* June/July 1906, 16-17, 19-20.

22. *Message of Governor George C. Pardee to the Extra Session of the Legislature of California, June 2, 1906* (Sacramento: State Printing Office, 1906), 4, 10.

23. The report of the State Board of Trade is reprinted in "Faith in City Is Unshaken," *San Francisco Call,* 27 May 1906.

24. Quoted in "Quake Caused But Little Damage," *San Francisco Bulletin,* 15 May 1906.

25. "The Future of the City," *San Francisco Chronicle,* 11 May 1906. See also "Height of Buildings," *San Francisco Chronicle,* 20 June 1906.

26. "Common Sense Prevailing Over Hysterical Terror," *San Francisco Bulletin,* 23 April 1906.

27. The report on the meeting is discussed in "Big Structures Now Planned," *San Francisco Chronicle,* 25 April 1906.

28. Francis G. Newlands, "The New San Francisco," *Independent,* 10 May 1906, 1093, 1094, 1095.

29. My thinking here was influenced by Mary Douglas and Aaron Wildavsky, *Risk and Culture: An Essay on the Selection of Technological and Environmental Dangers* (Berkeley: University of California Press, 1982), 29-30.

30. G. K. Gilbert, "Earthquake Forecasts," *Science,* 22 January 1909, 135.

31. J. C. Branner, "Earthquakes and Structural Engineering," *Bulletin of the Seismological Society of America* 3 (1913): 2-3.

32. Andrew C. Lawson, "Seismology in the United States," *Bulletin of the Seismological Society of America* 1 (1911): 3.

33. In addition to Gilbert, Branner, and Lawson, Harry Fielding Reid of Johns Hopkins and four other scientists were appointed to the commission.

34. The Lawson California Earthquake report was published in two volumes: volume 1 in 1908 and volume 2 in 1910. "No report of any previous earthquake has been issued on so liberal a scale," wrote Charles Davison some years later in his study of the early history of seismology. Charles Davison, *The Founders of Seismology* (Cambridge: Cambridge University Press, 1927), 152-53.

35. Separate insurance coverage for earthquake risk did not exist at the time. And the so-called "fallen building" clause contained in fire insurance policies protected companies from having to pay damages when a building collapsed or exploded before it caught fire. However, generally speaking, insurance companies did cover fire losses that were the indirect result of the seismic shock. It was thus in the best interests of insurers to figure out how much damage the earthquake caused directly so as to limit their liability.

36. "Adjustments Are Now at a Halt," *Insurance Field,* 24 May 1906, 6.

37. "California Not an Earthquake Country," *Coast Review,* September 1906, g, h.

38. Frederick L. Hoffman, *Earthquake Hazards and Insurance* (Chicago: Spectator Co., 1928), 128.

39. See "The Effects of the San Francisco Earthquake of April 18th, 1906, on Engineering Construction," *Transactions of the American Society of Civil Engineers* 59 (1907): 208-9, 211.

40. Ordinances of the City and County of San Francisco, The Building Law, Ordinance no. 31, § 69, approved 5 July 1906.

41. The Building Law and the Plumbing Law of the City and County of San Francisco, Bill no. 1121, Ordinance no. 1008 (New Series), § 89, approved 22 December 1909.

42. Official Building Laws, City and County of San Francisco (San Francisco: Daily Pacific Builder, 1921), § 89.

43. Bailey Willis, "Earthquake Risk in California," *Bulletin of the Seismological Society of America* 14 (1924): 15.

44. John Ripley Freeman, *Earthquake Damage and Earthquake Insurance* (New York: McGraw-Hill, 1932), 30.

45. After the development of the Richter scale, the establishment of an increasing number of seismograph stations across the world led to the development of a more refined measurement of magnitude called surface magnitude. Moment magnitude, however, is still the most reliable estimate of earthquake size.

46. Carl-Henry Geschwind, "Earthquakes and Their Interpretation: The Campaign for Seismic Safety in California, 1906-1933" (Ph.D. dissertation, Johns Hopkins University, 1996), 155, 156-57, 159.

47. Freeman, *Earthquake Damage,* 693-94.

48. Ibid., 11.

49. See Jerry L. Coffman, Carl A. von Hake, and Carl W. Stover, eds., *Earthquake History of the United States* (Boulder, Colo.: Department of Commerce, National Oceanic and Atmospheric Administration, and Department of the Interior, Geological Survey, 1982), 10.

50. Arthur Pound, "Conquering the Earthquake Crisis," *Independent,* 25 July 1925, 95.

51. In 1930, premiums on California properties alone were more than $2 million. See Freeman, *Earthquake Damage,* 658.

52. See C. T. Manwaring, "Report of Committee on Building for Safety Against Earthquakes: Preliminary Report on Guarding Against Panic," *Bulletin of the Seismological Society of America* 15 (1925): 213-221.

53. Issel and Cherny, *San Francisco,* 42.

54. See, e.g., Stuart Ewen, *PR! A Social History of Spin* (New York: Basic Books, 1996), 131-32.

55. "Murder in California," *New Republic,* 22 March 1933, 146.

56. Geschwind, "Earthquakes," 214.

57. Ibid., 228-31. Geschwind's dissertation argues against the views set forth in Arnold J. Meltsner, "The Communication of Scientific Information to the Wider Public: The Case of Seismology in California," *Minerva* 17 (1979): 331-54. Meltsner claims that scientific knowledge about California's earthquake risk was suppressed by business interests. Geschwind shows, however, that at the time of the 1906 earthquake, scientists themselves were ignorant of the region's seismic risk. In short, Geschwind explains, there was nothing for the business community to suppress. Although there is clearly some real merit to his critique, Geschwind tends to privilege science over popular knowledge. Clearly knowledge about the region's vulnerability to earthquakes dated back to at least the 1860s, even if scientists had yet to uncover the science behind these disturbances. Also, it is important to note that the scientists themselves discussed attempts to suppress the science behind earthquakes, as we have seen—an issue Geschwind overlooks.

58. *Fireman's Fund Record,* April 1936, 6, 7.

59. Meyer Levin, "The Candid Cameraman," *Esquire,* September 1936, 98.

60. "Cinema," *Time,* 6 July 1936, 48.

61. "Seismic Note," *New York Times,* 12 July 1936.

62. Wagner's review is reprinted in Anthony Slide, ed., *Selected Film Criticism 1931-1940* (Metuchen, N.J.: Scarecrow Press, 1982), 217.

63. Charles W. Jennings, "New Geologic Map of California: A Summation of 140 Years of Geologic Mapping," *California Geology* 31 (1978): 77. On the fault

map published by the Seismological Society in 1923, see Geschwind, "Earthquakes," 136-41.

64. "The Earthquake Taboo," *Nation,* 30 November 1964, 405.

65. John J. Fried, *Life along the San Andreas Fault* (New York: Saturday Review Press, 1973), 124-26.

66. "The Case of the Muzzled Geologists," *San Francisco Chronicle,* 24 January 1965, magazine section, 7; Fried, *San Andreas,* 128-30.

67. Fried, *San Andreas,* 133-36.

68. Karl V. Steinbrugge, *Earthquakes, Volcanoes, and Tsunamis: An Anatomy of Hazards* (New York: Skandia America Group, 1982), 32.

69. According to one estimate, California and western Nevada account for roughly 90 percent of all seismic activity in the contiguous United States. See Coffman, von Hake, and Stover, *Earthquake History,* 137.

70. Steinbrugge, *Earthquakes,* 3.

71. McPhee, *Assembling California,* 273.

72. Steinbrugge, *Earthquake Hazard,* 14.

73. See "Maps that Help to Spot Where Trouble Lies in Store," *New Scientist,* 12 May 1990, 58.

74. Quoted in Fried, *San Andreas,* 10.

75. Karl V. Steinbrugge et al., *Earthquake Planning Scenario for a Magnitude 7.5 Earthquake on the Hayward Fault in the San Francisco Bay Area* (Sacramento: California Department of Conservation, Division of Mines and Geology, 1987).

76. Risa Palm and Michael E. Hodgson, *After a California Earthquake: Attitude and Behavior Change* (Chicago: University of Chicago Press, 1992), 92.

77. *Who Perished: A List of Persons Who Died as a Result of the Great Earthquake and Fire in San Francisco on April 18, 1906,* comp. Gladys Hansen (San Francisco: San Francisco Archives, 1980), 3.

78. Thurston Clarke, *California Fault: Searching for the Spirit of a State along the San Andreas* (New York: Ballantine, 1996), 205-7. According to Clarke, Hansen predicts a final death toll of somewhere between 5,000 and 10,000.

79. Hansen and Condon, *Denial of Disaster,* 18, 20, 23.

80. McPhee, *Assembling California,* 301-302.

81. Mary C. Comerio, *Disaster Hits Home: New Policy for Urban Housing Recovery* (Berkeley: University of California Press, 1998), 67, 73, 81.

82. Steinbrugge, *Earthquakes,* 5.

83. Quoted in "Quake Improvements Put a Price on Life," *San Francisco Chronicle,* 22 January 1994.

84. Quoted in "Battle over Cost of Quake Retrofitting," *San Francisco Chronicle,* 6 February 1995.

PART II

FAITH

5

Faith and Doubt

The Imaginative Dimensions of the Great Chicago Fire

Carl Smith

Carl Smith reveals how two clusters of belief about Chicago and the modern city emerged from the Great Chicago Fire of 1871: a faith in the city's transcendent purpose and special relationship with God and history, and a deep concern that its social order would have to be carefully guarded since Chicago and places like it were tinderboxes ready to flare up in crime, degradation, and anarchy the moment restraints were relaxed. Together, Smith writes, these clusters of belief contributed to a complex understanding of contemporary events and the nature of urban reality, particularly in regard to the need for preserving and protecting a stable and structured society.

TWO LARGE, INTERRELATED clusters of belief regarding Chicago and the modern city emerged from the ashes of the Great Fire of October 8-10, 1871. Neither was new, but this major disaster reinvigorated both in significant ways. The first was a permutation of the outlook that had always been vital to Chicago's prodigious development. Faced with this terrible calamity, which destroyed about a third of the city, including the entire downtown, and left roughly an equivalent fraction of its population homeless, many paradoxically insisted that this ordeal reconfirmed Chicago's transcendent purpose and special relationship with God and history. Much of this thinking was expressed in a conventional rhetoric that emphasized both religious redemption and middle-class rectitude, prompted by a desire to see the conflagration as part of a morally, aesthetically, and politically appealing drama. Most commentators chose to

FIGURE 5.1. Residents of the city's South Division flee for their lives through the crush on the Randolph Street bridge as the firestorm consumes Chicago. From *Harper's Weekly*, October 28, 1871. (Special Collections, Northwestern University Library, Evanston, Illinois)

greet the fire, as many Americans had the Civil War, as an opportunity offered to the city to cleanse its soul and devote itself to an enlightened physical and spiritual discipline that would be a vital step in the march toward a more perfect community.[1] By this reasoning, the ordeal was part of the inscrutable workings of a divine hand. The scale of the destruction indicated not the degree of Chicago's venality or misfortune, but the grandeur of its destiny. Greater than the catastrophes that consumed Rome, London, and other world capitals, the fire proved that Chicago and America had already surpassed or would soon supersede these other cities in all respects.

The contrasting vision was steeped in some of the same antecedents but was more dubious about human nature and the future of urban culture if left unmonitored and unregulated by respectable and responsible citizens. Still highly moralistic but also protoprogressive in its emphasis on the need for rational control, this vision saw the American city, in normal as well as in such obviously exceptional moments as the

burning of Chicago, as a center of social conflict, with the eventual outcome still very much unsettled. Chicago might hold the key to America's future, but it would have to be carefully managed and guarded,
since the city was a tinderbox ready to flare up in crime, debauchery,
and anarchy the moment restraints were relaxed.

These two views were mainly held by the native-born Protestant
and middle-class Americans who controlled most political, social, and
economic institutions in the city and dominated cultural discussion in
Chicago and beyond during this period.[2] These outlooks vied with each
other in many places, moving along axes of uncertainty on which it is
possible to chart the imaginative dimensions of the fire. In some ways,
these attitudes were not very different—indeed, many people held both
at the same time—since each was based on a belief in the perils of urban
disorder and in the value of social control. Together they shaped a collective meditation on the relation of contemporary events to each other,
to the past, and to the future, expressed by a wide range of observers
whose common purpose was to discover through the fire the nature
and meaning of urban reality.

What exactly had happened in the burning of Chicago? What did the
future hold? These were the key questions those who considered the
meaning of the fire had to answer. In its interpretation of everything
from the smallest private action to the grandest public achievement,
the affirmative view of what had occurred found expressive form as
the story of a series of critical challenges that were decisively met by
the city and the nation. This view engendered a narrative of the fire
as a myth of *re*-creation in which Chicago was apotheosized into a
higher plane of civic being in an epic moment that made it pure,
heroic, and modern. The purpose of the myth was to banish the idea
that the fire was a threat to what had always been Chicago's most
valuable commodity: its future.[3]

The effort to interpret the fire as an act of purification was derived from a longstanding concern—especially on the part of the
"old settler" generation that had arrived around the time of the city's
incorporation in 1837 and of the new business leadership (including
such noted figures as Marshall Field and George Pullman) that had
moved to the city in the following decades and was now fully coming into its own around the time of the fire—that the moral condition
of the city was a source of embarrassment and shame.[4] "Pure" was

FIGURE 5.2. The city as beautiful young woman in distress was the theme of a number of allegorical depictions of what had happened to Chicago. In an engraving based on a painting by Alfred Fredericks, Chicago's sister cities both revive her and fend off the savage hounds that would prey on her in this moment of weakness, as the spirit of the fire hovers overhead. *Every Saturday,* November 4, 1871. (Chicago Historical Society ICHi-02915)

not an adjective commonly attached to pre-fire Chicago; the city had a well-earned reputation for tolerating gambling and prostitution.[5] Some commentators in other cities compared Chicago to Sodom and Gomorrah. The Reverend Granville Moody of Cincinnati, for example, saw the fire as punishment for the flouting of Sabbath and liquor laws and as "a retributive judgment on a city which has shown such a devotion in its worship to the Golden Calf." This kind of talk of sin and retribution was inevitable in the post-disaster mentality of any Christian nation, and was certainly one of the first cultural resources to which several Chicagoans themselves resorted both privately and publicly in an attempt to find a reason for their misfortune. William H. Carter, one of the three commissioners of the City's Board of Works, wrote to his brother, "Boastful Chicago lies prostrate and with outstretched arms is begging of her sister cities for relief," while customs official Francis William Test soberly told his mother, "We have been punished."[6]

The most pious of the several fire histories produced immediately following the event, the Reverend Edgar J. Goodspeed's *The Great Fires in Chicago and the West*, railed against all the breweries, brothels, theaters, "gambling-hells," and violations of the Sabbath in pre-fire Chicago, before asking rhetorically, "Will vice and crime riot as they have done, eating out the very vitality of the city? In the presence of death and woe will men forget the better part?" Mayor Roswell B. Mason's earliest emergency proclamations concentrated on social and economic concerns, but he attributed "this terrible calamity" to "the providence of God, to whose will we humbly submit." He duly designated Sunday, October 29, "as a special day of humiliation and prayer; of humiliation for those past offenses against almighty God, to which these severe afflictions were doubtless intended to lead our minds; of prayer for the relief and comfort of the suffering thousands in our midst; for the restoration of our material prosperity, especially for our lasting improvement as a people in reverence and obedience to God."[7]

Remarks like these were, however, a brief and relatively minor counterpoint to the view that not only dismissed the idea of the fire as proof of divine disfavor but embraced the disaster as a sign of Chicago's unique importance. The lead story of the *Chicago Weekly Post* of October 26, titled "Resurgam," stated, "People who see a Providential judgment in the destruction have very limited

FIGURE 5.3. This illustration was one of several like it throughout the fire literature, which heartily endorsed such vigilante justice. As the great fire burns indistinctly in the background, the fate that reportedly awaited thieves and incendiaries is vividly realized. (Chicago Historical Society ICHi-02906)

knowledge of Divine economy," while George Alfred Townsend, in his poem "The Smitten City," dated October 13, called the admonishments of those who read the fire as divine judgment "shallow platitudes from fool and foe." Townsend declared pre-fire Chicago a pillar of piety:

Bright, Christian capital of lakes and prairie,
Heaven had no interest in thy scourge and scath;
Thou wert the newest shrine of our religion,
The youngest witness of our faith.[8]

Explaining the destruction of Chicago this way was a somewhat tricky task since it required minimizing the disaster as an act of God while stressing the idea of holy purpose. It was important to observers both locally and nationally, whatever the contradictions, to attribute the fire to bad luck that could have struck anywhere, while at the same time connecting the monumentality of the experience to some intended sacred good divorced from the idea of direct punishment. Local author Alfred Sewell, who is credited with writing the first of the fire histories, stated that he would not treat "the divine or religious aspect" of the fire, "except so far as to express the opinion that, if the Almighty, in His government of our little world . . . employs what theologians term 'special providences,' then it may be accepted as a solemn fact that He smote Chicago not only for its own ultimate good, but as a warning and a lesson for all other cities, if not for all mankind."[9] Sewell's argument accepted the suffering as divine judgment, but diffused the blame. If anything, the city was not punished but honored by having been singled out for such a trial. The larger question, raised tentatively, of whether Chicago in particular or urban culture in general was in need of reformation was quickly buried under the theme of ultimate good.

This analysis conceptualized the fire less as a retribution for past sins than as a forward-looking and virtually instantaneous program of reform that was yet another sign of Chicago's brilliant destiny. The calamity seemed to transform this Gilded Age metropolis into a city on a hill inhabited by a spiritually reborn chosen people who had a covenant with God. The rebirth from the fire involved a conversion experience of the highest kind, as N. S. Emerson proclaimed in the last stanza of his poem "The Stricken City":

For he who walked of old on earth,
Is with us in this later birth:
We lost him in our greed for pelf,
But to his higher, purer Self,
He leads us through this golden tide,
And thus our loss is glorified.

In the months following the fire, this interpretation became the prevalent public reading of the event. Writing in an issue of the *Lakeside Monthly* marking the first anniversary of the fire, *Chicago Evening Journal* editor Andrew Shuman asked, "Was not the Great Fire a blessing in disguise?" and then answered his own question:

> If, as some of the severer school of religionists told us, Chicago's baptism of flame was an exhibition of God's vengeance upon a wicked, proud, and presumptuous community, then it must also be that He soon repented of his severity, and changed the curse into a blessing. . . . But turning from the consideration of individual unfortunates to that of the community and the city as a whole, it may, we think, be truthfully said that, all things considered, the fire will prove a benefit rather than a calamity.[10]

Virtually everyone who wrote about the fire was eager to read it in a very similar way as a trial of the city's character in which its mettle was tested in a literal crucible and found not wanting. The many stories that immediately appeared in print emphasizing individual bravery and selflessness were tributes to the human spirit that transcended the specific circumstances of the moment, but part of their message was that Chicago in 1871 was a community of valiant citizens who in this worst of times discovered the best in themselves.[11] This is evident in the "thrilling anecdotes" in the newspapers and histories that celebrated the courage of common citizens who were heedless of personal welfare, like quick-thinking Sherman House desk clerk John Hickie and his assistant, who saved the life of an ill female guest by dashing back into "the now trembling building," smashing in her door, drenching her bedclothes with water from a pitcher and basin in the room, and groping their way with her safely through smoke and fire, just a few minutes before this proud structure became "one of the most complete wrecks of the night."[12]

More common than the citation of such spectacular acts of bravery was the commendation of a quieter kind of courage that was evident in the dignity of Chicagoans amid terrifying danger. Eyewitnesses noted repeatedly how calm and civil people remained as they retreated from their lost homes. Like many others, Mary Ann Hubbard, the matriarch of the oldest of the old settler families, remembered being impressed by "the calm, courteous way in which people talked—if all had been serene and normal they could not have been more patient and respectful."[13]

As is commonly the case immediately following catastrophes in the United States, there was much talk of a refined post-fire "community of suffering" bonded by Christian faith and democratic feeling. Whether they asserted that the fire's effects were so utopian or not, Chicagoans were eager to point out that the destruction certainly seemed to have an egalitarian disregard for class distinctions that was beneficial even to those who seemed to lose the most. Emma Hambleton wrote to her mother a day after the fire that "in the streets were the families of the richest men in Chicago running, some lost, and many sitting right on the pavement for a moment's breath, dressed in velvets[,] silk, and jewels they were trying to save." She then reflected, if not without some dismay, "The fire was a wonderful leveler, if I may use that expression." In their fire history, Elias Colbert and Everett Chamberlin similarly maintained that one of the salutary consequences of the fire would be "the greater necessity for *work*" that would stir everyone into action. In a chapter titled "Good Out of Evil," they developed this theme at length:

> But the best work which the fire has wrought has been upon the character and habits of the people, rather than upon their business, political, or other material affairs. The people of Chicago were, before the fire, fast lapsing into luxury—not as yet to any such degree as the people of New York—but still more than was for their good. The fire roused them from this tendency, and made them the same strong men and women, of the same simple, industrious, self-denying habits, which built up Chicago, and pushed her so powerfully along her unparalleled career. All show and frivolity were abandoned, and democracy became the fashion.[14]

The fire literature maintained that the main effect of the flames was to burn away vain inessentials to reveal the sound and solid integrity of the people. One of the central figures in the Reverend E. P. Roe's immensely popular *Barriers Burned Away* (1872) remarks, "That which can vanish in a night in flame and smoke cannot belong to us, is not part of us. All that has come out of the crucible of this fire is my character, myself."[15]

The point of these comments was to testify that Chicagoans had displayed, in the words of one citizen writing a few days after the fire, "American character of the highest type," and thus had proved their city a coherent community.[16] Certain stories that appeared repeatedly in the fire literature developed this idea in greater depth. These generally evaded any serious critical reflection on the state of the pre-fire city by concentrating on effects and not causes of the disaster, and by seeing the benefits of the fire more as the source of a heightened self-awareness and maturity than as reform. Both personal correspondence and the instant histories singled out as a representative case the fate of Unity Church. Located in the city's best North Side neighborhood, Unity had as its spiritual leader Robert Collyer, who had established himself as one of the most popular preachers in the city. An outspoken abolitionist active in the Sanitary Commission during the war, Collyer was widely known as a humanitarian who embodied what many saw as the finest Chicago had to offer. The Sunday after the fire he met with the members of his congregation and of several others ("Denominations and creeds were forgotten") by the ruins of his sanctuary in a gathering that one fire history likened to "a convention of early Christians in the catacombs."[17] To post-fire Chicago, this gathering represented the moral and social core of a new urban dispensation that now better understood its responsibility to the future.

Several writers developed the theme of the multidimensional civic elevation of the burned-out city through a number of depictions of Chicago, "the Queen City of the West," as a woman. Colbert and Chamberlin concluded their lengthy history of the fire by comparing the effect worked by the fire on Chicago to the transformation of the "wild and wanton girl, of luxurious beauty, and generous, free ways," when "becoming a wife, a great bereavement, or the pangs and burdens of maternity overtake her, robbing her cheek of its rich flush, but at the same time ripening her beauty, elevating, deepening, expanding her character, and imbuing her with a susceptibility of feeling, a consciousness of strength, and an earnestness of purpose which she knew not before." They then folded this transformation into the mythology of national progress. By the time of the nation's centennial, now less than five years away, the "new Chicago" would "join her sisters in laying the laurel wreath upon the mother Columbia's brow," to be greeted warmly by all of them "and welcomed back from out her vale of affliction as one who had suffered that she might be strong."[18]

The visual interpretations of the meaning of the fire also expressed this idea of fortunate suffering (though not fortunate fall), working in the same vein as many other contemporary representations of the spirit of a particular country, city, or cherished national ideal (such as "liberty," "freedom," or "democracy") as a beautiful maiden with flawless classical features. The most ambitious example of this was a painting by Edward Armitage, a member of the Royal Academy, that the staff of the *London Graphic* commissioned and presented to Chicago. In the painting, the nude reclining figure that is stricken Chicago is attended by clothed sisters of mercy symbolizing Britain and America, respectively flanked by a lion and an eagle.[19]

The fire literature further explored the meaning of the occasion and indirectly offered a prescription for social conduct in its many different references to brides and weddings. Several private and commercially produced fire narratives made special note of what happened to the weddings (one involving Robert Collyer's son) that had been scheduled to take place in the days following the fire. The appeal of these anecdotes lay in the way they expressed optimistic sentiments about the future of the city. The focus in the wedding tales was on the bride, who, because of the fire, finds herself suddenly hard pressed to obtain a caterer, flowers, trousseau, license, and clergyman. She proves her pluck and character, as well as her "exceeding sweetness and womanliness" (which together form the female counterpart to the "manliness" that was elsewhere celebrated in the stories of courage and heroism), by fashioning a dignified ceremony from the humble possibilities available. In a story that appeared in the *New York Tribune* and was reprinted in several other places, one Chicago bride makes a cloth-covered soapbox do as an altar, on which she places a slop jar filled with a "bouquet" of autumn leaves. The story followed typical society-page language in describing her "gown," but now the point was the way its modesty demonstrated the bride's (and Chicago's) resourcefulness and sincerity. The *Tribune* correspondent informed the reader that the young woman adorned herself in a white cambric morning dress, a veil borrowed from her married sister, and her intended's gift of a string of "pearls" made from cotton ravelings.

Such episodes declared that Chicago had been stripped of affectation and rededicated to the responsibilities of the future. In one illustration, the bride and groom clasp hands to receive the benediction of a minister whose Bible rests on the remains of a chimney. The *Tribune* correspondent earnestly confessed that she had never seen, "among rich or poor, a sweeter and more holy-seeming wedding," which ended with the whole congregation dropping to their knees to thank God for their preservation, their "broken voices and tender heartfelt tones attest[ing] to the reality of the service." Conversing cheerfully with each other at a "marriage feast" of water and warm biscuit, "all felt that to be poor in such good company robbed ruin of half its sting."[20]

The handful of novels of the fire were likewise expanded moral melodramas in which the action moved toward marriage and a settled urban order purified by the fire. Conventional romances, they are full of improbable complications of plot that are sorted out by the conflagration, which occurs late in the book when the resolution is apparently beyond human reach. In Martha Lamb's *Spicy* (1873), narrator Melody Belmore is the wife of an army officer, and as the novel unfolds she furnishes the reader with such local color as descriptions of the wartime Sanitary Fair and of the city's reception of the news of Lincoln's death. The primary consequence of the fire in the context of the novel is that it removes the obstacles to the marriage of two major characters. While the book is filled with mysterious robberies, ghostly figures, hidden identities, family secrets, and noble sacrifices, it still depicts Chicago as a stable social order whose citizens are capable of the kind of selflessness and sympathy that has sustained this couple and will grace both their future and the city's.[21]

The broadest claims for the beneficial effects of the fire on Chicago—and on modern America—were made in the many retellings of the story of how the rest of the nation responded to the disaster. Like many of the anecdotes of how Chicagoans stayed calm and resolute as they watched their world disappear before their eyes, the depictions of the relief emphasized how determination, morality, sympathy, and self-control saved the day. But another of the purposes of these depictions was to bless the postwar economic and political order. The flood of contributions from around the nation and the world—valued at close to $5 million in all—seemed to prove that the developing national system through which the country circulated goods, capital, information, and people ultimately served universal democratic Christian sympathy. After all, the same telegrams and trains that carried the news and refugees out brought the pledges of relief and the carloads of food and supplies in. The fire histories reprinted verbatim the wires sent by dozens of mayors, governors, and heads of state pledging the essential resources that sped toward Chicago on the nation's rails. The story of the relief reaffirmed the manifold worthiness of Chicago and America. Americans expressed certainty that the city would inevitably prevail not just because the rest of the world's material progress needed a healthy Chicago, but also because this progress was allied with the finest human sentiments.

One of the most-repeated episodes in the accounts of the relief told of how New York financier Jim Fisk, after hearing the first bulletins of the disaster, loaded up a lightning express for Chicago, demonstrating that the economy that made such private fortunes possible also enabled an unprecedented display of charity and generosity. John Greenleaf Whittier, who interpreted the fire as a redemption from the "primal sin of selfishness" and a victory for Christ's "gospel of humanity," wrote:

> A sudden impulse thrilled each wire
> That signalled round that sea of fire;
> Swift words of cheer, warm heart-throbs came;
> In tears of pity died the flame![22]

Chicago, and the new urban order it represented, might be humbled overnight in a way that showed that God and not man was the ultimate ruler of earthly destiny, but through it all the city revealed itself to be astonishingly resilient because of its material and human resources, because of its vital connection to a far-flung yet tightly bound social and economic system, and because this system evidently had the blessing of the same God that in His wisdom chose to afflict Chicago for the nation's own good.

If the fire purified Chicago by burning away all but what was best within it, the challenge of the relief worked a similarly miraculous renewal and reunification of mankind elsewhere. In responding to Chicago's need, the rest of the country forgot its petty artificial divisions and rediscovered its finest collective self. That "so immense a destruction of actual wealth" did not cripple the economy and discourage the nation "is an inspiring proof both of its sound condition and of its cheerful confidence," wrote the editors of *Harper's Weekly*. Andrew Shuman observed that the terrible blow to Chicago "struck that chord of humanity which vibrates with the sympathetic thrill of a common brotherhood—the chord which unites us all, and makes the great family of man a grand unit in impulse, sympathy and a sense of dependence." It brought out the best in "close-fisted Yankees of New England," "slow-plodding capitalists of Canada," "lavish spendthrifts of the Pacific Coast," and the "'peculiar people'" of Utah. Even further afield, it leavened the souls of Germans "flushed with [their] freshly-earned triumphs in the land of the vanquished Gaul" and of "debt-burdened" and "tyrant-tied" Austria.[23]

The *New York Herald* of October 10 reported that groups of very different kinds of people pressed against the bulletin boards of newspaper offices, becoming one in their interest and concern: "From the kid-gloved exquisite, laying aside for once his nonchalant air, to the hard-fisted mechanic or apple woman, the same feeling of awe and sympathy prevailed, and from the lips of all, words of pity and kindness could be heard to fall."[24] The fire was as blessed a gift to the donors of aid as the relief was to its recipients, for it was the first major opportunity since the Civil War to pledge the nation to the unity for which so much had been sacrificed, and to prove that materialism and competition were not the governing spirits of the time. The rhetoric of relief was more pious than the accounts of the fire, conjuring up images of holy suffering and selflessness. Colbert and Chamberlin wrote that yet another indescribable aspect of the fire experience was "the acts in which all Christendom leant over Chicago and poured the precious balm of sympathy into her wounds, and bathed with the wine of relief her parched and blistered lips." There was "no acre of the United States but that some cinder from Chicago had lighted on it and kindled the fire of sympathy."[25]

Here again the fire literature construed the whole fire experience as ennobling. Bret Harte's poem on the fire, written the same day the flames finally went out, began with an image of the city as a noble young queen,

> Blackened and pleading, helpless, panting, prone,
> On the charred fragments of her shattered throne,

and moved toward assurance of salvation for all:

> She lifts her voice and in her pleading calls,
> We hear the cry of Macedon to Paul,
> The cry for help that makes her kin to all.

> But happy with wan fingers may she feel,
> The silver cup hid in the proffered meal,
> The gifts her kinship and our loves reveal.[26]

The relief efforts thus blessed all they involved.

Along with all these expressions of gratitude for the privilege of the fire there were, however, a few demurrals that, while still seeing the calamity in some senses as a valuable "lesson," argued that the most important thing it taught was Chicago's responsibility to itself and the country as a modern urban center. As the shock and euphoria of the days immediately after the catastrophe ebbed, important long-term policy decisions had to be made. Putting aside some of the moral and aesthetic terms in which the fire had been viewed in many accounts, several commentators reflected seriously on the need for new measures to deal with the problems posed by the sudden growth of large-scale industrial cities. They thought the fire was a blessing not because it purified the soul of Chicago, but because it might bring under control the sometimes shortsighted speculative ambitions that had led to the construction of shoddy buildings and inattention to zoning and fire prevention.

In its 1874 comprehensive review of its activities, the Chicago Relief and Aid Society, the private charitable organization managed by the city's business elite to whom the distribution of the relief resources was entrusted by Mayor Mason, blamed the fire on the city's rapid growth and hasty construction, and on public authorities who out of what had seemed "the necessities of the case" had provided mainly for the needs of "commercial interests rather than for the permanent security of the homes and property of the people." Frederick Law Olmsted similarly criticized Chicago's "weakness for 'big things,'" its pride in its belief that it would surpass New York, and its showy, shoddy commercial buildings. In yet another battlefield image that alluded to the Civil War, Olmsted contended that the fire might have been prevented, or at least controlled, with "honest architecture" and "good generalship, directing a thoroughly well-drilled and disciplined soldierly force of firemen and police." Eleven months after Olmsted's article was published, the *Chicago Inter-Ocean* stated that it was time to cut through the "fustian and hyperbole" of post-fire encomiums and acknowledge that the burning of the city revealed a civic fault of which the disaster was the correction: "The paramount need was harness, self-restraint, the temperance which comes by experience. What Chicago lacked was not pluck, but thoroughness; not thought or originality, but the embodiment of these in substantial forms."[27]

It should be kept in mind, however, that the people who were saying such things were for the most part spokespersons for the point of view of the leading businessmen both in the city and in financial centers like New York who were largely responsible for Chicago's rapid expansion. These businessmen naturally had a strong desire for the continuation of this expansion in ways that would serve their own interests. Their hope was that the fire would convince everyone that what was needed for the benefit of all was an effectively managed city in which their kind of enterprises would be better protected against such catastrophic dangers. They certainly had no desire to quell the booster spirit of Chicago, which, far from being discouraged by this apparent major setback, seemed to take heart from the disaster and expand to new proportions.

Modern discussions of the fire are fond of citing as a paradigmatic case the king of all Chicago boosters, John Stephen Wright, who came to Chicago with his father in 1832 and immediately entered the real estate business. His *Chicago: Past, Present, Future*, published three years before the fire (with a second edition two years later), was not only the culminating work of his career but arguably the masterpiece of the genre Ross Miller calls "Boosterature." Without reading some examples of this enormous body of writing, one cannot understand the imaginative power of the idea of the growth of Chicago and of other nineteenth-century cities (and would-be cities).[28] There appears to have been no economic or geographic fact, condition, or development Wright could not cite as incontrovertible proof that Chicago was destined to be the leading urban center in the whole wide world. His faith could be summed up in one of his sentences: "There never was a site more perfectly adapted by nature for a great commercial and manufacturing city, than this." By the time he wrote *Chicago: Past, Present, Future*, Wright could claim with some justification that his dream had been made reality. Indeed, the heading of one section is "The Basis of Our Prosperity is No Longer Hypothetical." When, with the ruins of Chicago all around him, Wright was asked about the prospects of this prosperity now, he is reputed to have predicted that Chicago would grow more in the next five years than if there had been no fire.[29]

Wright's response was typical rather than extraordinary among Chicago's entrepreneurs. Immediately after the fire, *Chicago Tribune* part-owner William Bross, whose family had just been burned out of their elegant new townhouse on Michigan Avenue, caught a train to New York (a major reason for Chicago's quick recovery was that its transportation infrastructure, and several of its major industries, were relatively uninjured by the fire). His purpose was to reassure the financial markets, and his major asset at this point was bravado. Upon arrival, Bross told reporters that the fire brought out the "true Chicago spirit" of pluck and determination: "Every one was bright, cheerful, pleasant, hopeful, and even inclined to be jolly in spite of the misery and destitution which surrounded them and which they shared."[30] Bross advised wealthy businessmen in New York and elsewhere to invest their fortunes and their sons in the unprecedented opportunities in Chicago created by the fire, and, like Wright, Bross assured them spectacular returns within five years. This faith animated the first post-fire issue of Bross's *Tribune*. It featured an editorial titled "Cheer Up," which confidently boasted, "As there has never been such a calamity, so has there never been such cheerful fortitude in the face of desolation and ruin." After asserting that "the forces of nature, no less than the forces of reason require that the exchanges of a great nation should be conducted here," it built to a lofty finish:

> Let us all cheer up, save what is yet left, and we shall come out all right. The Christian world is coming to our relief. The worst is already over. In a few days more all the dangers will be past, and we can resume the battle of life with Christian faith and Western grit. Let us all cheer up![31]

In two places the *Tribune* could not contain its enthusiasm and broke into capitals, stating first that "CHICAGO SHALL RISE AGAIN," and following this with the even more determined exclamation, "CHICAGO MUST RISE AGAIN!" The word "rise" was very popular among editorial writers, boosters, and poets determined to put the most optimistic face on this terrible event by viewing the city of Chicago as a spiritual force. Among the songs inspired by the fire was "From the Ruins Our City Shall Rise" by George F. Root, the Chicago composer who had rallied the North with "Tramp, Tramp, Tramp, the Boys are Marching," "Just Before the Battle, Mother," and "Marching Through Georgia," as well as "The Battle Cry of Freedom." The chorus of his fire anthem proclaimed:

> But see! the bright rift in the cloud. . . .
> And hear! the great voice from the shore. . . .
> Our city shall rise! yes she shall rise
> Queen of the west once more. . . .[32]

This kind of expression of faith in Chicago's resurrection soon was explicitly objectified in the adoption of the phoenix as the symbol of the city, and it was the essential message of the figurative language that continued to tie the fire to the Civil War as an experience that tested the spirit of Americans and, far from dividing and destroying them, ultimately created them anew and revealed their direction, purpose, and meaning.

But what if evil causes and purposes *were* behind the fire? Associations of Chicago's inferno with the forces of Satan abounded in contemporary accounts of the destruction. According to one account, witnessing the appalling spectacle was like "looking over the adamantine bulwarks of hell into the bottomless pit." In one of his numerous poems on the fire, N. S. Emerson personified it as

> *A demon whose power was stronger*
> *Than the strength of our puny hands,*
> *Who paused not to ask for favors,*
> *But took the wealth of our lands:*
> *We fought him with desperate courage,*
> *He laughed at our fruitless pain,*
> *We begged him to spare our treasures*
> *Alas! that we begged in vain.*[33]

Speaking in this manner hardly undermined the positive interpretation of the fire; it was instead yet another rhetorical means of declaring the disaster a victory of morality and character. Chicago was further elevated by having struggled with the devil. In any case, it is unlikely that most of those who discussed the fire this way thought they were doing anything other than talking figuratively.[34]

But the belief that the city had indeed been engaged in a battle with something sinister was in some respects deeply felt. Even as the commentary on the fire certified that Chicago had been sanctified and purified, it told another kind of story of how the flames unleashed many dangerous people and encouraged them to do their worst, putting the upstanding members of the population in peril. This narrative substantiated a view of what was wrong with the city as seen from the same middle- and upper-class, native-born perspective that formulated the affirmative view of this cataclysmic event. Speaking in an only partially veiled way about class and the need to draw the line on the thought and behavior of a social "other," this version of what had happened projected an idealized stable status quo based on a deep suspicion of urban society that viewed the fire as a metaphor for the dangers present in everyday experience.

Some raised the possibility that real demons in human form were responsible for what had happened. Immediately following the fire, the story circulated that it had been deliberately set by radicals with direct connections to the Paris Commune, which had been put down in late May 1871 in a bloody battle that ended with Paris set afire by radicals in a last-ditch act of defiance against the Versailles government, the bourgeoisie, the upper classes, and the monarchy. The *New York Evening Post* published a poem that wondered out loud about the relationship between the calamities that befell the sister cities of Paris and Chicago:

> *Did out of her [Paris's] ashes arise*
> *This bird with a flaming crest,*
> *That over the ocean unhindered flies,*
> *With a scourge for the Queen of the West?*[35]

In *The Lost City!*, the most melodramatic of the book-length fire histories, Frank Luzerne offered evidence of such a connection, a lengthy "alleged confession" of a "Member of a Secret Organization," based in Paris, dedicated to setting other leading cities ablaze as part of a war against wealth and property.[36] Such stories may have suggested that Chicago was the innocent victim of a foreign conspiracy from without, but to see the disaster as an extension of the Commune rather than of the Civil War turned it into a story of class conflict rather than of reunion and reconciliation.

Personal correspondence and newspaper reports in the days following the fire were more preoccupied with crime than with international conspiracy, however. Concerned that Chicago's misfortune, regardless of what had caused it, had created a golden opportunity for criminals throughout the country and within the city, they either predicted an outbreak of assaults on life and property or declared that one was already taking place. Cassius Milton Wicker wrote to his family in North Ferrisburgh, Vermont, "With the close of the fire, or rather conflagration, our troubles have not closed. Roughs and thieves from all parts of the country flocked here for plunder." The print coverage of this development was frequently lengthy and colorful, as professional writers seemed inspired by the chance to describe the secondary terrors of the catastrophe. In all cases, the point was how vulnerable Chicago was to these dangers. "The city is infested with a horde of thieves, burglars and cut-throats, bent on plunder, and who will not hesitate to burn, pillage and even murder, as opportunity may seem to offer to them to do so with safety," warned the *Evening Journal* a day after the fire. *Harper's Weekly* told of a "new reign of terror" marked by rape, arson, and murder, singling out four "ruffians" who were "well known to the police of every city in the Union—BARNEY AARON, BILL GRACY, JIM MUNDAY, AND JIM BROWN—as vile a set of scoundrels as ever picked a pocket or cut a throat."[37]

One of the purposes of such stories was to offer the same kind of assurances as did many of the tales of bravery and self-possession, to which they were often joined. The reports of terrorists, thieves, and murderers insisted that there was a saving majority of righteous people in Chicago. Most fire accounts that reported outbreaks of criminality called the malefactors "barbarians" to stress the point that they were external invaders foreign to the real Chicago. One of the earliest pulp fire histories described such low individuals as "black sheep and scabbed members of the flock" who were "hideous excrescences on the smooth surface of social life," opposed to the spirit of the "brave and noble-hearted sons of Chicago."[38]

But certain incidents that made their way into the fire narratives were far more unsettling. The most alarming effect of the fire from the point of view of many accounts, both public and private, was not that it attracted career criminals, but that it encouraged and permitted members of the city's underclass to follow their own base natures in ways that threatened the "better" elements in the city. This underclass was clearly identified with the substantial portion of the population whose background was different from that of the Yankee elite and the middle class. More shocking than any of the terrible things these people did was that they were able to assert their presence. The *New York Tribune* spoke approvingly of the imposition of a curfew, whatever its inconveniences, since it would restrict "that portion of the twilight population which always comes to the surface at such hours," whose "rascal faces and hang-dog air" now could be seen by day in parts of the city they had never ventured into before. "It would certainly not be prudent to give the city up to them," the *Tribune* advised, "and so at night they are kept in their own haunts on the West Side." One of the commonest features of accounts of the terrors of the night are scenes in which men and boys of a vulgar sort—often characterized as "roughs"—break into saloons and then proceed to commit outrages against wealth and respectability. Fire, whiskey, and the distraction of the authorities amidst the general chaos become a dissolving medium that removes whatever had restrained these people up to now, spurring them to give into "their slavish propensities" and terrorize others.

One of the earliest versions of this kind of wild moment appeared in the *Chicago Evening Post* a week and a half after the fire, and was soon reprinted in other places as well. Describing the inhabitants of a slum neighborhood in the fire's path as "[i]ll-omened and obscene birds of night," it continued in uncertain syntax:

> Villainous, haggard with debauch and pinched with misery, flitted through the crowd collarless, ragged, dirty, unkempt, these negroes with stolid faces and white men who fatten on the wages of shame, glided through the masses like vultures in search of prey. They smashed windows reckless of the severe wounds inflicted on their naked hands, and with bloody fingers rifled impartially till, shelf and cellar, fighting viciously for the spoils of their forays. Women, hollow-eyed and brazen-faced, with foul drapery tied over their heads, their dresses half torn from their skinny bosoms, and their feet thrust into trodden down slippers, moved here and there, stealing, scolding shrilly, and laughing with one another at some particularly "splendid" gush of flame or "beautiful" falling-in of a roof.[39]

The hollow-eyed hags, so physically repulsive and morally impure, were a striking contrast to the vibrant presence of Armitage's fair and full-bosomed representation of Chicago. They stood in the minds of respectable people for the undifferentiated rabble, who, if not directly responsible for the fire, possessed some half-articulated idea that anything bad that happened to their betters was a good thing. One of the consequences of Chicago's calamity was that it opened up opportunities for such people to invade the finer neighborhoods from which their own disorderly habits rightfully excluded them.[40] A visual representation of the fire, much more in keeping with the elevated tone of Armitage's painting than with the story in the *Evening Post*, appeared in the November 4, 1871, issue of the periodical *Every Saturday*. It depicted

Chicago as a beautiful young pre-Raphaelite princess being helped to her feet by four other maidens, representing the cities and countries that sent relief, each adorned identically with flowing dresses and coronets. The scene is one of apocalyptic destruction. Over fallen Chicago hovers a much larger and profoundly ominous winged female figure holding a torch, while in the murky background the other maidens struggle with their bare hands to fend off a pack of wild dogs with fearsome fangs. Dark birds on the horizon await the uncertain outcome.

Notably lacking in such depictions, and in the fire literature as a whole, is any significant attention to the losses and suffering of even the virtuous members of the lower class and of the enormous ethnic communities (including numerous middle-class Chicagoans), mainly German and Irish, that made up a majority of the city's population.[41] Despite the many assertions of universal spiritual awakening inspired by the fire, the authors of the commemoratives and instant histories reserved their sympathies mainly for the losses of "the landlord and aristocrat," who was to be pitied far more than "the boor who now jostles him," since his loss of property and prestige was far greater. What discussion there was of the tribulations of the economically marginal members of society was sometimes startlingly coldhearted. To some commentators the fire was a fortuitous piece of urban renewal that had cleared a few slums and, in so doing, raised property values. One noted that the city had, thanks to fire, gotten rid of some of its "old rookeries and riff-raff population near the river," while others reported with similar approbation that among the devastated areas were notorious immigrant neighborhoods like Conley's Patch, not far from the cottage of Catherine and Patrick O'Leary, in whose whereabouts the fire, whatever its precise cause, began.[42]

To the extent that it was victimized by the fire, this riffraff seemed to receive little more than what it deserved. Or so went the message of some of the fire accounts. Luzerne's *Lost City!* spoke of the fate of "women of the baser sort" in their "dens and haunts" drinking heavily and abandoning their children as the fire attacked their "squalid tenement." Those who did try to rescue one "painted Jezebel" were thwarted since "she had inhaled the intense caloric into a stomach already heated with alcohol, and fell dead before one could reach her." Others among the poor died because they evidently lacked the character and resolve to save themselves, which was also why they were poor in the first place. Their presence was felt to be a dangerous liability, and whatever misfortunes befell them were their own fault.[43]

More disturbing perhaps was how the fire brought out the worst in supposedly *good* people. Mary Ann Hubbard recollected the "universal thieving propensities let loose" that cost her many of her possessions, some of which she was sure were stolen by her own trusted servants. "I suppose the fact that things were lying round loose and would probably be destroyed by the advancing flames had the effect of weakening any principle of honesty," she reflected, raising the possibility that the calamity demonstrated that the city's moral fiber was perhaps not so strong after all.[44] William S. Walker attributed the fire-incited drinking to "physical and mental exhaustion" and "the inexplicable seeking for an assuage of trouble in potent alcohol," and he told (as many others did) of saloon keepers and liquor dealers who, knowing that their stock was lost in any case, rolled "barrels of the poison" out into the street and threw open their doors "to the overwrought and haggard populace." Walker's elevated diction dramatized his shock at the resulting loss of self-possession: "Men drank then whose lips had never before been crossed by alcohol; while those who had hitherto tasted of its Lethe-draughts only on rare occasions, now guzzled like veteran soakers."

The horrors knew no boundaries. Not only "were hardened women reeling through the crowds, howling ribald songs," and "coarse men . . . breaking forth with leering jokes and maudlin blasphemy," but there were even "women of the highest culture tossing down glasses of raw whiskey; ladies with cinder and tear-begrimed faces, pressing the cups with jewelled fingers." The fire seemed to have brought all down to the lowest level: "of rich and poor, well-bred and boors, the high and the lowly, there were few who did not appear to have been seized with the idea that tired nature must finally succumb unless the friendly stimulant was used."[45] Such Gothic scenes were riveting to the middle-class imagination, whose conception of social order was based on internal self-control, and which in its fixation on temperance in this period bolstered the traditional moralistic attack on drinking with "scientific" evidence that alcohol destroyed the prospects of an individual in an orderly society.[46] Those who let themselves go not only jeopardized their own well-being but also weakened the social order, which was ready to award money, status, and prestige to those who adhered to its strictures.

It is hard to square these anecdotes of debauchery with an interpretation of the fire as an invading enemy against whom the citizenry bravely rallied, let alone with the rhetoric of purification and positive purpose. What makes such stories all the more intriguing is that they, like the O'Leary legend and the Communard's confession, were based not on verifiable historical fact but on an anxiety about urban society that existed regardless of the fire. While there was some looting, theft, and drunkenness amid all the commotion, the tales of such behavior were greatly exaggerated and fed on each other.[47] In most instances, their authors confessed that they had witnessed no such atrocities directly; other trustworthy sources maintained that they were not true at all.[48]

Why did professional authors and private citizens describe events that never took place? Paranoid rumor and sensation are almost always among the aftershocks of any large-scale disorder, and so it was only natural that they would circulate locally for at least a brief time, especially in newspapers and periodicals vying for readers and sales.[49] Hinting that there was perhaps more fantasy than substance to some of these reports, bookkeeper Eben Matthews still recalled how powerful the rumors were: "In addition to the resident criminal class we were obliged to look out for persons of this character who began to come in great numbers, [which] added to our trouble. At this late date one, who was not an eye witness, can hardly imagine the fear of incendiarism, looting, etc. which prevailed. Stories of all kinds were afloat concerning thefts[,] murder and the like."[50]

But Chicago was perhaps particularly prone to becoming the subject of widely published tales of the eruption of criminal and destructively loose behavior because of a prevailing concern with urban vice and crime and with a postwar increase in the population of "floaters" and other suspect social types— including immigrants in general—who were drawn to the city.[51] Authors after a commercial audience were eager to exploit this concern and Chicago's existing reputation for loose and illegal behavior, joining their accounts of the fire to a lively literature of urban exposé that dated in the United States at least as far back as George Lippard's shocking treatment of Philadelphia in his *Quaker City* (1845) and George Foster's worldly-wise *New York by Gas-light* (1850). Such works purported to reveal to their audiences the shocking and otherwise hidden lives of those, usually the very wealthy and the very poor, who by choice or by necessity lived outside the boundaries of propriety.[52] The fire, which burned away all walls and masks and guards, offered an irresistible opportunity for professional writers ready to feed the fascination of respectable readers with stories of those at the margins.

But something more significant was also at work. Observers of the Chicago fire near and far saw in the smoke and flames a fulfillment of their deepest fears about urban life, fears that demanded realization, no matter what the facts, if the cherished prejudices that lay behind them were to be justified. Whether the specific cause of trouble was an international conspiracy of dedicated revolutionaries, an invasion of criminals, the unchecked flow of alcohol, or simply an ignorant Irish woman's clumsy cow, the basic problem was the precariousness of the social order. The tales of arson and drunkenness and crime spoke mainly on a symbolic level, revealing a desire for greater control of "dangerous" elements. The anxiety behind this desire was that social chaos, not fire, was the most severe threat to the future of the city.

This anxiety was most obsessively at work in one kind of story that appeared in most fire narratives: the lynching of incendiaries who, even if they did not start the conflagration, accelerated its spread. The motives of these individuals are not fully explained, though they are generally described as lower-class young men presumably acting out of a general antipathy to property and the settled order. Of all the kinds of stories that came out of the fire, the lynching tales had the highest ratio of reported to verified occurrences, of which there were none. Tales of street justice meted out to these arsonists (and to looters of all ages and sexes) appeared in the earliest newspaper dispatches. They figured prominently in the fire histories and the personal letters and memoirs, and they were a popular subject for the illustrations that accompanied the histories. On the page opposite the "Confession of a Member of a Secret Organization," Luzerne included a much-reproduced drawing (of which there were several variations) of a group of hearty male citizens hanging a young man from a lamppost. The men work together calmly, assisting each other in this grim errand with the same kind of cooperative spirit depicted in some scenes of rescue. The action takes place against a backdrop of smoke and fire that the assembled crowd of vigilantes and spectators ignores while it turns its attention to this spectacle. The caption reads: "Swift Justice. Fate of Thieves and Incendiaries."[53]

Authors and artists tried to outdo each other in their presentation of these grisly scenes. The "winner" in this strange competition was

George L. Barclay's *The Great Fire of Chicago!*, which contained an illustrated account of a would-be malefactor hanging barefoot and upside
down, about to be brained by two soldiers, one using a rifle butt and the
other an ax. The illustration is brutal, primitive, and direct, a kind of ritual exorcism of the devils that beset the city. Such vigilantes typically
are, like the hanged man, members of the working class, though they
are usually a little older. This suggests both that Chicagoans of the "better" sort would not participate in such activities and that responsible
citizens of all classes realize that property and order must be defended.
In any case, such scenes should be viewed in relation to the different
portrayals of Chicago as a beautiful young woman in distress. This
male incendiary, who is representative of the dangerously unstable elements of society, is ceremonially inverted, stretched, beaten, and dis-
membered for attempting to ravish the noble maiden.[54]

To read these anecdotes and view the illustrations is to marvel at
the foresight, presence of mind, and cooperative spirit of Chicago's citizens, who, in the midst of fleeing from a cataclysmic fire that destroyed
their every belonging and threatened their livelihoods and their lives,
found time to stop to apprehend such alleged villains, reach a consensus on what to do with them, procure a rope, and string them up. The
most remarkable thing about the lynching narratives was that the authors never failed to endorse the action of the vigilantes, thus declaring
that it was proper and perhaps necessary to take the law into "our" own
hands in order to defend the city against "them," the agents of disorder.
One fire history unabashedly saw the hangings as saving acts of moral
resolve that rescued Chicago from the same kinds of beasts that threatened the city in the more allegorical illustrations: "Let us thank God
that many of these monsters in human shape received the summary
punishment they so richly merited. And not forgetting the quality of
mercy, 'which is not strained,' let us heartily rejoice that in most cases
they were shot down like dogs, brained while they were in the act of
crime, or hung up high in the streets as a proof of good faith to other
members of the unholy pack."[55]

The reports of the lynchings—at once so unforgiving, bloodthirsty,
and untrue—were full of contradictions. While reasserting the primacy
of public order, they endorsed the most violent and irregular measures
in support of that order, carried out under the worst possible circumstances. The same accounts that recoiled from the thought of a reign of
terror thus contained a justification for one, as long as the right people

had the rope and acted against those who would set society aflame. The lynching narratives seemed to say that justice was preserved through the timely action of public-spirited citizens, even if this was accomplished only by ignoring some of the principles through which these same citizens claimed to be a civilized community. The best way to explain the lynching rumors, after conceding their sensational appeal, is on the level of a mass dream—or nightmare—that did not require consistency. These stories were the grimmer side of the hope that the fire was redemptive, a warning that saving the "life" of the city required not only heroic and selfless acts of rescue but also swift, sure, and even murderous measures against the enemies of society. On the deepest psychological level, authors and readers who participated imaginatively in the stories of hangings needed those arsonists and looters as focal points for their concerns about instability, and they needed to have them lynched. The fire gave these authors and readers the opportunity to assure themselves that these needs were real and that they would be able to identify and take arms against the enemy within.

The hanged incendiaries were born of concerns that urban order was inherently unstable, that the clarity of perception and action stability required—the ability to identify and remove sources of disorder as readily as did the vigilantes—was not available. The anxieties about the social order implicit in these narratives were in some ways more obviously present in the wild stories surrounding two other incidents of the fire: the release of prisoners from the jail in the Courthouse, the downtown building that housed most local government offices (it was situated in the same block as the present-day City Hall); and the gathering of fire refugees on "the Sands," which was located along the lakefront and just north of the main branch of the Chicago River. These incidents had some basis in fact, but the authors of the fire literature reworked both of them in order to express certain warnings about the nature of the urban populace and about social democracy.

To leave the prisoners incarcerated would condemn them to be burned alive, but the consequence of humanely letting them go was to allow these unreconstructed wretches to rejoin the law-abiding. Once liberated, they set the terrible tone of the night, at least according to such sources as the *Chicago Times*, which reported, "In view of the horrible scenes of incendiarism, robbery, and murder afterward enacted, it is almost a matter of regret that the entire batch of villains were not allowed to experience a hasty roasting." These prisoners, described elsewhere as "yelling like demons," thus came to be identified with the destructive spirit of the fire, which in turn was personified as a satanic being let loose in the city streets.[56]

This drama, in which the lowest and most dangerous elements of society, who had been captured and contained by the civilized order, were suddenly unleashed to do their worst, emphasized both the necessity and the vulnerability of social control in the same way the stories of lynching had. According to one improbable anecdote, the first thing the prisoners did was set upon a wagon full of clothing, which they "emptied . . . of its contents and fled to remote alleys and dark passages to don their plunder and disguise themselves."[57] They could then mingle undetected in the crowds, and amid the distraction and disarray caused by the fire there was nothing to stop them when they inevitably chose to turn on law-abiding citizens again. One kind of rumor here dovetailed with several others, as the story of the liberation of the prisoners helped to explain the reports of intemperance, crime, and barbarism, which in turn justified the much-celebrated vigilantism. Beyond that, however, the news of the prisoners' release warned post-fire Chicagoans that anyone among them could be an enemy of society, that the city was a place where such terrible villains were indistinguishable from respectable people, and that sparing these convicted criminals from what others like them—whether terrorists, arsonists, or Irish immigrants—had caused in the first place was perhaps a less wise policy than allowing them to perish.

Like the anecdotes of the lynchings, the stories of the escapades of the prisoners were untrue.[58] While some inmates were reportedly let go, the authorities evidently did not release the most dangerous criminals, but transferred them elsewhere in chains, and those who were freed, like most other Chicagoans, likely devoted their energies to self-preservation. The rumors of the release did, however, address the real fear that in such a large city with such a mixed population, any stranger might be suspect. The special problems that John J. Flinn, writing in his 1887 history of the Chicago police, said faced law enforcement officers following the disaster sound like those supposedly presented to Chicagoans by these prisoners:

> The city was undergoing a complete metamorphosis; locations were obliterated, old landmarks destroyed; the neighborhoods that had been respectable had become disreputable, the slums of ant[e]-fire

days had become purified; the streets were almost impassable for months after the fire; shelter and hiding places for criminals abounded in the ruins or in the rising buildings; new faces were in the majority among the criminals, and the most experienced officers had to learn their trade over again, just as if they had been assigned to duty in a new city.[59]

Flinn could have been describing the effects not just of the fire but of the rapid growth of the city, where neighborhoods and personal fortunes could seem to shift almost overnight, and where so many faces were unfamiliar. Chicago was continuously remaking itself into a new metropolis, with all kinds of individuals of questionable motives running free.

"The Sands" was genuine enough even if the fire-related events that supposedly took place there were also largely invented. The area had been notorious since the 1850s as a morally as well as geographically marginal neighborhood congenial to the most suspect human impulses and activities, notably gambling and prostitution, which were unofficially tolerated by the authorities. In April 1857, Mayor "Long" John Wentworth, determined to root out vice and corruption, led thirty policeman in a local raid. While this dramatic action added to the popular mayor's reputation, it proved to be counterproductive in that it scattered the men and women of shady repute all over the city, bringing "into hitherto law-abiding sections the fear and terror which only lawless elements create" and leading to the tacit acceptance of prostitution throughout the city.[60]

The proximity of the Sands to the lake made it a natural point of retreat from the flames. Here, closed off from other escape routes, the burned-out "shrank for refuge from the pursuing monster," only to find that the fire seemed to revive the old spirit of the Sands. Or worse. The point made in most descriptions of those haphazardly gathered here was how mixed the group was. The fire forced together "extremes of wealth and squalor" so that "inequalities of societies were now leveled off as smooth as the beach itself." "Such an assemblage as there congregated," Colbert and Chamberlin maintained, "Chicago never witnessed before and probably never will witness again."[61] The message here was clearly not a celebration of democracy but a reaffirmation of the value and desirability of class distinction and separation and of the need to be vigilant—forceful, if necessary—in their defense.

Like the liberation of the prisoners, and the fire in general, the community on the Sands pushed the "lowest" Chicagoans up against their betters, with no restraints and no fear of reprisals for acting out the impulses of their base natures. The situation on the Sands dramatized what Andrew Shuman said was taking place in the city as a whole: "There was no Power to control the confused elements, to protect the weak against the strong, or to enforce law, order or justice." Without this "Power," the "confused elements" would reign.[62] A. T. Andreas told how the well-to-do who were driven from their fine homes "found that they were between two deaths—the burning city on the one side and the lake upon the other," their only hope being "this stretch of sandy purgatory." Small hope it was, Andreas sadly recalled, enlisting the reader to share his own feelings of outrage at the violations of decency that were perpetrated. The fire played a scene that would cause a writer to pause "abashed and heartsick at the awful task before the worst was told," deeds so foul that "[n]o publisher would be permitted to preserve in type—no man of moral consciousness would place before his family—the volume that told what there transpired."

Tell he did, however, and with a flourish, to assure the reader that what had transpired was an appalling atrocity. The imaginative transformation of a social, political, and cultural concern into a sexual one, conveyed symbolically and obliquely in the narratives of the lynchings of young male arsonists, was in the stories of the Sands literal and inescapable. "There," Andreas continued, "on the scorching earth, that held the heat and sent a shimmering, ceaseless wave of blasting air and sand from underneath the feet, parching the flesh and drying up the fountains of blood and life, the spirit of infernal revelry prevailed." It was a hell on earth, full of "human creatures" and "maddened animals," where "delicate and refined women, pure and innocent children," "young girls, whose artless lives were unfamiliar with even the name of crime," and "men of well-ordered lives and Christian minds" suddenly found themselves cheek-by-jowl with "brutes in human form, who were not only ready to do acts of crime, but whose polluting wickedness was rank and cast off prison-fumes upon the air." It was as if the Courthouse convicts, by plan or by the destiny of their nature, had directly proceeded to the Sands to work their will on all that was most delicate and fine in Chicago. Here "purest girlhood was forced to endure the leering of the vile." The felons and the fire became indistinguishable fiendish forces:

> The creatures who there tortured the helpless were no longer human—vice had dulled their moral instincts, and despair transformed them, for the moment, into demons. Their orgies were born in malice, they delighted in their sins; they shrieked aloud with glee to see the innocent rush from them, and plunge into the lake, that, for the instant, the sight might be shut out.

These creatures and demons were, if anything, worse than the devil. "Could all the powers of hell itself," Andreas wondered, "devise a keener form of anguish?"[63]

Like the other talk of outbreaks of crime, passages like these recalled depictions of the lurid urban underworld, of ethnic-based riots, and of "the dangerous classes" in fiction, journalism, and social analyses over the previous decades.[64] In most instances, accounts of the Sands presented this gripping drama of defenseless virtue, assaulted by shameless vice, in order to express horror and alarm at the prospect of social mixing. Common to these accounts was the dramatization of the notion that urban order and decency, represented by the "delicate lady of highest social standing," was in terrible danger at the hands of villains who wanted to steal her wealth and violate her virtue. These beasts had always wanted to do this, but had had to refrain until this unexpected moment when this woman's protector—who might be her father, brother, husband, or suitor, but in any case represented moral authority in Chicago—had been separated from her. Left unshielded, she faced suicide or, far worse, pollution at the filthy hands of her vile attackers. The only thing that could save her from this terrible choice was the timely intervention of righteous male power.

The story of the imperiled maiden who, forced to choose between death and dishonor, is saved in the nick of time by a brave and noble gentleman, was by 1871 another well-worn turn of popular narrative, but the specific fears and hopes that invoked it—and the tales of the hanged man—were felt as real. They combined in the elite narrative of the fire to convey the idea that urban democracy was, if not "awful," extremely volatile. If the recognition of national and international interrelatedness that caused the country and the world to feel Chicago's loss as their own was a source of reassurance, the acknowledgment locally that different groups of people were forced to live together was unsettling. The lurking problem within the city was that the better sort of people who were concerned with the well-being of the community were always at risk of being victimized by the less virtuous, industrious, prudent, honest, and disciplined who also called Chicago home, and who had cows, barns, lanterns, whiskey—and the vote.

Reflecting on the losses to the population as a whole in an essay called "Political Economy of the Fire," D. H. Wheeler saw "new reasons for hopefulness" but "also for apprehension." He worried "that bad men, and careless good men, are not restrained from careless handling of great social concernments by the magnitude and range of the perils they thus invite, and when fools abound it is not cheerful to feel that any one of them may put us all to grief by one careless action or one piece of negligence."[65] Urban society, like the physical setting it inhabited, could burst into uncontrollable flame at any moment, and must be carefully watched. Rebuilding a city that was "fireproof" would require a wide range of regulation that would extend well beyond more stringent building codes and a better fire department. Measures that had any chance of being effective would have to be based on preserving and protecting a carefully structured social order.

NOTES

1. George Fredrickson, *The Inner Civil War: Northern Intellectuals and the Crisis of the Union* (New York: Harper & Row, 1965); Anne C. Rose, *Victorian America and the Civil War* (New York: Cambridge University Press, 1992); and James H. Moorhead, *American Apocalypse: Yankee Protestants and the Civil War, 1860-1869* (New Haven, Conn.: Yale University Press, 1978).

2. This excludes a large number of people, since almost half of the city's population at the time of the fire was foreign-born and a larger percentage working-class. Determining how attitudes varied by religion, class, and ethnicity (as well as by gender and race) is difficult, given that most reporters, editors, and publishers were middle- or upper-class males. The personal memoirs of the fire that are available in print or in archives, while running well into the hundreds (with probably a good many more in private hands), include a significant number of female voices, but the accounts are still mainly limited to native-born authors of some means. As Karen Sawislak points out, "almost no written accounts of the Great Fire by working people are readily available." Sawislak, *Smoldering City: Chicagoans and the Great Fire, 1871-1874* (Chicago: University of Chicago Press, 1995), 35. In several instances, information on the lesser-known authors of the sources cited here is provided. For population figures, see note 41, below.

3. A brief glance at the city's population statistics, extraordinary even in

this age of urbanization, gives a sense of why Chicago's high expectations about the future were justified. A tiny frontier settlement of a few hundred souls in the early 1830s, it was the home of almost 30,000 people by 1850, and eleven times that many by the time of the fire. It would pass half a million by 1880 and a million by 1890, by which time it had become the second largest city in the nation.

4. On the evolution of Chicago's elite, see Frederic Cople Jaher, *The Urban Establishment: Upper Strata in Boston, New York, Charleston, Chicago, and Los Angeles* (Urbana: University of Illinois Press, 1982), 453-575.

5. Bessie Louise Pierce, *A History of Chicago*, vol. 2: *From Town to City, 1848-1871* (New York: Alfred A. Knopf, 1940), 431-35. Chicago's unsavory reputation could be simultaneously a source of boasting and of embarrassment, depending on the circumstances.

6. Moody, quoted in Elias Colbert and Everett Chamberlin, *Chicago and the Great Conflagration* (Cincinnati: C. F. Vent, 1871), 522. Moody's comments may also have reflected Cincinnati's displeasure at being surpassed by Chicago as a commercial competitor. Letters of William H. Carter (15 October 1871) and Francis William Test (13 October 1871), Chicago Historical Society (hereafter CHS). The Chicago Historical Society has the largest single collection of fire narratives, partly because its members and employees made several efforts in the years following the fire to encourage eyewitnesses to record their experiences. Some accounts, including several not deposited in this collection, were published in newspapers or privately printed, and many have been gathered into fire histories and printed collections, including A. T. Andreas's section on the fire in his *History of Chicago*, vol. 2: *From 1857 Until the Fire of 1871* (Chicago: A. T. Andreas Company, 1885); Mabel McIlvaine, ed., *Reminiscences of Chicago During the Great Fire* (Chicago: The Lakeside Press, 1915); and Paul M. Angle, ed., *The Great Chicago Fire* (Chicago: The Chicago Historical Society, 1946). The text of McIlvaine's anthology, whose contents were published earlier in Andreas and other sources, is reproduced in David Lowe, ed., *The Great Chicago Fire* (New York: Dover Publications, 1979), which also contains an excellent selection of drawings of the catastrophe and photographs of the devastated city.

7. [Edgar John Goodspeed], *The Great Fires in Chicago and the West* (Chicago: T. W. Goodspeed, 1871), 55. *Report of the Chicago Relief and Aid Society of Disbursement of Contributions for the Sufferers by the Chicago Fire* (Cambridge, Mass.: The Riverside Press, 1874), 15, 21.

8. *Chicago Weekly Post*, 26 October 1871, 1; Townsend, cited in James W. Sheahan and George T. Upton, *The Great Conflagration* (Chicago: Union Publishing Company, 1871), 361-63. Sheahan was an editor at the *Chicago Tribune*. Upton also worked on that paper's editorial staff, and he wrote several works on music and composers.

9. Alfred L. Sewell, *The Great Calamity!* (Chicago: Alfred L. Sewell, 1871), 77. On Sewell as the author of the first fire history, see Andreas, *History of Chicago*,

vol. 2, 759; vol. 3: *From the Fire of 1871 Until 1885* (Chicago: A. T. Andreas Company, 1886), 684; and Joseph Kirkland, *The Story of Chicago* (Chicago: Dibble Publishing Company, 1892), vol. 1, 306.

10. N. S. Emerson, "The Stricken City," in Frank Luzerne, *The Lost City!* (New York: Wells, 1872), 117-18; Andrew Shuman, "One Year After," *Lakeside Monthly*, October 1872, 246-47.

11. This narrative squared with a general middle-class outlook toward apparently undeserved personal misfortune. As Burton J. Bledstein argues, "Mid-Victorians believed that worldly reversals were tests of will, commitment, and endurance. A fall now and then would eventually prove to have been 'fortunate,' when one looked back from the heights after the long race upward." Bledstein, *The Culture of Professionalism: The Middle Class and the Development of Higher Education in America* (New York: W. W. Norton, 1976), 113; see also 147 on the relationship of character, faith, and meaning.

12. William S. Walker, cited in Andreas, *History of Chicago*, vol. 2, 727. Walker's account appeared earlier in *The Lakeside Memorial of the Burning of Chicago*.

13. Mary Ann Hubbard, *Family Memories* (privately printed, 1912), 127. The Cleveland narrative is in the collections of the Chicago Historical Society and also appears in several printed collections. Cleveland was a major figure in the development of the city's park system in the late nineteenth century. Olmsted, "Chicago in Distress," *Nation*, November 1871, 303. As Michael Barkun points out, this heightened sense of community transcends local cultural conditions and is linked to a universal millennial impulse. "One of the curious ambiguities of disaster," Barkun writes, "is that, while it is by definition a form of intense deprivation, it produces feelings of well-being that sometimes verge on euphoria. This is often referred to as *disaster utopia*." Barkun, *Disaster and the Millennium* (New Haven, Conn.: Yale University Press, 1974), 163.

14. Letter of Emma Hambleton (10 October 1871), CHS; Goodspeed, *The Great Fires in Chicago and the West*, 21; Colbert and Chamberlin, *Chicago and the Great Conflagration*, 364, 450-51. Colbert and Chamberlin's book is arguably the best contemporary history of the fire. Colbert was commercial editor of the *Chicago Tribune*, while Chamberlin worked for the *Chicago Times*.

15. E. P. Roe, *Barriers Burned Away* (New York: Grosset and Dunlap, n.d.), 419. This is one of several reprints of the original 1872 edition. Roe's novel was probably the best-selling book about the fire, and one of the great commercial successes of its time, with sales in various editions ultimately totaling a million copies. See John Tebbel, *A History of Book Publishing in the United States*, vol. 2: *The Expansion of an Industry, 1865-1919* (New York: R. R. Bowker, 1975), 228-29.

16. Letter of James W. Milner, CHS.

17. On Collyer, see Colbert and Chamberlin, *Chicago and the Great Conflagration*, 268, 404-5.

18. Colbert and Chamberlin, *Chicago and the Great Conflagration*, 462.

19. The original painting was given to the Chicago Historical Society but was itself lost in a fire. Several lithographs were produced that differed from the original in making the identification of the two clothed figures with England and America more explicit and in taking care to drape the recumbent Chicago more modestly. A. T. Andreas reproduced a lithograph version of the Armitage painting as the frontispiece illustration of the second volume of his *History of Chicago*. On such representations of women in America, with particular application to the period from 1876 to 1918 but with much relevance to the period before, see Martha Banta, *Imaging American Women: Idea and Ideals in Cultural History* (New York: Columbia University Press, 1987).

20. *New York Tribune*, 26 October 1871, 4. For a wedding illustration, see Luzerne, *The Lost City!*, 165. Variations on these kinds of wedding stories appear often in the wake of natural disasters. In its coverage of the blizzard of the late winter of 1993 that paralyzed much of the eastern portion of the country, the *Chicago Tribune* of March 15 carried the feature, "'The Wedding Nobody Would Forget': Giant Storm Can't Delay Wedded Bliss."

21. Mrs. Martha J. Lamb, *Spicy* (New York: D. Appleton, 1873).

22. Lamb, *Spicy*, 164; Whittier, in Colbert and Chamberlin, *Chicago and the Great Conflagration*, 524. John J. Pauly, who discusses the response to the fire in the context of anxieties about cities and modernity, points out how the press served as a symbolic domain in which the fire could be seen as melting away day-to-day differences based in hard political and economic problems, and in the process created at least the appearance of consensus, stability, unity, and progress without sacrifice of traditional values. Pauly, "The Great Chicago Fire as a National Event," *American Quarterly* 36 (1984): 682-83.

23. "The Silver Lining of the Cloud," *Harper's Weekly*, 28 October 1871, 1002; Andrew Shuman, "The Burnt-Out People, and What Was Done for Them," *Lakeside Memorial of the Burning of Chicago*, 49-50.

24. *New York Herald*, quoted in *The Ruined City; or, The Horrors of Chicago* (New York: Ornum, 1871), 23.

25. Colbert and Chamberlin, *Chicago and the Great Conflagration*, 408-9, 515, 523.

26. Bret Harte, "Chicago," in Sheahan and Upton, *The Great Conflagration*, 364.

27. *Report of the Chicago Relief and Aid Society*, 6; Olmsted, "Chicago in Distress," 304-5; *Chicago Inter-Ocean*, 10 October 1872, 3. Mason's decision to put the Relief and Aid Society in charge of fire relief and the Society's subsequent conduct have a complicated history. For critical analyses of this history, see Sawislak, *Smoldering City*, chap. 2: "Relief, Aid, and Order," 69-119; and Carl Smith, *Urban Disorder and the Shape of Belief: The Great Chicago Fire, the Haymarket Bomb, and the Model Town of Pullman* (Chicago: University of Chicago Press), 65-77.

28. Ross Miller, *American Apocalypse: The Great Fire and the Myth of Chicago* (Chicago: University of Chicago Press, 1990), 49. William Cronon discusses the conventions of booster thought and its combination of fantasy and serious theorizing in regard to frontier economic growth in *Nature's Metropolis: Chicago and the Great West* (New York: W. W. Norton, 1991), 33-34. As he points out, much work has been done in this field by Charles N. Glaab, David Hamer, and others. On early boosterism in Chicago, see also Carl Abbott, *Boosters and Businessmen: Popular Economic Thought and Urban Growth in the Antebellum Middle West* (Westport, Conn.: Greenwood Press, 1981), 126-47.

29. John S. Wright, *Chicago: Past, Present, Future* (Chicago: Horton and Leonard, 1868), 249, 25. On the Wright anecdote, see Harold M. Mayer and Richard C. Wade, *Chicago: Growth of a Metropolis* (Chicago: University of Chicago Press, 1969), 117.

30. William Bross, *History of Chicago* (Chicago: Jansen, McClury, 1876), 96; *New York Tribune,* 14 October 1871, 1.

31. *Chicago Tribune*, 11 October 1871, 2.

32. George F. Root, *From the Ruins Our City Shall Rise* (Chicago: Root & Cady, 1871). Lloyd Wendt states that the *Tribune* editorial was the source of Root's title. See Wendt, *Chicago Tribune: The Rise of a Great American Newspaper* (Chicago: Rand McNally, 1979), 237. Root's other fire songs included "Passing Through the Fire," and they joined a medley of inspirational melodies prompted by the calamity.

33. *Chicago Evening Post*, 18 October 1871, 2; N. S. Emerson, "Call for Help for Chicago," in Luzerne, *The Lost City!*, 199.

34. Likewise, descriptions of the first tentative inspections of the ruins compared the experience to a descent into the underworld. See Miller, *American Apocalypse*, 93.

35. "Paris and Chicago," quoted in Sheahan and Upton, *The Great Conflagration*, 367. In his comparison of views of the ruins of Chicago with those of the Civil War, Miller also includes photographs of the devastation of Paris. *American Apocalypse*, 94-95. Cecilia Tichi offers a similarly suggestive comparison of stereographs of the damage caused by the Galveston hurricane of 1900 and by the Homestead strike of 1892. See *Shifting Gears: Technology, Literature, Culture in Modernist America* (Chapel Hill: University of North Carolina Press, 1987), 48.

36. This anonymous figure, "one of the prime movers in this fiendish work," revealed that the organization had its start "during the troublous times that preceded the election of Louis Napoleon to the Presidency of France." Luzerne explained, "It is the startling theory that a secret organization conceived and matured the diabolical plot for the destruction of the city, and sent their agents here to execute it." Luzerne, *The Lost City!*, 185-86, 189. Karen Sawislak indicates that the confession first appeared in the *Chicago Times* on October 23. Sawislak analyzes this invention of an international terrorist network

and the angry denial of it in the pages of the German-language *Illinois Staats-Zeitung*, describing this story and the harsh treatment of Mrs. O'Leary in the press as appealing to ethnic and class fears. See Sawislak, *Smoldering City*, 46-48. These rumors may have been based on similar stories of female incendiaries, or *pétroleuses*, on the loose in Paris during the Commune. See Gay L. Gullickson, "The Unruly Woman of the Paris Commune," in Dorothy O. Helly and Susan M. Reverby, eds., *Gendered Domains: Rethinking Private and Public in Women's History* (Ithaca, N.Y.: Cornell University Press, 1991), 135-53.

37. Letter of Cassius Milton Wicker, CHS; *Chicago Evening Journal*, 9 October 1871, 2.

38. *The Greatest Calamity of Modern Times* (Toronto: Richardson and Punchard, 1871), 26.

39. *New York Tribune*, 13 October 1871, 2; *Chicago Evening Post*, 18 October 1871, 2. The racially mixed nature of the mob described here increased its terrors. The accuracy of the report is questionable. There were fewer than 3,600 African Americans in Chicago in 1870, or slightly more than 1 percent of the population. Pierce, *A History of Chicago*, vol. 3: *The Rise of a Modern City, 1871-1893* (New York: Alfred A. Knopf, 1957), 48. See also Miller, *American Apocalypse*, 46-47.

40. Such fears had been voiced before. For example, Richard Bushman cites Philip Hone's revulsion at "the miserable wretches who prowled about the ruins" of a fire in Manhattan in 1835, turning into beasts from drinking the alcohol they found. "At least in the imaginations of the wealthy gentility," Bushman writes, "this horde of discontented back-street barbarians threatened to invade the genteel city whenever suffering or disaster stirred them." See Bushman, *The Refinement of America: Persons, Houses, Cities* (New York: Alfred A. Knopf, 1992), 366.

41. Chicago's foreign-born population comprised half of the city's residents by 1850, and while this percentage gradually decreased to 48.35 percent in 1870 and 40.7 percent in 1880 (where it remained for the next decade), the proportion of Chicagoans who were either immigrants from abroad or children of at least one foreign-born parent was just under 80 percent by 1890. In 1870, 17.73 percent of the city's residents had been born in Germany, 13.37 percent in Ireland. The 1890 census was the first to note the number of native-born residents with at least one immigrant parent. Pierce, *A History of Chicago*, vol. 3, 21, 515-16; Wesley D. Skogan, *Chicago since 1840: A Time-Series Data Handbook* (Urbana: University of Illinois Institute of Government and Public Affairs, 1976), 15, 19. On the very complex ethnic and class dimensions of the fire experience, see Sawislak, *Smoldering City*, esp. chap. 2, 21-67; and Smith, *Urban Disorder and the Shape of Belief*, esp. chap. 4, 64-87. Sawislak argues convincingly that the working class, whether foreign-born or not, generally suffered more than the more well-to-do because their homes were more vulnerable, their resources for

recovery (including insurance) were either negligible or nonexistent, and their network of support was less substantial. She also points out that they were often treated with suspicion by the Relief and Aid Society following the fire, and even skilled workers faced difficulties in dealing with employers and landlords during the rebuilding.

42. Colbert and Chamberlin, *Chicago and the Great Conflagration*, 223; E. O. Haven, "Commercial and Public Institutions," in *The Lakeside Memorial of the Burning of Chicago*, 71.

43. Luzerne, *The Lost City!*, 121. In one of the few expressions of sympathy for the condition of working people after the fire, a survivor wrote to his parents, "We can't tell yet what effect this will have upon labour and wages and the price of provisions but we are inclined to think it will be a bad job for the labouring classes." Letter of H. Hartley (10 October 1871), CHS. Sawislak asserts that the fire literature did single out Mrs. O'Leary for class-motivated attacks. *Smoldering City*, 44. On the mistreatment of the beleaguered Kate O'Leary in the popular press, see Perry R. Duis and Glen E. Holt, "Kate O'Leary's Sad Burden," *Chicago*, October 1978, 220-24. For a recent examination of the source of the fire, including an ingenious theory about the specific culprit, based on property records and testimony at the official inquiry of late November and early December 1871, see Richard F. Bales, "Did the Cow Do It? A New Look at the Great Chicago Fire," *Illinois Historical Journal* 90 (1997): 2-24. The precise source of the O'Leary legend, which began almost immediately following the fire, is as hard to determine as the origin of the fire itself, since different reporters later claimed credit or offered varying versions of how the story first appeared. The O'Learys denied any knowledge of the origins of the fire during the official inquiry, which assigned no individual blame. In October 1997, the Chicago City Council officially exonerated Mrs. O'Leary, adopting Sawislak's view of why she was singled out in the first place.

For more on the O'Learys and the fire, see "The O'Leary Legend," in the Chicago Historical Society and Northwestern University Web site *The Great Chicago Fire and the Web of Memory*, http://www.chicagohistory.org/fire /oleary.

44. Hubbard, *Family Memories*, 126, 136.

45. William S. Walker, "Description of the Great Fire," in *The Lakeside Memorial of the Burning of Chicago*, 31-32.

46. Burton J. Bledstein notes that "science as an attitude for professional discipline required inner control and an individual respect for rules, proven experience, and a system of hygienic laws concerned with such personal habits as diet, bathing, sex, dress, work, and recreation. Typically, middle-class Americans with professional pretensions translated the moral cause of temperance into a scientific truth for successful living." Bledstein, *The Culture of Professionalism*, 90-91.

47. Exactly how much objectionable behavior can be attributed to the fire is very hard to reconstruct. Perry Duis points out, however, that the same railroad system that brought the relief trains in did make it easier for criminals (as well as reporters) to get to the city. Duis, "Whose City? Public and Private Places in Nineteenth-Century Chicago," *Chicago History* 12 (Spring 1983): 14.

48. In an uncharacteristic moment of authorial restraint, Frank Luzerne framed the terrorist's "confession" with the disclaimer that he offered it "without the expression of any opinion as to its authenticity," admitting that it seemed to be "utterly romantic and improbable." Olmsted told of "respectable citizens who hold to the opinion that the fire was started and spread systematically by incendiaries," and mentioned that he had spoken with one person, "lately from Paris, who is sure that it was part of a general war upon property," but he then dismissed the story outright: "Numerous alleged facts are cited to sustain this view, but I believe them generally to be delusions growing out of the common excitement, or accidental coincidence." Luzerne, *The Lost City!*, 186; Olmsted, "Chicago in Distress," 303.

49. For example, similar rumors of foreign incendiaries appeared in London in 1666. See *The Diary of Samuel Pepys*, ed. Robert Latham and William Matthews (Berkeley: University of California Press, 1966), vol. 7, 275; and *The Diary of John Evelyn*, ed. E. S. de Beer (Oxford: Clarendon Press, 1955), vol. 3, 462.

50. Eben Matthews, CHS. This undated account was probably written well after the fire.

51. Robin Einhorn points out that some of the support in the mid-1850s for a powerful, uniformed, centralized police force in Chicago was aimed at controlling transients who were thought responsible for virtually all of the city's crime problem. Einhorn, *Property Rules: Political Economy in Chicago, 1833-1872* (Chicago: University of Chicago Press, 1991), 148. On the widespread concern, from the antebellum period on, over the large number of recently arrived single men in the city thought to be in danger of falling prey to the temptations of urban life, see Paul Boyer, *Urban Masses and Moral Order in America, 1820-1920* (Cambridge: Harvard University Press, 1978), 109-10.

52. There has been a rise in scholarly interest in this literature in recent years. Stuart M. Blumin offers an excellent overview in his recent edition of Foster's writing, *New York by Gas-light and Other Urban Sketches by George G. Foster* (Berkeley: University of California Press, 1990), 1-61. See also Blumin, *The Emergence of the Middle Class: Social Experience in the American City, 1760-1900* (New York: Cambridge University Press, 1989), 286; and John F. Kasson, *Rudeness and Civility: Manners in Nineteenth-Century Urban America* (New York: Hill and Wang, 1990), 74-80. Note that much of this writing had to do not with crimes directly against property, but with vice, mainly gambling and prostitution. Note also that some of it, including the work of Lippard and Foster, attacked the moral hypocrisy of America's urban social and political elite as a betrayal of

American political ideals. Virtually all of the fire literature sides with the comfortable classes and treats the working poor with suspicion. For the broader literary context, see David S. Reynolds, *Beneath the American Renaissance: The Subversive Imagination in the Age of Emerson and Melville* (Cambridge: Harvard University Press, 1988), esp. chaps. 6 and 7, 169-224.

53. Luzerne, *The Lost City!*, 187.

54. Barclay, *The Great Fire of Chicago!* (Philadelphia, 1871), 32.

55. *The Greatest Calamity of Modern Times*, 26.

56. Walker, "Description of the Chicago Fire," in *The Lakeside Memorial of the Burning of Chicago*, 28; *Chicago Times,* 18 October 1871, 1; Andreas, *History of Chicago*, vol. 2, 725.

57. Andreas, *History of Chicago*, vol. 2, 725.

58. Closer to actuality were two other accounts of the release that appeared in several places. The first told how A. H. Miller, owner of a handsome four-story building across from the Courthouse that was the home of his well-known jewelry store, simply handed his doomed wares to surprised ex-prisoners as they hurried to find refuge. The prisoners also figured in one of the heroic legends of the fire, real estate man John G. Shortall's quick-thinking rescue of records from his office near the Courthouse. Since the city's documents and those of every other similar firm were lost to the flames, the files from Shortall's firm were thought to be the only documentary proof of ownership of property that survived the evening. With the assistance of associates and a borrowed pistol that he kept cocked, Shortall commandeered a wagon that he and the others filled; they then "recruited" two prisoners to help him manage the overloaded vehicle as it pulled away. But both the Miller and the Shortall narratives, and especially the prisoners' unthreatening role in them, received much less attention than the dangers supposedly posed by the escaped demons.

The fullest version of the Miller story is his widow's privately published *Reminiscences of the Chicago Fire* (n.p., n.d.), which was written at the urging of her friends. Mrs. Miller's *Reminiscences* is one of the few memoirs, and certainly one of the very few that were published, that depict the fire as the source of sustained personal misfortune. John G. Shortall's personal recollection is in the Chicago Historical Society collection of fire narratives, and is reprinted, with a flattering photographic portrait, in Joseph Kirkland's *The Story of Chicago*, vol. 1, 310-15.

59. John J. Flinn, *History of the Chicago Police from the Settlement of the Community to the Present Time Under Authority of the Mayor and Superintendent of the Force* (Chicago: The Police Book Fund, 1887), 136-37.

60. Pierce, *A History of Chicago*, vol. 2, 433-34. See also Flinn, *History of the Chicago Police*, 82-83.

61. Colbert and Chamberlin, *Chicago and the Great Conflagration*, 223.

62. Shuman, "The Burnt-Out People, " 43.

63. Andreas, *History of Chicago*, vol. 2, 754-55.

64. Paul Boyer describes the decades before the war as "a time of almost continuous disorder and turbulence among the urban poor." Boyer, *Urban Masses and Moral Order in America*, 69.

65. D. H. Wheeler, "Political Economy of the Fire," in *The Lakeside Memorial of the Burning of Chicago*, 99.

6

Distant Disasters, Local Fears

Volcanoes, Earthquakes, Revolution, and Passion in The Atlantic Monthly, 1880–84

Sheila Hones

Sheila Hones focuses on The Atlantic Monthly's *Gilded-Age fascination with catastrophes: its reporting on sensational but distant natural disasters, such as the volcanic eruption of Krakatoa in 1883; and its frequent use of the images of earthquakes and volcanoes, made familiar by this reporting, in discussions of perceived instabilities that were social rather than geographical and local rather than distant. Hones studies the ways in which representations of natural disasters in the Boston-based* Atlantic's *nonfiction and fiction simultaneously articulated and assuaged the pressing social and political concerns of its community of writers and readers.*

INTRODUCTION

WRITING ABOUT NATURAL disasters in the center of an earthquake zone has turned out to be a disturbing but at the same time strangely reassuring experience. Disasters epitomize loss of control and the triumph of disorder, but the organization of chaos into text seems to be an effective strategy for coping with the sharp edges of hazard perception. Whether the textualization takes the form of an objective scientific description, a conventional narrative fiction, or a passing figure of speech, the imposition of a secure rhetorical point of view renders the flood, the fire, or the earthquake not only distant but also meaningful and comprehensible, reaffirming the bounds of familiar order. It helps, of course, that in my case I am writing about old disasters, fictional floods and metaphorical volcanoes. Distance certainly makes disorder less personally overwhelming, and it is much easier to see periodic natural upheavals as normal elements of an essentially stable physical world from a position of personal safety. But just as the actual experience of a natural disaster reveals a great deal about the daily patterns of life in the affected area—its routines, assumptions, and dominant social values—so the way in which people report, describe, or explain natural disasters, even distant disasters, is also culturally revealing. The reporting of distant disasters often not only "organizes" the event reassuringly through an objective and controlling narrative point of view, but also uses the dramatic incident as a safe theater in which to explore areas of immediate cultural or social concern. In this way, the report or analysis takes on a further narrative dimension in its displaced or metaphorical articulation of social problems or shared areas of cultural or political concern. Distant disasters thus provide the textual framework for an exploration of local anxieties.

This essay will focus on the description of natural disasters and the use of disaster images in a large collective text, the Boston-based monthly magazine *The Atlantic Monthly,* in the five-year period from 1880 through 1884. Following a convention in the discussion of periodical literature, it will deal with the ten volumes of the *Atlantic* in this period as a single text with a "corporate author" and will assume that the text represents the characteristic voice of its implied reader/writer community, a Boston-oriented social group which in this period spoke from a sense of social leadership and cultural authority.[1] The natural disasters that figure most prominently in this text during the five-year period under consideration are the earthquake, the volcano, and the flood. Hurricanes and tornadoes are also mentioned, as are severe storms and the danger from lightning, but it is large-scale disruptions of the earth's surface that are discussed most extensively and referred to most often, even though the Boston area was clearly more likely to suffer from a storm than from a volcanic eruption. Indeed, a book review from 1880 criticizes a recent novel for its wild inaccuracy by remarking that while the action takes place in New England, "the story is as inexact as would be a picture of that part of the country representing a volcano in active eruption, with pirates capturing the inhabitants who were setting out to sea in gondolas."[2] This criticism not only points out the relative distance that separated Bostonians from the threat of volcanic eruption, but also contains a clue to their fascination with natural explosions. Volcanoes are as unlikely in Boston as pirates, but while the physical eruption represented by the volcano was obviously unlikely, the social upheaval represented by the pirates seemed all too possible, even imminent, to this elite community. By classing the volcano with the pirate, the *Atlantic* here reveals dramatically the figurative connection it makes between distant disaster and local fears.

This figurative connection between social unrest and disturbances in the natural order has some basis in the assumptions of a broadly Social Darwinist world view that Mike Hawkins argues regarded the natural world as both a model and a threat. According to Hawkins, the "need to show that the social order in some way mirrored the natural order . . . created a potential for the production of a whole range of equivalences, analogies, images, and metaphors." Metaphors and images were for this reason central to the construction of a link between society and nature that showed "how human culture was governed by the inexorable laws of nature."[3] In the *Atlantic* of this period, such a link would have seemed reassuring because the text generally insists that the natural world is not only ordered but also meaningful, that it is the physical manifestation of a divine intelligence, and that its laws can be discovered and relied upon. "All about the human world, so chaotic and incomprehensible, lies the world of nature, strong, serene, beautiful, and harmonious," writes one contributor, confident that even as disaster strikes locally, this ordered and meaningful natural context survives, serenely "undisturbed by our disasters, as if knowing them to be ephemeral and unreal."[4]

The *Atlantic* of this period takes it to be the duty of society to emulate this natural order, to create a "social atmosphere" that will keep things (and people) in their place and allow a civilized culture to rise above turmoil and achieve a social serenity that can emulate the harmony of nature. Thus in 1882, a contributor to the *Atlantic* can write admiringly of the "natural" and "not disagreeable" separation of social classes that he discovered in a public garden in England, based, he imagines, on the fact that there is "a social as there is a natural atmosphere, which acts powerfully but invisibly, compelling objects to maintain their position, yet exerting no violence."[5] Chaos and agitation are local and human; stability and order characterize the natural ideal.

The *Atlantic*'s characteristic belief that the large natural world is meaningful and ordered while the local social world is prone at any particular moment to turmoil and disruption has obvious implications for its attitude toward natural disaster. First, the text tends to rationalize disaster as much as possible, working to achieve a firmly objective point of view that can include disastrous natural events within an overarching sense of nature's ultimate stability. For this reason, it tends to focus on causes, distribution patterns, and long-term natural results, not on local disruption or human suffering. Second, the text then uses this particular construction of natural disaster to defuse social or personal turmoil and instability by articulating it figuratively through the image of a momentary disruption—a natural part of an essentially ordered environment. Both of these textual responses to disorder demand strong rhetorical control, a control that in the textual world represents or parallels the meaningful organization of a divinely ordered nature. The narrative voice has to position itself firmly inside the text and away from the disaster, and the reader, too, must be able to feel sufficiently secure in the narrative conventions of the text to be able to approach the topic at hand without trepidation.

The *Atlantic*'s most direct approach to the topic of natural disaster is made in essays such as "The Floods of the Mississippi Valley," "The City of Earthquakes," and "The Volcanic Eruption of Krakatoa." Less obvious but just as significant is its widespread use, in essays, serialized novels, and short stories, of the images of earthquake, volcano, flood, and storm in discussions of perceived instabilities that were social rather than geographical. And the third way in which natural disaster is worked into the text, linking these literal and metaphorical references, is in the use made of dramatic natural events as plot devices in fiction.

SWEPT AWAY

In an anonymous short story from the *Atlantic* of November 1880, "His Best," the action revolves around class distinction, a romantic triangle, and a devastating flood.[6] The tragedy of Joseph Lafferty, a West Virginia Irish immigrant butcher who dies doing "His Best" to save lives in a sudden Virginia flood, is the tragedy of a man swept away as much by a flood of inappropriate emotion for an upper-class summer visitor as by the waters of the roaring Shenandoah. Actually, Lafferty is "swept away" three times—by emotion, by flood, and by a tidy narrative conclusion. For while his death in the story's final paragraphs illustrates the awful human devastation of a natural disaster, at the same time, in its radical removal of the unsuitable suitor from a love triangle, it solves a problem of community instability and restores order to the social universe. In this way, the fearsome power of the flood is acknowledged but the story is able to end with a narrative resolution that emphasizes continued order. This effect depends entirely on the identification of the implied reader with the story's upper-class characters, particularly Helen Franklin and her fiancé Philip Spalding.

Romantic affection is not inherently disastrous in the *Atlantic* of this period, but it is nonetheless not hopeful for a country butcher to fall in love with a genteel summer visitor from the city. And Joe Lafferty's helpless attachment to Helen Franklin, who is happily engaged to the suitable Philip Spalding, while far from being a threat to social order in any real sense, is a narrative thread that demands a firm resolution. The turmoil of his impossible feelings, the social instability implied by the situation, and the community disruption brought about by the flood all demand a conclusion, a transcendence into the safe zone of the *Atlantic's* much-valued "repose." The triple conclusion is achieved at the moment when Lafferty loses his life saving a group of neighbors trapped by the rising waters. The turmoil of his feelings comes to an end—in death, he looks "perfectly calm and peaceful"—and the mending of community disruption is suggested when the last man rescued "lands in his wife's arms." As for the social instability threatened by his infatuation, that, too, is conclusively resolved.

One of the ways in which Lafferty is marked as an unsuitable match for Helen Franklin, the representative of the text's reader/writer community, is through a detailed explanation of his immigrant Irish, Roman Catholic background. He is not only a working man with little formal education, but a man whose "Celtic blood" is taken to "assert itself" violently when he is overwhelmed by strong feeling. Such a feeling is the anger and frustration he experiences when he learns of Helen's impending marriage, a turning point in the narrative at which his unruly emotion and the threatening storm and rising water become explicitly connected. A "flood of fancies surged through his mind all day" and grows upon him towards evening, "when the storm redoubled in violence." In the passage describing his despair and the rising storm, it is often impossible to distinguish literal from metaphorical description, as his resentment and social frustration become merged with the physical storm bearing down on the small community in which he lives. Even though Joe Lafferty is "a gentleman, at heart," he is not a gentleman in life; even though he was a brave soldier, reads surprisingly good books, "always vot[es] for the right man," and is, in fact, "a *mighty* good fellow," he is sharply separated from the "higher and more cultivated class," which, in the *Atlantic* of this period, is the narrating class. All of the upper-class characters in this story are related, by blood or by marriage—even the engaged couple are already cousins—and this is the class of people that is taken throughout the magazine's scientific articles to represent "our race."

NARRATIVE DISTANCE

The maintenance of a measured and confident narrative tone as well as a consistent and secure point of view are essential elements of the *Atlantic's* essays on natural hazards. All of these essays have clear and conventional rhetorical structures. They move reassuringly from introduction to development to conclusion, and they always bring the reader in the end to some sense of closure and security—textual, at least, if not literal. The voice, we could say, is Philip Spalding's, and it seems to survive (just as he does) past the end of the narrative and into an always improving future. One group of hazard essays deals with natural phenomena liable to occur in the United States, although not, generally, in New England, and tends to emphasize the relationship between national geography and national identity. A second, larger group of essays focuses on volcanic eruptions and earthquakes, both past and recent, and always occurring outside the United States. This group is in a sense the more unlikely and the more interesting. Why should there be five major articles on foreign earthquakes and volcanoes in the Boston-based *Atlantic* in the space of five years? Of course, the globally disruptive eruption of Krakatoa took place in August 1883, bringing with it spectacular effects that would have been very obvious even in Boston; but that event could not have been the impetus for an interest first evident in an 1880 article on Mt. Aetna. And this interesting focus on volcanic and seismic events is paralleled in the incidence of related figurative images used in other articles and in the fiction of this period.

What was it about volcanoes and earthquakes that made them so interesting? In part, the *Atlantic's* fascination with large-scale natural disasters seems to have been linked to a continued interest in the geological debates of the 1840s that had focused on the question of whether the earth's geological history was fundamentally repetitive or had included extreme or even supernatural events.[7] Readjustments of these apparently polar positions ("uniformitarian" and "catastrophist") were still being worked out in 1880s' discussions of seismic or volcanic events. The Harvard geologist Nathaniel Southgate Shaler, who contributed several articles to the *Atlantic* in this period and who (according to his biographer, David Livingstone) "interpreted the world of nature as a place of purpose and design incarnating the plan of a beneficent Providence," wrote from a position that incorporated an interest in catastrophe into a fundamentally uniformitarian methodology.[8] As Livingstone explains: "His method was clearly uniformitarian or actualist; his system, however, not at all inconsistently, allowed for quite sudden and dramatic changes in nature, catastrophes that were in fact fundamental to drawing the vital gradualist analogy between the history of life on earth and the history of the earth itself."[9] Writing from "a deep-seated belief in a designed world," Shaler was clearly interested in demonstrating and sustaining natural and social order through his work on natural catastrophes: "Only by evolutionizing traditional religion's teleology and ethics, he believed, could nature, humanity, and God be prevented from a collapse into chaotic naturalism."[10]

The *Atlantic*'s interest in natural disasters also no doubt sprang from the fact that they were romantic, shocking, and newsworthy. As one contributor points out, while "a single bad sewer may, in its time, kill more people than all the shocks of earth and air within the bounds of an empire," still, "the great incidents of nature are picturesque; they have the noble charm that belongs in things terrible."[11] But there is something more than "noble charm" that makes the volcano so interesting to the *Atlantic*, and this particular fascination has a well-documented provenance. In his work on the idea of American freedom in the period from 1815 to 1860, the historian Fred Somkin showed in some detail how the image of the volcano was conventionally used in the early United States to suggest "concealed menace"—to represent the "essential fragility of [American] civilization and its liability to instantaneous and utter destruction."[12] This metaphorical association of the volcano with social insecurity, Somkin argues, already possessed in the early nineteenth century a considerable history dating back at least as far as Michael Wigglesworth's "Day of Doom," a particular connection with the volatile nature of the democratic experiment that was encapsulated in 1788 by Fisher Ames in the view that a democracy "is a volcano, which conceals the fiery materials of its own destruction." These "fiery materials" (personified, perhaps, in the 1880s by a less noble and more politicized version of Joe Lafferty the passionate butcher) were bound to "produce an eruption, and carry desolation in their wake."[13] James Fenimore Cooper's 1847 novel *The Crater* provides an extended metaphor for the dramatic end to American democracy through social cataclysm, as Somkin points out, in its story of a Utopian community created by an earthquake and completely destroyed by a volcanic eruption.[14]

If the volcano (and to a lesser extent the earthquake) quite conventionally represented the fragility of the familiar social structure in the 1880s, then the scientific interest in those natural events that is evident in the *Atlantic* from 1880 through 1884 becomes understandable in one sense as a form of displaced control. Here, at a time of intense social anxiety, within a self-consciously elite community adapting to sudden change, the textual taming of such a potent image of instability would have been very reassuring. In a collective text where socialist or revolutionary ideas, political reorganization, immigration, sexual passion, repressed anger, and spiritual unrest are all at various moments "volcanic," it makes sense that there would have been a strong incentive to imply some control over seismic activity, if only through scientific analysis and explanation. In the end, however, each of the five essays of the volcano/earthquake group slides away from its implied scientific objectivity and relies for its sense of conclusiveness on a strong rhetorical organization in which it achieves its effects of closure without even attempting any explanation of why volcanic eruptions or earthquakes occur, or how they could be predicted or prevented. The essays feel finished, the narrative voice gives the impression of having brought the reader to a secure conclusion, but the central topic—the volcano or the earthquake—remains as mysterious as ever.

Two of these essays, "Wintering on Aetna" and "Volcano Studies," open from an overtly tourist point of view. The narrator of the piece on Aetna, for example, is returning to the area some years after his first view of the peak, made on a pleasure trip as he "coasted the Sicilian shores," and the volcano is once more initially viewed from a safe and an aesthetically pleasing distance, even though the purpose of this second trip is to take up residence on the volcano and study it. "Volcano Studies," too, opens like a travel article on South America. In the opening sentence, the reader is placed in the "little mountain village" of Guanarete "on the line of the projected railroad from Guayaquil to Quito," told that it "is destined to become the Chamouni of the American continent," and directed toward the view of the "grandest mountain panorama of the western hemisphere."[15] The middle essay of this first group of three, "The City of Earthquakes," is somewhat different, recounting as it does the author's personal experience of a strong earth tremor in the South American city of Caracas; nonetheless it manages throughout to maintain its "visitor's distance."[16] The way it achieves this is evident in compressed form in the opening paragraph, where, in presenting earthquakes as a form of underground storm, the author emphasizes the language of scientific prediction over a suppressed but still present counter-register recording subjective impressions. Thus, the opening sentence highlights words and phrases like "observations," "established," "fact," "accurately predicted," "routine," "repeat," "regularity," and "accuracy," giving much less space to the subcurrent represented by words such as "mysterious," "dreaded," and "epidemics." The paragraph's consistent emphasis on "prediction" nonetheless disguises the fact that this foretelling is limited to an estimation of an earthquake's duration, direction, and average destructiveness—not its occurrence. It is only at the end of three lengthy paragraphs that the author openly admits that his experience of an earthquake during his stay in Caracas impressed upon him "how impossible it is to predict the day of their advent."

Casually referring to a connection between natural and social upheavals he takes as obvious, the American tourist describing "The City of Earthquakes" observes that "Caracas has got used to earthquakes as Mexico to revolutions."[17] But he creates his narrative closure with the prediction that despite their resigned attitude the inhabitants of Caracas will eventually relocate the city; in spite of the earthquakes, the population will increase, and in time the city will abandon its present site and move slightly to the east. In ending with this prediction, the essay appears to finish with a solid conclusion, despite the fact that the site of the city has not been the essay's main concern, has not, in fact, been mentioned as an issue at all until this concluding paragraph. The other two essays also end by creating strong narrative closures that are surprisingly off the apparent point. "Wintering on Aetna" turns out by the end to be not the report of a scientific investigation at all, but the humorous account of a largely unsatisfactory attempt to study the volcano at close range, bad weather finally having prevented the author from reaching the summit and furthering his research. The volcano remains metaphorically as well as literally hidden in the mist and clouds.

The natural and social disorder experienced by the author who tried "Wintering on Aetna" turns out in the end to have been nothing but trivial and humorous, even though the essay's opening pages describe the city of Catania, "which has been cut through and through by lava streams, and shaken down by earthquakes in recent times," and even now "lives from day to day at the mercy of its terrible neighbor." It is "an outlet of those very infernal regions whose existence some deny," the visitor writes, sounding almost enthusiastic about the rivers of fire, devastating quakes, and "death in sudden forms, for thousands at once," the "ever-impending terror, against which science is unavailing and man's strength impotent."[18] The essay quickly abandons this alarming topic, however, and slides instead into a much gentler form of natural and social disorder in the entertaining story of an upside-down world in which the far-off Mediterranean appears to be nothing more than a nearby pond, the clouds roll away below the visitor's hut to allow the sunshine to stream up, and altitude creates the appearance of dramatic reversal in the social status of the narrator and his guards. "My men they were, up here," the narrator remembers, "though down below they perhaps considered me their man."

The connection between brigands and volcanoes suggested in an 1880 essay on "Sicilian Hospitality," in which the townspeople themselves "seem brigandish . . . with their impulsive, volcanic nature," is worked out to humorous effect at the end of the essay on Aetna. Down below, on their return journey to Catania, the ensemble passes through "sun-lit streets" followed by "shouts of delight and interest." This time "the coming wonder" is not at all life-threatening—nothing, in fact, more dangerous than a scientist mistaken for a bandit.[19]

"Volcano Studies," too, maintains its distanced point of view through to the end, concluding with a return to the theme of South America's challenge to Europe as tourist attraction. A controlled and limited hint of disorder or change is presented in "Volcano Studies" in the idea that Guanarete, introduced in the opening paragraph as "the Chamouni of the American continent," will in the future actually supplant the Swiss town in tourist popularity. Offering the visitor a view that "transcends the grandest panoramas of the European

Alps," and located on "the route of the predicted intercontinental railroad," Guanarete will be able to serve a memorable New Year's dinner to Bostonians who have spent Christmas at home.[20]

Strangely enough, Bostonian Christmas dinners feature in two of these three volcano essays. The festive meal functions in "Volcano Studies" to highlight the future role of Guanarete as an easily accessible and comfortable tourist spot, while in "The City of Earthquakes" it serves to point up the contrast between the narrator's familiar comforts and his uncomfortable experience in the hut on Aetna. On his first night on the mountain the scientist goes to bed cold and wet, in a room decorated with "several rather curious printed prayers against earthquakes, stuck up on the lava walls" and disturbed by the noise of horses and mules "fighting and screaming" in the next room. Falling asleep "to the sound of the rain dripping on the floor," he thinks "of a house on the other side of the Atlantic, where certain people would be gathered round the dinner-table, for this was Christmas Day."[21] Part of the effect of these two references to Bostonian Christmas celebrations is to remind the reader of the distance between a warm, safe New England home and the location of the narrative; they reconnect the text to its context and reaffirm the fact that the implied reader/writer community does not normally belong in a hut on the top of a volcano. This kind of small but repeated reference to familiar contexts beyond the setting of the essay works to place the natural threat within a comfortable frame in the same way that the reassurance of a conventional narrative structure, which creates the appearance, at least, of conclusion and safe arrival, defuses threat. But in the two essays dealing with the eruption of Krakatoa and its effects, both published in 1884, the authors are faced with a new order of disaster, a vast and destructive event whose effects were still visible worldwide, even in Boston, and the form of rhetorical conclusion and contextualization develops in a new direction in accordance with the greater challenge.

OF A NATURE NOT UNUSUAL

When the spectacular skies described in Shaler's essay on "The Red Sunsets" first appeared in Boston in 1883, their connection with the August eruption of Krakatoa was not obvious. At first, Shaler explains, "all the experts in meteorology were at sea in their explanations," although he is happy to note that it was explanations and not interpretations that the population in general was seeking. In America, he remarks with satisfaction, the scientific attitude had made considerable progress even among "the less cultivated class," so that by the 1880s "even the least educated no longer ask, What does this presage? but What is its cause?" It was up to "the experts in meteorology" to supply the answer, and fortunately they were not "at sea" for long, reaching dry land in time for his article in the April 1884 issue of the *Atlantic* and thus proving that Boston remained metaphorically as well as literally unthreatened by the tidal waves, of ocean waters and of scientific doubt, that had been caused by the explosion.[22]

"The Red Sunsets" has a relatively limited goal. It sets out to provide explanations for the change in Boston's skies and does not seriously engage with the volcanic eruption itself either as a natural phenomenon or as a human disaster. Instead, what it emphasizes about the eruption are its "grandeur" and the fact that despite its unusual size "its nature was not unusual." Even though it completely redesigned the geography of a large area, "destroyed somewhere near one hundred thousand lives," and sent atmospheric as well as tidal waves all the way round the globe, "it differed from a thousand similar accidents of this troubled world only in degree."[23] The essay thus depends for its containment of the disaster on two lines of contextualization. On the one hand, it aestheticizes the event, and on the other, it insists on its essential normality. It is a fundamentally unexceptional event that nonetheless, in its size, should remind the reader of the grandeur of nature. Thus, in his conclusion, Shaler presents the eruption and the subsequent red sunsets as "a lesson in favor of a little more humility on the part of those semi-scientific men who fancy that they know the world as a watchmaker knows the wheels of a watch." In the face of an event on this scale, he suggests, science can only stand back and marvel; the concluding paragraph of the essay finds the significance of the eruption and associated red skies in the way in which they serve to remind the viewer of the glory of nature. "When this volcanic dust ceases to glorify our skies at dawn and eve," he writes, "we shall part with what has probably been the most remarkable and picturesque accident to the earth's physical life that has been known within the limits of recorded history."[24] Focusing, as he does, on the red sunsets that followed the eruption of Krakatoa, Shaler is able to regard the explosion primarily as an "accident to the earth's physical life" and not an accident erasing the lives of thousands of people.

The author of the later article, "The Volcanic Eruption of Krakatoa," writes from a position much closer to the event itself and probably for this reason finds it much more difficult to achieve a secure and objective tone. The opening paragraph oscillates rapidly between a language of scientific observation and a language of dramatic experience. The essay opens confidently—"We know that . . ."—but moves on immediately to acknowledge that what "we know" is really only how "stupendous" the eruption of Krakatoa was. The second sentence again begins with an assertion of organized knowledge—"From the newspapers of the day we learned much"—but then admits that what we learned was of "the horrors" of "this unusual convulsion" and "the disasters" that followed it. The third and final sentence of the introduction follows the same pattern, beginning calmly with the assertion that "as information is gathered and collated, it is possible to present an interesting summary," but the sentence and the paragraph end with a return to the awestruck—"of this great effort of nature."[25]

This movement between the registers of calm objectivity and subjective excitement continues throughout the essay, which frames a two-page quotation taken from the "especially graphic and thrilling" description given at the San Francisco Hydrographic Office by the captain of a British ship in the vicinity of Krakatoa at the time of the explosion. The introduction to the captain's report is especially dramatic:

> On the afternoon of the 26th there were violent explosions at Krakatoa, which were heard as far as Batavia. . . . During a night of pitchy darkness these horrors continued with increasing violence, augmented at midnight by electrical phenomena on a terrifying scale. . . . The lurid gleam that played on the gigantic column of smoke and ashes was seen in Batavia, eighty miles away. . . .
>
> On the morning of the 27th there was a still more gigantic explosion . . . which produced an immense tidal movement, occasioning . . . great loss of life. . . . The matter expelled rose to an elevation so tremendous that, on spreading itself out, it covered . . . hundreds of square miles with a pall of impenetrable darkness. . . . Between ten and twelve o'clock in the forenoon of that day the subterranean powers burst their prison walls with a terrific detonation, which spread consternation and alarm among the dwellers within a circle whose diameter lay across nearly three thousand miles.[26]

But by the time it reaches its last few pages, the essay has regained its composure and its passive constructions: "coincident with [the resulting] atmospheric fluctuations," the final paragraph begins, "magnificent sunlight effects, lurid skies, prolonged dawns, and lengthened twilights were observed." We have left behind by now the drowned inhabitants of the area surrounding Krakatoa, represented even as they were only by "their scattered and ghastly relics," and are focusing (as we did at the conclusion to "The Red Sunsets") on nature's power and beauty. We are left contemplating the volcanic cloud, at first "a comparatively narrow column," which in time "gradually spread out north and south, until the inhabitants of all lands obtained a view of the beautiful effects of broken and absorbed sunbeams, and a demonstration of the power of that steam which was imprisoned by the last convulsion of nature."[27]

In the light of the apparent connection made in the *Atlantic* at this time between social instability or disruption and natural disaster, it is interesting to note that twice the author uses the image of an escape from prison to suggest the unleashed power of a volcanic eruption. The original explosion is described as the moment when "the subterranean powers burst their prison walls with a terrific detonation," spreading "consternation and alarm" among the people living in the area. In the last paragraph, the author refers to the release, by "a convulsion of nature," of "the power of that steam which was imprisoned." At a distance of thousands of miles, and represented in Boston only by stupendous sunsets, this sudden release and bursting of prison walls is not directly alarming, only awesome to consider. But when the figurative relationship is reversed, and it is local social insurrection that is articulated in the terms of volcanic explosion, then the awesome image of the literally distant volcano serves to defuse the awful idea of the apparently imminent local disruption of order.

ELEMENTAL ENEMIES

Despite the occasional incidence of the kind of "wide-spread destruction" represented by the volcanic eruption of Krakatoa, Shaler assures the *Atlantic* readership in 1882, "the general physical order of our universe is singularly well suited to the needs of organic life." "Departures from the calm order of physical events of our earth fall into a few classes," he explains: "the earthquake, the lightning, and the violent movements of the atmosphere, known as cyclones, typhoons, or hurricanes." And while these events "fill a large place in the fears of man," they will be sufficiently unfamiliar to the reader/writer community of the *Atlantic* that, according to Shaler, "few of those who read these lines will have seen any deadly effects from their action." Having made this apology for the irrelevance of his topic, he announces that he is going to rely instead on the picturesqueness and the "noble charm" of natural disasters to attract the reader's interest in his paper on hurricanes. Actually, despite this reticence, Shaler must have been quite confident of the attraction of the "great incidents of nature" as an essay topic for the magazine, for in the space of four years he presented readers of the *Atlantic* with three essays on the subject in addition to his piece on the red sunsets of 1883: "The Future of Weather Foretelling" in 1880, "Hurricanes" in 1882, and "The Floods of the Mississippi Valley" in 1883.[28] These three essays form an interesting group in that they deal with natural hazards characteristic of the interior of the United States and thus have a markedly different tone from the earthquake and volcano essays, set abroad, which are characterized by the tourist point of view. Shaler draws overt social and political lessons from the geographical incidents of the United States, at times giving the natural hazards the same kind of double significance, as actual events and as metaphors, that the anonymous author of the short story "His Best" gave Joe's flood.

Like the contributors writing for the *Atlantic* about the distant earthquakes and volcanoes, the author of these essays on American storms and floods prefers not to focus on the local tragedies or the disruptions of human life caused by the disasters. Shaler clearly perceives his task to be scientific analysis or commentary, and not eyewitness reporting or tales of human interest: "If space permitted," he remarks in the essay on hurricanes, "it would be interesting to trace in detail the circumstances that attend these calamities," as they "afford scenes of terror to which the most dreadful earthquake can scarcely furnish a parallel."[29] But in fact, the *Atlantic* in this period seems to have little taste for "scenes of terror," greatly preferring simply to "note the purely natural side of the convulsion." Even in this reference to the terrifying impact of natural disaster, the language is controlled and the disastrous results of the hurricane are simply "circumstances" and "incidents." This, "for our purpose," we are told, "will be sufficient."

The focus of these essays is not, then, found at the level of the individuals who experience disaster at terrifying first hand; rather, it is at the national level, and explicitly at the level of the nation's political and cultural life and development—a nation that is identified as the embodiment of "our race," motivated by "the genius of its people," and united by "the bond of common interest."[30] In a sense, the belief in the importance of a concerted and intelligent response to the threat of national natural disasters (even those as "distant" to the *Atlantic*'s implied readership as the floods of the Mississippi Valley) is taken in these essays to represent the containment and control not only of the nation's dramatic geography but also of the nation's alarming potential for social disruption. In an interesting displacement, "Science" has become the empire being won, and knowledge the frontier, while the undeveloped areas of the United States are simply "the wild countries that fall to their lot," as if they had been bestowed upon the nation by destiny rather than acquired by design.[31] Faced, therefore, even in Boston, with a responsibility for the problem of the Mississippi water system, Americans are under a heavy obligation to regard any natural hazard within its wide geographical boundaries as "a national problem" and not a distant, localized threat; the imposition of scientific order and regulated response at the federal level is taken to be an essential indication or even reaffirmation of the nation's political health and unity.

Given the conventional figurative connection widely assumed in nineteenth-century America between natural hazard and the political instability of the nation's democratic experiment, this emphasis on the "empire" of Science and the need for a federal response to local disaster is interesting. The course of empire, in this configuration, takes its way not so much westward as toward "the cause of law and order," in a metaphorical expansion of intellectual and scientific territory. This is clearly evident in the introduction to "The Future of Weather Foretelling," where Shaler contrasts the situation in the study of the "solid earth" and the "far-off heavens," in which Science's "empire is affirmed," with that in the "unstable" air "between these two well-possessed provinces," a "region that is not yet subjugated."[32] While there have been "some gains to the cause of law and order" in the region of weather foretelling, the project is far from complete, and in pursuing its development "science has made its greatest success in extending the limits of the known rather than in opening altogether new fields of knowledge."[33] After laying out a program to further the cause of meteorological exploration and recommending that it be undertaken by an international commission, Shaler concludes with the idea that if the other nations prove unwilling to join in, then the United States should take on the job alone. "The United States," he explains, "have already won an enviable prominence for their surveys of the wild countries that fall to their lot," and from its unique position as "the only state that lies upon the two great climate-making seas of the earth," the United States should be prepared to proceed alone, following up the investigations it had already initiated, "lines of inquiry . . . which are clearly adapted to the genius of its people."[34]

The United States is in several ways uniquely positioned to "[extend] the limits of the known," according to Shaler, partly because its very identity depends on its ability to control the internal and geographical threats to its survival, not the external and military threats that challenge the nation-states of the Old World. "Ancient regimes," he argues, "maintained themselves by the power with which they resisted armies," but "the governments of the practical age we are entering," of which the United States is a prime example, "will stand or fall by their power to combat the elemental enemies."[35] In the United States, the "elemental enemies" represent for Shaler a threat to the nation as potent as any foreign force; indeed, the natural hazards common to the American continent are several times presented in these essays in the terms of an invading army. A midwestern tornado, for example, appears in the essay on hurricanes as if making a sudden attack; the clouds gather as if "coming from nowhere, growing at once in the lurid air," and "in less than half an hour the forces of the storm are organized and the dreadful advance begins."[36] Possibly because Shaler associates these storms with battlefield advances, they are also several times presented in unusually mechanical terms. Hurricanes are "dreadful engines" set in motion by mysterious causes; cyclones and earthquakes are the "inorganic machinery" of "wide-spread destruction."

Internal, "elemental" threats, sometimes articulated in the language of invading armies, are identified in these essays then as the source of potentially fatal disruptions to national survival and federal control—not primarily because they are so physically destructive, but because of the frightening possibility that their attacks will divide the nation into interested sections. In the case of the floods of the Mississippi Valley, Shaler argues, if the federal government does not respond to the problem, then some kind of association of the most immediately affected states will take up the burden, and this will create the "gravest political dangers." Such an association would be the first step toward national disruption or even political secession, a threat that had only recently been averted during the devastating conflict of the Civil War. Shaler's reference to the still painfully and personally memorable events of that war is clear in his warning that any association of states formed to react to the problem of the Mississippi water system would be

> a federation within the nation for mutual protection against a danger that the general government had failed to repel. It could not fail to weaken the bond of common interest, the source of common obligation, which we gave a generation of life and labor to affirm. . . . Such a sundering of the moral union of the people would pave the way to, if it did not in itself warrant, a political disintegration of the nation.[37]

For the *Atlantic* in the early 1880s, then, the greatest real threat posed by natural disaster is its challenge to the nation's "moral union," "bond of common interest," and self-control or self-regulation at the national level. Believing the natural world to be orderly and meaningful, the implied reader/writer community of the *Atlantic* in this period appears also to believe that for the nation to be most healthy, it, too, should be "strong, serene, beautiful, and harmonious," able to find itself—to use two key words from the text—in repose and not in turmoil. The nation should not be indifferent to disaster or physical threat; rather, it should possess the collective power to absorb "departures from . . . calm order" that in the national time scale will turn out to be simply "momentary in their action." Reflecting on the question "Is Nature Merciful?" in 1881, a contributor balances the cruel fate of "cities that confide in a crater, and in an hour are seething into lava," with Nature's "immense and kindly recuperative force" and the fact that "the grass grows over her extinct volcano" in the end. Secure in its construction of a nature characterized by inevitable progress, the *Atlantic* recognizes a natural disaster even on the scale of a Krakatoa as a part of large-scale, long-term natural improvement.[38]

A VAST POWER CHAINED DOWN

Nature repairs and improves itself naturally; humans and nations must do so through will and determination, aiming always to move through turmoil, however creative, toward repose. In the *Atlantic,* "nature's forces" seem to be "working always and by impulsion towards what is highest," and in the same way, it assumes, the natural "progress of mankind" will move civilization "from fragmentariness to solidarity," through disruption toward stability.[39] Thus a book review talks admiringly of a character who by falling in love achieves her essential nature and discovers her life's purpose: "The woman in her asserts herself, not in violent or conflicting emotions, but attains to a domination, as the sun rises above the mists."[40] Or, in a short story, as a man comes to terms with the death of an old childhood friend, "the storm of feeling passed away, and . . . having gained control of his emotions, [he] slowly lifted his face from his hands. . . ." At this moment in the story, the landscape surrounding the man reflects his attainment of tranquility: "It was very still," "the softest breath of June scarcely whispered in the pines overhead," and the landscape seemed "strangely at rest in the fervid brightness of the summer noon."[41]

The *Atlantic* acknowledges that natural as well as social upheavals can be ultimately progressive, admitting the often beneficial or creative aspects of turmoil and explosive energy, as long as that turmoil is to some extent contained and the explosive energy merely one part of a larger stable state. But the text's broad emphasis on calm and control clearly sits well with a conservative view of social order and a strong attraction to authoritarian intellectual and legal control. This attitude, in fact, is what seems to connect the text's apparently detached geographical/scientific interest in distant natural disasters with its more alarmed interest in the less concrete forms of destabilization that were apparently threatening familiar social or political relationships. Not surprisingly, faced with rising immigration, political uncertainty, the intellectual shock of theories of evolution, shifts in morals and in normative social behavior, and the rapid expansion of both the national territory and the empires of science and technology, the reader/writer community implied by the *Atlantic's* text in the early 1880s has a strong incentive to reassure itself by rehearsing its faith in its own control of circumstance.

"In America," says Shaler, writing on the floods of the Mississippi Valley, "there is far more unity in the destiny of the land" than existed in Europe, and so "blessings and curses have a wider, freer range."[42] He goes on to imply that this geographical unity, this common vulnerability, demands of Americans a unified sense of destiny and purpose. Just as the nation should respond as one to the problems of the Mississippi water system, so it should respond, for example, to the apparently looming threat of "a really serious fight between capital and labor, or between wealth and poverty."[43] A character in W. H. Bishop's serialized novel *The House of a Merchant Prince* describes the problem in a speech that hints at the figurative connection between communism and volcanoes, riots and earthquakes:

> An alarming spirit of socialistic revolt has already appeared, and who shall say to what lengths it may reach? Communism in a republic, with all our safety-valves, our opportunities for expansion and legal redress, our equality of rights, which should obviate the need of it, is a more dangerous symptom perhaps than under monarchical governments. . . . Abroad there are great standing armies always ready to put down disturbances. But here . . . suppose the mob take it into their heads to be offended at the kind of dwelling our host lives in: what is to prevent their bringing it clattering down about his ears?[44]

Quite conventionally, the *Atlantic* identifies conservative values and social tradition with mountains, associating movements toward change—viewed with alarm as forms of social disorder—with storms and tremors. For the *Atlantic*, "the two summits" of social stability are church and state; "often clouded, covered with snow, or hidden by mist," these twin mountains are nonetheless "resting on foundations adamantine, immovable"; and as long as the peaks "are seen to abide, the race of men rests in security." But "when [they] seem to disappear, a sense of uneasiness disturbs the foundations of mind." "In America," we are warned, "effort is being made to remove both of these pillars," as "the swelling tide of agnosticism washes away the shores of belief."[45] In the same vein, a prominent poet is revered as a "venerable and sturdy product of American democracy," as, indeed, "a sort of human mountain."[46]

While William Cullen Bryant can be both a democrat and a mountain, there is at the same time a strong line of figurative expression in the *Atlantic* that connects democracy itself with storm and tremor. An 1880 essay on "Equality" assumes that "some notion of 'the equality of men'" led to "the socialistic and communistic ideas which . . . broke out with volcanic violence" in ancient Greece and Rome, and the same volume of the magazine describes how when the French revolution "swept like a whirlwind" through royal apartments, bringing a "wild blast" of change, a Madame Vigée le Brun floated through the "unprecedented convulsions and catastrophes it was her lot to witness" just as "a bit of thistle-down might float over a lava torrent."[47] Still, the reshuffling of established social structure could be creative as well as destructive. A description of the European origins of modern democracy emphasizes both aspects of the cataclysm:

> This vast power had been so chained down that men had almost ceased to reckon upon it, and when it burst its bonds in France, and made Europe quiver from centre to circumference, every one was aghast at the mighty force which had slumbered hardly dreamed of at their side. The first effects of this unfettering of the popular strength and energy were of course terribly destructive, and then came the ebb of the tide; but the democratic movement has, through all, gone steadily forward, and is to-day the dominant impulse and influence in the affairs of men.[48]

The very foundation of the American republic, then, is potentially explosive, and not unnaturally it is the past eruptions that are taken to be creative while those in the future still seem only terrifying. Harriet Beecher Stowe's enormously influential novel *Uncle Tom's Cabin* can thus be comfortably remembered for its role in the eventual (creative) destruction of the slavery system as "the murmur which precedes the earthquake" of "the greatest social revolution of ancient or modern times," while in the present moment in 1882, caught between unions and capitalists, "we hear mutterings of a coming storm" or "feel ourselves caught in the whirl of new forces, and flung forward every day a step farther into a future dim with the portents of a struggle between Titans reared on steam, electricity, and credit." Meanwhile, popular political feeling was decidedly volcanic. So (for example) in the widespread grassroots determination to rise up against "machine politics," a commentator in 1884 could see that "there [was] likely to be considerable fire and lava thrown up, and some political burials under the ashes of the volcano."[49]

The volcano is ambiguously energetic, devastating in the short term but creative in the end, a potent symbol for a conservative community proudly finding its roots in revolution. Disruption is interesting after all as long as it eventually comes to an end and everyone gets what they deserve. The reconstruction of a sense of order takes time, as does the reconstruction of a building. The restructuring of the college curriculum, criticized in the *Atlantic* of 1883, seems at the time to be less a reordering than a collapse, leading to "a confused jumble of studies," and "creating the painful impression that the old curriculum has been shaken by an earthquake." On the other hand, the intellectual confusion in Shakespeare studies that had sprung from the comparison of two competing editions of *Hamlet* had reached a slightly later stage in the aftermath of disaster—in 1881, it still clearly represented "the confusion of an intellectual earthquake" but, "as after an earthquake," the scholar writing on the topic admits, it was clear that "although some parts of what has gone to ruin have been lost in the catastrophe, we have around us the scattered fragments of the whole."[50]

Covering the breadth of the field of social relations, from national politics to family arguments, the image of the natural disaster, like a volcano, itself provides a safety valve for trapped heat. Applied to situations of stress and conflict from revolution to romance, it defuses the moment by containing it within a familiar image of ultimately creative energy itself contained within the norms of nature. People, of course, are volcanic and stormy: Andrew Jackson had his "violent prejudices, uncurbed and stormy passions"; John Quincy Adams's strong feelings would sometimes "burst forth like a volcano, as if beyond his control"; Thomas Carlyle, when excited, "was like the eruption of a volcano,—thunder and lightning, hot stones, and smoke and ashes"; the election of a country boy to attorney general in one of C. E. Craddock's mountain stories shows how "his talents had burst through the stony crust of circumstance, like the latent fires of a volcano."[51] Volcanic politicians and national leaders become so common after a while in these pages that when Henri III is described as having "a compressed energy and a certain elevation of manner," that oblique phrase alone seems enough to make the point.[52] The *Atlantic*, in its privileging of repose, does not deny the need for the expression of turmoil, and perhaps these public figures fulfill some social function as representative vents for general frustration, as one of Sarah Orne Jewett's sea captains, being "an uncommon swearer," is described as belonging to that group of people who "seem to serve as volcanoes or outlets for the concealed anger of poor human nature." The explosions that accompany these moments of intense energy seem often to be taken as healthy and natural, like the tears of anger that "are geyser-jets dashed over volcanic fires, fervent extinguishers and not unaccompanied by vapor, smoke, and detonation."[53]

Perhaps the closest the reader of the *Atlantic* gets to the core of creative disaster is in the love scenes of the magazine's fiction; there, "the passion of the story is powerful," the reader experiences "a pent-up energy," and "when the storm of love bursts the reader is swept along by it"—this, from a review of short stories by the Scandinavian writer Björnstjerne Björnson. But these moments of passion, when the readers come closest to finding themselves swept off the bridge and into the flood, are always firmly located in the safe structures of a reliably conventional house of fiction. Nonetheless, they are volcanic moments. As G. P. Lathrop explains in his serialized story "An Echo of Passion":

> The stream of human passion is poured out from unseen sources like a living fire, but it hardens on the top in a thin lava surface, upon which we walk in all the security of convention. It needs only a narrow seam to let the burning reality jet upward and melt away the crust we are treading. A few words had placed those two on a totally altered footing.

"Those two" now find themselves on the unfamiliar but exciting footing of the naval officer and the dweller in a city of earthquakes.[54]

Nonetheless, even romance is not consistently volcanic, and "the normal condition of a healthy society is not . . . fierce conflict . . . any more than a thunderstorm is the normal condition of any tolerable climate." Moments of stormy passion are incidents within what the *Atlantic* needs to understand as the large-scale stability of a natural and a social world, and the narrative voice is there at all times to provide that sense of context. As obedient readers, we are obliged, in general, not to be "swept along" by anything, but instead to look for "the foundations of order and stability." He "who can look beneath the surface of the political froth that obscures the deep-moving currents" has the discernment to see "the real power" where it moves, we are told, and we need to understand, as did the ancient Greeks, "that what seems to us evil is often in reality a great good, and that the destructive forces are as essential as the productive." We must move on from turmoil to true repose, "the repose of the strong artist, who has overcome" figurative disaster—"the searchings, the explorations, the deep discouragements, of a spirit stormy and passionate, moved by noble impulses, but driven from without by forces not yet subdued to its high will."[55] It is the "high will" of the artist that contains disaster in text, as it is the high will of the American people that must, for the *Atlantic*, absorb threats both geographical and social within the unified nation.

One of the most basic rhetorical problems of the *Atlantic* in the period from 1880 through 1884 is its need to acknowledge social and cultural instability in such a way as to suggest that while it is explosive, it is either progressive or containable, or both. One way it achieves this is by articulating these instabilities in figurative images of natural disaster. By identifying (for example) an explosive politician as "volcanic," the text associates the unpredictability of the man's behavior with a force it believes to be part of an essentially ordered and meaningful nature. By reconfiguring the real threat of a disruption in the human world in the form of a relatively conventional reference to a natural context, the text defuses the potency of the social threat and even manages to contain or embed it within a well-wrought sentence produced by a confident and controlling narrative voice. Not only is the original anxiety-producing danger defused by displacement; the very act of expressing that danger through a figure of speech carries with it the reassuring implication of a level of detachment and an undisturbed intellectual power. As Shaler observes in his essay on hurricanes, there is a problem involved in studying disasters at close hand: "such conditions as they bring about are not favorable to close observation," because "no mind can see calmly when the body is in the very hands of death."[56] This is an unfortunate fact for the scientist, but an encouraging one for the reader of the *Atlantic*. If the text appears to be seeing things calmly, outlining even imminent disaster in a neatly crafted metaphor, then neither the writer nor the reader would appear to be "in the very hands of death." They are instead, at the closest, simply in the enthralled but safe position Shaler himself occupied as he stood "during the time of [a] February flood, on a bridge over the Ohio at Cincinnati, looking at the roaring mass of waters, full of wreckage of fences, bridges, houses, and barns, that gathered in quivering, changing heaps against each of the massive piers."[57] The key point here is that we are on the bridge, we are on the banks. While Joe is swept away, we are still standing on the safety of solid ground with Helen and Philip. And so when in the text we come upon floods of immigrants, floods of emotion, or floods of atheism, we are safe with the narrator on a bridge supported by massive piers, in a position of relative security metaphorically provided by the articulation of local fear through distant disaster, the containment of crisis by rhetoric.

NOTES

1. Louis James, "The Trouble with Betsy: Periodicals and the Common Reader in Mid-Nineteenth-Century England," in *The Victorian Periodical Press: Samplings and Soundings,* ed. Joanne Shattock and Michael Wolff (Leicester: Leicester University Press, 1982); Ellery Sedgwick, *The Atlantic Monthly 1857-1909: Yankee Humanism at High Tide and Ebb* (Amherst: University of Massachusetts Press, 1994). References to *The Atlantic Monthly* 1880-84 will give the author's name when it was included in the original Table of Contents. "Review" refers to an unsigned book review; "Contributor's Club" pieces come from a collection of unsigned comments and short essays printed at the end of each monthly issue.

2. "Some Recent Novels" (review), July 1880, 124.

3. Mike Hawkins, *Social Darwinism in European and American Thought, 1860-1945: Nature as Model and Nature as Threat* (Cambridge: Cambridge University Press, 1997), 18, 34.

4. Caroline E. Leighton, "Sylvan Station," July 1883, 118.

5. O. B. Frothingham, "Care for the People under Despotism," July 1882, 23.

6. "His Best," November 1880, 624-37.

7. Robert C. Bannister, *Social Darwinism: Science and Myth in Anglo-American Social Thought* (Philadelphia: Temple University Press, 1979; reprint with new preface, 1988), 17.

8. David N. Livingstone, *Nathaniel Southgate Shaler and the Culture of American Science* (Tuscaloosa: The University of Alabama Press, 1987), 86.

9. Livingstone, 219-20.

10. Livingstone, 86.

11. N. S. Shaler, "Hurricanes," March 1882, 330.

12. Fred Somkin, *Memory and Desire in the Idea of American Freedom, 1815-1860* (Ithaca, N.Y.: Cornell University Press, 1967).

13. Somkin, 38-39.

14. Somkin, 41.

15. Horace D. Warner, "Volcano Studies," October 1883, 508-15.

16. Horace D. Warner, "The City of Earthquakes," March 1883, 397-403.

17. Ibid., 398.

18. S. P. Langley, "Wintering on Aetna," July 1880, 38–47.

19. Luigi Monti, "Sicilian Hospitality," August 1880, 164; Langley, 47.

20. Warner, "Volcano Studies," 515.

21. Langley, 42.

22. N. S. Shaler, "The Red Sunsets," April 1884, 475-82.

23. Ibid., 475.

24. Ibid., 482.

25. E. W. Sturdy, "The Volcanic Eruption of Krakatoa," September 1884, 385-91.

26. Ibid., 386-87.

27. Ibid., 390-91.

28. N. S. Shaler, "The Future of Weather Foretelling," November 1880, 645-51; "Hurricanes," March 1882, 330-36; "The Floods of the Mississippi Valley," May 1883, 653-60.

29. Shaler, "Hurricanes," 331.

30. Shaler, "Floods," 660.

31. Shaler, "Weather Foretelling," 651.

32. Ibid., 645.

33. Ibid., 647.

34. Ibid., 651.

35. Shaler, "Floods," 660.

36. Shaler, "Hurricanes," 331.

37. Shaler, "Floods," 660.

38. Elizabeth Stuart Phelps, "Is God Good?" October 1881, 535-36.

39. "The Artist as an Individual" (Contributor's Club), July 1881, 139; John Fiske, "The Theory of a Common Origin for All Languages," November 1881, 664.

40. "Hardy's But Yet a Woman" (review), May 1883, 708.

41. P. Deming, "Tompkins," July 1883, 48.

42. Shaler, "Floods," 653.

43. W. H. Bishop, "The House of a Merchant Prince," August 1882, 232.

44. Ibid., 232.

45. O. B. Frothingham, "Art and Wealth," December 1882, 747.

46. "Two Journalists" (review), September 1883, 412.

47. "Equality," January 1880, 20; Henry James Jr., "En Province," August 1883, 172; "Madame Le Brun," May 1880, 703.

48. "Lecky's England in the 18th Century" (review), September 1882, 412.

49. "The Holmes Breakfast," Supplement to the *Atlantic* of February 1880, 3; M. H. Hardaker, "A Study in Sociology," August 1882, 219; Henry D. Lloyd, "The Political Economy of 73 Million Dollars," July 1882, 70; Laurence J. Laughlin, "The New Party," June 1884, 840.

50. Albert S. Bolles, "What Instruction Should Be Given in Our Colleges?" November 1883, 686; Richard Grant White, "The Two Hamlets," October 1881, 473.

51. "Andrew Jackson and John Randolph" (review), January 1883, 131; "Reminiscences of Washington," June 1880, 811; "Froude's Carlyle" (review), July 1882, 133; Charles Egbert Craddock, "Electioneerin' on Big Injun Mounting," January 1880, 102.

52. J. Brander Matthews, "The Dramas of the Elder Dumas," September 1881, 386.

53. Sarah Orne Jewett, "An Only Son," November 1883, 675; "A Plea for Tears" (Contributor's Club), August 1882, 281.

54. "Björnstjerne Björnson's Stories" (review), January 1883, 129; George Parsons Lathrop, "An Echo of Passion," April 1882, 446.

55. "Julian's Political Recollections," April 1884, 562; Edward Atkinson, "The Unlearned Professions," June 1880, 751; Elizabeth Robins, "Evil in Greek Mythology," September 1882, 323; "Björnson's Stories," 130.

56. Shaler, "Hurricanes," 331.

57. Shaler, "Floods," 655.

7

"Nothing Ends Here"

Managing the Challenger Disaster

Ann Larabee

When the space shuttle Challenger *exploded in 1986, defenders of the space program and the technocultural order of which it is a part scrambled to shore up their project. Through the lens of the shuttle disaster, Ann Larabee investigates the visions of domestic safety and harmonious social order advanced by promoters of a utopian future of life in self-contained microenvironments. Their utopian visions, Larabee contends, actually present a destitute, fatalistic, homogeneous cultural future in which survival becomes containment—a reign of threat that demands rationing, regulation of movement, forced production, sanctions against intimacy, and constant surveillance.*

THE COLD WAR'S endlessly replayed rhetoric of security and containment culminated in 1983 with Ronald Reagan's proposal of the Strategic Defense Initiative (SDI), a space-age umbrella that would deflect a storm of nuclear weapons. Such a technology would need a means of deployment, a way of getting the hardware—including counterattack weapons and satellite surveillance systems—into space. That was to be a primary task of NASA shuttle missions. Although Reagan had initiated the idea of a teacher in space as part of his 1980 presidential campaign, the space shuttle's unifying nationalist spirit was closely allied with strategic defense.

The optimistic rhetoric of the Reagan years asserted that complex technological systems were the answer to technological apocalypse. As Reagan would explain ten years after introducing SDI, "If our nation and our precious freedoms are worth defending with the threat of annihilation, we are surely worth defending by defensive means that ensure our survival."[1] Those means were to be a technological fix created and maintained by a patriotic workforce. In his first call for the project, Reagan urged the nation to begin a "formidable, technical task" by "turning to the very strengths in technology that spawned our great industrial base."[2] The import of Reagan's rhetoric extended beyond state-supported space projects to a national philosophy that technological systems would protect citizens from the very dangers these systems created. Thus, SDI was a symbolic modernist project of what Ulrich Beck has termed the "risk society."[3] The circular production of danger and safety played against media coverage of technological accidents, most spectacularly the Three Mile Island nuclear plant's radiation leak in 1979 and Union Carbide's chemical release in Bhopal in 1984. While these could be dismissed as corporate mishandling, the *Challenger* space shuttle disaster in January 1986, followed within months by the Chernobyl meltdown, called into question a national identity embodied in the rhetoric of high-tech development, necessitated by competition with an Evil Empire.

Although in his speech honoring the *Challenger* crew, Reagan was quick to say that "nothing ends here," the national media was asking, "Why so many disasters? What has happened to the technological fix?"[4] Throughout the rest of the 1980s and into the 1990s, as the cold war waned, these questions prompted a review of national identity, with frequent solicitations of a renewed technological faith. The beleaguered NASA provided a working model not only for fixing a faulty organization and restoring space projects, but for imaginatively projecting versions of a safety culture, a technoculture in which even the smallest everyday dangers might be closely monitored and contained. From the politicians and astronauts presiding over the *Challenger* hearings to the sociologists, political scientists, organizational theorists, and spaceologists who acted as consultants, professional knowledge workers projected their high-tech anxieties into survival fantasies of escape in technological lifeboats, where safety became the organizing principle.

LIFEBOAT

A symbol of preparedness and accurate prediction, the lifeboat is both a physical and a psychological escape from technocultural terrors and, more ambiguously, a condensed version of that same technoculture. It is an institutional answer to disaster: a scaled-down model of institutional systems in which people are rendered beholden to an authority that may be exercised in extreme ways. The lifeboat presents concentrated power as essentially beneficent, the only solution to disaster, and therefore worthy of cooperation. And exercises of power are justified by the limited technological structure that determines survival, a determinism not possible in more open, expansive ecologies.

In a radioactive, polluted, terrorist, and generally chaotic world, one must move to a smaller, safer box, ideally the hermetic world of the harmoniously functioning, disaster-resistant enclosure, an artificial biosphere that will ensure extraplanetary human survival. The spaceship is a grander version of the lifeboat, designed to move the postindustrial knowledge class away from earthly disasters and into biotechnical systems thinking. Space advocates have long promoted the idea of space travel as a hedge against disaster, most extravagantly the threat of a dying sun: "Remember, the sun blows up in ten billion years, so it's quite clear—we either blow up with it, or it blows up with human descendants remaining alive somewhere beyond the solar system."[5] But the disaster has also been constructed more locally as a nuclear holocaust or the population "explosion": "It is possible . . . to list many excellent practical reasons why Mankind ought to conquer space, and the release of atomic power has added a new urgency to some of these. Moreover, the physical resources of the planet are limited."[6] Because the spaceship has even more limited resources and drifts through a hostile environment replete with cosmic radiation, it is a scaled-down rendering of disaster culture, in which safety and survival provide the overriding logic and in which survivors are selected on the basis of professional skill. These survivors not only are subjected to, but participate in the disciplinary work of surveillance and observation that seemingly keeps the lifeboat safe, a work possible only in such a microenvironment.

However, the spaceship/lifeboat began to look dangerous indeed when the *Challenger* space shuttle exploded, after being heralded as "one of the most significant technological achievements of the century" and the solution to human survival in a rejuvenated space program.[7] Critics of NASA asked why there were no lifeboats for the lifeboat, no means of escaping a largely untested, inevitably disastrous technology, made up of more than 700 critical components, any one of which might cause a fatal accident. Although space enthusiasts may have promoted the spaceship as a lifeboat in itself, a way of escaping a doomed planet and sowing the seeds of *Homo sapiens* across the universe, the shuttle disaster demonstrated that the lifeboat is not especially life-sustaining. The *Challenger* seven lived to experience a gruesome drift, the long descending spiral to the ocean where impact crushed the crew cabin. One of the media lessons of the *Challenger* disaster was that in high-tech enclosures, catastrophe is inescapable and its victims—even friendly teachers—have no viable means of ejection. This televised spectacle of claustrophobia and futility riveted millions, who helplessly watched the exploding microcosm of postindustrial life. Gregory Whitehead writes that the media's construction of the *Challenger* disaster was a "thanaturgical excess of fire + fire + light," a Futurist's necrodrama provoking dread and shock.[8]

The Rogers Commission investigation of the accident attempted to restore this faith in the safety of all human-technology relations, not only in high-tech microenvironments such as space shuttles but in the more familiar technosphere of daily life as well. The Rogers Commission determined that the shuttle exploded because of the hot gas breach of a seal, an O-ring. In an effort to make this understandable to the public, government officials and journalists made these faulty parts seem as simple as putty and rubber washers, familiar to anyone with a leaky faucet. In her thorough investigation of the organizational communications leading to the shuttle disaster, sociologist Diane Vaughan describes her own difficulties in understanding the technical details of the leaky joint, first imagining it to be a Nerf ball and then a "rubber ring between a Mason jar and its lid."[9] The booster seal was the central focus of testimony from engineers, who described evidence from earlier shuttle flights of "blow-by"—the leaking of hot gases from the booster seals. Blow-by was indicated by the presence of soot, ranging in color from gray to black. According to Morton Thiokol engineer and whistle-blower Roger Boisjoly, black soot, which appeared when the seal was subjected to cold temperatures, indicated that it was going "away from the direction of goodness."[10] When the *Challenger* was launched under cold temperatures on the morning of January 28, the seal failed completely and the shuttle caught fire. The Rogers Commission verified suspicions that the poorly designed seal of the right solid rocket booster was the technical cause of the accident. But it also accused the managers of NASA and its contractor for the solid rocket boosters, Morton Thiokol, of not heeding early warnings from engineers about the faulty seals.

Consisting of five published volumes, including 1,700 pages of testimony and numerous appendices containing charts, graphs, and parts lists, the Rogers Commission report resembles the documentation in product liability trials that sets out to allocate the responsibility for the technological failures of daily life—faulty wiring, exploding gas tanks, toys small enough to choke infants. According to Elaine Scarry, the product liability trial is a *"cultural self-dramatization*: The courtroom is a communal arena in which civilization's ongoing expectations about objects are overtly (and sometimes noisily) announced."[11] Here, a narrative of disaster is constructed in order to restore civilization:

> Implicit in this mimesis of restorability is the belief that catastrophes are themselves (not simply narratively but actually) reconstructable, the belief that the world can exist, usually does exist, should in this instance have existed, and may in this instance be "remakable" to exist, without . . . slippage.[12]

Part of this remaking is enacted through compensation for bodily injury, a healing of technological wounds through judgment and financial reward.

Like the judge and jury in a product liability case, the Rogers Commission was certainly engaged in a remaking of civilization and its projects. Revisionist risk theorists see disasters as opportunities for reconstructing dangerous institutions through a minute investigation: "each piece of physical evidence . . . becomes a kind of fetish object, painstakingly located, mapped, tagged, and analyzed, with findings submitted to boards of inquiry."[13] But there is a larger necessity embedded here: regaining public trust in big technological projects that reify national identity. The trial was enacted before the public eye, a national demonstration to restore the narrative of technological progress by means of testimony from scientific experts. The Commission's broad mandate was to "review the circumstances surrounding the accident" and "develop recommendations for corrective or other action."[14] And this mandate was framed by a "firm national resolve"[15] to restore the space program—a program that has reified cultural identity around a supposedly common endeavor that transcends cultural differences, preservation of the species from wholesale disaster. In the many reiterations of the steps that led to disaster, in the meticulous documentation of the shuttle components' performance and NASA decision-making hierarchies, the Rogers Commission report sought to reinvent the nation and its technological projects without blow-by and slippage.

The most spectacular moment in the Rogers Commission's testimony was when Commission member and eminent physicist Richard Feynman dropped a bit of O-ring material into a glass of ice water to prove its lack of resiliency under cold temperatures. Immediately picked up by the press, who lionized Feynman, this simple impromptu experiment seemed to cut through the waffling, confusing, jargon-riddled rhetoric of the NASA decision makers' testimony. But perhaps more importantly, the experiment demonstrated that catastrophic failure occurs in basic technological parts and everyday household experience. As Boisjoly later claimed, "most failures usually occur because some minor subsystem gives: 25-cent washers, $2.50 bolts, $25 clevis pins."[16] The press claimed whistle-blowers Feynman and Boisjoly as heroes precisely because they seemed to expose the simple truth about quotidian life in the technological age. Our most familiar objects carry incipient, unforeseen, body-threatening dangers. The preface to the Rogers Commission report states,

> The Commission construed its mandate somewhat broadly to include recommendations on safety matters not necessarily involved in this accident but which require attention to make future flights safer. Careful attention was given to concerns expressed by astronauts because the Space Shuttle program will only succeed if the highly qualified men and women who fly the Shuttle have confidence in the system.[17]

As a public hearing on body-technology relations, the Commission's report attempted to restore confidence in even minor subsystems, to reinstate a national faith in technological existence, made safe through vigilance and the most minute surveillance, down to the thumbtacks.

DISAPPEARING BODIES

Most strikingly absent from the remade world of the technocratic Rogers Commission report is any effort to reconstruct and assess bodily damage. Although it opens with the now famous photograph of the smiling shuttle astronauts and payload specialists in their shiny sky-blue space suits, posed with an American flag and a toy

FIGURE 7.1. The crew of the space shuttle *Challenger*. Courtesy of NASA.

model of the *Challenger*, the report contains no discussion of the bodies. Often working on their hands and knees in low-visibility conditions, salvage divers found the corpses several weeks after the accident. After a civilian diver spotted a space suit, the Navy team discovered the crew compartment where they "could read the nametags on the astronauts' blue flight suits."[18] The Rogers Commission took testimony until early May but received almost no forensic evidence, nor did the Commission express any desire for such evidence, stating publicly that this would be inappropriate and outside its jurisdiction.[19] The only exception lies in the testimony of FBI special agent Stanley Klein, who reported on February 7:

> We do have human hair, Negro hair, Oriental hair, and hair from two different brown-haired Caucasians, and what is interesting, according to the laboratory, is that there were no signs of heat damage to any of the hair, which was surprising. The hair came from face seals, fragments of helmets, and helmet liners, and headrests.[20]

This reduction to anonymity of NASA's highly touted racially and ethnically diverse shuttle crew was quickly passed over in favor of a discussion of possible laser terrorism by Libyan dissidents and Puerto Rican pro-independence groups.

The Rogers Commission followed NASA's lead. NASA's position in the disaster's aftermath was that the astronauts and payload specialists had died instantly, or at least were rendered instantly unconscious, an assumption easily accepted by television viewers who had watched the fiery crash. However, careful study of footage from the disaster clearly revealed that the crew compartment had hurtled to the ocean intact during a nearly three-minute descent, and NASA later revealed that some crew members had activated and used their emergency air packs. Controversy arose over NASA's original transcript of the voice recorder, in which pilot Michael Smith's ominous "Uh-oh" was elided. Attempting to restore public faith in technology, neither NASA nor the Rogers Commission was very willing to admit that the crew might have known its fate and suffered.

The strict control of information surrounding the bodies of the lost *Challenger* astronauts and payload specialists had purposes beyond delicacy and respect for the crew's loved ones. Their drawn-out and horrifying deaths had to be suppressed in the interests of continuing manned space flight. With eminent astronauts Sally Ride and Neil Armstrong participating, the presidential investigative committee remained committed to manned space flight, hearing from other astronauts such as former *Challenger* pilot Paul Weitz, who testified that "man can do many wonderful things in orbit."[21] However, Weitz also suggested, "Every time you get people inside and around the Orbiter you stand a chance of inadvertent damage of whatever type, whether you leave a tool behind or whether you, without knowing it, step on a wire bundle or a tube or something along those lines."[22] Although the enormously complicated technologies of the space shuttle might, in ideal circumstances, provide a secure enclosure for experimental human and animal bodies, those bodies are marked by mundane clumsiness, inadvertent behaviors, everyday chance, and uncertainty.

Furthermore, bodies are not especially suited to life in space. On long flights they are subject to muscle and bone deterioration and weight loss, and ubiquitous radiation may damage reproductive organs. As NASA consultant Harry Shipman explains in his book about the future of space flight after the *Challenger* accident, bodies pollute spacecraft, contaminating them with sweat and transforming them into smelly "urine dumps."[23] While male astronauts in the good old days used catheters and plastic bags, the presence of women necessitates more elaborate plumbing—the shuttle's zero-gravity toilet, the "slinger," caused "serious problems in actual use and . . . required a good bit of cleaning."[24] During the May 1985 flight of the *Challenger*, twenty-four rats and two squirrel monkeys being tested for their responses to weightlessness produced an unanticipated "flood" of feces, so that the uncomfortable crew had to wear face masks.[25] The scatological body, especially the female or animal body, mars the strictly hygienic myth of the clean machine. A dead body is even worse.

The fundamental question in the decades-long argument over manned space flight is whether bodies need to be present at all. As the eminent physicist James Van Allen wrote in the wake of the *Challenger* disaster, "all the truly important utilitarian and scientific achievements of our space program have been made by instrumented, unmanned spacecraft controlled remotely by radio command from stations on the earth."[26] If humans on Earth can operate highly sensitive space robot arms and eyes or drift remotely through hallucinatory worlds more fantastic than alien planets, why are their bodies necessary in space? Recommending entirely automated extraplanetary operations for a renewed space program, artificial intelligence expert Marvin Minsky writes, "As for safety, *no one gets injured when no one is there*."[27] The loss of the *Challenger* seven called into question NASA's commitment to the "man-machine mode" in space travel and made its defense of a human presence in space even more controversial. In its 1985 study *The Human Role in Space* (THURIS), NASA laid out its theory of cybernetics, insisting on the presence of humans in a largely autonomous system:

> There is no such thing as an unmanned space system: everything that is created by the system designer involves man in one context or another; everything in our human existence is done by, for, or against man. The point at issue is to establish in every system context the optimal role of each man-machine component.[28]

THURIS created a taxonomy for human-machine interactions: manual (hand tools), supported (manned maneuvering units), augmented (power tools, microscopes), teleoperated (remote control systems), supervised (computer functions with human supervision), and independent (artificial intelligence). These categories do not make much sense in themselves; clearly some manual manipulation is required for power tools, and microscopes, wrenches, and hammers augment and support human capabilities. But the taxonomy inscribes a fossil record, a technological evolution toward "self-actuating," "self-healing," independent machines.[29] The THURIS authors hoped that such independent machines would require human intervention and attempted to describe uniquely human contributions to largely automated space enterprises. Humans, they argued, possess the unique capacity for visual evaluation, motor coordination appropriate to complex assembly, and mental powers of interpretation, innovation, deduction, and judgment. (Recent developments in artificial neural networks and fuzzy logic call even these "human" powers into question.)

This discussion of what makes a human presence necessary to space technologies reflected broader cultural anxieties about the changing nature of work, an apparent shift to an "informated" postindustrial society, identified by work historian Shoshana Zuboff in *In the Age of the Smart Machine* (1984). Zuboff argues that new computer technologies have destabilized traditional work hierarchies and erased embodied techniques. Unlike automating, the "informating" of production not only replaces the laboring body, but puts production under continuous surveillance, redefines skill as symbol manipulation, and redeploys the body as a social instrument for organizational communication.[30] Zuboff proposes two possible scenarios for the future of the informated workplace: one in which managers reconstruct their authority by emphasizing a panoptic, "fail-safe" machinic intelligence over worker knowledge, and one in which workers are encouraged to use new "critical judgment" in "understanding and manipulating" instrumentalized information, resulting in a blurring of traditional power relations and greater collaboration.[31] Clearly promoting the second alternative, Zuboff argues for a "fertile interdependence between the human mind" and its machines and a "comprehensive vision" of harmonious domestic relations and individual fulfillment made possible through this interdependence.[32] Like the THURIS authors and many other critics of artificial intelligence in the 1980s, Zuboff defends human contributions, unparalleled by the machine: "The informated organization . . . relies on the human capacities for teaching and learning, criticism and insight."[33] *In the Age of the Smart Machine* articulated a new technorational, utopian organization for fertile knowledge workers, decontextualized from other ecologies and social relations.

This dream of a productive informed worker, unique and essential to the corporate machine, took a nationally symbolic shape in the promotion of the space program, always a public forum for elites invested in high technologies. The knowledge worker, proficient at operating, interpreting, and mediating new technologies, replaced the cold war's spaceman, who displayed physical endurance and psychological stamina within the hostile technosystem of the claustrophobic capsule. Thus, the *Challenger* crew included a social studies teacher, an electrical engineer, a physicist, and a corporate representative from the Hughes Aircraft Company. The crew represented a populist presence in space: entirely informed workers living happily within the machine, untainted by global political and environmental concerns, their function to dispense information to outside observers. Dwarfed by the massive shuttle, their mission was to mediate and domesticate the machine for a young television audience—Christa McAuliffe was to have taken her remote students on a video field trip around the Orbiter. But after the destruction of the harmonious technoworld presided over by a teacher mom, psychologists and grief specialists raced in to erase the spectacle of graphic technological violence and the imagination of Christa McAuliffe's body. In the discourse of the *Challenger* disaster, the corpses of the shuttle crew had to remain behind the technological veil, in the interests of continuing manned space flight and the cultural renegotiation of the necessary body.

However, the many popular jokes emanating from the *Challenger* disaster often involved those bodies in quite graphic ways. These jokes present the body/technology interface as a spectacularly violent one, in marked contrast to the cultural ideal in which interaction between the human body and the machine is a flow state:

Q: What do you call a burnt penis on the Florida shore?
A: A shuttlecock.[34]

Q: What was the last thing that went through Christa McAuliffe's head?
A: A piece of fuselage.[35]

Q: Why didn't they put showers on the *Challenger*?

A: Because they knew that everyone would wash up on shore.[36]

Based on familiar rhetorical patterns and cycles, these "sick" jokes have been called political cynicism, a rebellion against the mass media's pompous reverence, a critique of national institutions, and an alleviation of death anxieties in the nuclear age.[37] We expect our technologies to be transparent so that ideally we are scarcely aware of the machine's presence in the cybernetic flow. Skilled operators are supposed to become one with their machines; distinctions between the organic and the technological disappear in harmonious signal and response. Technological disaster shifts the terms of that interaction, for here technology violently entraps, penetrates, and chars the body locked in its embrace. It is this possibility that evokes both national efforts at repression and the return of the repressed through the joke cycle. In a national spectacle of disaster, the body is the pain of technological violence that can never be represented, but only displaced by word and image. Thus, the body must be reconstructed within an organizational safety model, a lifeboat, that denies any further possibility of collapse.

GROUPTHINK

The national hearing on the space shuttle disaster attempted to restore the idea of a safe and efficient manned organization, made possible through more fluent exchanges of information. The Rogers Commission report made it clear that NASA's organizational culture was to blame in the decision to launch the space shuttle despite icy weather and faulty booster seals. Thus, NASA's management, as well as failed machine parts, became an object of study. NASA's organization was represented in the Rogers Commission report as a self-regulating system without external surveillance or intervention, a situation sociologist Diane Vaughan credited, in part, to NASA's secret military projects.[38] An effective external regulator would have had access to classified materials, an unacceptable risk in the cold war climate. Without external reality checks, many critics suggested, NASA had become isolated in its own delusional can-do ideology, derived from its Apollo mission successes. Furthermore, observing the "contradictory" and "rancorous" displays of agency infighting at the hearings, *The New Re-*

public suggested that NASA itself seemed to be experiencing a midlife crisis.[39] The modern organizational man was exposed and displayed through the figure of the NASA administrator, locked in a decaying airtight compartment of his own making and possessed of the wrong stuff.

In the scientific press, especially in the first assessments of the disaster, some attempt was made to blame NASA's rank and file. A few weeks after the disaster, *Science* twice reported that an internal review of the shuttle had found "relaxed workplace standards" including "worker inexperience, lack of motivation, and faulty equipment."[40] Furthermore, it indicated that NASA's investigation included speculation that workers had forgotten to plug a hole in the faulty booster after a leak test.[41] Despite the search for "inadvertent damage" caused by flawed workers, blame was soon leveled at NASA's and Morton Thiokol's decision makers, who came to represent a nationwide corrupt power elite, now open to investigation. Charles Perrow, whose study of accidents in complex systems would often be evoked in discussions of the *Challenger,* decried the "Pentagon effect" at NASA that created a climate of managerial self-aggrandizement and toadying to corporate and military sponsors and the media.[42] Journalist and longtime NASA observer Malcolm McConnell blamed ambitious policy makers engaged in "the political intrigue and compromise, the venality and hidden agendas" that led to disaster.[43] In another account, Joseph Trento called the disaster a political failure, quoting shuttle mission specialist John Fabian on the *Challenger* investigation: "It just unraveled like Watergate."[44] Thus, discussions of the *Challenger* disaster spread beyond mechanical error to wide critiques of postindustrial capitalists, skilled at political manipulations in a secretive high-tech world.

The national media hearkened back to NASA's glory days, suggesting that the organization had devolved, degenerated, decayed from a golden age of right rule, benevolent and safety-conscious. The same space journalists who attacked a highly politicized NASA rhapsodized about the pride and the glory, the "heroic neoclassical élan of the moon race."[45] Little connection was made to NASA's ever-recurring technical failures, including the horrifying Apollo space capsule fire that trapped three screaming astronauts in a fiery furnace and melted them into a nylon puddle. Nor was much mention made of NASA's origins: the "Rocket State" developed in tandem with nuclear weapons and fueled by cold-war paranoia.[46] This lack of a thorough cultural critique left a way open to NASA's salvation from a wholesale attack on the disastrous, deviant operations and inevitable risks of complex systems.

The vision of NASA as a once effective, now decadent organization was very appealing to academic theorists who set about to "fix" the agency, using it as a research model. In the flurry of sociological studies that followed the *Challenger* disaster, NASA's homogeneity and in-group ambience, its hidden agendas, political maneuvering, and back-stabbing, came to signify the internal workings of all corporations. Social theorists searched for ways to explain and heal the breach in orga-nizational systems, dissected and exposed in a public hearing, fanned by a nationally televised tragedy. Academia, in itself a largely homoge-neous entity with its own industrial and military affiliations, responded to the *Challenger* disaster with a corporate consultant's enthusiasm. Dis-cussions of what went wrong with NASA became a common pedagog-ical tool in public administration, political science, and sociology courses.

Ensconced in university government documents sections, the five-volume Rogers Commission report provided an easily accessible text for application of organizational theory and systems models, based on information flow within conveniently closed circuits. According to or-ganizational theorists, NASA was, like the space shuttle itself, a mal-functioning but correctable system with faulty components—namely, NASA's and Morton Thiokol's managers and engineers and NASA's external and internal regulatory units. NASA had experienced blow-by and slippage in its communication linkages: some of Morton Thiokol's engineers had attempted to voice their fears about the faulty booster seals and cold-temperature launches to their bosses, who had essen-tially ignored what they considered unproven speculations.

Many theorists attributed the communication failure to NASA's fall from grace. According to this scenario, NASA once had "a less hierar-chical and flexible matrix structure" that relied on "nurturing consen-sus."[47] From these days of childhood innocence, the agency had grown increasingly isolated, streamlined, and pressurized, indulging in over-weening bureaupathological fantasies about its abilities despite budget cuts. In addition, NASA's components had become so highly special-ized in their activities, languages, and fundamental worldviews that, for example, the professional ethics of engineers did not match the ex-pedient decisions of managers.[48] Isolated from engineers, NASA's man-agement engaged in groupthink, driven by fantasies of invulnerability and a need for unanimity and cohesion.[49] Thus, the decision to launch the *Challenger* was a technocracy's "major malfunction."

Despite rumblings in the media that the space agency was in its last hours after an apocalyptic failure, academic theorists accepted NASA's continuing existence at face value. Like the shuttle, it was a machine that could be repaired through better interactions and linkages among its components.

The *Challenger* disaster provided organizational theorists with an opportunity to show that the systems model applied equally well to machines and to human societies. Using Charles Perrow's work on accidents in complex systems, Diane Vaughan wrote that technological failures could not be separated from organizational failures and that the language of systems applied to both. NASA "malfunctioned" because "The failure of one component interacts with others, triggering a complex set of interactions that can precipitate a technical system accident of catastrophic potential."[50] The use of systems theory in critiques of post-*Challenger* NASA is disputed by G. Richard Holt and Anthony W. Morris using Yrjö Engeström's activity theory, acknowledging that human activity is not technologically determined, but "messy, disorganized, seemingly chaotic, and hence endlessly fascinating."[51] To ensure safer space flights, Holt and Morris argue, NASA had to accept the internal contradictions and wide possible outcomes inherent in such human activity. Although the authors exposed gaps in systems models of NASA, their aim was to fix the agency as an information-processing system, a contradictory position in itself.

The *Challenger* catastrophe threatened political mythologies of the final frontier and, in a larger sense, cast doubt on systems theories and the entire cultural project of systems building. The models of organizational theorists reflected the strict methods of disciplines and vested interests in the national space program. A radical sense of discontinuity, uncertainty, potentiality, and violence—the ontological complexity of disaster—threatened the fundamental order of disciplines, apparatuses, and methods. Charles Perrow, who has argued against the indiscriminate, myopic building of dangerous complex systems, put this most forcefully: "Risky systems are full of failures. Inevitably, though less frequently, these failures will interact in unexpected ways, defeat the safety devices and bring down the system."[52] Thus, the academic response to the *Challenger* disaster was an effort to restore stable systems and, in an entirely self-referential mode, to reassure its academic audience of information workers that their systems, ideologies, disciplines, and bodies were still in place and all was right with the world. There might yet be a teacher in space.

TO THE STARS

One of the broader political outcomes of the *Challenger* disaster was a massive public relations campaign by space enthusiasts to resell the idea of manned space flight. In 1986, the National Commission on Space, appointed by Ronald Reagan, produced a strategic planning report on the future of space ventures that included renewed shuttle flights, construction of space station *Freedom,* increased space surveillance of the biosphere, and human settlement on the moon and Mars. In 1989, George Bush called for a lunar settlement by 2004 and a manned trip to Mars by 2019. In 1990, the United Nations endorsed 1992 as International Space Year (ISY), the quincentenary of Columbus's landing, inflaming the usual cant among U.S. politicians and space enthusiasts about human destiny, pioneering spirit, and life on the new frontier.

In that same year, Philip Robert Harris, a "management and space psychologist" and NASA consultant, published *Living and Working in Space: Human Behavior, Culture and Organization,* an attempt to justify the use of the behavioral sciences in space settlement design, using James Grier Miller's living systems theory. The book is introduced by Jesco von Puttkamer, a NASA program manager and strategic planner, who briefly describes the post-*Challenger* NASA as rejuvenated, ready to "penetrate the new frontier of space."[53] Von Puttkamer argues that the *Challenger* disaster provoked a public outpouring of support for manned space flight because of an "unconscious, unspoken feeling that we are dealing here with evolutionary forces at work."[54] In behavioral science, evolutionary biology, and artificial intelligence research, systems theory proposes that the biosocial world is made up of systems with interactive components that allow flows of information and energy.[55] According to these theorists, a natural, intuitive law dictates that systems evolve into more and more complex entities (for example, molecules-cells-organisms-ecosystems-biospheres, or cells-organisms-groups-societies-supranational sys-tems). Thus, the worldwide cybernetic information exchanges of the postindustrial world are seen as the result of thermodynamic, evolutionary processes leading to higher organizational levels.

Systems theorists associated with space programs see human expansion into space as the next organizational level beyond the biosphere. Thus, von Puttkamer writes that manned space travel allows "Man," "Earth," and "Space" to be "one single creative system," an "intricately closed-loop feedback system, a super-ecology."[56] In addition, extraplanetary artificial biospheres will be designed for what von Puttkamer predicts will be a new cybernetic species, a weightless species, floating in a space womb, transcending gravity and "entropic deterioration."[57]

The idea of an impending catastrophe is a favored reason for human extraplanetary expansion. During International Space Year, Charles Walker, assistant to the president at McDonnell Douglas and president of the National Space Society, explained his support of manned space exploration:

> Human survival. Political and economic survival in technical competition within the global economy, sure. But more than that: All human creation, all life as we know it, is here on earth. All our eggs are in one basket, one planet. But our embryonic resources are diminishing, and our nest becoming fouled. Our technological nature has given us the means to remove that risk.[58]

Here, haunted by the specter of catastrophe, the dreams and aspirations of the postindustrial knowledge class[59] have been given the shape of science fiction and justified through the nineteenth-century language of evolution and nature and the twentieth-century language of systems. Frequent evocations of "eggs," "embryos," "cradles," and "wombs" reinscribe sexual reproduction within an entirely mechanical environment, an exoskeleton of metal plates that will protect, control, and manage the human body and ensure the genetic continuation of the chosen spacefarers. Ironically, human sexual reproduction in space may actually be impossible under weightless, radioactive conditions.

In this fantasy of a postindustrial army in space, fears of impending accidents like the *Challenger* make all cultural expression a safety function. Indeed, space planners have invented a culture of catastrophe based on faith in prediction. Catastrophe provides the rationale for subsuming the disciplines under "spaceology," the transformation of the body into a stable energy-matter-information channel, and the continual mapping and surveillance of biotechnical system components. This national vision of the human future counters (and thus depends on) the construction of the thrilling and threatening mass media cyborg, imaged as the Terminator or Robocop, who performs destabilized and penetrated social identities.[60] Furthermore, the national science fiction of space travel seems reassuring next to the spectacles of disaster in the 1980s—not only the real-life disasters of leaking toxic chemicals and exploding machines, but those designed for entertainment: graphic nuclear holocausts with shriveling humans in flames; raging dinosaurs ripping men in half; artificially intelligent computer systems trapping and suffocating workers; buildings exploding and falling into rifts in the earth, crushing their inhabitants; planes crashing in an elegant bloody montage of flying shrapnel. Space planners reassure us that catastrophe is our origin and our nature: the Earth-crossing asteroid or comet that destroyed the dinosaurs "allowed a tiny creature, the ancestral mammal, to grow, differentiate, and fill vacated ecological niches, giving rise eventually to *Homo sapiens*."[61] Those asteroids can now be mined for hydrogen, carbon, and nitrogen to feed the transcendent biotechnical organism of the postindustrial knowledge class, emptied of troublesome memory, safe at last.

The political and social meanings of this consensual future are quite apparent in the imagined space settlements of *Living and Working in Space*. Philip Harris refers to the expansion of the human species, the global human family, into the solar system, fulfilling a natural urge for frontier exploration. But his space settlements are built and inhabited by only a segment of that family, the postindustrial knowledge class, envisioned as a cross-disciplinary group of scientists, engineers, technicians, corporate managers, psychologists, sociologists, anthropologists, physicians, teachers, journalists, lawyers, politicians, architects, filmmakers, and designers. Harris writes:

> The colonists to the New World during the eighteenth century were largely poor, ill-used white artisans and indentured servants, as well as African slaves. The prospects are that the space colonists of the twenty-first century will be more affluent and self-directed, better educated and chosen. Expertise is required of specialists in cross-cultural relocation and living in exotic environments to design systems for deployment and support of spacefarers.[62]

Thus, the *Challenger* disaster provided the text for the post-catastrophe survival of the knowledge class, constructed and maintained through systems theories. It suggested that technological and organizational systems were ever on the verge of collapse; the massive public relations campaign for space settlements imagines a safe new artificial biosphere, a closed ecology, for the chosen: academics, civil servants, and corporate managers, freed from environmental disaster, atmospheric impurity, starvation, poverty, disease, and gravity. Harris suggests that this cross-disciplinary community will result in a transformation of human consciousness, a spirit of fertile interdependence and informated collaboration that will trickle down to the problematic Earth populations left behind. A compendium of recent work in space settlement planning, *Living and Working in Space* promotes the use of the behavioral sciences in mediating a technological environment for human habitation. As part of the space team, anthropologists, psychologists, and sociologists will maintain continual surveillance of human bodies, studying reproduction, sleep cycles, time sense, physical and mental stress, and the effects of weightlessness, isolation, and noise. "Artificial life" may produce time sense warps, "psychotic reactions," "spatial illusions," interpersonal conflict, depression, boredom, "anger displacement," a "need for dominance," motion sickness, water retention in the face, and a loss of body mass.[63] In addition, conflict might arise among disciplines, cultures, and ethnic groups.

The answer to controlling these human disturbances in techno-utopia is the application of James Grier Miller's general living systems theory, a complex symbol language of subsystems and processes. In a space environment, bodies become ingestors, distributors, converters, producers, extruders, and decoders, components in a biotechnical system for control of matter, energy, and information flows.[64] Thus, differences are transcended as humans become synergistic, ergonomically conditioned components in the metamachine. Here, the "informating" of knowledge workers in a postindustrial economy based on instantaneous communications, erosion of managerial hierarchies, the formation of strategic alliances and teams in electronic exchanges, and the potential for virtual universities and corporations is given stability under the rubric of mission success and safety.[65] Living systems theory provides the paradigm for a new, entirely planned microculture that will determine every facet of a spacefarer's existence, from decor to diet, from language to sex, for harmonious system functioning. Space planners stress the safety of their rationally managed synthetic biospheres, which include "storm shelters" for protection against solar flares.[66] As longtime space consultant David Criswell explains in his discussion of future space biospheres, inhabitants of "s'homes" (space homes) will have "feelings of safety [that] reasonably spring from the certain knowledge that their advanced technologies constructed, operated, and can constantly refine their places and build new ones."[67] Space planners construct the s'home as a protective technological matrix where consensual decision making takes place among productive knowledge workers devoted to mission safety. Thus, Ronald Reagan's dream of scientists gathering to create a space shield has been given a more sweeping iteration in the interdisciplinary fictions of artificial biospheres.

Lifeboat dreams such as these are not purely escapist fantasies but reproductions of disastrous conditions under apparently controllable circumstances. They imaginatively contain the disaster within narrow, conceivable parameters. As an expression of survival, they simply reiterate and summarize the technocultural formations that produce disaster in the first place. Such microenvironments present a destitute, fatalistic, homogeneous vision of a cultural future, despite their promoters' soothing rhetoric of domestic safety and harmonious social order. Survival becomes containment, a reign of threat under which rationing, control over movement, forced production, sanctions against intimacy, and constant surveillance are normalized. Workers participate willingly for protection from a destruction that is produced by the structure itself. For despite the rhetoric of a great ship launching humans into a utopian future, the lifeboat is a disaster waiting to happen.

NOTES

1. Ronald Reagan, "Statement on the Occasion of the Tenth Anniversary of the Strategic Defense Initiative," Washington, D.C., 23 March 1993.

2. Ronald Reagan, "Address to the Nation on National Security," 23 March 1983.

3. Beck argues that in risk societies, the production of hazards and their subsequent management create a modernist logic that revolves around control of anxieties rather than fulfillment of human needs. Ulrich Beck, *The Risk Society: Towards a New Modernity*, trans. Mark Ritter (Newbury Park, Calif.: Sage, 1992).

4. Abigail Trafford, "Living Dangerously," *U.S. News and World Report*, 19 May 1986, 19.

5. Jerome Clayton Glenn and George S. Robinson, *Space Trek: The Endless Migration* (Harrisburg, Pa.: Stackpole, 1978), 184.

6. Arthur C. Clarke, *The Exploration of Space* (New York: Harper & Row, 1959), 179.

7. Jerry Grey, *Beachheads in Space: A Blueprint for the Future* (New York: Macmillan, 1983), 3, 5.

8. Gregory Whitehead, "The Forensic Theatre: Memory Plays for the Postmortem Condition," *Performing Arts Journal* 12 (Spring 1990): 100-101.

9. Diane Vaughan, *The* Challenger *Launch Decision: Risky Technology, Culture, and Deviance at NASA* (Chicago: University of Chicago Press, 1996), 40.

10. Testimony of Roger Boisjoly, U.S. Presidential Commission on the Space Shuttle *Challenger* Accident, *Report to the President* (Washington, D.C.: The Commission, 1986), 785.

11. Elaine Scarry, *The Body in Pain* (New York: Oxford University Press, 1985), 304.

12. Ibid., 298.

13. Malcolm Gladwell, "Blowup," *New Yorker,* 22 January 1996, 32.

14. William P. Rogers, "Preface," *Report to the President,* 1.

15. Ibid.

16. Roger Boisjoly, "Interview with Tony Chiu," *Life*, March 1988, 220.

17. Rogers, "Preface," 1.

18. E. Foster-Simeon, "Picking Up the Pieces," *All Hands*, June 1986, 22.

19. Storer Rowley, "NASA Debates Whether Crew Was Aware in Shuttle Plunge," *Chicago Tribune,* 25 April 1996, C2.

20. Testimony of Stanley Klein, *Report to the President,* 213.

21. Testimony of P. J. Weitz, *Report to the President,* 1437.

22. Ibid.

23. Harry L. Shipman, *Space 2000: Meeting the Challenge of a New Era* (New York: Plenum, 1987), 315.

24. Ibid., 331.

25. Anastasia Toufexis, "Good Data and a Feces Crisis," *Time,* 13 May 1985, 61.

26. James A. Van Allen, "Myths and Realities of Space Flight," *Science* 232 (1986): 1075.

27. Marvin Minsky, "NASA Held Hostage: Human Safety Imposes Outlandish Constraints on the U.S. Space Program," *Ad Astra,* June 1990, 36.

28. Stephen B. Hall, ed., *The Human Role in Space: Technology, Economics and Optimization* (Park Ridge, N.J.: Noyes, 1985), v.

29. Ibid., 63.

30. Shoshana Zuboff, *In the Age of the Smart Machine: The Future of Work and Power* (New York: Basic Books, 1984), 23.

31. Ibid., 6.

32. Ibid., 7, 414.

33. Ibid., 414.

34. Collected by Elizabeth Radin Simons, "The NASA Joke Cycle: The Astronauts and the Teacher," *Western Folklore* 45 (1986): 269.

35. Ibid., 272.

36. Collected by Willie Smyth, "*Challenger* Jokes and the Humor of Disaster," *Western Folklore* 45 (1986): 244.

37. See Simons, "NASA Joke Cycle," 261-77; Smyth, "*Challenger* Jokes," 243-60; Patrick D. Morrow, "Those Sick *Challenger* Jokes," *Journal of Popular Culture* 20 (Spring 1987): 175-85; Elliot Oring, "Jokes and the Discourse on Disaster," *Journal of American Folklore* 100 (1987): 276-87; and Nicholas von Hoffman, "Shuttle Jokes," *The New Republic*, 24 March 1986, 14.

38. Diane Vaughan, "Autonomy, Interdependence, and Social Control: NASA and the Space Shuttle *Challenger*," *Administrative Science Quarterly* 35 (1990): 232.

39. Robert Bazell, "NASA's Mid-Life Crisis," *The New Republic*, 24 March 1986, 12.

40. Eliot Marshall, "The Shuttle Record: Risks, Achievements," *Science* 231 (1986): 664; R. Jeffrey Smith, "Shuttle Inquiry Focuses on Weather, Rubber Seals, and Unheeded Advice," *Science* 231 (1986): 911.

41. Smith, "Shuttle Inquiry," 911.

42. Charles Perrow, "Risky Systems: The Habit of Courting Disaster," *Nation*, 11 October 1986, 354.

43. Malcolm McConnell, *Challenger: A Major Malfunction* (New York: Doubleday, 1987), x.

44. John J. Trento, *Prescription for Disaster* (New York: Crown, 1987), 4.

45. McConnell, *Challenger*, 12.

46. Dale Carter, *The Final Frontier: The Rise and Fall of the American Rocket State* (New York: Verso, 1988), 6-7.

47. Barbara S. Romzek and Melvin J. Dubnick, "Accountability in the Public Sector: Lessons from the *Challenger* Tragedy," *Public Administration Review* 47 (1987): 233, 230. See also Howard S. Schwartz, *Narcissistic Process and Corporate Decay: The Theory of the Organization Ideal* (New York: New York University Press, 1990), 107-26; and C. F. Larry Heimann, "Understanding the *Challenger* Disaster: Organizational Structure and the Design of Reliable Systems," *American Political Science Review* 87 (1993): 421-35.

48. Michael Davis, "Thinking Like an Engineer: The Place of a Code of Ethics in the Practice of a Profession," *Philosophy and Public Affairs* 20 (1991): 150-67. Diane Vaughan disputes the idea that engineers deserved no blame for the disaster, while managers carried the guilt of poor decision making. She argues that both were involved in flawed communications and technical decisions. *Challenger Launch Decision*, 61-62.

49. Gregory Moorhead, Richard Ference, and Chris P. Neck, "Group Deci-

sion Fiascoes Continue: Space Shuttle *Challenger* and a Revised Groupthink Framework," *Human Relations* 44 (1991): 539-51.

50. Vaughan, "Autonomy, Interdependence, and Social Control," 225.

51. G. Richard Holt and Anthony W. Morris, "Activity Theory and the Analysis of Organizations," *Human Organization* 52 (1993): 102.

52. Perrow, "Risky Systems," 354.

53. Philip R. Harris, *Living and Working in Space: Human Behavior, Culture and Organization* (New York: Ellis Horwood, 1992), 9.

54. Jesco von Puttkamer, "Introduction," in Harris, *Living and Working in Space*, 9.

55. This work stems from Ilya Prigogine's and Isabelle Stenger's hypothesis that chaotic systems may take up energy and begin to manifest orderly behavior. See Prigogine and Stengers, *Order Out of Chaos: Man's New Dialogue with Nature* (New York: Bantam, 1984).

56. Puttkamer, in Harris, 17-18.

57. Ibid., 22.

58. Charles D. Walker, "Why We Must Sail On," International Space Year special insert, *Ad Astra,* January-February 1992, 7.

59. Daniel Bell predicted that the industrial labor force would be replaced by workers skilled in the production and dissemination of information in *The Coming of Post-industrial Society: A Venture in Social Forecasting* (New York: Basic Books, 1973). For a discussion of the cybernetic goals and fantasies of these knowledge workers in the late twentieth century, see Grant H. Kester, "Out of Sight Is Out of Mind: The Imaginary Space of Postindustrial Culture," *Social Text* 35 (Summer 1993): 15-32.

60. Cynthia S. Fuchs, "'Death is Irrelevant': Cyborgs, Reproduction, and the Future of Male Hysteria," *Genders* 18 (Winter 1993): 114.

61. National Commission on Space, 65.

62. Harris, *Living and Working in Space,* 68.

63. Ibid., 95.

64. Ibid., 102. James Grier Miller began his work on general living systems theory in the 1950s at the University of Chicago's Institute of Behavioral Sciences and the University of Michigan's Mental Health Research Institute. Later, he would propound the potential contributions of behavioral scientists to spaceology, arguing that they could plan a highly engineered human society. James Grier Miller and Jesse L. Miller, "Living Systems Applications to Space Habitation," in *Space Resources: Technological Springboards into the 21st Century,* ed. M. F. McKay (Houston: NASA Johnson Space Center, 1992); James Grier Miller, *Living Systems* (New York: McGraw-Hill, 1978); James Grier Miller, "Applications of Living Systems Theory to Life in Space," in *From Antarctica to Outer Space: Life in Isolation and Confinement,* ed.

Albert A. Harrison, Yvonne A. Clearwater, and Christopher P. McKay (New York: Springer-Verlag, 1991), 177-98.

65. The term "informate" was first used by Zuboff. For a managerial view of the growing information economy, see Stephen P. Bradley, Jerry A. Hausman, and Richard L. Nolan, eds., *Globalization, Technology, and Competition: The Fusion of Computers and Telecommunications in the 1990s* (Boston: Harvard Business School Press, 1993).

66. National Commission on Space, 71-72.

67. David R. Criswell, "Solar System Industrialization: Implications for Interstellar Migrations," in *Interstellar Migration and the Human Experience,* ed. Ben R. Finney and Eric M. Jones (Berkeley: University of California Press, 1985), 58.

PART III

COMMUNITY

8

"It Must Be Made Safe"

Galveston, Texas, and the 1900 Storm

Patricia Bellis Bixel

Devastated by a hurricane in 1900, the island community of Galveston, Texas, vowed to rebuild and to regain its preeminent economic position in the state. An elaborate plan to protect the community from future storms was central to the recovery, and city leaders and a traumatized population looked to the professional engineering ranks for guidance. Retired army personnel worked with newly professionalized civilian engineers to offer salvation and safety through mechanical means, suggesting an aggressive modification of the land upon which the city was built. The eventual solution—constructing a seawall and elevating the city's height above sea level—testified to a great faith in modern technology and an equal resolve to remain on an unprotected sandbar. Patricia Bellis Bixel examines the decision to rebuild the city after the storm and the heavy reliance on the technical expertise of professional engineers to formulate a long-term plan for island protection.

ON SEPTEMBER 8, 1900, a hurricane swept across Galveston Island, devastating the thriving Texas port city. Death toll estimates ranged from 6,000 to 8,000 people, and property damage was calculated at approximately $30 million (1900 dollars).[1] Dealing with the storm's immediate aftermath kept everyone busy for months, but as the cleanup and recovery progressed, city leaders were forced to consider the long-term effects of the hurricane and how best to regain the island's premier economic position within the state and region. The civic leaders of Houston, fifty miles to the north, were always ready to capitalize on

Galveston's misfortune, and now they cautioned investors away from the island. The precarious physical location, the destruction of the tax base and infrastructure, the massive loss of life and subsequent departure of thousands of residents—all suggested that Galveston's heyday was over. Yet the port still boasted a deep-water channel, largely intact piers, and a committed business community. The island had always been vulnerable to tropical weather systems, but the extent of the damage from the 1900 storm and fears of future inundations sent leaders searching for ways to guarantee the city's safety and to encourage citizens to return, rebuild, and invest.

The city would not only rebuild, leaders decided; it would also refashion itself in such a way as to eliminate the dangers of disaster. Crucial to this reconstruction were a massive sea wall that would barricade the island from the pounding of storm-driven seas and a citywide grade elevation that would literally raise the surface of the land—an extraordinary proposal to pull land from the sea as a bulwark against nature. This solution testified to a great faith in modern technology and an equal resolve to live on an unprotected sandbar.

Besides being a dramatic story of community survival, Galveston's response to its catastrophe reflected a national current of reform. In its program of post-hurricane restoration and reconstruction, Galveston's experience highlights two particular aspects of the Progressive period: an agenda of political reform to eliminate what reformers saw as corruption and inefficiency and a reliance upon the efficacy of experts and modern technology to solve the larger problems of urban life. As a southern city, Galveston also implemented these reforms against a backdrop of regional racial norms. As Jack Temple Kirby has shown, the move to a commission form of government removed black residents— and many members of the white working class—from the decision-making process.[2] Their absence from the voting booths—or the dilution of their participation—eased the way for plans and policies sponsored by the middle- and upper-class white citizens of the island.

While no one would have wished for a hurricane to destroy the city, the storm and the subsequent necessity of clearing wreckage, distributing relief, and planning recovery facilitated the acceptance of reform proposals that had been simmering since the 1890s. To the leadership of Galveston, developing and realizing plans for rebuilding depended upon first the replacement of the existing political structure of the city with a commission and then the completion of two huge civil engineering projects. Galveston after the 1900 storm became a laboratory for Progressive reform and professionalism.

Days after the hurricane, citizens vowed to return and rebuild. "It is not time yet to talk of the future," commented the Galveston *Tribune* on September 12, "except to say it is all ours, and when we are fed, clothed and healed we shall seize it all and make it glorious." In reply to an inquiry from "a great New York paper" as to whether the community would rebuild, the Galveston *Daily News* answered "that Galveston did not intend to succumb to her crushing misfortune, but would again resume her place as the great port of the gulf."[3] Optimistic but wary, the *Engineering Record* gravely counseled that "before the city can assume the importance its geographical position renders possible, it must be made safe against such inundations as wrecked it a fortnight ago."[4]

There was no public discussion about abandoning the island. Just after the storm, W. L. Moody Sr. told an interviewer:

> Galveston will be rebuilt stronger and better than ever before. It is necessary to have a city here. Even if the storm had swept the island bare of every human habitation and every structure and left it as barren as it was before civilized man set foot on the place, still men would come here and build a city because a port is demanded at this place.[5]

The Southern Pacific railroad, a crucial corporate presence in the port and on the island, had invested $1 million in the construction of facilities at the port in 1899 and wasted no time in announcing the order of a new two-track bridge to cross the bay.[6] Perhaps most significant, if Galveston did not rebuild, many wealthy individuals stood to lose millions of dollars that were already invested in island enterprises. As relief efforts were scaled down and some kind of normalcy returned to the town, thoughts turned to the future and how to make it bright.

Immediately after the hurricane, a Central Relief Committee (CRC) was appointed to oversee relief and recovery efforts. The committee was composed of prominent members of the community, many of whom were also active in local politics. CRC member Isaac Herbert ("Ike") Kempner, also the city treasurer, considered what would be necessary for Galveston's business resurgence. Building a sea wall or taking other precautionary measures seemed to acknowledge the city's dangerous position, yet without some moves by

Galveston leaders to calm fears of future calamity, people would not remain, return, rebuild, or invest. Any actions taken had to be framed very carefully for the public. Galveston would take steps to protect itself, leaders agreed, because the city was too important *not* to rebuild in the best and safest manner possible and in order to pacify and appease those who would feel more secure if such measures were implemented—just in case, many years down the line, another hurricane might threaten. Galveston's problems were simply technical—issues to be resolved through political reform, expert professional advice, and modern technology. Where, then, to begin?

As a member of the finance subcommittee of the CRC, Kempner knew firsthand the state of the city's coffers.[7] Somewhat troubled before the storm, municipal finances were appalling in the aftermath. Besides pre-storm indebtedness, the city carried a staggering load of relief debt and faced the ongoing responsibility for repairing or replacing city services and equipment. In addition, leaders agreed that some steps had to be taken to guarantee that such overwhelming damage would never recur; the island had to protect itself from future hurricanes. From 1901 until 1904, Kempner and other Galveston officials and businessmen worked to develop plans that addressed all of these issues. Their solution—a radical change in government and two amazing civil engineering projects—brought Galveston back as an economic player in the region and inspired confidence in both residents and investors.

For decades, local residents and entrepreneurs had seemed oblivious to the threat posed by Gulf waters. As Galveston's seashore began attracting visitors, islanders removed indigenous groupings of salt cedar trees and sand dunes to improve access to the beach, which further eased the water's way into low-lying areas.[8] In addition, as island development moved westward, builders took sand from the dunes as fill for marshy areas upon which to build.[9] By the late nineteenth century, the trees and dunes—natural barriers protecting the island's interior—no longer impeded waves from the Gulf.

The city's problem was compounded by its openness to flooding from the bay side of the island. Water from Galveston Bay rose even more than the daily tide, depending on the direction of the wind or the level of the rivers that flowed into the bay; the city faced high-water dangers on two sides. Though aware of these threats, prominent businessmen and politicians had been reluctant to commit the funding necessary to achieve any level of protection for the city or to stop activi-

ties—the removal of trees and dune sand, for instance—believed to encourage economic growth. Discussion of building a sea wall came and
went with each storm season; and every time Galveston escaped without serious damage, calls for such safeguards faded.

The idea of building a sea wall to protect portions of Galveston
Island was not new. All kinds of barricades—dikes, levees, or
berms—were standard engineering methods used to protect vulnerable shorelines and riverbanks. Damage caused by a severe hurricane
in 1875 prompted discussions of building such a structure, but
Galvestonians were unwilling to pay for the project themselves and
unable to convince the state legislature to fund the work in the interests of regional commerce.[10] In 1878, salt cedar trees were planted
along the old dune line in an effort to accumulate sand and to form a
natural barrier to waves and rising water.[11] After another storm in
1886 destroyed the coastal community of Indianola, a group of thirty
businessmen formed the Progressive Association and issued a public
resolution calling for the construction of a sea wall. This group lobbied the state legislature and secured passage of an amendment to
the city charter that authorized issuance of bonds to fund protective
works. In addition, the group contacted James B. Eads, an engineer
famous for improvements to the mouth of the Mississippi, who submitted a plan for a twelve-foot embankment. A bond issue met with
fierce resistance, and as the years passed with no storm-driven damage, the island lapsed into a false sense of security.[12] On September 1,
1900, with eerie prescience, Colonel H. M. Robert, then Divisional
Engineer of the U.S. Army, presented to the Galveston City Council a
plan for the "improvement, protection, and development of Galveston Harbor" that included construction of a dike "that would form
a wall diverting the heavy storm tides from the northeast and thus
protect Galveston from overflow."[13] On September 16, 1900—only
eight days after the storm—David Hall, "one of the creditors of the
city," wrote the *Daily News* to advocate the building of a sea wall.[14]

And supporters were not without other suggestions. By September
28, 1900, the New York *Herald* had published suggestions for Galveston's safety that included a sea wall, a daytime Galveston for business
on the present site and a nighttime Galveston for sleeping on the mainland, rebuilding the city on steel or wooden piles as a "modern Venice,"
consolidation with Houston, or complete removal of the city to Port
Arthur, Sabine Pass, or Aransas. One of the most creative suggestions

came from France, where a colonel in the artillery advocated "a plan to erect a battery for destroying hurricanes close to Galveston. . . . If a West Indian cyclone approached he would fire at it and . . . break its back."[15]

Probably no municipal government could have met the demands of so vast and complete a disaster, but Galveston political leaders were perceived by the white elite of the city to be more ill-equipped than most. The city was governed by a traditional mayor/council system with twelve aldermen elected by wards, and some local residents, inspired by national Progressive reform efforts, had been trying since the early 1890s to combat what they saw as the corrupt, self-interested, unbusinesslike administration of city operations. Despite changes made to Galveston's electoral process during the 1890s, reformers urged more drastic action.[16]

Political and economic leadership circles in the city only rarely overlapped. Elective office carried little prestige and paid poorly. Real political power lay with a committee unique to Galveston and focused on economic development of the island port.

When engineer James B. Eads proved that properly designed jetties could result in the scouring, or deepening, of a channel, Galveston leaders formed a "Committee on Deep Water" in 1881 to meet with Eads and explore the possibility of building such jetties for Galveston. After meeting with the engineer and being convinced that such a scheme would work, what became known as the Deep Water Committee (DWC) began serious lobbying efforts at all levels of government to gain funding for the deepening of Galveston channel. This effort ended successfully when in 1889 Galveston was selected by the federal government as the primary port for the western Gulf of Mexico. Washington appropriated the necessary funds for jetty construction, and by 1897 the jetty system was complete and a channel depth of almost thirty feet secured. Membership on the DWC was confined to a wealthy and powerful elite; most participants were bank and corporate leaders and some served on the Wharf Company board of directors as well.[17]

Once they had secured their goal of a deep-water channel for Galveston, the committee did not disband. Members took to heart their reason for being—the economic health of the city—and simply moved on to other issues that they believed affected the island business climate. And, the committee came to think, there were serious concerns to be addressed at city hall. Quietly, and always behind the scenes, the committee began to formulate suggestions for reform even before the storm.

City streets were in widespread disrepair and sanitary conditions were abominable. The council did not meet its September 1899 payroll until December, and it was plagued by charges of favoritism and mismanagement.[18] Constant deficits required the regular floating of bonds to cover the shortfall, and nothing indicated that the situation was likely to improve. Even before the storm, Alderman C. H. McMaster requested that the council obtain copies of other city charters from around the country so that the group could explore alternatives.[19] Repair of the system would not go far enough, thought many; radical action was in order. Members of the DWC and other local business interests strongly supported efforts to alter dramatically the political landscape.

After the storm, infrastructure and services were nonexistent; water, power, and communications were restored only after the most extreme exertions. When Mayor Walter C. Jones named many members of the Deep Water Committee to positions on the Central Relief Committee, it seemed an admission that city government was not up to the task at hand. With almost half of the city's taxable property destroyed and upwards of $200,000 of floating debt—not to mention the expense of repairing city property—there seemed no doubt, at least to the DWC, that drastic measures were essential.[20]

In November 1900, two months after the storm, members of the DWC began meeting on a regular basis to draw up a proposal for a new city charter. They looked toward appointed commissions as a viable alternative. Commissions that governed Memphis, Tennessee (during a yellow fever epidemic in 1878) and Washington, D.C., were instructive examples of what might be achieved. Most of all, the men wanted a body that would organize and operate city government like a business, imposing regulation and administration to discharge municipal responsibilities and provide necessary services. Their condemnation of the existing system was scathing:

> Certainly no set of public officials ever seemed so indifferent to the welfare, safety, and health as the ruling majority of those now in office.
> . . . Businessmen and methods are what we need now in Galveston, men who know their duty to the city and are not afraid to perform it.[21]

Their plan called for the governor to appoint five city commissioners—one to serve as mayor-president, each of the others to administer a single department: finance and revenue, police and fire, waterworks and sewerage, streets and public improvements. The entire commission, sitting as a body, would make policy decisions.[22]

New city charters had to be approved by the legislature, and the DWC worked to obtain the broadest possible base of support, lobbying locally as well as statewide for passage.[23] There was little opposition to the proposal in print, but a few citizens read the proposal and thought through its implications. As written, the commission plan called for the governor to appoint all five members, effectively banishing democratic government from the island. Supporters claimed that provisions for electing commission members would be implemented after recovery from the storm was complete, but this seemed disingenuous to some. The sitting city council eventually developed its own proposal for a new city charter that left the system largely intact. Both bills were introduced in the legislature by Galveston Representative Thomas H. Nolan.[24]

Both sides tried to show broad support for their respective plans. The city council focused on the DWC plan's elimination of elections, while the DWC staked its claim on efficient, businesslike management. Island residents appeared to be quite willing to give up their right to elect their leaders, and the DWC plan received surprisingly widespread backing from most Galvestonians. The performance and integrity of the CRC suggested to most that a city government run by the same people would be equally efficient and successful.[25]

Some non-Galveston lawmakers, however, were deeply troubled by the abandonment of democratic principles and sided with the opposition. Threatened with failure and strongly committed to the passage of the plan, commission-backers and legislators negotiated an amendment that made the proposal acceptable. Two of the commissioners would be elected at large, thus providing at least an appearance of popular participation without endangering the appointed majority. The bill granting a new city charter to Galveston became law on July 7, 1901, and the new city commission took office on September 18 of that year. Judge William T. Austin, one of the elected commissioners, was named mayor-president, and the other elected commissioner, A. P. Norman, a livestock dealer, was placed in charge of police and fire. The governor appointed the other three commissioners: Isaac H. Kempner, finance and revenue; Herman C. Lange, waterworks and sewerage; and Valery Austin, streets and public improvements.[26]

Was there truly a need for a completely new form of city government? Historians examining the issue differ in their responses. Mayors and council members prior to the commission were not of the same class as members of the DWC or most of the other business leaders of the community, nor did they possess anywhere near the financial clout. Critics of the DWC and their ostensible reform efforts charge that Galveston's city government was no worse than any other nineteenth-century urban center, but there were ongoing financial problems that hampered city operations. An audit in 1895 revealed that no trial balance had been taken since 1891 and that the official accountant knew no bookkeeping. The issuing of bonds to cover unfunded debt rankled businessmen, and poor services were a continual annoyance. No doubt the Progressive movement heightened awareness of both problems and potential solutions, and the destruction caused by the September hurricane forced the issue. To commission supporters, if Galveston was to recover for the long term and to regain its commercial prominence, the city had to prove that it could solicit, obtain, and administer millions of dollars in a responsible way. Through the commission form of government, Galveston got its municipal house in order before entertaining prospective investors, even as it placed power in the hands of a wealthy elite and curtailed popular participation in electoral politics.[27]

Once installed, the new commission moved rapidly to develop long-term plans for the island's safety. On September 25, 1901, a resolution was passed to appoint a committee charged with selecting competent engineers to report on protection plans for the city. On November 20, based on recommendations from the committee, the city commission appointed a board of engineers composed of General H. M. Robert, Alfred Noble, and H. C. Ripley to plan protective measures for Galveston.

At a public meeting on January 25, 1902, the engineers submitted their report. In it, they described original grading surveys initiated in 1875, outlined conditions under which the island regularly flooded, and offered anecdotal evidence as to the heights of each of these floods. The 1875 grading survey fixed the elevation of Broadway at 8 feet, a level that was later raised to 9, with the grade descending from that point toward the Gulf and the bay. Nowhere on the island was the elevation higher than 8.9 feet, and the average elevation from Sixth to Thirty-ninth Street was 5.8 feet. West of Thirty-ninth Street the elevation declined to an average of 3.7 feet. The first flood in recorded memory occurred in 1834, when, elderly Galvestonians recalled, the island had been completely submerged. The engineers listed six other inundations that had resulted in floodwaters up to 9.5 feet in some places. But the worst had been the storm of the previous year, when "the water reached a height exceeding by far any previous records at Galveston." The deepest flooding had been at Shulte's store, located at Eighth Street and Avenue B (The Strand), where the water measured 15.7 feet, but depths of 10 to 14 feet were recorded at twelve other locations.[28] They went on to recount that "the greatest destruction was caused by currents and wave action." It was this wave action, in conjunction with the absolute increase in water volume, that was responsible for the horrendous destruction visited upon the island in 1900.[29] The engineers concluded that

> Protection from storms is not only required for the preservation of life and property, but also . . . to give confidence to the people of Galveston and to others who may be drawn here by business interests, in the absolute safety of the city. . . . The Board is of the opinion that it is practicable, at an expense not large . . . to place Galveston entirely out of reach of any storm like those from which she suffered previous to 1900 . . . and at the same time make the city safe from any serious damage from water in a storm like the one of 1900.[30]

The engineers recommended the construction of a sea wall more than three miles long, the raising of the city grade, and an embankment connecting the sea wall to the raised island.[31]

Because the island faced the possibility of flooding from both the Gulf of Mexico to the southeast and its channel to Galveston Bay on the northwest, any protective measures had to address rising water on either side of the narrow land mass. The engineers outlined a system whose three components worked together to prevent wave and water damage associated with the periodic hurricanes that ravaged the city. The raising of the city grade was necessary to get the streets and lots sufficiently high to ensure the safety of life and property "in severe storms. The seawall was necessary to protect the filling from the force of the waves." They went on to stress the importance of the filling. "The filling proposed to be made over the city, together with the embankment immediately behind the seawall, is hardly less indispensable than the seawall itself. It places the entire city area above the height of ordinary floods."[32]

The three advisors calculated both unit prices and total costs. The sea wall was determined to cost $66.50 a linear foot. With engineering fees and contingencies added, Galveston could have its bulwark for $1,294,755. The grade raising, second component of the plan, was determined to require 13,873,000 cubic yards of fill costing $.10 a yard. After adding expenses of paving and soil placement at $7.40 a linear foot, the projected cost of raising large sections of the island was $2,210,285. "Total cost of entire project recommended by the Board, $3,505,040, or say, $3,500,000."[33]

Residents were more than willing to accept the advice and recommendations of these engineers. Galveston's experience with technology had always been positive; such expertise had already resulted in the deepening of the port's channel in the 1890s and continued improvement of the harbor facilities. Besides possessing a genuine desire to rebuild their city, islanders also had great faith in the committee called upon to solve their problems. Robert, Ripley, and Noble were prominent members of a growing class of urban planning professionals. Robert and Ripley were both retired from the U.S. Army Corps of Engineers; both had visited or served many years in Galveston and had worked throughout the Galveston District. Alfred Noble was an engineer as well; he had been involved with the construction of Chicago's breakwater and was serving as president of the American Society of Civil Engineers. Such experts in technology had great status within the Progressive movement as holders of highly specialized knowledge whose employment could lead to the creation of safer, healthier, and more beautiful urban environments. They were believed to be above petty politics and dedicated to making cities less hostile to their inhabitants. And they possessed enormous faith in their expertise as well. An *Engineering News* editorial concluded that "if the city desires to save itself from a repetition of the recent calamity, it is quite within the resources of engineering to furnish the desired protection."[34]

Public and private moral support for the proposal came quickly. Financing was another question. The new city commissioners had allowed the city to default on $17,500 worth of forty-year bonds issued in 1881. Negotiations with bondholders resulted in the lowering of interest rates on remaining outstanding issues. But given the decimation of the tax base, the existing bonded indebtedness, a new and untried government, and the size of the bond issue required, the city of Galveston could not issue bonds to cover sea wall construction and the grade raising.[35] Contemporary accounts of this period make no mention of the city's bonded indebtedness problem but claim overriding community support for underwriting the costs. Using as evidence the amount of taxes paid to the county by residents of Galveston, city and county commissioners reached an agreement whereby the county would issue bonds for sea wall construction and the city would finance the grade raising. Issuing the bonds for sea wall construction, however, required the consent of two-thirds of the county's taxpayers. By the time the county's request for a $1,500,000 issue came to a vote, 84 percent of the bonds' purchase price had been pledged. With a 98 percent turnout, the bond issue authorization passed 3,119 to 22. The newspaper noted "A Grand Jollification" in response to the vote. In addition, the state legislature donated, for grade-raising purposes, two years' worth of the city's ad valorem taxes and a portion of the occupation and poll taxes. The following session of the legislature extended the period of donation to fifteen years.[36]

With financing secured, Galveston County proceeded with planning and construction of the first segment of the sea wall. Technology for such building was well known, and work progressed quickly. Specifications for the sea wall were published in June 1902, the construction contract was let to J. M. O'Rourke and Company in September, and the first pile was driven on October 28.[37] Supporters of organized labor pressed for union workers in the project, and the *Galveston Journal* noted that labor support of the city commission had helped gain approval of the project. Besides, as evidenced by the construction of the commissary houses, union workers did good work at good prices. In the end, union workers were utilized where possible, but there was little call for skilled labor in sea wall construction.[38]

In their report, the three engineers described the project as "a solid concrete wall, over 3 miles long. . . . The top of this wall to be 17 feet above mean low water, or 1.3 feet higher than the highest point reached by the water in the storm of 1900." The Gulf face of the wall was curved so that waves would be forced upward, and the structure's foundation was to be piles protected from undermining by sheet piling and riprap. At the bottom the wall would be sixteen feet wide, at the top five feet.[39]

The first sea wall segment, completed in 1904, ran along the Gulf side of the island for 17,593 feet. While Galveston County was building the sea wall, the federal government authorized construction and extension of the wall across the front of the Fort Crockett military installation located from Thirty-ninth Street to Fifty-third Street. This added 4,935 feet to the island's bulwark and connected three gun emplacements. Construction of the federal segment began in December 1904; the segment was finished in November 1905 at a cost to taxpayers of $295,000.[40]

The sea wall has been extended several times since this initial effort. The first extension, completed in 1921, was a lengthening of the wall eastward from Sixth Street to the first battery at Fort San Jacinto. That segment was extended in 1926 all the way across to the south jetty. Westward expansion soon followed. In 1927, Galveston County finished extending the wall from Fifty-third Street to Sixty-first Street. The final three-mile extension of the bulwark was completed in stages from 1951 to 1962. Today the sea wall extends almost ten miles along the Gulf of Mexico side of Galveston Island, protecting nearly one-third of the beachfront.[41]

One unforeseen consequence of the sea wall construction involved erosion of the beach in front of the wall. A hurricane in 1915 washed away most of the sand, and subsequent cycles of tides, winds, and storms did not replenish the area. By 1934, Gulf waters had reached the riprap in most places and threatened the sea wall itself. Engineering studies determined that the erosion process could be stopped and reversed if a system of rock groins were built perpendicular to the wall. Completed in 1936, these groins extend 500 feet into the Gulf and help to collect and retain sand below water level and somewhat along the beach. In the 1990s, Galveston paid for "beach renourishment," a process by which sand is dredged from nearby Gulf waters and deposited along the shoreline. This procedure is not permanent, however, and must be repeated every few years to maintain wide stretches of beach for the tourism industry.[42]

The city's grade raising efforts proceeded along a slightly different path. Amendments to the city charter specified that the governor appoint a board of "resident citizens" to supervise and administer the grade raising process.

On May 15, 1903, Governor Samuel Willis Tucker Lanham announced the appointments of Captain J. P. Alvey, John Sealy, and E. R. Cheesborough. All three men had been active in Galveston business and politics for many years. Alvey was general manager of the Texas Guarantee and Trust Company and a member of the Texas Land and Loan Company and the school board. John Sealy, scion of a prominent Galveston family, was a member of the banking firm of Hutchings, Sealy and Company, president of the Galveston Wharf Company, and an officer of many other local institutions. Edmund R. Cheesborough was the youngest of the board of managers but was equally well considered. As secretary of the Blum Land Company and secretary-treasurer of the Texas Cement Company, he brought strong administrative talents to the body.[43] Moreover, he had been heavily involved in founding the Galveston Good Government Club, having written the New York City Good Government organization in 1894 about establishing such a group in the island city.[44] He brought credibility and integrity to the grade raising effort and quickly assumed responsibility for administering the massive project.

Once the Grade Raising Board was in place, events proceeded apace. Final specifications for the grade raising were completed September 15, 1903, and bid solicitations were placed in appropriate publications throughout the United States at the beginning of October. In the document, the bid requested proposals to "raise the grade of the City of Galveston" for four large areas that encompassed approximately 500 blocks.[45]

By the 2 P.M. deadline on December 7, 1903, only two bids for the work had been received. After some consultation, the contracts were awarded to the firm of Goedhart and Bates of New York on December 12, 1903. The plan outlined by P. C. Goedhart and Lindon Bates was bold. Dredge material would be taken from Galveston Bay by self-loading and -discharging, self-propelled hopper dredges that would then steam through a distribution canal and pump fill under the raised and waiting structures. Once finished, the dredges would fill up the canal as they left; buildings removed from the canal right-of-way would be replaced on the newly raised ground. The sea wall embankment, controlled by the County Commissioners Court, was to be filled within twelve months from February 18, 1904, and the raising of the city was to be completed by that date in 1907.[46]

The authors of this plan could claim great authority for such work. P. C. Goedhart was the senior member of the Goedhart Brothers engineering firm of Dusseldorf, Germany. That company had worked in the harbors of Dusseldorf, Neuss, Danzig, and Kiel, as well as in the Dortmund-Ems and Amsterdam-Rhine canals. Lindon Bates was the American partner of the firm Goedhart and Bates of New York; the inventor of a system of high-powered hydraulic dredges, he had been engaged in the design and implementation of harbor improvements for numerous nations, including the United States, Belgium, Egypt, Australia, and India.[47]

What appeared to be a reasonably straightforward plan required a monumental administrative effort. Early in the planning process, city leaders had agreed that the city would be responsible for raising streets, trolley lines, gas, water, and sewer pipelines, and whatever other municipal service properties lay in the areas to be raised. The city would also provide the fill for the rest of the process. Private property owners would be responsible for the raising of their houses, barns, stables, and any other structures located on the blocks to be raised. Excavating the canal by which the dredges would transport fill material necessitated another kind of negotiation with private property owners. The canal route ran parallel to the sea wall and also required a turning basin so that the dredges could discharge their fill and return to gulf waters to reload. In order to acquire the land for the canal right-of-way, the city agreed to lease the necessary lots from their respective owners, paying as rental fees the taxes covered by the period of the lease. At no cost to the property owner, the contractors moved any structures from the property to sites provided by the city for that purpose. Once the grade raising was completed and the canal filled, the structures would be returned to their original locations and placed on the newly raised lots.[48]

Edmund R. Cheesborough was responsible for the bulk of leases. Corresponding directly with property owners or working through local realtors with information supplied by the tax assessor-collector, he eventually obtained 284 leases to lots in the canal right-of-way.[49] As fewer and fewer leases were outstanding, he chivvied the realtors to complete the task of obtaining leases for all affected properties.[50]

The grade raising forged ahead. Quarter-mile sections were enclosed by dikes. Structures, sewers, pipes, trolley tracks, and gas lines were lifted precariously, and fill was pumped in underneath until the grade level met the survey requirement. While fill was being pumped, residents negotiated the neighborhood by way of temporary catwalks and trestles, resulting in what the *Daily News* referred to as "A City on Stilts."[51]

As secretary to the grade raising board, Cheesborough handled the day-to-day inconveniences. He cajoled Bates into moving more quickly, pacified residents fearful of the expense, modified and cancelled leases when the contractors changed the western canal terminus, and saw to the operation of pontoon bridges across the canal. He intervened when residents' services were not restored correctly and chided those in the canal right-of-way who expected the city to raise chicken houses, outhouses, and fences.[52]

One of the most unfortunate aspects of the massive filling project was its effect on the island's vegetation. Any trees and plantings completely buried under dredge material would be killed, but even oaks or oleanders lovingly lifted by their owners along with buildings were endangered. Since the fill was 15 to 45 percent sand and the rest salt water, the resulting soil composition was not suited to grow much of anything.[53]

The Women's Health Protective Association (WHPA) took the revegetation of the island as one of its missions. The need for replanting the island after the grade raising coincided with national campaigns for city beautification, and the women found sources of support among national "City Beautiful" organizations. The WHPA consulted agricultural experts, obtained cuttings and seedlings, and convinced the railroads to carry thousands of palm trees without charge from California and Florida. Beginning with parks and boulevards most heavily used by residents and visitors to Galveston, the WHPA worked its way throughout the raised area and encouraged other groups and organizations to take responsibility for the replanting of their buildings and grounds. The organization operated a nursery and gave away or sold at cost seeds, rose bushes, oleander cuttings, and other plants to property owners wanting to restore their home gardens. Contests were held and prizes awarded to acknowledge residents' efforts to beautify recently raised structures and lots. For several years, starting in 1906, an annual horse show funded WHPA civic improvement programs, and the event quickly became a focal point of the social season on the island. When the shows ceased in 1910—largely due to the advent of the automobile and a lack of horses to show—organizers could claim their efforts had been a great success.[54]

In all, 2,156 structures of various kinds were raised during the course of the filling.[55] The most spectacular of these was St. Patrick's Church, one of the largest churches in the city. Located at Thirty-fourth Street and Avenue K, it measured 53 feet by 140 feet and was estimated to weigh approximately 3,000 tons. Its tower alone accounted for 1,400 tons. The church was lifted from its foundation by excavation underneath and placed in a cradle of heavy timbers and iron girders. Seven hundred jackscrews were then distributed under the cradle and the structure was very slowly and carefully raised five feet. "Owing to the nature of the construction of this building," wrote the *Daily News*, "fears were entertained as to the feasibility of raising it. It is virtually a big brick shell with the exception of the solidly constructed tower." The paper went on to observe, "No accidents occurred during the operation and services have never been discontinued while the raising was in progress. On St. Patrick's Day, March 17, a record-breaking congregation attended the services while the church was elevated high in the air."[56]

Work continued, slowly and steadily, for years. By September 26, 1906, the halfway mark had been reached, but in February 1907 the contractors requested and received a three-year extension on the time for completion. In 1910, North American Dredging Company took over the contract and pumped sand from Offat's Bayou to finish the work.

Goedhart and Bates claimed to have lost $400,000 on the project, but they received the praise of a grateful city. When the work was finished in 1911, five hundred blocks had been filled with 16,300,000 cubic yards of sand.[57] Other parts of the island have been filled as development has moved west, but nothing has been done of the magnitude of this initial effort.

The sea wall and grade raising were tested periodically during this time. A hurricane in 1909 caused some scouring and deterioration of the sea wall and necessitated repairs and modifications recommended by General Robert. But the greatest test of both efforts came on August 17, 1915, when a storm comparable to the 1900 hurricane hit the island. The storm passed just south of Galveston, and while the barometric readings remained higher than those taken in 1900 (28.63 inches versus 28.42), the tide was half a foot higher. The highest wind speed was 93 mph at 2:37 A.M. on August 17, and hurricane-force winds continued on the island for nineteen hours. The highest wind speed documented in 1900 was 84 mph, but the anemometer blew away; officials estimated that winds reached 120 mph before the end of the storm. Meteorologists in 1915 calculated that the storms "were of about equal intensity."[58] Results of the storm, fortunately, were not.

"Great Hurricane Sweeps Texas Coast; Galveston Seawall Again Paramount," read the headline in the *Daily News* on August 17. "Subjected to a test that could hardly have been more terrific, the great Galveston seawall again was tried and not found wanting. Against the battering of giant seas it stood stanchly throughout every foot of its five miles."[59] "The sea-wall at Galveston, Tex., was the city's salvation during the hurricane of Aug. 16-17. This is the outstanding feature, from the engineering viewpoint, of the effect of the recent storm," reported the *Engineering Record*.[60] In *Engineering News*, R. P. Babbitt was even more congratulatory: "Had it not been for the seawall there would now be only a heap of ruins to mark the site of this great Texas seaport. This magnificent wall, extending . . . along the Gulf front of the city, was impregnable to the fury of the waves which beat against it but were baffled at every point."[61]

All of this tribute notwithstanding, portions of the wall were undermined, its concrete sidewalk seriously damaged, and areas of backfilling washed away. The greatest storm damage befell the causeway connecting Galveston Island to the mainland. Approaches to the 2,455-foot reinforced concrete viaduct (completed in 1912) were washed out, and the pipe carrying the city's water supply was also destroyed.[62] But the loss of life and property experienced in 1900 was not repeated, and urban engineers and planners basked in self-satisfaction:

> Amid the chaos in the wake of the Galveston storm of August 17 one structure stands out in bolt [sic] relief, a monument to engineering skill and foresight—the seawall. . . . Galveston's seawall was the city's salvation, and to the engineers who designed it and to the contractors who built it the Texas town owes a debt of gratitude which can never be adequately repaid. . . . It takes a catastrophe like the Galveston storm to demonstrate to a public, often forgetful of those to whom it owes its safety, that the civil engineer is the foundationstone upon which the physical welfare of cities must be built. . . . City officials . . . may well ponder over the Galveston lesson and take inventory of their own state of preparedness against unforeseen catastrophes which engineers can aid them in preventing.[63]

Citizens felt secure enough after the storm to send a telegram to the Associated Press refusing any form of relief and expressing their profound thanks "in this triumphant battle with the elements that similar assistance [to that offered in 1900] is unnecessary." They went on to "assure friends and admirers everywhere of this sincere pledge to strive diligently and heartily to attain that superior success which last night's victory promises for the community."[64]

The sea wall, a visible and formidable construction separating land from sea, received the bulk of the credit for preserving the city. The grade raising, largely completed and invisible by 1915, was no less a factor in the city's survival. Constructing the sea wall and raising the city's grade—projects that were inextricably interrelated—brought with them a host of environmental ramifications. Raising the grade was pointless without building a wall to keep the new high ground from washing away into the Gulf. And the wall was essential to block potentially destructive wave damage from future storms. As noted above, however, the wall was quickly undermined due to the extensive erosion of the Gulf-side beaches. Rock groins, added years after the fact, do help accrue and retain sand in front of the wall, but city leaders are faced with the prospect of eternal vigilance—and expense—if they want to keep beaches for tourists and protection for residents. In addition, the effects of Galveston's various jetties, groins, and sea wall extend to beaches both east and west, where ongoing erosion processes threaten more recent development.

Galveston learned early on what the rest of coastal America is only now comprehending: barrier islands, while magical spaces, are not necessarily appropriate for major human habitation. Even as Galveston struggled throughout that first agonizing year of recovery, city leaders took a long, hard look at the island's future and made decisions they believed were essential for its survival. A dramatic change in government assured investors and calmed critics of earlier administrations; constructing the sea wall and completing the grade raising were physical actions taken to guarantee protection from future hurricanes. And all of the decisions for change were grounded in ideals of reform and professionalism that also resulted in the effective removal of large numbers of black men from the electoral pool—a distinctively southern aspect of Progressive reform.

In January 1904, E. R. Cheesborough contacted W. H. Plummer in Millbridge, Maine, to secure a lease for the canal right-of-way. "The Grade Raising Board," he wrote, "is doing everything that mortal men can do to succeed in their stupendous undertaking, and we believe that success is assured." With an administration that was perceived to be more "businesslike" and the most modern of civil engineering amenities, the island city reentered the battle for economic success in the growing Southwest.

NOTES

1. This essay comes from a larger work, Patricia Bellis Bixel and Elizabeth Hayes Turner, *Galveston and the 1900 Storm: Catastrophe and Catalyst* (Austin: University of Texas Press, 2000), which examines the storm and the city's recovery from a variety of perspectives. For members of the middle and upper

classes, mainly professionals, business people, and their families, the hurricane recovery afforded an opportunity to obtain what they perceived to be major political reforms and secure the island's future through construction of the sea wall and grade raising. For black Galvestonians and the white working class, the fruits of storm recovery were less clear-cut and more ambiguous, in ways that are explained more fully in the book. This essay focuses on the technological response to the hurricane and does not try to explore long-term social consequences attendant on the recovery.

The city of Galveston is located on the eastern end of a barrier island of the same name that parallels the Texas Gulf Coast. Located approximately 50 miles southeast of Houston, Texas, the island is 27 miles long and ranges in width from 1 to 3 miles. "The Great Storm," as it has come to be called, has been extensively documented in articles and books. This hurricane still ranks as the worst natural disaster, in terms of loss of life, to strike North America. Because of the significance of the tidal surge accompanying the storm and the number of deaths due to drowning, the event is sometimes called "The Galveston Flood." See also Eric Larson, *Isaac's Storm* (New York: Crown Books, 1999); John Edward Weems, *A Weekend in September* (College Station: Texas A&M University Press, 1957, 1980); Herbert M. Mason Jr., *Death from the Sea* (New York: Dial Press, 1972); and Stephen P. Kretzmann, "A House Built Upon the Sand: Race, Class, Gender, and the Galveston Hurricane of 1900" (Ph.D. dissertation, University of Wisconsin, Madison, 1995). Numerous sensationalist accounts were published immediately after the storm. See, for example, Paul Lester, *The Great Galveston Disaster* (Philadelphia: Globe Bible Publishing Co., 1900); John Coulter, ed., *The Complete Story of the Galveston Horror, Written by the Survivors* (Chicago: United Publishers of America, 1900); Nathan C. Greene, ed., *Story of the Galveston Flood: Complete, Graphic, Authentic* (Baltimore, Md.: R. H. Woodward, 1900); and Murat Halstead, *Galveston: The Horrors of a Stricken City* (Chicago: American Publishers Association, 1900). To refute these narratives, Galveston newspaper editor Clarence Ousley authored *Galveston in 1900* (Atlanta: W. C. Chase, 1901). See also E. B. Garriott, "The West Indian Hurricane of September 1-12, 1900," *National Geographic* 2 (October 1900): 384-88.

2. Jack Temple Kirby, *Darkness at the Dawning: Race and Reform in the Progressive South* (Philadelphia: J. B. Lippincott Co., 1972), 4. All southern historians of the Progressive period wrestle with the role of racism and its practical manifestation—black disfranchisement and Jim Crow laws—in the southern Progressive movement. Kirby specifically cites "black disfranchisement and segregation . . . [as] the seminal 'progressive' reform of the era. . . . [C]ounting out Negroes politically and socially made possible nearly every other reform" (Kirby, 4). For a discussion of southern historiography of the Progressive period, see Richard L. Watson Jr., "From Populism through the New Deal," in John B. Boles and Evelyn Thomas Nolen, *Interpreting Southern History: Historiograph-*

ical Essays in Honor of Sanford W. Higginbotham (Baton Rouge: Louisiana State University Press, 1987), 308-89, esp. 329-49.

3. "The Future is Ours," *Galveston Tribune,* 12 September 1900; and *Galveston Daily News,* 14 September 1900 (hereafter *GDN*).

4. *The Engineering Record* 42, no. 12 (22 September 1900): 267.

5. Quoted in Mason, *Death from the Sea,* 229. For a discussion of the question of Galveston's recovery, see Kretzmann, "A House Built Upon the Sand," 98-99.

6. Mason, *Death from the Sea,* 230.

7. Besides being the head of a prominent Galveston family, Isaac Herbert ("Ike") Kempner (1872-1967) was a director of the Galveston Cotton Exchange, a member of the Deep Water Committee, the Galveston City Treasurer, and the head of the firm of H. Kempner. Chairman of the finance committee of the Central Relief Committee after the hurricane, Kempner became the city's finance director under the new commission form of government. See Harold M. Hyman, "I. H. Kempner and the Galveston Commission Government," *The Houston Review* 10, no. 2 (1988): 56-85.

8. Lynn M. Alperin, *Custodians of the Coast: History of the United States Army Engineers at Galveston* (Galveston District: U.S. Army Corps of Engineers, 1977), 237.

9. Albert B. Davis Jr., "History of the Galveston Seawall: Galveston's Bulwark against the Sea," paper presented at the Second Annual Conference on Coastal Engineering, Houston, Texas, November 1951, 1. Copy in possession of the author.

10. David G. McComb, *Galveston: A History* (Austin: University of Texas Press, 1986), 29-30.

11. Kretzmann, "A House Built Upon the Sand," 76.

12. Alperin, *Custodians of the Coast,* 238.

13. *GDN,* 1 September 1900.

14. *GDN,* 16 September 1900.

15. "Some Wild Projects," *GDN,* 28 September 1900.

16. Bradley R. Rice, "The Galveston Plan of City Government by Commission: The Birth of a Progressive Idea," *Southwest Historical Quarterly* 78 (April 1975): 369. See also Bradley Robert Rice, *Progressive Cities: The Commission Government Movement in America* (Austin: University of Texas Press, 1977), 3-33 and Kretzmann, "A House Built Upon the Sand," 88.

17. For Eads's influence on Galveston, see Alperin, *Custodians of the Coast,* 47-48. For the creation of the Deep Water Committee, see McComb, *Galveston,* 59-60, and Rice, "Galveston Plan," 380-81.

18. Rice, "Galveston Plan," 376.

19. Ibid.; and Kretzmann, "A House Built Upon the Sand," 133.

20. Rice, "Galveston Plan," 378.

21. Galveston *Tribune*, 9 January 1901, quoted in Rice, "Galveston Plan," 385.

22. Rice, "Galveston Plan," 390.

23. Ibid., 390-91.

24. Ibid., 391; and Kretzmann, "A House Built Upon the Sand," 86.

25. Historians Bradley R. Rice and Stephen P. Kretzmann point to four reasons the commission plan was so easily accepted. First, many believed that only a radical and complete change in government would provide the organization and stability needed to obtain funding for rebuilding, refinancing debt, and constructing protective measures against future hurricanes. Second, most believed that the commission would eventually be elected, that a completely governor-appointed body was only temporary. Third, given the extent of the disaster and the road the city faced to recovery, most people simply trusted the judgment of the DWC and its adherents. And finally, members of the working class believed their interests would be protected. See Rice, " Galveston Plan," 391-96, and Kretzmann, "A House Built Upon the Sand," 236-38.

26. Rice, "Galveston Plan," 402

27. The various positions in the historiographical debate about the necessity of implementing such complete governmental change may be found in McComb, *Galveston*, 134-37; Rice, "Galveston Plan," 396; Kretzmann, "A House Built Upon the Sand," 280-81; Harold M. Hyman, "I. H. Kempner and the Galveston Commission Government," *Houston Review* 10 (1988): 81-85; Harold M. Hyman, *Oleander Odyssey: The Kempners of Galveston, Texas, 1854-1980s* (College Station: Texas A&M University Press, 1990), 146-63; and Bixel and Turner, *Galvaston and the 1900 Storm* (Austin: University of Texas Press, 2000), 93-94.

28. Galveston County Board of Engineers Records, Galveston and Texas History Center, Rosenberg Library, Galveston, Texas, 73-0371, Folder 34-0021, Reports to the Galveston County Commissioners Court, 4 (quotation) and 5. Several versions of this report exist. Page numbers for subsequent citations in this essay come from a published version, "Plans for the Protection of Galveston: Report of the Board of Engineers on Plans for the Sea Wall and Raising the Grade of the City" (Galveston: Clarke and Courts, 1901). Hereafter cited as *Engineers Report*.

29. Ibid., 5.

30. Ibid., 6-7.

31. Ibid., 7.

32. Ibid.

33. Ibid., 11-12.

34. For insight into the role of engineers and city planning professionals during this period, see Stanley K. Schultz and Clay McShane, "To Engineer the Metropolis: Sewers, Sanitation, and City Planning in Late-Nineteenth-Century

America," *Journal of American History* 65 (September 1978): 389-411; and *Engineering News* 44, no. 12 (20 September 1900): 196 (quotation).

35. Hyman, *Oleander Odyssey*, 162-63; and McComb, *Galveston*, 138.

36. For the necessity of the bond election, *GDN*, 1 September 1904; election returns and tax rebates by the legislature, *GDN*, 23 March 1902; "Memorial of the City of Galveston to the Democratic State Convention at Galveston, July 14, 1902 and to the Twenty-Eighth Legislature of the State of Texas," Texas Book Collection, Galveston and Texas History Center, Rosenberg Library.

37. Patricia Bellis Bixel, "Working the Waterfront on Film: Commercial Photography and Community Studies" (Ph.D. dissertation, Rice University, 1997), 220.

38. Kretzmann, "A House Build Upon the Sand," 273.

39. *Engineers Report*, 7.

40. Davis, "History of the Galveston Seawall," 4.

41. Ibid., 10-12; and Alperin, *Custodians of the Coast*, 242-50.

42. Davis, "History of the Galveston Seawall," 7-8 (1915 storm erosion), 13-14 (development of groin system). For a cogent description of the Galveston sea wall project and the perils of sea wall construction for beaches, see Cornelia Dean, *Against the Tide: The Battle for America's Beaches* (New York: Columbia University Press, 1999), 6-14.

43. *GDN*, 16 May 1903.

44. Rice, "Galveston Plan," 369.

45. "Advertisement, Instructions, Specifications and Proposal for Grade Raising, Galveston, Texas," Edmund R. Cheesborough papers, 22-0024, Box 1, folder 1, Galveston and Texas History Center, Rosenberg Library, Galveston, Texas. Hereafter cited as ERC papers.

46. "Raising the Grade of Galveston," *Engineering Record* 51, no. 10 (11 March 1905): 284; Report to Governor Lanham, 2 June 1904, ERC papers, letterpress book 2, 448.

47. E. R. Cheesborough, "The Grade Raising," *GDN*, 1 September 1904.

48. Ibid.

49. E. R. Cheesborough to Mayor and City Commissioners, 10 March 1904, ERC papers, letterpress book 3, 321.

50. E. R. Cheesborough to John Adriance, Trueheart Family Papers, 22-0023, Box 2, folder 16, Galveston and Texas History Center, Rosenberg Library, Galveston, Texas.

51. *GDN*, 14 April 1905.

52. For the raising of chicken houses, outhouses and fences, see E. R. Cheesborough to Messrs. E. L. Reading and Co., 1 December 1904, ERC Papers, letterpress book 3, 158.

53. W. T. Hornaday, "Lifting a City," *Wide World Magazine*, 1908, 503.

54. Elizabeth Hayes Turner, *Women, Culture, and Community: Religion*

and Reform in Galveston, 1880-1920 (New York: Oxford University Press, 1997), 206-10.

55. McComb, *Galveston*, 142.

56. *GDN*, 7 April 1907.

57. McComb, *Galveston*, 143.

58. "Meteorological Analysis of Storm Indicates Similarity to Hurricane of 1900," *Engineering Record* 72, no. 9 (28 August 1915): 275-76.

59. *GDN*, 17 August 1915.

60. "Galveston's Sea-Wall Checks Hurricane's Devastation," *Engineering Record* 72, no. 9 (28 August 1915): 271.

61. "Effect of Galveston Storm on Seawall and Causeway," *Engineering News* 74, no. 9 (26 August 1915): 427.

62. See *Engineering News* 74, no. 10 (2 September 1915): 469-72; and *Engineering Record* 72, no. 9 (28 August 1915): 271-76.

63. "Galveston Sea-Wall the City's Salvation," *Engineering Record* 72, no. 9 (28 August 1915): 247.

64. *GDN*, 17 August 1915.

9

Chicago on the Brink

Media Trauma and the 1977 L-Train Crash

Andrew Hazucha

On a freezing February day in 1977, an elevated train dropped out of the sky into the rush-hour crowds in Chicago's Loop. Reporters were on the scene immediately, trying to make sense of the crash for themselves and a shocked public. The death of the city's longtime mayor and power broker Richard Daley earlier that winter had been equally sudden and traumatic. In a civic culture rooted in the cocksure self-image of "the city that works," Andrew Hazucha explains, these paired disasters evoked "a sense of despair and dislocation." The L-train crash "happened precisely at a moment in Chicago history when the city was most vulnerable to a cataclysmic event." To contain the shock, Chicago's newspapers ended up representing the crash as inevitable rather than unimaginable—"a symbol of Chicagoans' particular mix of defiance and anxiety," another sign of the city's brawn and resilience.

> . . . the El
>   careening thru its thirdstory world
> with its thirdstory people
>   in their thirdstory doors
> looking as if they had never heard
>   of the ground . . .
>   —Lawrence Ferlinghetti,
>   "Reading Yeats I do not think"

THE WINTER OF 1977 was the coldest in Chicago history, made even colder by the sudden and unexpected death of Richard J. Daley, the

247

city's longest serving mayor. First elected in 1955, the seventy-four-year-old Daley had served an unprecedented six terms as mayor, a two-decade tenure that transformed him into an enduring and revered symbol of, as he liked to phrase it, "the city that works." While such other major American cities as New York, Los Angeles, and Philadelphia suffered from paralyzing union strikes in sectors providing essential city services, throughout his reign Daley boasted that Chicago's streets remained clear of snow, Chicagoans' garbage was always picked up, and the vast transportation network that served the city was always in service. In Daley's twenty-one years as mayor, the city had never had a crippling strike and had ended each fiscal period in the black. At the time of his death, the *Chicago Tribune* noted that while other cities had become "political graveyards for their mayors," Daley had become the most powerful mayor in the nation by building a political machine that consolidated all its power in the mayor's office and seemed to operate on the premise that he would live forever.[1]

Daley's popularity as Chicago's leader even among his sometime detractors was due largely to his success as an urban developer. The day he died Chicagoans could say of Daley that he had suffered only two notable disappointments as mayor-builder: he had failed in numerous attempts to convince the Illinois legislature to release state funds to help the city construct a proposed Crosstown Expressway, and he was never able to marshal the financial resources or public support to build a subway to replace the antiquated elevated train tracks in the downtown Loop.

Daley's death from a heart attack on December 20, 1976 was particularly discomfiting for Chicago because he had never indicated a favorite who might become his successor, and now that he was dead there was no heir apparent to assume control of his power base. The ensuing struggle over who would act as interim mayor quickly developed into an all-out war between feuding factions on the Chicago City Council that threatened to involve the city's top brass in a lengthy and bitter affair. A week after Daley's death, Michael Bilandic, an alderman from Daley's own Bridgeport neighborhood, emerged from the succession battle as a compromise candidate. The City Council appointed him acting mayor until such time as the Council could call a general election. The election eventually took place on June 7, 1977, some five months later.

CHICAGO AFTER DALEY: THE DEEP FREEZE

On February 4, 1977, Chicago had already endured thirty-nine straight days and nights of subfreezing temperatures, a siege of frigid weather that would reach a record forty-three straight days of below-freezing readings. The string of cold weather shattered the previous record of twenty-nine consecutive subfreezing days, set almost a century before, from December 18, 1878 to January 15, 1879. The streak, which began at 10:00 P.M. on December 27 (a week after Mayor Daley's death) and ended at 10:10 A.M. on February 9, included an incredible twenty-two days of below-zero temperatures and a record −19° F on January 19, the coldest day of the century. (The typical Chicago winter has only eight days of below-zero weather.)[2] The deepest and most prolonged freeze in the city's history slowed its transportation system to a crawl, with breakdowns and delays on Chicago Transit Authority trains and buses. At the end of January, CTA officials had put out an advisory urging riders to stay home if possible, and the entire city began to pay a price in lost wages and revenues from businesses unable to stay open due to weather-related labor shortages. It was almost as if nature were mocking the city now that its leader, who always said that he never aspired to a higher political office than mayor of Chicago, was gone.

To compensate for fifty-two lost CTA train cars whose electric motors had been shorted out by blowing snow and corrosive road salt, officials shifted fifty subway cars from the State Street line after a January 28 snowstorm to prevent a loss of service on the Dan Ryan line. This line, which started on the south side of the city at 95th Street, ran northbound along the median of the Dan Ryan Expressway all the way into the Loop, where it became elevated and then continued out to the western suburb of Oak Park along Lake Street.[3] There were no notable service delays on the Lake-Dan Ryan line on February 4, although because of weather-related problems on another line—temperatures hovered in the teens all day and it had been snowing off and on in the afternoon—all Evanston Express trains were diverted at 5:00 P.M. to the outer track of the Loop elevated section, a track already shared by Dan Ryan and Ravenswood trains. As dusk descended on the Loop, Chicagoans who worked downtown began filing out of their offices as usual for their last commute of the

FIGURE 9.1. Two cars of a Lake-Dan Ryan L train lie in the street and another two dangle from the elevated tracks after it rammed a Ravenswood train (right) at Lake Street and Wabash Avenue. *Chicago Tribune* photo by Walter Kale.

week. It was an unexceptional day for a city in hibernation, caught in the malaise of a frigid winter, inert, seemingly catatonic. But the city's malaise was about to rupture.

A TERRIBLE AWAKENING

> . . . no need then to detail the Loop, in death like the center of every other American city, but what a dying! Old department stores, old burlesque houses, avenues, dirty avenues, the El with its nineteenth-century dialogue of iron screeching against iron about a turn. . . .
> —Norman Mailer

Despite some added congestion on the outer track of the Loop elevated line that Friday afternoon, CTA trains were running on schedule. At approximately 5:27 P.M. a rerouted Evanston Express train pulled into the elevated station at the corner of State and Lake Streets. As a trailing Ravenswood train approached the State-Lake station, it slowed and then stopped on the bend above Lake Street and Wabash Avenue, waiting for the Evanston Express train to clear the station before proceeding. It was now 5:29 P.M., the height of Chicago's rush hour. For reasons never determined, at that moment an eight-car Lake-Dan Ryan train rounded the northeast corner of the Loop at roughly six miles per hour and rammed into the rear end of the Ravenswood train. The first four cars of the Lake-Dan Ryan train, each filled to standing-room capacity with between fifty and seventy-five commuters, slowly began to sway, and an instant later they heaved and slipped the tracks, toppling to the street twenty feet below. Two of the cars landed on their sides near the intersection of Wabash and Lake; the other two hung at an angle from the tracks, each with one end still on the elevated platform and the other end resting on the pavement at street level. During the ensuing terror and confusion—266 people were injured and 11 were killed, among whom were two pedestrians crushed by the falling cars—the streets, as one reporter described it, "rang for hours with the siren wails of patrol cars and ambulances."[4] Priests rushed on foot from two nearby Roman Catholic churches to administer last rites to the dead and dying as fire department helicopters daringly maneuvered between tall buildings and street lamps to airlift the most critically injured from the site. Reports of the accident flashed across the country in time to interrupt dinner-hour news telecasts, while in Chicago phone circuits were jammed with incoming long-distance calls from commuters' relatives in every region of the nation. One eyewitness at the scene, a woman who was sitting in the Lakeview Restaurant on Wabash Avenue just yards from where one of the cars came to rest, described how an elderly female passenger crawled out of a broken window in one of the cars that still dangled from the edge of the L tracks and climbed onto its roof, raving and threatening to jump. The witness also recorded how the restaurant was converted into a temporary emergency room where the injured were brought in and left "lying there with broken arms, legs . . . lying on the floor, bleeding, with the medics working on them as fast as they could."[5] The magnitude of the carnage, the scope and severity of the injuries to passengers, the surreal element of a busy city center witnessing train cars

FIGURE 9.2. Its undercarriage twisted by the impact, the third car of the Lake-Dan Ryan train rests on its side while the fourth car remains upended in front of the Lakeview Restaurant on Wabash Avenue. *Chicago Tribune* photo by John Bartley.

falling from the sky at rush hour—all these circumstances created an atmosphere of horrified disbelief akin to what one would expect at the scene of a plane crash. What fixed this disaster forever in the collective psyche of all Chicagoans, however, was that it happened within three city blocks of the *Sun-Times, Daily News,* and *Tribune* newspaper offices. The press was at the scene before the police were.

Although the L-train crash would never make a top-ten list of Chicago disasters in terms of sheer numbers of people killed and maimed, it nonetheless earned the status of a catastrophe in terms of how it was perceived by the public and reported by the press. For Chicagoans, who had throughout the Daley era always prided themselves on living and working in a brawling industrial city of "big shoulders," a place where, as Norman Mailer phrased it, "life was in the flesh and in the massacre of the flesh," the event could not have seemed more catastrophic had an atomic bomb been dropped in the Loop.[6] The witness in the restaurant who blandly stated later that "it never dawned on me that the dangling cars might fall" may therefore stand as an antistrophe to the wailing chorus of print reporters who, in the immediate aftermath of the accident, likened it to some of the bloodiest battle scenes of Vietnam.[7]

Of the city newspapers covering the crash the next day, the *Sun-Times* devoted the most pages of print, using twenty reporters to produce seven separate stories that, with accompanying photos, completely filled the first eight pages of the Saturday morning edition. The lead headline on the front page read "L DISASTER" in bold two-inch type, a stark, terse proclamation underscored by a page-wide aerial photo of the wrecked L cars. Offering an unrehearsed response to horror incarnate, the news articles employed the immediacy of eyewitness accounts given just minutes after the crash: five of the seven articles contained lengthy quotations from victims and bystanders at the site of the accident. A page 4 article quoted a doorman from a nearby hotel who sprinted a half block to the crash site, where he happened upon several fatalities. His description is revealing in that it provides relatively few hard details about the scene he encountered:

> It was just so awful. One lady looked like her whole head was broken open. There was so much blood. There was another lady, on the ground in front of the sporting goods store. She was dead. There was a blond girl in her 20s. She was dead, too. Right after I got there the police covered her head. They don't do that for nothing.[8]

Other witnesses quoted in the *Sun-Times* coverage were more forthcoming with details, but perhaps because their comments were issued spontaneously at the scene, without the benefit of their having processed what they saw, the descriptions seem disembodied, unreal, even to the point of defying the laws of physics. "I saw a whole line of people pinned under the car," Agnes McCormick, the woman in the Lakeview Restaurant, was quoted as saying in the same article. "Only their heads and shoulders were showing. There were pools of blood. I've never seen so much blood." A patrolman who was walking the beat with his partner near Wabash and Randolph, one block from the falling cars, said that several passengers "came right through the windows from that car that's hanging up there. Some screamed. Others just seemed to fall silently. By the time they hit the ground, [my partner] Jerry Windham and I were there." Another eyewitness who had looked down at the accident from the fourteenth floor of the Loop City College building insisted that the last two cars of the Ravenswood train had derailed before the crash and damaged the tracks, whereupon the Lake-Dan Ryan train approached the damaged area and "just peeled off," falling from the elevated platform. Subsequent investigations of the crash by the CTA and the National Transportation Safety Board revealed that the Ravenswood train never left the tracks, which were unscathed in the accident and allowed Loop trains to run their normal routes around the Lake-Wabash curve the very next day.[9]

While the scores of print reporters covering the disaster for city newspapers had little difficulty finding loquacious (albeit unreliable) witnesses willing to provide narratives of what they had seen, many of the reporters found themselves becoming sources in their own stories. Because the reporters were on the scene so quickly, before emergency medical personnel could negotiate the busy downtown streets to reach the crash site, some of them became participants in the rescue effort, pulling the injured from the wreckage and comforting shock victims. The phenomenon of reporters turned rescue workers added a subjective dimension to the news coverage, their personalized descriptions of the disaster punctuated by snippets of ad-libbed moral commentary. A *Tribune* reporter concluded his Sunday feature story on the crash by suggesting that the disaster had already assumed mythic status, adding that future generations of Chicagoans would look up at the elevated tracks "reflexively . . . [a]nd remember Feb. 4."[10] One veteran *Sun-Times* news reporter, Bill Braden, was so shaken by his encounter with a dazed twenty-year-old woman whose mother had died in the free-fall of the lead car of the Lake-Dan Ryan train that he refused to preface his article with the customary byline. Underneath the story's headline, which read "Vickie Survives, but Mother is Dead," a disclaimer appeared in italics, stating that the reporter wished to remain anonymous due to the extraordinary circumstances under which he conducted his "interview" with his subject. "The reporter who wrote this story did not want his name used," the disclaimer stated. "He got involved—to help, not to get a byline." In place of Braden's name the byline read "By a *Sun-Times* Reporter."[11]

That Braden felt compelled to renounce publicly many of the expectations associated with his role as reporter suggests that the disaster had fractured, or at least redefined, those expectations. His poignant first-person narrative, he knew, simply did not read like a typical news story, and his involvement with his subject's personal tragedy—he ended up driving her home, a distance of more than forty city blocks, after he and *Chicago Daily News* columnist Mike Royko tried unsuccessfully to call her relatives from a pay phone—indicates a reluctance on his part merely to write a descriptive piece about the disaster. His lead paragraph, decidedly thin on details, hints at the difficulty of constructing a coherent drama from the disaster:

> I can't tell you much about Vickie Wojs. Only that she is a 20-year-old Chicagoan. That she was in an L crash. And that her mother, Lorraine Wojs, is dead.

In his column in the Saturday-Sunday issue of the *Daily News*, Royko details how Braden, who "was very close to tears," had "put his arm around her shoulder and spoke soothingly," coaxing the L-crash victim to let him drive her home. Both reporters unashamedly provide first-person glimpses into their own disordered states of mind, Royko declaring that the two blocks he walked alongside the victim were the "longest two blocks I've ever walked," and Braden stating, "I didn't know what to tell her" and "I can't tell you much more about Vickie. Only that her mother is dead."[12]

If the seasoned reporters Braden and Royko were unable or unwilling to attain a critical distance from the L disaster, rendering raw accounts of their own psychic experiences in relation to the event rather than simply describing the chaos, other reporters were similarly reluctant to provide objectively realistic representations, emphasizing instead the fantastical element of the scene before them. A *Daily News* reporter began his story on the disaster by referring his reader to the movie *King Kong*, which was playing at the State-Lake Theater just one block from the intersection of Wabash and Lake.

> The confusion of mangled steel, flashing lights and frenzied rescue work looked almost unreal, as if the L had been plucked off the tracks.

> Some inhuman force had to be responsible for the carnage underneath the 19th-century vintage L structure. How else could it have happened?

The reporter went on to describe how two of his colleagues saw "firemen cut through metal with blowtorches and buzzsaws to free twisted, bleeding bodies from the wreckage. They saw seemingly lifeless forms laid on stretchers and then suddenly twitch and writhe in agony."[13] *Sun-Times* columnist Roger Simon likewise described the cinematic quality of the emergency efforts: "A huge battery of searchlights lit the scene, making it all look like a Hollywood movie set. . . . There were the shrill whine of the power saws, growling when they bit into the metal cars and the hiss of acetylene torches as they reached where the saws could not."[14] A *Tribune* article quoted a commercial artist who, upon seeing the cars tumble off the tracks, declared, "It was like a fantasy"; a *Sun-Times* article quoted the same man as saying, "Things like this just don't happen."[15] Another *Tribune* reporter who was off duty and saw the accident happen described it as if he were viewing it on film. For him, however, the event appeared in miniature, as a diminution of reality rather than a larger-than-life event. Saying that he was underneath the intersection at the time of the crash, he added, "At first it reminded me of a toy train set, moving too fast, squealing on the tracks. Then the cars began to fall, one at a time. It was happening right above me—but in slow motion."[16] Even Vickie Wojs perceived the crash in terms of Hollywood. "All these disaster movies," Wojs told Braden, disoriented and still in a state of shock. "You see this in disaster movies. I couldn't believe it would happen to us."[17]

The impressions offered by print reporters and their sources at the scene of the L crash produced a cumulative and consensual feeling in the city newspapers, a sense not only that this was the worst transportation disaster Chicago had ever experienced, but that it was the worst urban catastrophe imaginable. Their collective assertion that the disaster had a cinematic, unreal dimension suggests the difficulty of processing what they saw; a train that appeared to fall in slow motion from the sky amid flakes of snow afforded no analogy to urban catastrophes they had known or might anticipate. In comparing the crash to scenes from disaster and horror movies, eyewitnesses proved themselves unable to create metaphors from contemporary life that would accurately describe the large-scale urban destruction they saw dramatized before their eyes. That some eyewitnesses to the L crash described the movement of the falling train cars as a series of super-slowed freeze-frames indicates how radically alien this sensory experience was to them. Similarly, the imprecision of some of the reporters' impressions was due in part to the accident having no recent memorable precedent. For many, it was an event without a referent save wartime massacre.

The emergency personnel at the scene, hardened to the grim spectacle of urban accidents involving large numbers of fatalities, employed metaphors of war to describe the slaughter they found. Chicago Fire Commissioner Robert Quinn, who helped pull bodies from the mangled cars, told a *Daily News* reporter, "I saw people upside down—it was just like the war." When interviewed by other reporters, Quinn called the crash "one of the worst wrecks I've seen" and added, "We broke every goddamn window to get people out. . . . The firemen worked like hell."[18] Dr. Bernard Feldman, who was on duty at Northwestern Memorial Hospital in the northern Loop area when the injured crash victims began pouring into the emergency room, said, "I didn't serve in Vietnam, but several staff members have. They said it looked like it—one patient after another."[19] A paramedic at the scene was similarly struck by the massive trauma he encountered inside the train cars. He described the difficulty of getting to all the injured commuters:

> They were all piled on top of each other. We immediately began triage . . . but first we had to pull them all apart. . . . When we got to the bottom, we could see through the windows, there were people down there crushed underneath. . . . there were a lot of people in shock, totally stunned, they had no idea what had happened. . . . Some of them simply wouldn't respond. It was [as] if they couldn't even hear me. So we led them around like sheep. Take a person in shock by the hand, and he'll respond like a little child.[20]

A twenty-nine-year-old seriously injured in the crash corroborated much of what the medical personnel were saying about the violent nature of the wounds they encountered at the site of the disaster. Interviewed by the *Tribune* from his hospital bed, he said that after the car in which he was riding hit the ground, he was able to survey his immediate surroundings.

> I looked at the woman in front of me. She was half out of the car window. Her head was under the car. I told the policeman to help her, but

he said, "Forget it. She's gone." I went through Vietnam and I never saw anything like this.[21]

The newspapers' repeated references to scenes of war, their emphasis on the surprising brutality of the injuries, their cataloguing of wounds (both the *Tribune* and the *Sun-Times* published lists of the dead and injured the day after the crash, with descriptions of the injuries), their insistence on the sheer horror of the task of rescuing the maimed and dying—such coverage kept Chicago readers mindful that in the annals of urban disasters this one was monumental, an event requiring as formidable a civic leader as Richard J. Daley to interpret its meaning and console the public. To make sense of the calamity in a post-Daley world became the newspapers' most difficult task.

IN THE WAKE OF DISASTER

Although the first day's coverage of the crash collectively conveyed an urgent, univocal despair, some of these early stories also offered concerted attempts to contain the horror. A *Daily News* story pointed out that no less than seven priests were on the scene, including Chicago's John Cardinal Cody, who administered some of the last rites. Also at the site, according to other stories that appeared on February 5 and 6, were "many dignitaries," among them Acting Mayor Michael Bilandic, Police Superintendent James Rochford, City Public Works Commissioner Marshall Suloway, Human Services Commissioner Cecil Partee, Chicago Transit Authority Chairman James McDonough, Regional Transportation Authority Chairman Milton Pikarsky, U.S. Representative Abner Mikva (D-Evanston), and, although his presence was never explained, heavyweight champion Muhammad Ali.[22] Implicit in this listing of important figures at the scene of the disaster was the notion that together they would explain how and why it happened, bring order out of chaos, and read meaning into the wreckage left in its wake. The day after the crash the newspapers also reported that Bilandic had visited hospitalized victims, called Illinois Governor Jim Thompson to discuss the status of the investigation, and personally requested $400 million in federal funds from President Jimmy Carter to begin work on a new subway system that would replace many of the downtown elevated train routes. The *Tribune* revealed in its Sunday edition that Bilandic also had arranged to meet with Carter the following day "to discuss the future of public transportation in Chicago," an indication that the mayor's attempts to console the public were based not on assurances that the L system was safe, but on the intention that it eventually would be replaced. The *Daily News* announced that RTA Chairman Pikarsky had appointed "a blue ribbon panel of national transportation experts" to investigate the accident; the *Sun-Times* noted that the National Transportation Safety Board would be conducting its own independent investigation.[23] Other articles, challenging earlier reports that in the aftermath of the tragedy the northern Loop area resembled "bedlam," were quick to emphasize how orderly and professional the rescue and cleanup operations were. A *Sun-Times* article detailing the expertise with which nearby Northwestern Memorial Hospital handled the crisis affirmed that every hospital worker knew exactly what to do, concluding, "And so the scene was one of order, not chaos; hurry, but not haste."[24] The *Daily News* made even broader claims for the city's emergency operations, declaring that "Every ambulance in the city and every doctor on the Near North Side had been put on alert by the fire department in the first hectic minutes after the crash and there was no shortage of medical help."[25] The *Tribune* joined the chorus of newspapers praising the area hospitals' emergency procedures, noting that each hospital "reported receiving an orderly flow of injured" and could have handled even more.[26] "Triage had gone into effect at 5:30 and ended at 7:15 P.M.," the *Sun-Times* proclaimed triumphantly. "The emergency was over."[27]

As joint investigations of the crash turned up evidence that the CTA motorman of the Lake-Dan Ryan train had overridden an automatic braking system and failed to follow proper slow-down procedures when approaching the Ravenswood train, the press became disinclined to print more stories that offered forms of consolation. Public discourse about the disaster became increasingly critical of the CTA and its operations, even to the point of questioning official explanations of the event. The *Tribune* ran a February 6 article under the headline "CTA Blames 'Human Error'" in which CTA Chairman James McDonough was quoted as saying that the preliminary findings should "assure the public that our equipment is safe, that our trains are safe to ride." Unwilling to let McDonough's statement stand on its own, the *Tribune* commented, "When asked how such a system could be 'fail-safe' if it allowed human error to cause a crash, McDonough said he couldn't discuss that until a later time." The story added, "McDonough also declined to assure the public that another crash would never occur on rapid transit trains."[28]

Five days after the crash the *Daily News* ran a page-5 story quoting Acting Mayor Bilandic as saying that the L disaster "brought out the best in everybody"; on page 3 of the same issue, columnist Mike Royko wrote a scathing indictment of Bilandic's response to the event. Criticizing Bilandic for using the disaster as a way to get "TV and newspaper coverage for his election campaign," Royko questioned the mayor's usefulness at the scene:

> He mouthed a lot of platitudes about how the police and firemen and hospitals were all pitching in and doing a good job. Apparently he doesn't know that they ALWAYS pitch in after a disaster. That is their work. They get paid for it. . . . He next rode along with investigators who tried to duplicate the conditions of the crash. The investigators didn't need him there. More TV publicity.

Royko suggested that instead of worrying about whether to seek $1 billion in federal funds to build a new Crosstown Expressway, Bilandic ought to use his administration's influence to "[demand] that the management of the CTA explain why so many of their passengers get killed and maimed."[29]

The *Sun-Times* ran several stories that did little to soothe the anxieties of a public already jittery about getting back on the city's L trains. Under the headline "Could Old Ways Avert L Mishap?" a February 9 article questioned the effectiveness of the relatively new electronic cab signaling system that the CTA employed on its elevated routes to prevent one train from ramming into the rear of another. Noting that the old mechanical system of metal "trip arms," still in use on the CTA's subway lines, had never allowed a rear-end collision, the *Sun-Times* concluded that the current system on the elevated lines had a dubious safety record by comparison. A February 6 story included the opinions of commuters on CTA Loop-bound trains about riding into the city to the downtown area, where the trains become elevated. Many of the passengers said that they would disembark before reaching the Loop and finish their commute by bus, cab, or on foot. One passenger said she would never ride the L trains again, adding, "I think the structure is old. It's antiquated. I'm surprised the city fathers haven't torn it down."[30] A second *Sun-Times* story appearing the same day revealed that two of the eleven people who died in the L crash were a young married couple who, although they regularly commuted together to their jobs in the Loop, had entertained fears about riding the train. The story quoted the sister-in-law of the deceased woman as saying that she "was afraid of the L. . . . I remember that she was stuck on the L about two hours once and she came home and cried."[31]

The editorials that appeared in the newspapers in the wake of the disaster were on balance quite unforgiving in their criticisms of the CTA and its operations. Noting that the L's "fail-safe" cab signaling system did not prevent the crash, the *Sun-Times* bluntly declared, "It should be modified to prevent *Titanic*-like failures." Arguing that elevated trains represent an outdated and unsafe technology, the editorial concluded, "the day of trains above Loop streets should be over. We can't think of a better time to begin the transition to a Loop subway system."[32] Five days later the *Sun-Times* reiterated its appeal that the CTA build a Loop subway, pointing out that CTA leaders "spent $25 million for a 'fail-safe' system that was supposed to guarantee that such crashes couldn't happen." The L disaster, said the *Sun-Times*, "is a reminder to all CTA employees that their own lives and others are in their hands."[33] A third editorial appearing more than a month later criticized the CTA for failing to train its motormen properly in the safe operation of elevated trains. Citing the National Transportation Safety Board's report that gave CTA employees a failing grade for "confusion and a lack of understanding of operating rules and of the cab signal indications," the *Sun-Times* argued that CTA officials "may have been too quick . . . to put sole blame on one man."[34]

A more strident tone characterized editorials that appeared in the *Daily News* during the weeks following the crash, influenced largely by columnist Mike Royko's interview with a CTA motorman. The motorman, who asked to remain anonymous, told Royko that in order to endure their jobs he and many of his coworkers took "drugs or drink to get us through it." When asked to elaborate on the unsavory elements of his job, the motorman spoke at length of the CTA's shortcomings.

> I hate being cooped up in that metal box. . . . Not everybody has the temperament or judgment to run a train. And a lot of us shouldn't be doing it. But they don't have psychological profiles on us. If I take a few drinks before I go to work, who's going to know it? . . . I'm looking for another job. I know that I've got to get out. It's just a matter of time

until I do something wrong. When you hate a job that much, and you don't have any confidence in yourself, it's bound to happen. You'll do something wrong to get back at the job you hate.

A *Daily News* editorial appearing two days after Royko's column pleaded that the CTA begin "the simplest kind of psychological screening" of motormen in order to weed out "a variety of hostile or suicidal potential killers." Noting that the motorman who was driving the fateful Lake-Dan Ryan train had been cited for several safety violations over his eight-year career with the CTA, the *Daily News* asked, "How can sane men put the job security of single individuals, with a history of repeated failures, ahead of the peril to life and limb of the thousands who have no choice but to ride with them?"[35] Joining the voices of discontent, the *Chicago Defender* published an article that attempted to shift attention back to the CTA leadership and away from the individual motorman involved in the crash. Quoting a member of the newly organized Transit Riders Authority, an African-American citizens' watchdog group formed to monitor the CTA, the article began, "For too long, the citizens of Chicago have remained silent, docile and obedient passengers to an unresponsive, inefficient and inexpert public transportation system."[36]

The *Defender's* response to the crash delineated significant differences between the way the white and black communities viewed the disaster. Whereas the *Daily News* had been quick to fault the CTA for hiring "aberrant personalities," thereby producing the kind of motorman who "seeks solace in drink or drugs," the *Defender* was inclined to point an accusatory finger at the hierarchical structure of an organization in which management was largely white and "upwards to 60 per cent" of motormen were black. Quoting two spokespersons from the Transit Riders Authority, the *Defender* noted that a "substantial part of the black community and the poor community" rides CTA trains, a situation that puts its members at risk when "the crashes on the Chicago public transit system add up to more fatalities than [those on] all of the other systems in the country."[37]

The *Defender* also scooped the other Chicago metropolitan newspapers when it obtained a rare interview with Stephen A. Martin, the black motorman of the Lake-Dan Ryan train. Saying that Martin was finally given an opportunity "to tell his side of the story" before a hearing of the National Transportation Safety Board, the *Defender* suggested that the motorman had been tried by the CTA and pronounced guilty by the mainstream press before he ever issued any public statement in his own defense. "The entire CTA system," the *Defender* thundered, "sounds antiquated and patronizing which smaks [*sic*] of plantation politics where Big Daddy rules and gives orders and token power to the worker." A month later the *Defender* reported charges of racism leveled against the CTA by a group of black CTA employees. Citing statistics supplied by the group making the charges, the *Defender* noted that 87 percent of the CTA workforce was now black and that the CTA was very quick to assign blame to a motorman in the event of an accident without first launching an investigation.[38]

The *Defender's* editorial position received significant support from its readers, one of whom, a Presbyterian minister, wrote a letter to the editor that depicted CTA officials as perpetrators of crimes against humanity. Arguing that the CTA should have much stricter standards in place for recruiting and evaluating motormen, he suggested that not having such standards was tantamount to murder:

> The horrifying accident that slaughtered so many lovely people and damaged the emotional systems of so many others going home from work is a tragedy that lingers in my mind as being the job of murderers. . . . It is time for the people to speak, and so articulately that the possibility of something like this happening again will be very unlikely.[39]

Letters to the editors of the other city newspapers voiced similar concerns with CTA management, but many of the letters also implicated the socioeconomic class and, in coded ways, the race of the motorman. In the wake of reports that Martin had been suspended from his job three times and cited for nine safety violations in 1975 alone, a week after the crash the *Sun-Times* ran two letters that condemned the undereducation and carelessness of motormen who drive the L trains. Stating that the CTA's problem "is not faulty equipment, but faulty personnel," one reader claimed that he had friends who had applied for jobs with the CTA but were turned away on the grounds that they had earned college degrees. He ended his letter by calling for a "thorough investigation of CTA hiring practices, ideally by a grand jury."[40]

With varying degrees of subtlety, the editorials and letters to the editor of the three major daily newspapers seemed to seek the cause for the crash solely in the CTA's force of ill-trained, poorly educated, and (though not stated explicitly) black motormen—the same "aberrant" and "incompetent" motormen referred to in the columns and letters. It should come as no surprise, then, that the newspapers themselves mirrored a rather exclusive white power structure in the city, a structure that Mayor Daley not only had never questioned but had helped to establish even as black migration to Chicago steadily increased the city's minority population throughout the 1960s, and to upwards of 40 percent by the late 1970s. A September 1976 study of Chicago's newspapers in the *Chicago Reporter*, a monthly periodical devoted to racial issues in metropolitan Chicago, found that none of the three major Chicago newspapers had significant minority representation in its corps of reporters. Five months before the L-train crash and three months prior to Mayor Daley's death the *Sun-Times* had nine black reporters on an editorial staff of 230; the *Tribune* had eight on a staff of 400; and the *Daily News* had seven on a staff of 195. The fact that in late 1976 no black journalist sat on the editorial boards or worked at the major bureau offices of any of the big three Chicago papers indicates clearly that the papers' coverage of both Daley's death and the L-train crash offered a "white" perspective of these events, a phenomenon that tended to lionize Daley and condemn the CTA's hiring of purportedly underqualified minorities.[41]

Taking a retrospective look at Daley's mayoral reign in its December 1976 issue, the *Reporter* offered a counterpoint to the opinions of the popular press, criticizing Daley's performance on race relations. Arguing that the late mayor "consistently refused to lead on the issue of race," the *Reporter* added, "If O'Hare Field and the new Loop skyline are Daley's monuments so are the Robert Taylor Homes."[42] The Robert Taylor Homes, a two-mile strip of low-income high rises on the city's south side, represented to many observers the mayor's attempt to contain blacks in undesirable areas of the inner city, a policy that created concentrated areas of poverty and despair. A decade after Daley's death the Robert Taylor Homes had decayed so badly that a *Newsweek* special report on the public housing project called it "a place where hope died," declaring gloomily that "to be a boy in the Taylor Homes is to apprentice at becoming an invisible man."[43]

At the time of the mayor's death, however, this legacy of housing large numbers of blacks in drug-infested, war-torn encampments within the city did not find its way into the major newspapers' eulogies. If Daley refused to use the power of his office to lead Chicago toward economic and educational reform in the face of growing racial segregation, none of the three major daily newspapers seemed inclined to criticize very persistently his performance on race. The papers' criticisms of CTA hiring practices, moreover, reflected a general reluctance on their part to confront veiled forms of racism in the city's institutions, much less within their own ranks. To members of Chicago's black community, the papers' condemnation of the CTA motormen looked and sounded like the reaction that might have come from the mayor's office itself were Daley alive to respond to the L-train crash.

Perhaps the most fascinating development in the written discourse about the tragedy as time went on was the shifting of public attitudes about it. As the days turned into weeks, letters to the editors of the major Chicago newspapers began to construe the crash as both an inevitable and an expected event. It seemed as if Chicagoans' paralytic horror had turned, in a matter of days, to bland acceptance. In the public debate over whether the CTA should replace some of its elevated routes with subways, for example, one *Tribune* reader argued that constructing subways would be self-defeating since they "would merely make it more difficult to rescue accident victims." A letter the next day pointed out that "Chicago's transit lines have the sharpest curves in the world, and even a slow collision may lead to what happened Feb. 4." A *Sun-Times* reader demonstrated a similar fatalism, saying that because crashes on the flawed CTA system were unavoidable, "Putting the problem underground will solve nothing."[44]

It is significant that readers of the city's major newspapers were beginning to view the subway as a more dangerous version of rapid transit than the L, and that they considered either system as doomed to failure. In light of the newspapers' coverage of the disaster and subsequent editorials in favor of a new subway system, one would expect the public to be sympathetic to the idea of abandoning the L for an underground transportation system. In a sense, however, Chicagoans had processed the tragedy as an event that, because it confirmed their worst fears about the unreliability of technology, precluded the possibility of their accepting the mere substitution of one technology for another. Moreover, for those who rode the L and viewed it as part of Chicago's sky-defying architecture, a symbol of Chicago's brawny, self-confident civic character, the calamitous event of February 4 was not reason enough to abandon a technology that in eighty years of operation had become a defining feature of the city.

In place of an initially unanimous disbelief that such a disaster could happen, then, public discourse about the event eventually came to articulate a quite different position. The L-train disaster had forced upon the people of Chicago perhaps only one abiding truth: trains, like planes, are subject to catastrophic failures. And like the sudden and disastrous death of Mayor Daley, an event that came before the city could prepare for it, this particular accident required interpretive strategies that offered not only consolation but preparedness for future calamities. With the help of the city newspapers, Chicagoans had come around to the notion that when a train falls out of the sky, the only way to salvage meaning from its wreckage is to transform it over time into an expected event. It meant, in effect, transforming the broken L train into something else.

RECONSTRUCTING THE WRECKAGE

Now, between the wavering warning flares, the all-night locals paused, as always, and passed across the thousand-girded El down the tunnel of old El dreams and were gone.

—Nelson Algren

A potentially poignant moment occurs in the eighteenth-century novel *Tristram Shandy* when one of the main characters, Walter Shandy, receives by letter the news of the sudden and unexpected death of his eldest son Bobby. The eccentric Walter, however, surprises the reader with his emotionless and oddly amusing response. "If my son could not have died," he says, "it had been matter of wonder,—not that he is dead."[45] Walter Shandy's remark epitomizes a familiar twentieth-century response to technological disasters, especially airplane crashes. On some level, those of us who live in the modern era of air transportation know that airplanes are *supposed* to fall out of the sky; we have cultural rituals in place to prepare us for such an event. Such rituals include, among other things, flight attendants' preflight safety instructions involving the proper use of oxygen masks, seat cushions, and exit chutes in the event of an emergency; standardized protocol governing the dissemination of information from cockpit to cabin when a plane encounters trouble during a flight; the speedy arrival of airline psychologists and the National Transportation Safety Board at the scene of the inevitable crash; and the eventual release of edited versions of black box voice recordings of the pilot's communications with the control tower. Any passenger who takes a seat on a commercial airliner must listen to a litany of emergency procedures before the plane begins its journey; and even though the effect of repetition over many flights dulls one's response to this routine, it does not erase one's awareness of the possibility of mechanical failure, loss of airspeed, rapid descent, and death. Furthermore, the airline commuter is forced continually to contemplate—because of frightening vibrations caused by takeoffs and landings, the sensation of falling due to sudden patches of turbulence, and in-flight messages from the pilot that punctuate the constant hum of the plane's engines—the extent to which the journey's success depends upon thousands of details working themselves out behind the curtain of the cockpit. Even the calmest air traveler has prepared for the possibility of those details not working out, and the price one pays for that preparedness is an ever-present, subconscious anxiety.

Freud has argued that fright is caused "by lack of any preparedness for anxiety," a theory he formulated to account for traumatic neurosis. This condition, which Freud observed in response to "railway disasters and other accidents involving a risk to life," was in his view a direct result of experiencing an unexpected fright. According to Freud, anxiety and fright are two entirely separate emotions deriving from separate causes. Anxiety, he theorized, "describes a particular state of expecting the danger or preparing for it, even though it may be an unknown one." By contrast, fright "is the name we give to the state a person gets into when he has run into danger without being prepared for it; it emphasizes the factor of surprise." If we apply Freud's notion to modern forms of transportation, we might conclude that those who travel by plane are familiar with anxiety, feeling it initially as a kind of low-level background emotion as the plane throttles up its engines and prepares for takeoff. According to Freud's theory, the airline passenger avoids fright precisely by maintaining a continual state of anxiety, erecting at the same time a kind of "stimulus shield" against the various disconcerting noises and vibrations one experiences in flight. By undergoing preparations for anxiety while at the same time providing a protective shield against unwelcome stimuli, the airline passenger can endure the mental strain of air travel. Only when the external stimuli are powerful enough to break through the stimulus shield, such as in the case of a rapid and unaccountable loss of altitude or smoke filling the cabin, does the passenger experience a trauma that would induce fright.[46]

Modern commuter train passengers, by contrast, have little reason to prepare for danger by entering into a continual state of anxiety. This is true in large part because the train passenger has no access to ritualized procedures that would prepare one for disaster. Commuter trains generally have no seatbelts, no attendants issuing safety instructions, no disembodied voice over an intercom recommending that passengers remain seated when the train negotiates a tricky bend in the track. In a sense, the technology of rail transportation has advanced to a stage at which the disquieting stimuli so prevalent in air travel are no longer present. Compared to the stimuli an airline passenger receives during a flight, a train's consistency of motion and noise produces a relatively smooth and anxiety-free journey for the typical commuter.

On the other hand, it is true that in the early days of locomotives the railway caused tremendous anxiety both in Europe and in America when city planners began admitting trains into heavily populated urban areas for interstate travel. Wolfgang Schivelbusch demonstrates how in the first half of the nineteenth century an imperfect technology led to widespread fears of derailment, particularly in the aftermath of a tremendous railway disaster on May 8, 1842, in France that killed fifty-five passengers and injured more than a hundred more. According to Schivelbusch, moreover, frequent derailments in the early days of the locomotive constituted just one reason for travelers' anxieties. The isolation of the compartment in which passengers were typically enclosed led to a "feeling of helpless passivity," a sense that one was unable to influence the machinery that carried one pell-mell through a landscape from which one was alienated. One of the psychological effects of early train travel was that passengers used to traveling by horse-drawn coaches began to think of themselves as commodities, as parcels shot through time and space like projectiles shot from a cannon.[47] Other historians of early modern transportation have pointed out how the first generation of steam-powered locomotives were often banned from the downtown streets of America's largest cities. By 1839, public fears of high speeds and all-too-frequent boiler explosions led to rioting by New York City residents along the inner-city streets where railroads ran their steam engines.[48] Such fears prompted experimentation in the late 1860s with an alternative technology, the elevated railroad, which eventually was designed to run on electric power, considered a much safer energy source than steam. At the same time, high-speed interurban trains were largely banished to the peripheries of the city, and new train stations were built there to accommodate rapid passenger movement from one urban area to another.[49] The result was that intracity commuter trains, slower and domesticated versions of their interurban counterparts, came to be seen as a safer, less threatening technology as the conversion of steam- to electric-powered railroads proceeded over the last third of the nineteenth century. Into this milieu the elevated train was born.

The elevated train came to Chicago at the beginning of the 1890s, hastened along by a recommendation from the city's new mayor, Hempstead Washburne, that the public needed relief from dangerous traffic congestion in the city center. To remedy the situation, Mayor Washburne created His Council's Special Committee on Intramural Transportation, which advocated the development of elevated railways in the city center. The mayor's committee viewed the elevated railway as not only a way to relieve downtown traffic congestion, but a means by which Chicago could catch up to eastern cities such as Philadelphia that already employed the new technology for their commuters.[50]

The elevated railroad was not, however, without its critics. Largely because the majority of Chicago's elevated lines were rapidly constructed by the unscrupulous financier Charles Tyson Yerkes—a man who in his heyday had a virtual monopoly on Chicago's rail system, owning more than five hundred miles of railway, including forty miles of elevated electric railway—the L was developed haphazardly and at minimal cost, giving it a reputation for poor service. Yerkes, in fact, spent much of his time in court as a defendant in personal injury suits brought by passengers of his trains.[51] When asked to explain why he did not attempt to relieve the overcrowding and delays on his streetcars, he is reported to have said, "It is the straphangers that pay the dividends." He also once told an acquaintance, "The secret of success in my business is to buy up old junk, fix it up a little, and unload it upon other fellows."[52] In the face of growing public indignation over the dubious safety record of his rail lines, Yerkes eventually departed Chicago for New York and then London, leaving behind him an elevated railway system that was, in the opinion of some transit watchers, "obsolete even before it was finished."[53]

In the seventy-seven years between Yerkes's departure from Chicago and the February 4, 1977 L-train crash, the Chicago elevated railway had no less than eight major accidents, including a November 24, 1936 crash at the Granville Street station that left ten people dead and 234 injured. In the eleven-year period from 1964 through 1975, CTA trains experienced 219 collisions and derailments, with injuries to more than 1,700 passengers. During the fifty-year period between 1927 and 1977 there were thirty-two fatalities from CTA accidents—more than for all the other rapid transit lines in the entire United States combined. One of these accidents, on December 7, 1966, came about when the last two cars of an L train inexplicably detached from the rest of the train and left the tracks, falling into a yard below. Only one person died in that incident; twenty-five others were injured. On six separate occasions prior to 1977, a CTA accident involved train cars falling off the elevated tracks.[54]

Although taken individually none of those accidents caused as many casualties as the 1977 crash, the question remains why this most recent crash, neither unprecedented nor wholly unthinkable, became in the minds of many Chicagoans the most catastrophic event of their century. Why did this accident, which in the annals of Chicago transportation history was far from anomalous, remain so uniquely horrific, so capable of provoking a kind of hysteria in both the press and the public? And how was the horror ultimately contained?

The answer to the first question lies partly in the geography of the event and partly in its timing. Because members of the Chicago print media were so proximate to the disaster that they saw it unfold through their office windows—one *Sun-Times* reporter remarked twenty-two years after the crash that he and his colleagues that day were "[watching] it out the city room windows as if it were on TV"—they reported it as history in the making rather than as a finished event.[55] Rendered largely in first-person, present-tense narrative, much of the newspaper coverage conveyed an urgency and immediacy not normally found in most stories about technological disasters. That the train fell off its tracks in the middle of a busy city center at the height of rush hour, at a time when reporters from both the day and night shifts of the three major city newspapers were on duty, ensured maximum coverage as well. Perhaps most importantly, however, the crash happened at a moment in Chicago history when the city was most vulnerable to a cataclysmic event. The three major Chicago newspapers had reported the death of Mayor Daley as a ringing climax to an era that had seen Chicago grow and flex its muscles as the "Second City"; their perception was that the post-Daley city, by contrast, was stagnating. Quoting from such longstanding and vociferous Daley critics as the Reverend

Jesse Jackson, Illinois Governor Dan Walker, and Governor-elect James Thompson (who as U.S Attorney had prosecuted many of Daley's corrupt political friends), the *Tribune* had offered only words of praise from his former antagonists the day after Daley's death. "We will miss him," said Thompson, echoing the words of other Daley detractors quoted in the same article. "[H]e was a great mayor, a fact not always understood by his critics."[56] Despite some dissenting opinions in the occasional article that questioned Daley's authoritarianism even as it praised his reign (the *Tribune* noted in its very laudatory eulogy of the mayor that he "possessed vast and unquestioned power," which he sometimes wielded "unmercifully"), the newspapers' coverage of his death conveyed for the most part a sense of despair and dislocation.[57]

The protracted cold spell that followed Daley's death only seemed to confirm the media's fatalistic opinion that no civic leader of Daley's stature would ever emerge to take the city back to its previous grandeur. Plunged into the deepest freeze in the history of their once proud city, Chicago's mainstream print journalists now feasted on the notion that no living contemporary of Daley had power enough to keep the CTA trains on schedule, much less the personal influence and authority to deliver singlehandedly, as they believed Daley had once done, Chicago, the state of Illinois, and ultimately the Presidency of the United States to John F. Kennedy.[58] As the paralyzing cold gripped the city, a telling metamorphosis occurred: the Chicago newspapers became increasingly impatient with the monotone character of Daley's replacement, a man the *Daily News* would eventually call "the unlikely politician with the mortician's manner."[59] In the colorless Bilandic, Chicago in early February 1977 had a new leader who, unlike his predecessor, could not bully or cajole Chicagoans into a comfortable belief that their city was working on all fronts. He could not so easily downplay its deep racial divisions, cover up its corrupt patronage politics, or defend its reputedly brutal police force. If a city in some small way takes on the character of its mayor, the Chicago newspapers saw their city as mirroring its new leader's lethargy. And so the L-train crash hit at the heart of Chicago when the city was comatose, its pulse slowed to a dull throb. It shocked into wakefulness a hibernating giant.

How the horror was contained once the newspapers began their initial coverage owes something to the character of Chicago-style journalism. Despite their reputation for turning out as hardened a group of reporters as ever penned a story, the major daily newspapers saw this tragic drama as both utterly apocalyptic and transformative, as a climactic event that somehow, amid all the terror and suffering it engendered, legitimized Chicago's claim to greatness at the very moment when that greatness seemed on the wane. They knew, even if they could not articulate it, that the L-train crash was a more significant indicator of the failures of modern technology than even a downed airliner; Americans grown accustomed to news footage of smoldering fuselages had never before seen a train fall from the sky. Out of the first day's coverage was born a bravado, a sense that this event was uniquely terrible in scope, even if the rest of the nation looked on with comparatively mild interest.[60] For those who lived and worked in the city, this was a monumental event, an epic catastrophe that helped Chicagoans define themselves anew as gritty survivors, the true inheritors of Carl Sandburg's laughing, brawling, defiant city. In the pages of the city papers, the L-train crash became the defining moment of a modern city that, having recently lost its greatest mayor, sought to renew its own grandeur by itself, alone, with no outside help.[61]

Perhaps the greatest irony of the disaster is that the Chicago newspapers ultimately reconstructed it as an expected event. Initially unimaginable, the L-train crash became over a few weeks the seminal event of Chicago's modern history, the transitional moment marking the end of Mayor Daley's long, storied reign and the start of a new epoch. On another level, however, the print media's reconstruction of the fallen train cars into recognizable wreckage meant, in effect, transforming the shattered L train into a downed airliner in the public's imagination. As the major daily newspapers sought to console and control the astonished public in the aftermath of the crash, the people of Chicago needed to know that it was not a harbinger of the apocalypse, but rather an inevitable event in a world made dangerous by technology. Preparing the public for future anxiety became the newspapers' task even as they attempted to explain away the present horror of 266 injured and eleven dead. To normalize the horrific, to willingly suspend a city's disbelief, the reporters who saw it happen ultimately construed the crash as the natural outcome of running a number of trains around sharply curved rails twenty feet in the air. From this day forward, the L became a symbol of Chicagoans' particular mix of defiance and anxiety, and in preparing for the disconcerting possibility of future disaster the public simply accepted the inevitability of this one.

And so in the weeks following the crash, the city awoke to the terrible truths of its imperfect transportation technology. Having prepared themselves for the worst, city planners ultimately decided to forgo immediate plans for a new downtown subway, opting to keep its elevated train system in place no matter the cost in future accidents. As the temperature broke the freezing mark on February 9 and a portent of a spring thaw wafted in on southerly winds, the people of Chicago resumed their daily commutes, from the suburbs to the edges of the city, from there to downtown, riding the several arteries of the L system into the Loop, defying the curves around which the L trains screeched, knowing that this journey, though subject to disaster, was a civic responsibility for all who drew sustenance from the perilous city.

NOTES

1. "Daley: City's Boss for 21 Years," *Chicago Tribune*, 21 December 1976, sec. 4, 12.

2. "Freezing Streak Snapped; Thaw May Stay," *Tribune*, 10 February 1977, sec. 1, 5; "Superfreeze Letting Go After 43-Day Siege Here," *Chicago Sun-Times*, 9 February 1977, 5.

3. "Weather Is Costly to CTA," *Tribune*, 3 February 1977, sec. 3, 6.

4. "2 Yrs. Old: 'The Crash' Lingers On," *Sun-Times*, 4 February 1979, 47.

5. Ibid., 67.

6. Norman Mailer, *Some Honorable Men: Political Conventions 1960-1972* (Boston and Toronto: Little, Brown, 1976), 174.

7. "2 Yrs. Old," 67.

8. "'It Was the Most Fearless Thing I've Ever Seen,'" *Sun-Times*, 5 February 1977, 4, 6.

9. Ibid.; "Ls Fall, 13 Die, 165 Hurt," *Sun-Times*, 5 February 1977, 2, 16.

10. "'My God, the Car is Coming Through!'" *Tribune*, 6 February 1977, sec. 1, 15.

11. *Sun-Times*, 5 February 1977, 2.

12. Ibid.; "'I Can't Go Home . . . My Mother Died,'" *Chicago Daily News*, 5-6 February 1977, 1, 4.

13. "Like a Movie—but Horror Here Was Real," *Daily News*, 5-6 February 1977, 4.

14. "'Cars Coming Off . . . Oh God,'" *Sun-Times*, 5 February 1977, 6.

15. "'L' Train Plunges to Loop Street in Rush Hour," *Tribune*, 5 February 1977, sec. 1, 4; "'It Was the Most Fearless Thing,'" 6.

16. "'The Train's Cars Began to Fall, One at a Time . . .,'" *Tribune*, 5 February 1977, sec. 1, 3.

17. "Vickie Survives, but Mother is Dead," *Sun-Times*, 5 February 1977, 2.

18. "Disaster Plan: A Call to Action" and "20-Foot Plunge: `4 Seconds—We Were on the Ground,'" *Daily News*, 5-6 February 1977, 3; "'L' Train Plunges to Loop Street in Rush Hour," *Tribune*, 5 February 1977, sec. 1, 4.

19. "16 Die in Rush-Hour El Crash," *Arlington Heights Herald*, 5 February 1977, 1.

20. "Crash Horror: A Paramedic's View," *Sun-Times*, 6 February 1977, 2.

21. "Victims Recall Grim Scene: Confusion, Screams, Blood," *Tribune*, 6 February 1977, sec. 1, 14.

22. "20-Foot Plunge,'" 3; "'My God, the Car is Coming Through!'" sec. 1, 15; "Ls Fall, 13 Die, 165 Hurt," 2.

23. "Bilandic, Percy Support a Subway," *Tribune*, 6 February 1977, sec. 1, 15; "Did L Driver Bypass CTA Safety System?" *Daily News*, 5-6 February 1977, 1, 4; "Ls Fall, 13 Die, 165 Hurt," 2, 16.

24. "Hospital Goes to Disaster Plan," *Sun-Times*, 5 February 1977, 8.

25. "Disaster Plan: A Call to Action," 3.

26. "Disaster Aid Plan Passes the Test," *Tribune*, 6 February 1977, sec. 1, 13.

27. "Hospital Goes to Disaster Plan," 8.

28. *Tribune*, 6 February 1977, sec. 1, 1.

29. "Everyone Was Great in Disaster—Bilandic," *Daily News*, 9 February 1977, 5; Mike Royko, "Bilandic Off the Track on His CTA Solution," *Daily News*, 9 February 1977, 3.

30. *Sun-Times*, 9 February 1977, 5; "Take the L Again? Riders Split," *Sun-Times*, 6 February 1977, 2, 32.

31. "Disaster Ended Daily Trip of Oak Pk. Couple," *Sun-Times*, 6 February 1977, 3.

32. Editorial, "To Deter L Disasters," *Sun-Times*, 7 February 1977, 29.

33. Editorial, "More 'Human Error'?" *Sun-Times*, 11 February 1977, 57.

34. Editorial, "Tightening CTA L Safety," *Sun-Times*, 6 July 1977, 73.

35. Mike Royko, "Nerve-Shattering Job of a CTA Motorman," *Daily News*, 10 February 1977, 3; editorial, "Screen the Motormen," *Daily News*, 12-13 February 1977, 16; editorial, "Safety First on the CTA," *Daily News*, 6 July 1977, 10.

36. "Ask Safety Probe of 'L' Trains," *Defender*, 16 March 1977, 4.

37. "Screen the Motormen," 16; "Ask Safety Probe of 'L' Trains," 4.

38. "Martin Fights 'Fall Guy' Rap," *Defender*, 22 March 1977, 4; "Blacks Hit CTA on Racism," *Defender*, 26 April 1977, 4.

39. "Improve the CTA . . ." *Defender*, 15 February 1977, 7.

40. "Blame CTA Hiring," *Sun-Times*, 11 February 1977, 57.

41. "Who, What, When, Where, Why of Race Relations at Chicago's Major Dailies; More Black Reporters in Newsrooms, but Editorial Influence Blurred," *Chicago Reporter*, September 1976, 1-5.

42. "Looking Back on the Daley Era: His Legacy Holds Lessons for the Future," *Chicago Reporter*, December 1976, 5.

43. Peter Goldman, et al., "Inside Trey-nine," *Newsweek*, 23 March 1987, 60.

44. "After the L Crash," *Tribune*, 10 February 1977, sec. 3, 2; "After the Accident," *Tribune*, 11 February 1977, sec. 2, 3; "Can't Bury L Problem," *Sun-Times*, 11 February 1977, 57.

45. Laurence Sterne, *Tristram Shandy*, ed. James A. Work (Indianapolis, Ind.: Bobbs-Merrill, 1982), 353.

46. Sigmund Freud, *Beyond the Pleasure Principle*, trans. and ed. James Strachey (New York: W. W. Norton, 1989), 10-11, 30-36.

47. Wolfgang Schivelbusch, *The Railway Journey: Trains and Travel in the 19th Century*, trans. Anselm Hollo (New York: Urizen Books, 1979), 58, 83, 127. Schivelbusch argues that early train travel caused passengers to feel as if they had lost contact with the landscape outside, in part because the terrain on which the railway companies laid their railroads was necessarily straightened and smoothed over, resulting in "the loss of the sense of space and motion that was based on it." See Schivelbusch, 25; also chap. 3, "Railroad Space and Railroad Time," 41-56, and chap. 4, "Panoramic Travel," 57-72.

48. Clay McShane, *Down the Asphalt Path: The Automobile and the American City* (New York: Columbia University Press, 1994), 12.

49. See McShane, *Down the Asphalt Path*, chaps. 1 and 2; and Winfried Wolf, *Car Mania: A Critical History of Transport*, trans. Gus Fagan (London: Pluto Press, 1996), esp. part 1, "The Eighteenth and Nineteenth Centuries: Railways and Canals."

Wolf describes how the early railroads built their routes to expedite interurban transport, a circumstance that led them to avoid linking city center with city center. Schivelbusch also discusses the relegating of interurban trains to the margins of major cities in chap. 11, "The Railroad Station: Entrance to the City." Schivelbusch states that in the industrial era the "railroad station is not an integral part of the city: it is located outside the traditional city walls, and for a long time it remains an alien appendage." Schivelbusch, *Railway Journey*, 161.

50. Homer Harlan, *Charles Tyson Yerkes and the Chicago Transportation System* (Ph.D. dissertation, University of Chicago, 1975), 122-33.

51. Gavin Stamp, "Say Yes to Yerkes," *Spectator*, 13 April 1996, 52-53; "Yerkes: Real Crash Culprit?" *Sun-Times*, 13 February 1977, 5.

52. Peter Baida, "Dreiser's Fabulous Tycoon," *Forbes*, 27 October 1986, 97-102.

53. "Yerkes: Real Crash Culprit?", 5.

54. "Worst L Crash Here," *Sun-Times*, 5 February 1977, 8; "Loop Tragedy Was Second Major Crash in 13 Months," *Tribune*, 5 February 1977, sec. 1, 2; "CTA: Deadliest Transit Line," *Daily News*, 8 February 1977, 1, 12.

55. Zay N. Smith, personal communication, 14 July 1999.

56. "Leaders, Citizens Mourning," *Tribune*, 21 December 1976, sec. 1, 1, 8.

57. "Daley: City's Boss for 21 Years," sec. 4, 12.

58. That Daley was unable to deliver Illinois to Jimmy Carter in the 1976 presidential election was an indication to some observers that the mayor's power was waning. That same year Michael Howlett, Daley's handpicked Democratic machine candidate, lost the Illinois gubernatorial election to Republican Jim Thompson by the astounding margin of 1.39 million votes.

59. "Bilandic: The Reluctant Politician," *Daily News*, 9 June 1977, 6.

60. *Newsweek* ran a seven-paragraph story on the L crash in its 14 February 1977 issue; *Time* failed to mention the crash in its February issues.

61. Acting Mayor Michael Bilandic boasted to a group of Rotarians on February 8, 1977 that when President Carter phoned a few hours after the L disaster to offer the city federal assistance, he told the President, "we have everything under control with our own resources here in the city of Chicago." "Everyone Was Great in Disaster—Bilandic," *Daily News*, 9 February 1977, 5.

10

The Day the Water Died

The Exxon Valdez *Disaster and Indigenous Culture*

Duane A. Gill and J. Steven Picou

Alaska Natives were devastated by the Exxon Valdez *oil spill of 1989. The spill destroyed more than economic resources; it shook the core cultural foundations of Native life. Alaska Native subsistence culture is based on an intimate relationship with the environment. Not only does the environment have sacred qualities for Alaska Natives; Natives' very survival depends on the preservation of the ecosystem and the maintenance of cultural norms of subsistence. Duane A. Gill and J. Steven Picou discuss the consequences the spill had for Native people in terms of subsistence, cultural traditions, and psychosocial well-being.*

The excitement of the season had just begun, and then, we heard the news, oil in the water, lots of oil killing lots of water. It is too shocking to understand. Never in the millennium of our tradition have we thought it possible for the water to die, but it's true.

—Chief Walter Meganack[1]

ON MARCH 24, 1989, the largest oil spill in North American history occurred when the supertanker *Exxon Valdez* ran aground on Bligh Reef in Prince William Sound, Alaska. Within three hours of the grounding, the tanker lost more than 10 million gallons of Prudhoe Bay crude oil. The accident was exacerbated by lack of preparedness and inadequate response. After a three-day period of calm seas during which no significant oil containment or recovery occurred, a violent storm broke up the massive slick, and oil soon washed ashore on the western edge of Prince William Sound. Oil then drifted and spread southwest along the Kenai Peninsula, up Cook Inlet, into the Gulf of Alaska, around Kodiak Island, and along the Aleutian Peninsula. In all, more than 1,300 miles of rugged Alaskan coastline and 10,000 square miles of coastal seas were oiled.[2]

There is no good place to have an oil spill, but Prince William Sound has to be one of the worst. Described as one of the two most beautiful places on earth,[3] the Sound is characterized by a 2,000-mile shoreline of bays, fjords, islands, and tidewater glaciers. The area is accented by a mountain landscape covered by a temperate rainforest. The region's ecosystem is rich and diverse, supporting an abundance of birds, fish, marine mammals, and wildlife.

Prince William Sound's ecosystem was the first to suffer the effects of the oil spill. Early spring in Alaska signals the beginning of a season of high biological activity. As a result, many birds, animals, and fish were exposed to oil during various stages of migration and reproduction. The initial casualty list included more than 300,000 birds, 3,500 sea otters, 300 harbor seals, 15 killer whales, and an unknown number of young fish.[4]

Cleanup techniques such as pressurized hot water and chemical treatments worsened the disaster by destroying microorganisms that form the base of the ecosystem's food chain. The ecological devastation was so great that ten years after the spill, only two of twenty-four affected animal species (bald eagle and river otter) had been declared "recovered."[5] Among the twenty-four species, seven (including black oystercatchers and common loons) were listed as "recovery unknown" and eight (including killer whales, harbor seals, and Pacific herring) were listed as "not recovering."[6] Although some species (for example, harbor seals) were experiencing problems prior to the spill, the disaster exacerbated their decline.

The ecological destruction also had profound effects on human communities, especially those dependent on renewable natural resources such as fish.[7] Commercial fishing communities in oiled areas experienced disruptions within the fishing industry that, in some places, continued almost a decade after the spill.[8] Although many fishermen made money from the cleanup, all have suffered from the decline in the commercial fishing economy. According to Bob von Steinberg, "Since the spill, the value of fishing permits have plummeted, effectively destroying the collateral and equity of most fishermen. Hundreds have quit the business. As many as half of the 700 boats in Cordova's port have been idle in recent seasons. In 1987, the Cordova fleet landed 70 million pounds of fish worth $60 million in current dollars; that fell to 59 million pounds worth $26 million in 1997."[9] The damage to economic resources reverberated throughout the community, affecting commercial fishermen, cannery workers, and other industry-related groups.

Of all groups touched by the disaster, in many ways Alaska Natives were most affected. The disaster damaged more than economic resources; it attacked subsistence, the defining characteristic linking modern Natives to their traditional culture. Not only does the environment have sacred qualities for Alaska Natives; their cultural survival depends on a healthy ecosystem and maintaining subsistence norms and values. The spill threatened the well-being of the environment, disrupted subsistence harvests, and severely impaired Alaska Natives' sociocultural milieu.

CULTURAL CONTEXT

Historically, Prince William Sound was a melting pot of various Alaska Native groups, including Eskimos, Aleuts, Athapaskans, Eyaks, and Tlingits.[10] Through centuries of group succession, trade, intermarriage, and warfare, a distinct group, Alutiiq, emerged to dominate the region. Villages were located along coastal areas with a high confluence of fish, marine mammals, and wildlife.

The abundance of renewable natural resources and the development of harvest techniques gave rise to a subsistence culture that persisted for several millennia prior to Western contact. Since contact, however, Alaska Native culture has experienced numerous assaults and transformations.[11] Russian occupation in the mid-1700s exposed Alaska Natives to diseases that decimated the population and to alcohol, which further disrupted social life. When Alaska was transferred to the United States in 1867, Natives became a major component of the commercial fishing labor force.[12] This helped accelerate cultural change toward a mixed economy of capital and subsistence and was accompanied by an increasing reliance on Western technology in pursuit of traditional subsistence activities.[13]

American occupation of Alaska brought more disease and alcohol, further decimating the Native population. In 1900, an influenza epidemic known as the Great Death killed more than half of the Eskimo and Athapaskan people exposed to it. Harold Napoleon, an Alaska Native spiritual healer, noted that "this epidemic killed whole families and wiped out whole villages. It gave birth to a generation of orphans—our current grandparents and great-grandparents."[14] In the 1930s, Native children were forced into boarding schools, where they were usually punished for speaking their Native language. The ensuing demise of their language further eroded traditional culture, and the diminished contact with elders reduced opportunities to pass on cultural traditions to new generations.[15]

Native culture became more modernized in 1971 when federal legislation allocated 44 million acres of land and $962 million to Alaska Natives. Natives were organized into a framework of village corporations to manage their resources. Three Native corporations were established in Prince William Sound for the villages of Chenega Bay and Tatitlek (each with a population of less than 100) and the village of Eyak located in Cordova, where nearly 500 Natives reside.

Although much of traditional Native culture has been lost through population loss and modernization, subsistence continues to be an important part of the self-identity of many Alaska Natives.[16] As one Native noted:

> When we worry about losing our subsistence way of life, we worry about losing our identity. . . . It's that spirit that makes you who you are, makes you think the way you do and act the way you do and how you perceive the world and relate to the land. Ninety-five percent of our cultural tradition now is subsistence . . . it's what we have left of our tradition.[17]

Many Natives living in towns and urban areas continue to participate in subsistence activities, particularly through social networks that share traditional foods and resources. These activities reaffirm their Native identity and maintain part of their cultural heritage.

Although many Alaska Natives live in urban areas, others reside in small towns and isolated villages where they practice a subsistence economy and lifestyle. Like other subsistence cultures, Native village economies are quite different from industrial economies. Since residents produce and consume their own products, most Native villages have no stores or markets. Resource distribution is based on communal networks of family, extended kinships, friendships, and the village. Subsistence resources are not thought of in terms of dollars, and there are few jobs for pay. Much of the cash that occasionally comes into the community is spent on modernizing subsistence operations (for example, snowmobiles and guns). Instead of the job specialization found in industrial economies, a villager has a broad range of skills and works with a wide variety of natural resources.

Compared to Western capitalist culture, a subsistence culture has more direct and intimate links to the environment. Cultural activities of Alaska Natives are intertwined with seasonal cycles.[18] Chief Walter Meganack explains:

> Our lives are rooted in the seasons of God's creation. Since time immemorial, the lives of Native people harmonized with the rhythm and cycles of nature. We are a part of nature. We don't need a calendar or clock to tell us what time it is. The misty green of new buds on the trees tell us, the birds returning from their winter vacation tell us, the daylight tells us. The roots of our lives grow deep into the water and land. That is who we are. The land and the water are our sources of life. The water is sacred.[19]

Subsistence harvests also serve as a context for teaching skills and lessons of life, storytelling, and other cultural activities. Eyak Native Patience Faulkner states:

> It is during the cycles of subsistence that bonding is strengthened and expanded. The sense of worth is solidified and new skills are learned. It is during these bonding times that our individual value is placed within our community, and we are able to understand what we must do to preserve our lives and to live in harmony.[20]

Rita Miraglia, a subsistence specialist for the Alaska Department of Fish and Game, observes:

> When someone goes out harvesting, they're not just doing it for themselves; they're doing it for their community. It gives them connection

to the generations before them. It gives them connection to the generations to come. So it's all about community.[21]

Subsistence is the remaining link most Alaska Natives have with their
traditional culture. This intimate relation to natural seasonal cycles includes symbolic definitions and expressions of a way of life. As an Eyak
Native describes it, "This is a way of life for us, not just subsistence. It's
part of us. We *are* part of the earth. We respect it."[22]

Alaska Natives have endured many traumatic encounters with the
West and, as a result, their culture continues to change. Throughout
these changes and declines in environmental resources, fragments of
their traditional culture have survived, particularly subsistence. When
the *Exxon Valdez* ran aground, Alaska Natives experienced a serious
threat to their subsistence culture.

INITIAL EFFECTS OF THE SPILL: YEAR ONE

Alaska Natives encountered many problems after the spill and during
the cleanup. The timing of the spill was particularly disruptive since it
occurred as spring was breaking the long, cold grip of winter.

As news and images of the oil spill spread, Natives experienced a
mixture of emotions: denial, outrage, sadness, numbness, hurt, confusion, and grief. "First I cried, and then I was mad and then cried. It was
just really mixed."[23] "This is hurting more than anything else we ever
experienced. It's like losing everything you had."[24] "Some people were
depressed and suicidal. Even nonfishermen felt somebody had broken
in and entered their house. [There was a] terrible feeling of rape, viola-
tion."[25] "Seeing the dead animals day after day really got to me. I found
myself standing in the middle of Main Street crying."[26] "Those days
were horrible. . . . Dying animals were floating around. Dead animals.
. . . It's beyond imagination. Oil everywhere. . . . Dead otters. Dead deer.
Dead birds."[27] "When you pick up these dead carcasses day after day,
you go through a mourning process. It's not only death in your environment, but, in a sense, it's a death of yourself. Because you're part of
that environment."[28]

Residents of Tatitlek experienced fear because the tanker was
grounded a few miles from their village and they could smell the fumes
from the leaking oil. As Tatitlek Village Council president Gary Komp-

koff recalls, "It's not something that people can easily forget. The smell made some people sick. The herring season was about to open; our first harvest after winter. The government had to shut it down. Shut down our salmon too. We lost it all."[29]

Chenega Bay villagers endured additional pain because the *Exxon Valdez* grounded 25 years to the day after their village was completely destroyed in the Great Alaskan Earthquake and all the residents were forced to move. The people had managed to maintain their spirit of community and had just recently completed rebuilding and resettling their village. "And then the oil spill hit," explained Gail Evanoff, a village resident. "It was like . . . that I felt a very deep hurt. That the pain they had suffered in '64. Not even 20 [*sic*] years later that we would have to endure this kind of devastation again down here."[30]

Throughout the spill area, village residents experienced trauma as oil washed up on their shores and they witnessed the environmental destruction. Shock overcame many who witnessed the massive death brought about by the spill. Chief Meganack said, "We walked the beaches, but the snails and the barnacles and the chitons are falling off the rocks, dead."[31]

Like emergency response workers at the site of a disastrous crash, Alaska Natives were numbed by the total devastation they witnessed from the oil. An Eyak Native leader noted, "The morning after the spill I got calls from the elderly saying 'I feel like someone has died, like a part inside me is gone.'"[32]

Alaska Natives had never experienced such environmental destruction and contamination. Contamination intruded into the very fabric of their spiritual beliefs and day-to-day behavior. Many believed the oil spill had damaged their relationship with the environment. Kai Erikson's interviews with Alaska Natives revealed the depth of their feelings[33]: "They killed something vital in me when they spilled that oil. You see, there's a rapport, a kind of kinship you sometimes develop with a particular place. It becomes sacred to you. That connection has been severed for me."[34] "People around here are closely related to the land and the ocean, so the death of birds and animals and seeing so much oil in the water has a deep impact on their lives. . . . This is their home, and it's been violated."[35] "I was born of this land, these waters. . . . I'm as infected as mother nature is, suffocating and gasping for breath. . . . As the environment deteriorates, we too deteriorate."[36] "The beach was sick, the water was sick. We couldn't give it medicine to make it well. . . . It was sick and there was nothing I could do to fix it."[37] "It's not only death in your environment, but in a sense it's a death of yourself, because you're a part of that environment."[38] "The Sound isn't dead, but it is very, very sick. My heart is sick, too. . . . Along with the countless birds, otters, and other casualties of the spill, a part of me has died."[39]

Natives were concerned about the environmental damage, the loss of subsistence resources, and the safety of subsistence food. Because the spill occurred at the beginning of the traditional harvest season, subsistence activities were disrupted all year. The decline in subsistence harvests meant that "store" food had to be shipped to many villages.

Oil covered many of the areas traditionally used to harvest subsistence foods. This created concern about the safety of subsistence foods that may have been exposed to the oil. As Chief Meganack observed, "We caught our first fish, the annual first fish, the traditional delight of all; but it got sent to the state to be tested for oil. No first fish this year."[40] Chenega Bay residents Larry and Gail Evanoff related the following:

> We always say "the tide goes out, the table is set." But not anymore. You're going to have to be really picky and choosy when the table is set. What's all this oil going to do to our food; our supermarket out there?[41]

Natives experienced a further loss of traditional authority as they had to rely on outside authorities for food safety. Daryl Totmoff explained, "You can't have a scientist in a white coat come up and tell you everything is safe. It's going to take a long time to feel comfortable again. It's going to take a long time even if they give us a clean bill of health. We're still really wary and unsure about a lot of things. The big question mark is still there."[42]

In addition to the social disruptions caused by the decline in subsistence, the disaster response also took a toll. Exxon's cleanup strategy of hiring an army of workers to treat the shoreline and recover oil had disruptive effects. Native villages were inundated with a seemingly unending influx of people and technology. Chief Meganack explained:

> Before we have a chance to hold each other and share our tears, our sorrow and our loss, we suffer yet another devastation. We are invaded by the oil companies offering jobs, high pay, lots of money. We need to clean the oil, get it out of our water, bring death back to life. We

are intoxicated with desperation. We don't have a choice but to take what is offered. So we take the jobs, we take the orders, we take the disruption, we participate in the senseless busywork.[43]

Native villages experienced a "human spill" as corporate and government officials, cleanup crews, scientists, lawyers, and media personnel traveled through the oiled communities. Village populations also increased as relatives of villagers came to work on cleanup crews. Most outsiders, particularly the media, were ignorant of Alaska Native culture. Eric Morrison, a Tlingit Native who conducted research in the village of Tatitlek, observed, "It did not matter where the news people came from or their particular field of media, they all were insensitive to the community, arrogant, frightening to the children, and abusive to the elders. Reportedly they chased children and elders into homes, attempted to take pictures through residents' windows, and laughed at people who were caught off guard."[44]

The arrival of so many strangers in such a short time caused many Natives to feel threatened and uneasy in their own communities. A Chenega Bay resident said, "It was like living in an apartment and then all of a sudden there are ten people that you don't know who come in and live with you."[45] The high number of strangers led many villagers to lock their doors, something most had never felt the need to do. The human spill became such a problem that some local leaders issued informal bans on travel into the village. A village official in the Native village of Karluk reported, "Finally, we decided to keep the reporters out. I remember getting on the radio when a plane showed up and telling the pilot that if there were any reporters on the plane don't think about landing. They are not welcome here!"[46]

Along with the "human spill" came a "money spill." Many Natives experienced a sudden and dramatic increase in cash income from working on the cleanup. Instead of providing a boost to the community, the influx of cash was perceived by some as "money pollution." Most villagers were not accustomed to dealing with large amounts of cash, and oftentimes it was poorly managed. Some Natives used money to purchase alcohol and drugs and smuggle them into the village. The income also forced some to confront the Internal Revenue Service for the first time. In subsistence villages, cash can become a disruptive intrusion. As Cordova resident David Grimes explained, "The people of Tatitlek don't really measure their life in dollars. If you screw up the environment, you've screwed everything up. If you make a cash settlement, you screw them up."[47]

Authorities in charge of the cleanup ignored the Natives' knowledge of the local area. Chief Meganack observed, "Our people know the water and the beaches, but they get told what to do by people who should be asking, not telling."[48] A Native official of Chugach said, "The people there [in the villages] know the current flows of Prince William Sound. They knew there was no way the oil spill could be contained, we knew it would impact Seldovia, English Bay, Port Graham, and other areas but we were not asked, we were ignored when we went to the meetings to give input."[49] Officials often overlooked the fact that some Natives were highly educated (for example, some are scientists and attorneys), and in some cases they displayed blatant racism.

Cleanup activities disrupted families, especially those with children. Many children received less care as parents worked on cleanup crews or became involved in other spill-related activities. As one villager described it, the jobs "were not just 8 to 5 jobs. They were like 7 to 12 [at night] and sometimes longer. They worked until midnight unloading boats, got home, slept three hours, and got up and went back to work."[50]

In some families, one or both parents were gone for weeks working on cleanup crews. Declining parental supervision led to increased drinking and drug use among some teenagers.[51] Within a month of the spill, the village of Tatitlek requested $40,000 from Exxon to provide adequate child care in the village. Exxon did not respond to this request despite the efforts of state officials. A Tatitlek village administrator expressed his frustration: "It was pretty incredible that Exxon would spend eighty thousand dollars to save an otter but they weren't willing to spend any money on the children."[52]

Social life was also disturbed by the disaster. Research indicated that individuals working on the spill reported significant increases in domestic violence and abuse of alcohol and drugs in their communities and among their families and friends.[53] Dr. Bill Richards, the Chief of Behavioral Health for the Alaska Area Native Health Service, observed:

> I know of villages that had many alcohol-related problems in the past, but had begun a slow and painful process of recovery, with many villagers sober prior to the spill. After the spill, village leaders began drinking again, and many in the village have now "fallen off the wagon" with

re-emergence of the numerous alcohol-related problems—child-abuse, domestic violence, accidents, etc.—that were there before.[54]

The assault on the environment, disruption of subsistence activities, and strains on family and village life affected the transmission of traditional culture to new generations. As Chief Meganack explained, "Our elders feel helpless. They cannot do all the activities of gathering food and preparing for the winter. And most of all, they cannot teach their young ones the Native way. How will the children learn the values and the ways if the water is dead? If the water is dead, maybe we are dead, our heritage, our tradition, our ways of life and living and relating to nature and each other."[55]

LONG-TERM EFFECTS OF THE SPILL: 1990–1996

The effects of the disaster on Alaska Natives and their culture did not end after the first year. Chronic ecological effects emerged as the ecosystem struggled to recover and Natives tried to cope with the consequences. Commercial fishermen, Alaska Natives, and other groups economically or culturally tied to the damaged environment experienced uncertainty, distrust, and cultural disorganization in the aftermath of the disaster. Natives experienced continued disruption in subsistence as well as persistent social strains and chronic psychological stress. They also experienced a "secondary disaster" when they became embroiled in litigation against Exxon.

Alaska Natives in the spill area experienced a sharp decline in subsistence harvests following the disaster.[56] Subsistence harvests in all communities in the spill area declined in 1989, and many remained below pre-spill levels in 1990. By 1991-1992, however, most had recovered to levels comparable to those observed prior to the spill.

Subsistence recovery was slower in Prince William Sound. Prior to the disaster, Tatitlek and Chenega Bay harvested more than 600 pounds of wild foods for every person in the village. Harvests dropped to 225 pounds in 1989 and 150 pounds in 1990. The harvests for the two villages increased to 345 pounds in 1991, but fell again to only 275 pounds in 1993. Although yields continued to improve gradually, subsistence harvests had not recovered to pre-spill levels by 1996. A U.S. Department of the Interior study reported that "This decline in subsistence, reliance on store bought groceries, and other economic hardships related to the oil spill increased personal and family friction and stress."[57]

Part of the decline in subsistence harvests can be attributed to safety concerns about subsistence foods. Residents were particularly concerned about mussels, clams, and other shellfish. Fears about the safety of subsistence foods were reinforced when the Prince William Sound herring population crashed in 1993. Villagers observed surface hemorrhages, deformities, and abnormal behaviors among the herring, and laboratory tests concluded that the population had a viral infection. This supported the perceptions of many elders that the harm to the environment was long-term.

Villagers were skeptical when officials announced that the virus posed no human health threats and the herring were safe to eat. Tatitlek village council president Gary Kompkoff summarized the issue:

> Prior to the oil spill, our people never had to worry about their resources, for generations we have been able to harvest whatever we wanted without worrying about the safety of consuming anything. The total failures of the herring and salmon seasons this year have made residents of Prince William Sound wonder what the true impact of the oil spill has been on the sound. The herring are an integral part of the food chain, almost all of the subsistence resources we rely on depend largely on herring for their sustenance. When the herring returned to the sound with sores and lesions on them, we became extremely concerned about the safety of harvesting any and contacted the Alaska Department of Fish and Game and the Department of Environmental Conservation about their condition; we were told that while both agencies were not sure what was affecting the herring, they were safe for human consumption. This made absolutely no sense at all to us. Suppose there were meats in the American supermarkets that had sores and lesions on them, do you think that either agency would have told the consumers that the meats were safe, even before they had determined what was affecting the meats?[58]

Subsistence harvests also declined because resources were more scarce. Chenega Bay villagers reported fewer birds, fish, marine mammals, and wildlife. "This was the poorest year we ever had for seal. I looked for sea lion, but I didn't get any."[59] "There are no more octopus along the beach [on Evans Island] and no gumboots."[60] "I couldn't find any shrimp in the normal hot spots. I used to be able to get shrimp just a couple hundred yards in front of my cabin. They're not there now."[61] "Seals are scarce. When you go out on a boat, you seldom see seals or sea lions like before. Man, the water is just dead. Along eighteen miles of Knight Island where we used to harvest, I didn't see even one. Now we have to go thirty miles by boat to find seals. We used to get them less than two miles away from the village."[62] "Most all the animals use the ocean for salt, for kelp, and it's still oiled. [The] land otters and mink are dead. I haven't seen an ermine in four years."[63] "We were out for six hours. [We] saw not one [bird] at Cape Elrington. [The] oil spill killed them all. Oil is at Bishop Rock, Sleepy Bay, Pt. Helen, and it comes through here. I have been here [in Prince William Sound] 17 years. Now you can run all day and count all the birds you see on one hand."[64] "[Marine mammal harvest numbers] are a lot less because they are more scarce. There are not as many around and they're dropping yearly. We think the *Exxon Valdez* oil spill had a lot more to do with it than people believe. The pups sank. We saw it. How can a mother seal identify its pup if it's covered with crude?"[65]

The decline in subsistence resources disrupted culture in a variety of ways. Many people, especially elders, hungered for foods that were no longer available. As an elder from Chenega Bay explained, "I still hunger for clams, shrimp, crab, octopus, gumboots. Nothing in this world will replace them. To be finally living in my ancestors' area and be able to teach my kids, but now it's all gone. We still try, but you can't replace them."[66] When asked about the importance of subsistence foods to Native identity, a Cordova Native replied, "Without those things, a part of *us* is missing. Because we were raised that way."[67] When asked what would happen if there were no game, another Cordova Native answered, "A part of our lives would be missing. We'd be craving something we can't get. It would bring a void."[68]

Social disruption continued in the years following the disaster. There were declines in social relations among spouses, children, relatives, friends, neighbors, and co-workers, and more conflicts with outsiders and friends[69]: "The oil spill has drifted people apart. We used to help each other. Before, these people were one big family, but after the oil spill I noticed the village—that it's pulling away again, people started going into their own shell, and just pulling away."[70] "That's one of the saddest things that came out of this. This was a very tight-knit, close community, and it's really been fragmented, you know, the trust. People are uncertain."[71] "You can deal with the dead salmon and the dead otters, but you can't deal with the damage done to the social fabric of the community."[72] Natives exposed to the spill tended to have problems with alcohol, drugs, and fighting and observed these problems in their communities and among their families and friends.[73]

Problems also persisted among Native children. For example, there were reports of children not liking to be left alone, of children fighting with other children, having trouble getting along with their parents, and suffering declines in academic performance.[74]

This chronic pattern of stress was worsened by limited mental health resources. Native villages in the spill area relied on professionals from larger communities. However, the disaster overburdened mental health services, and in many communities the turnover rate of personnel increased. As Patience Faulkner explained:

> The social service people are good at their jobs. [But] these people were damaged by the spill, just like everybody else. They tried to cope, their work load went up, but it was like the hurt helping the hurt. It was very difficult for them. And we would not accept at all a stranger coming in from Fairbanks, or Juneau, or Nome, to be our social worker, and sit there and say, "Yes, I know how you feel." No, you don't know how I feel, because you were not here. You did not go through the scare, the trauma, the fright, the financial disaster. There was nothing a social worker from anywhere else can say to help us. We have got to heal from within.[75]

As a result, most Alaska Natives did not receive adequate assistance to help them cope with the personal, family, and community stress they were experiencing.

Litigation created additional problems. Alaska Natives were among the many groups that filed a class-action lawsuit against Exxon.[76] Natives claimed the disaster damaged subsistence resources and thereby disrupted their culture. Lawyers argued that the Natives' "subsistence way of life was central to their culture in a way that was fundamentally different from the noncommercial resource uses of other Alaskans."[77]

The Natives' claims of cultural damage were rejected in a 1994 court ruling by Judge H. Russel Holland. Judge Holland ruled that such claims were not recognized by maritime law. He further stated:

> The Alaska Natives' non-economic subsistence claims are not "of a kind different from [those] suffered by other members of the public exercising the right common to the general public that was the subject of interference." Although Alaska Natives may have suffered to a greater degree than members of the general public, "differences in the intensity with which a public harm is felt does not justify a private claim for public nuisance."[78]

The judge acknowledged a universal right to lead a subsistence lifestyle:

> All Alaskans, and not just Alaska Natives, have the right to obtain and share wild food, enjoy uncontaminated nature, and cultivate traditional cultural, spiritual, and psychological benefits in pristine natural surroundings. Neither the length of time in which Alaska Natives have practiced a subsistence lifestyle nor the manner in which it is practiced makes the Alaska Native lifestyle unique.[79]

Under the law applied to this case, the subsistence activities of Alaska Natives were indistinguishable from those of non-natives.

Judge Holland did recognize a cultural difference between Alaska Natives and non-native Alaskans, but he declared:

> The affront to Native culture occasioned by the escape of crude oil into Prince William Sound is not actionable on an individual basis. . . . The Alaska Natives' claims for non-economic losses is [sic] rejected, and the plaintiffs must find recompense for interference with their culture from the public recoveries that have been demanded of and received from Exxon.[80]

Specifically, Judge Holland reasoned that Exxon's legal settlement with the state of Alaska and the federal government provided compensation for "lifestyle" damage claims. He later noted:

> The value Alaska Natives place on their choice to engage in subsistence activities is a non-economic "way-of-life" claim which this court has already rejected. In the case of subsistence harvests, to place a

value on anything other than the lost harvest itself is to place a value on lifestyle. The court recognizes that lifestyle has a value, but the value is non-economic. Quite simply, the choice to "engage in [subsistence] activities" is a lifestyle choice. . . . The lifestyle choice was made before the spill and was not caused by the spill. . . . Lest there be any doubt, the claims of the Native subsistence harvesters are limited to the economic value of the lost subsistence harvest.[81]

The result of Judge Holland's rulings was a rejection of cultural damage claims and a narrowing of claims to the economic value of damaged resources.

Class-action litigation caused many Natives to feel further victimized because damages to their culture were disregarded. These feelings intensified when the case went to trial in 1994. The Natives were among several groups seeking compensation for damages caused by the disaster. The jury awarded $20 million to Native corporations for damage to subsistence resources. Natives were also one of many parties awarded a share of $5 billion in punitive damages. However, the case was appealed and Exxon has vowed to appeal all the way to the Supreme Court. Twelve years after the spill, the damages remain unpaid.

CULTURAL REVITALIZATION: 1996–2001

Alaska Natives in Prince William Sound experienced a turning point in 1996 that led to a revival of their culture. Subsistence was slowly improving, but people were still concerned about recovery of the ecosystem. Social disruption continued, but it resembled stressful patterns that existed prior to the spill. Communities continued to experience mental health problems, and attempts were made to remedy these through innovative programs. Natives also began to experience the effects of a 1991 legal settlement between Exxon and the Alaskan and federal governments.

Twelve years after the spill, subsistence harvests have returned to pre-spill levels, even in the heavily oiled areas of Prince William Sound. Certain resources are still scarce or unsafe to use, so Natives have increased their harvests of other resources. They also report spending more effort and money and traveling further to harvest subsistence foods. However, there is still concern about the recovery of the environment. Valdez charter boat operator Stan Stephens observed:

> It'll probably take another 20 years for the Sound to be back as it was. When you go out, you can tell there's not the bird life there was. There are problems with the whales. We lost almost all our herring, and everything that feeds off herring had to find another food source. Some of the marine life had to go someplace else, but it's slowly coming back.[82]

Social disruption continues, particularly in Native villages where high rates of suicide, alcohol and drug abuse, domestic violence, and child abuse exist.[83] Because many of these patterns existed prior to the spill, it is difficult to determine the role the disaster had in intensifying them. Traditional community mental health services have been ineffective in responding to the unique problems posed by the oil spill disaster. A research project to develop, implement, and evaluate an alternative community mental health program was initiated in 1995 under the direction of Dr. J. Steven Picou.[84] The program has been effective in informing the public and reducing some of the mental and social stress. However, mental health problems remain as the environment and economy struggle to recover and the litigation languishes in the courts.

Litigation between Exxon and the Alaskan and federal governments has brought significant changes to Natives' lives and communities. In 1991, Exxon agreed to pay $900 million over a ten-year period. The settlement created the Exxon Valdez Oil Spill Trustee Council, made up of representatives from six state and federal agencies, to manage the settlement fund. The fund was targeted for recovery and restoration of damaged resources. The budget included about $180 million for scientific research on injured species and construction of a state-of-the-art aquarium and research laboratory. The bulk of the funds, however, went into restoration efforts to buy, preserve, and protect lands adjacent to heavily oiled areas. More than 650,000 acres, including 1,400 miles of shoreline, were purchased to provide damaged species with a habitat untouched by logging and other development activities. As the executive director of the Trustee Council, Molly McCammon, explained, "We've gotten incredible resources into the public domain. We wanted to insure there'd be no further harm to wildlife resources and provide a safety net by providing a long-term recovery area."[85]

The Trustee Council land purchase posed another dilemma for Alaska Natives because much of the land needed for restoration was owned by Native corporations. The financially strapped corporations were caught between a need for money and a need to maintain their cultural heritage. With many Natives living in poverty amid continuing uncertainty about subsistence, most corporations decided to sell large tracts of land. The Eyak Native Corporation in Cordova earned $45 million, Tatitlek $34.5 million, and Chenega Bay $34 million from land sales to the Trustee Council.[86]

Decisions to sell land were reached differently among the six corporations involved. Although one corporation, Port Graham, decided not to sell, three, including Tatitlek, were mostly in favor. The Chenega Bay and Eyak corporations experienced more debate and contention.[87] Eyak village council vice president Glenn Ujoka stated, "We lose our identity when we lose our land."[88] Likewise, Mark Hoover, an Eyak council member, explained, "Most of the Native corporations are in dire financial need—this one's always in trouble. This was our land, our way of life. They only came to the Natives so they could get the land back. The money's only going to mean $70,000, $80,000 over five years and you can't live on that. Maybe if we'd had part of that $5 billion, we wouldn't have had to sell."[89] Eyak member Sylvia Lange lamented, "But it's so pathetic. We have sold our children's birthright. It has made the land into something it never should have been. This has pulled the rug out from under any kind of tribal feeling among us. Now, it's all about individual gain. I didn't think I was in it for me—I thought we were in it for us. They dangled $45 million in front of people who desperately needed it, and we sold our heritage. It's human nature. It's not fair to hold Natives to a higher standard than anyone else. Most of them understand it's more money than they've ever seen in their lives."[90] Luke Borer, a former Eyak corporation official, summarized the situation when he said, "I'm sure everybody will look back at this and regret it. Remember, the Indians on Manhattan thought those beads were a good deal, too."[91]

Despite these continuing problems, Native culture has experienced a sense of revitalization in recent years. The decline of subsistence and uncertainty regarding its recovery increased awareness of the importance of traditional culture. Many Natives felt the need to re-energize their local communities by holding more community events and teaching traditional arts and crafts. Money from land sales has assisted in this effort, but a more significant event occurred in 1996 when a "Talking Circle" ceremony was held by the Native Village of Eyak and residents from Tatitlek and Chenega Bay were invited to participate.

A Talking Circle is a ceremony where individuals share experiences, feelings, and thoughts with others. It is open to all village members, and all who attend are "welcomed and openly received by the circle."[92] Talking Circles are flexible enough to accommodate various groups and situations. Participants "can come together to share themselves," and "truth can be spoken about all things communal, familial, and personal."[93]

The 1996 Talking Circle was organized by the Native Village of Eyak as part of a community mental health research program sponsored by the Prince William Sound Regional Citizens' Advisory Council.[94] The *Exxon Valdez* oil spill was the focus of the Talking Circle, and the objective was to assist in healing spill-related cultural and personal problems. The two-day event received assistance from Native spiritualists from Alaska, an American Indian outreach specialist, and the Northern Light Drummers, a Native group who performed traditional music.[95] More than eighty-five people participated in the ceremony, including local Natives and their non-native spouses and friends. Natives from Tatitlek and Chenega Bay also attended, including some Elders from both villages who brought special significance to the ceremony. Dr. Picou was one of several non-Natives who participated by talking about research findings on the disaster's damage. His observations of the ceremony provided a firsthand account of this unique event.[96]

The opening ceremony focused on healing relationships between the people and their environment. An apology was formally offered to the sea otters through a ritual conducted on the shores of Orca Inlet in southeastern Prince William Sound.

A variety of topics emerged from the Talking Circle. Picou identifies five themes: ecological damage, Exxon, traditional culture, the group, and the self.[97] Many participants expressed sorrow for the injuries suffered by various species in the ecosystem and apologized for the hurt caused by human beings. In addressing Exxon, participants talked about Exxon's failure to live up to promises and the corporation's disregard of Native subsistence culture as part of its legal defense. Native cultural tradition was reasserted through expressions of a "cultural spirit" of harmony with nature, the need to return to more traditional ways, and the therapeutic performances of

the Northern Lights Drummers. Participants addressed group conflicts, and many talked about the positive healing they were experiencing from the ceremony. During the ceremony, some individuals
made public commitments to change their lives.

The Talking Circle has had a revitalizing effect on traditional culture. In Cordova, the Native Village of Eyak has become more active in
organizing cultural events and teaching traditional arts and crafts. Villages are using money from land sales to send the youth to "Spirit
Camps" where traditional culture is passed on to the next generation.[98]
One Talking Circle participant summarized the event: "The Talking Circle was important because it gave everyone a sense of knowing that we
all shared a common hurt. It also gave direction to all Native people
who were there. The way for us should be the Native way. We now realize that it is important for us and our children to embrace our elders
and our heritage."[99]

CONCLUSION

The *Exxon Valdez* oil spill cannot be described simply as a supertanker
impaled on a reef, spewing millions of gallons of oil into a pristine natural environment. Oil not only discharged into the environment, it
coursed throughout the subsistence culture of Alaska Natives. The disaster directly challenged a culture with traditional subsistence bonds to
the environment, producing emotional responses and long-term psychological distress within Native communities. These effects have continued and are among "the most lingering and measurable of the
spill."[100]

Since contact with Western civilization, Alaska Native culture has
been repeatedly assaulted. In response to these challenges, Alaska Natives have been able to retain and transmit to their children a core element of their identity—subsistence. The ability to endure the "Great
Death," attempts at cultural genocide, loss of resources, and the delayed trauma of these events is a testament to a commitment to survive
the *Exxon Valdez* disaster as a living culture. More than a decade ago, the
late Chief Walter Meganack described this resolve:

> A wise man once said, "where there is life, there is hope." And that is
> true. But what we see now is death, death not of each other, but of a

source of life, the water. We will need much help, much listening in order to live through the long barren season of dead water, a longer winter than ever before. I am an elder. I am chief. I will not lose hope. I will help my people. We have never lived through this kind of death, but we have lived through lots of other kinds of death. We will learn from the past, we will learn from each other, and we will live. The water is dead, but we are alive, and where there is life there is hope.[101]

NOTES

This essay was originally published in J. Steven Picou, Duane A. Gill, and Maurie J. Cohen, eds., *The* Exxon Valdez *Disaster: Readings on a Modern Social Problem* (Dubuque, Iowa: Kendall/Hunt Publishing Company, 1997). Used with permission.

Research for this essay was supported in part by the Mississippi State University Social Science Research Center, Mississippi Agricultural and Forestry Experiment Station (Project No. MIS-605080), and the College of Arts and Sciences, University of South Alabama. Additional support was provided by grants from the National Science Foundation, Polar Social Science Division (DPP 9101093), the Earthwatch Center for Field Research, and the Prince William Sound Regional Citizens' Advisory Council. The authors are solely responsible for the contents of this essay.

1. Walter Meganack Sr., "Coping with the Day the Water Died," *Anchorage Daily News*, 5 August 1989, B1.

2. R. B. Spies, et al., "The Effects of the *Exxon Valdez* Oil Spill on the Alaskan Coastal Environment," *American Fisheries Society Symposium* 18 (1996): 1-16.

3. *Voices of the Sound*, produced by David Grimes and Michael A. Lewis, Film Center for the Environment, 1989. Videocassette.

4. Alaska Wilderness League, "*Exxon Valdez* Oil Spill: Could It Happen Again?" Available from http://www.exxonvaldez.org/report.html.

5. Doug O'Harra, "Sound Battles Back, But Threats Linger," *Anchorage Daily News*, 13 May 1999, M1.

6. Ibid.

7. J. Steven Picou and Duane A. Gill, "Commercial Fishers and Stress: Psychological Impacts of the *Exxon Valdez* Oil Spill," in *The* Exxon Valdez *Disaster: Readings on a Modern Social Problem*, ed. J. Steven Picou, Duane A. Gill, and Maurie J. Cohen (Dubuque, Iowa: Kendall/Hunt, 1997), 211-35.

8. J. Steven Picou, G. David Johnson, and Duane A. Gill, *Mitigating the Chronic Community Impacts of Localized Environmental Degradation: A Case Study*

of the Exxon Valdez *Oil Spill.* Report to the Prince William Sound Regional Citizens' Advisory Council. (Mobile: University of South Alabama, 1997).

9. Bob von Steinberg, "Decade Later, *Exxon Valdez* Spill Lingers," *Minnesota Star Tribune*, 7 March 1999, metro edition, A1.

10. Nancy Yaw Davis, "Contemporary Pacific Eskimo," in *Handbook of North American Indians*, ed. D. Dumas (Washington, D.C.: Smithsonian Institution Press, 1984), vol. 5, 198-204.

11. Mary Childers Mangusso and Stephen W. Haycox, eds., *Interpreting Alaska's History: An Anthology* (Seattle: University of Washington Press, 1989).

12. Ronald Jensen, "Russia Sells Alaska," in *Interpreting Alaska's History: An Anthology*, ed. Mary Childers Mangusso and Stephen W. Haycox (Anchorage: Alaska Pacific University Press, 1989), 122-40.

13. Joseph G. Jorgenson, *Oil Age Eskimos* (Berkeley: University of California Press, 1990).

14. Harold Napoleon, *Yuuyaraq: The Way of the Human Being* (Fairbanks: University of Alaska Fairbanks Center for Cross-Cultural Studies, 1991), 10.

15. Ibid.

16. Kai Erikson, "Preface," in *The* Exxon Valdez *Disaster*, ed. Picou, Gill, and Cohen, ix–xiii.

17. Lawrence A. Palinkas, et al., "Social, Cultural, and Psychological Impacts of the *Exxon Valdez* Oil Spill," *Human Organization* 52, no. 1 (1993): 8.

18. Christopher L. Dyer, Duane A. Gill, and J. Steven Picou, "Social Disruption and the *Valdez* Oil Spill: Alaskan Natives in a Natural Resource Community," *Sociological Spectrum* 12, no. 2 (1992): 105-26.

19. Meganack, "Coping," B1.

20. Riki Ott, *Sound Truth: Exxon's Manipulation of Science and the Significance of the* Exxon Valdez *Oil Spill* (Anchorage: Greenpeace Report, 1994), 47.

21. Debra McKinney, "Spill-Linked Fears Color Subsistence Life," *Anchorage Daily News*, 22 March 1999, A1.

22. Minerals Management Service, *Social Indicators Study of Alaskan Coastal Villages: IV Postspill Key Informant Summaries, Schedule C Communities, Part 1 (OCS Study MMS 92-0052)* (Anchorage, Alaska: U.S. Department of the Interior, 1993), 178.

23. Alaska Public Radio Network, *Poisoned Waters: Alaska Natives and the Oil Spill* (Homer, Alaska: True North Productions, 1991), radio broadcast.

24. Ibid.

25. Minerals Management Service, *Social Indicators Study: Part 2*, 701.

26. Erikson, "Preface," x.

27. Ibid.

28. Ibid.

29. John G. Mitchell, "In the Wake of the Spill," *National Geographic*, 195, no. 3 (1999): 101.

30. Alaska Public Radio Network, *Poisoned Waters.*

31. Meganack, "Coping," B1.

32. Minerals Management Service, *Social Indicators Study: Part 1*, 210.

33. Erikson, "Preface," xi.

34. Ibid.

35. Ibid.

36. Ibid.

37. Ibid.

38. Ibid.

39. Ibid.

40. Meganack, "Coping," B1.

41. Alaska Public Radio Network, *Poisoned Waters.*

42. Ibid.

43. Meganack, "Coping," B1.

44. Eric Morrison, "Tatitlek," in *Social Indicators Study: Part 1*, 432-33.

45. Impact Assessment, Inc., *Social and Psychological Impacts of the* Exxon Valdez *Oil Spill. Interim Report #3 Prepared for Oiled Mayors Subcommittee, Alaska Conference of Mayors* (Anchorage, 1990), 272.

46. Minerals Management Service, *Social Indicators Study: Part 2*, 764.

47. Jack Kruse, *Communities' Mitigation Strategies Project Progress Report: Phase 1. Report Prepared for the Regional Citizens Advisory Committee* (Anchorage: Institute of Social and Economic Research, University of Alaska Anchorage, 1992), 69.

48. Meganack, "Coping," B1.

49. Christine E. Klein, "The Disaster of 'Disaster Response': The *Exxon Valdez* Oil Spill, Alaska, 1989." Paper presented at the Annual Meeting of the Society for Applied Anthropology, York, England, 1990.

50. Impact Assessment, Inc., *Economic, Social and Psychological Impact Assessment of the* Exxon Valdez *Oil Spill. Final Report Prepared for Oiled Mayors Subcommittee, Alaska Conference of Mayors* (Anchorage, 1990), 46.

51. Impact Assessment, Inc., *Interim Report #3*, 281.

52. Ibid.

53. Ibid., 27-28.

54. Bill Richards, "Mitigating Psychological and Social Impacts of the *Exxon Valdez* Spill on Small Villages." Paper presented at the Annual Meeting of the Society for Applied Anthropology, Charleston, South Carolina, 1991.

55. Meganack, "Coping," B1.

56. James A. Fall and Charles J. Utermohle, eds., *An Investigation of the Sociocultural Consequences of Outer Continental Shelf Development in Alaska, II Prince William Sound. (OCS Study MMS 95-011)* (Anchorage: U.S. Department of the Interior, 1995).

57. Morrison, "Tatitlek," 435.

58. Fall and Utermohle, *Investigation*, V-22.

59. Ibid., IV-9.

60. Ibid., IV-11.

61. Ibid.

62. Ibid., IV-9.

63. Ibid., IV-13.

64. Ibid., IV-10.

65. Ibid., IV-13.

66. Ibid., IV-16.

67. Minerals Management Service, *Social Indicators Study: Part 1*, 222.

68. Ibid., 220.

69. Palinkas, et al., "Social, Cultural," 5.

70. Erikson, "Preface," xii.

71. Ibid., xiii.

72. Ibid.

73. Palinkas, et al., "Social, Cultural," 9.

74. John C. Russell, Larry A. Palinkas, and Michael Downs, *Social, Psychological, and Municipal Impacts Related to the* Exxon Valdez *Oil Spill* (Portland, Ore.: Briker, Nodland, Studenmund, Inc., 1993), 47-49.

75. Christopher L. Dyer, "Tradition Loss as Secondary Disaster: Long-Term Cultural Impacts of the *Exxon Valdez* Oil Spill," *Sociological Spectrum* 13, no. 1 (1993): 82-83.

76. William B. Hirsch, "Justice Delayed: Seven Years Later and No End in Sight," in *The* Exxon Valdez *Disaster*, ed. Picou, Gill, and Cohen, 271-307.

77. Fall and Utermohle, *Investigation*, I-25.

78. Ibid.

79. Ibid.

80. Ibid., I-25–26.

81. Ibid.

82. Paul Nussbaum, "The Sound and the Fury," *Inquirer Magazine*, 7 March 1999, 17.

83. Natalie Phillips, "Sound Use Doubles Since '89," *Anchorage Daily News*, 25 March 1999, B1.

84. Picou, Johnson, and Gill, *Mitigating*.

85. Nussbaum, "Sound," 17.

86. Natalie Phillips, "Spill Funds Aren't End of Trouble: Money has Downside, Says Anthropologist," *Anchorage Daily News*, 26 March 1999, C1.

87. Ibid.

88. Mitchell, "In the Wake," 113.

89. von Sternberg, "Sound," A1.

90. Nussbaum, "Sound," 17, 28.

91. Ibid., 28.

92. Napoleon, *Yuuyaraq*, 28.

93. Ibid.

94. Picou, Johnson, and Gill, *Mitigating*.

95. J. Steven Picou, "The 'Talking Circle' as Sociological Practice: Cultural Transformation of Chronic Disaster Impacts." Paper presented at the Annual Meeting of the Society for Applied Sociology, Chicago, Illinois, 1998.

96. Ibid.

97. Ibid.

98. McKinney, "Spill-Linked Fears," A1.

99. Picou, "Talking Circle."

100. Ernest Piper, *The* Exxon Valdez *Oil Spill: Final Report, State of Alaska Response* (Anchorage: Alaska Department of Environmental Conservation , 1993).

101. Meganack, "Coping," B1.

PART IV

POSSIBILITY

I I

"Unknown and Unsung"

Feminist, African American, and Radical Responses to the Titanic *Disaster*

Steven Biel

Steven Biel describes how oppositional groups—feminists, African Americans, labor radicals—challenged a conventional narrative of the 1912 Titanic *disaster that celebrated the heroism of the first-cabin male passengers in order to shore up orthodoxies of gender, class, and race. Many suffragists contrasted the chivalry on the* Titanic *with the failure of men to protect women and children on shore and argued that women empowered by the vote would bring a "new chivalry" to American politics and society. African Americans alternatively celebrated the fact that there were no blacks on board and made claims for black heroes whose good sense and skill allowed them to escape while the wealthy and powerful went down. Labor radicals debunked the myth of first-cabin heroism, railed against the greed and privilege represented on the ship's upper decks, and substituted an alternative roster of working-class heroes.*

THE *TITANIC* DISASTER, the subject of hundreds of books, is the stuff of what academically trained historians sometimes condescendingly refer to as "popular history," in which complex processes are ignored in favor of antiquarianism or reduced to single dramatic moments. We are uncomfortable with unselfconscious narrative, with arguments that seem insignificant or too bold. A statement like Walter Lord's, that "the *Titanic* more than any other single event marks the end of the old days, and the beginning of a new, uneasy era," makes us squirm. In my opinion, the disaster changed nothing except shipping regulations. It did not, as Wyn Craig Wade writes, produce a "loss of innocence" and replace "certainty" with "doubt." It was not "the birth cry of a growing animosity" between Great Britain and Germany; despite Charles Pellegrino's suggestion, the *Titanic* wireless operator's snub of his counterpart on the *Frankfurt* had nothing to do with the coming of the First World War.[1] Any search for the social effects of the disaster is bound to yield facile generalizations and tenuous connections.

But the importance of an event doesn't necessarily reside in its effects; we need not treat the *Titanic* disaster as the "end of an epoch" to recognize its cultural significance. It was, as Lord and others have noted but professional historians have not, an event of deep and wide resonance in Progressive Era America. Beyond shock and grief, the disaster produced a contest over meaning that connected the sinking of an ocean liner on calm seas in April 1912 with some of the most important and troubling problems, tensions, and conflicts of the time. If not a transformative event, it was nonetheless a highly dramatic moment—a kind of "social drama" in which conflicts were played out and American culture, in effect, thought out loud about itself.[2] Whatever "timeless" messages the disaster may convey about heroism or cowardice, about complacency or technological hubris, it tells us a great deal about how American culture worked in the Progressive Period.

At the center of the contest over the disaster's meanings was a conventional narrative that emerged in the commercial press, genteel magazines, poems, popular songs, pictures, eulogies by public officials, sermons by mainstream religious leaders, and efforts to build *Titanic* memorials. I choose the term "conventional" to describe an interpretive framework that affirmed existing power relations—that made sense of the disaster according to dominant conceptions of gender, class, ethnicity, and race. I also call it conventional because it was pervasive, defying clear-cut divisions between conservatives and reformers, between high culture and low culture, between staid and sensational reporting, between sections and regions of the country. It was a collective work of interpretation (though the interpreters often claimed only to be telling the truth) constructed and reinforced in the days, weeks, and months after the wreck by people who consciously or unconsciously needed to understand and represent a shocking event in familiar and comfortable terms.[3]

Briefly summarized, this conventional narrative was centered around a myth of the heroism of the first-cabin male passengers—a myth based on reports that women and children had survived in much greater numbers than men. According to this myth, wealthy and successful men willingly died so that their weaker charges might live. Repeated celebrations of the chivalry and Christian sacrifice embodied in this act reinforced conservative views of gender and class relations in which both women and workers were best served by accepting the authority and protection of paternalistic elites. The myth emphasized natural and immutable gender differences while it denied class conflict. Meanwhile, any incidents of panic were attributed to "crazed" or "frenzied" immigrants and stokers. The first-cabin men and the British officers received credit for preserving order when chaos threatened. Chivalry was often described as an exclusively "Anglo-Saxon" virtue. Probably the most succinct version of this narrative can be found in a wire service report that appeared in papers across the country on April 17—two days before any reliable information, except for lists of survivors, had reached shore. "The picture that invariably presents itself, in view of what is known," said the report, "is of men like John Jacob Astor, master of scores of millions; Benjamin Guggenheim of the famous family of bankers; Isidor Straus, a merchant prince; William T. Stead, veteran journalist; Major Archibald W. Butt, soldier; Washington Roebling, noted engineer—of any or all of these men stepping aside, bravely, gallantly remaining to die that the place he otherwise might have filled could perhaps be taken by some sabot-shod, shawl-enshrouded, illiterate and penniless peasant woman of Europe."[4]

But if the conventional narrative met the expectations of most Americans, it did not meet the expectations of all. Marginalized people and oppositional groups responded differently, drew divergent implications from the *Titanic* story, and constructed alternative narratives of their own.

By 1912, the suffrage movement was gaining new momentum. After fifteen years of defeats and stagnation, suffragists were encouraged by their successful campaign in California in 1911 and by the revitalization of the National American Woman Suffrage Association (NAWSA) beginning in 1910.[5] With this momentum came an ideological shift. The movement's earlier approach, dating from the Seneca Falls Convention of 1848, had been to argue for the vote on the grounds of natural rights. Suffrage was a matter of justice, based on the assumptions of equality and common humanity embodied in the Declaration of Independence and later in the movement's Declaration of Rights and Sentiments. Near

VOTES FOR WOMEN TO THE RESCUE

FIGURE 11.1. Suffragists compared the *Titanic* to the ship of state. With the vote, they argued, women would steer the ship clear of all sorts of dangers. The sea monsters are labeled "smallpox," "saloons," "fire traps," "graft," "sweatshops," "white slavery," "poverty," "gambling," "social diseases," "diptheria [*sic*]," "child labor," "impure food," and "consumption." (State Historical Society of Wisconsin, negative number N13283)

the turn of the century, suffragists developed new arguments based on expediency rather than on rights and "stressing what enfranchised women could do for the government and their communities." These arguments were compatible with prevailing conceptions of gender differences; women, as moral exemplars, had special gifts to bring to the polity. As one historian summarizes the shift, "the new era saw a change from the emphasis by suffragists on the ways in which women were the same as men and therefore had the *right* to vote, to a stress on the ways in which they differed from men, and therefore had the *duty* to contribute their special skills and experience to government."[6]

Though the *Titanic* provided fodder to the antis, it is not surprising that supporters of woman suffrage also accepted and fostered the chivalric myth. Suffragists who argued for the vote on the basis of difference easily defended themselves against claims that suffrage would destroy chivalry. The president of the Maryland Equal Suffrage League dismissed the antis' "supposition that the ballot makes men and women equal and that therefore neither should have preference in the recent maratime [sic] disaster" as "a misunderstanding of the position of the advocates of the vote for women." The sexes, she explained, "play a different part in the scheme of life, and to woman will ever be shown a chivalry and a respect that fittingly adorns her. I believe this spirit will make ever-unchanging the unwritten law of the sea, which recognizes the weakness of women in physical strength, but her worth in other directions."[7] From genuine belief and for strategic purposes, many suffragists made their own case for immutable gender differences.

Opposition to suffrage came, for the most part, from conservatives who read the *Titanic* disaster as a vindication of their beliefs. In Denver, however, suffragists were forced to defend themselves against an attack from the Left. Emma Goldman, in town for a lecture when news of the *Titanic* broke, used the occasion to denounce the "present-day woman" for her weakness and dependence, her willingness "to accept man's tribute in time of safety and his sacrifice in time of danger, as if she were still in her baby age." The women on the *Titanic* should have chosen the path of equality and died "with those they loved." In showing themselves unequal and unemancipated, they had dealt the cause of women a severe blow. As an anarchist, Goldman viewed suffrage as a red herring; electoral politics could not produce meaningful change even if women were allowed to vote. As a feminist, she rejected affirmations of inequality and difference regardless of the uses to which such affirmations were put.[8]

Denver suffragists answered Goldman by arguing that women "seemed to show their bravery as well as the men, though perhaps in different ways." Just as there was "an unwritten law of the sea which makes it imperative for men to stand back," there was "also some intuitive principle which makes women, regardless of who or what they are, inclined to obey and not dally or complicate dangers by hysterics and argument." By demonstrating that women were capable of "discipline" and "self-control," the disaster proved that they were "eligible for the ballot." Judge Ben Lindsey, the pioneer of the juvenile court system, insisted that even "if suffrage were the rule all over the world," the heroic response of the men would have been the same. "Men are better fitted physicially [sic] than women to battle with wind and waves. Suffrage cannot affect this one way or the other." A former Colorado attorney general said that it was a simple "matter of the strong protecting the weak. If the theory of suffrage calls for strong men not to give way in time of danger, why I say give it up. But no such demand is made."[9] Suffrage, according to such views, posed no threat to essential gender roles. Women's increased participation in public life would preserve the kinds of distinctions that the *Titanic* disaster exhibited.

Not all feminists were suffragists—Goldman is a case in point— and certainly not all suffragists were feminists. The term "feminism"— signifying opposition to sex hierarchy, the belief that gender roles are socially constructed and therefore changeable, and a commitment to activism based on common experience—came into widespread use between 1910 and 1913.[10] Situated at the radical end of progressive reform, feminists redirected the *Titanic* disaster and its chivalric myth to their own purposes. Moving beyond the call for specific reforms concerning speed, the provision of lifeboats, and wireless transmissions, they read the disaster as a lesson in the need to extend protective legislation to cover all aspects of American life. To feminists, memorializing the *Titanic* meant more than paying lasting tribute to the "noble altruism" of the first-cabin heroes.

Some accepted the chivalric myth but described it as the exception rather than the rule. Rheta Childe Dorr chose "Women and Children First" as the title of an article describing her experiences working in a "dismal" sweatshop in Brooklyn with its "foul odors" and "locked doors" that prevented mothers from going home to take care of their children. Her conclusion was blunt: "The law of the sea: women and children first. The law of the land—that's different." Dorr converted the claim that the men on the *Titanic* had sacrificed themselves for motherhood and childhood from celebration into criticism. "[I]t is known on land as well as at sea that the race is carried on by children and that women are needed to care for the children," yet only in a rare circumstance had men acted on this knowledge. Alice Stone Blackwell, editor of NAWSA's *Woman's Journal*, generously noted that "chivalrous things were done even by men who had not been chivalrous in their past lives, as well as by those who had always been so," and she was touched "to see how many people were able to die bravely though they had not been able to live bravely." But Blackwell went beyond the conventional homage to call for a "new chivalry" that would transform protection into a general principle and apply it universally. The only way to achieve such a goal, she contended, was for women "to secure the ballot, the prime weapon in the modern warfare against oppression and wrong." Inez Milholland, an organizer of the New York parade, argued that the best way to extend the heroism and chivalry of the *Titanic* men was to give women the freedom to exercise these admirable qualities.[11]

The chivalry displayed on the *Titanic*, which proved to many that women didn't need the vote and that American society was basically sound, demonstrated precisely the opposite to feminists such as these. Comparing the captain of a ship to a captain of industry, Blackwell observed that

> the "law of the sea" is quite different from the custom on land. The captain is expected to be the last man to leave his ship; all other lives must be saved before his. The captain of industry makes sure first of a comfortable living for himself, even if the workers in his employ die of tuberculosis through insufficient food and unsanitary conditions. The chivalry shown to a few hundred women on the Titanic does not alter the fact that in New York City 150,000 people—largely women and children—have to sleep in dark rooms with no windows; that in a single large city 5,000 white slaves die every year; that the lives and health of thousands of women and children are sacrificed continually through their exploitation in mills, workshops and factories. These things are facts.

An editorial in the *Progressive Woman* went further in contrasting chivalry at sea with exploitation on land by exposing the hypocrisy of the *Titanic* heroes themselves. "Most of those men, no doubt, stubbornly opposed the idea of the rights of women in participation in governmental affairs. Exploited them in industry, voted for the white slave pen, sent the daughter to the street, the son to the army, the husband to tramp the streets for a job."[12] They may have redeemed themselves in the end, but their lives up to the moment of redemption had been anything but chivalrous. It was women, this point of view suggested, who were best equipped to universalize the self-sacrificing behavior that surfaced in men only in extraordinary circumstances.

Male chivalry, for example, had done nothing to prevent the disaster, only to mitigate its effects. Such "wholesale, life-taking disasters must almost be expected," wrote Agnes Ryan, as long as "the laws and the enforcement of the laws are entirely in men's hands."

From Blackwell's perspective, "[t]here was no need that a single life should have been lost upon the *Titanic*. There will be far fewer lost by preventable accidents, either on land or sea, when the mothers of men have the right to vote." Drawing an analogy from the *Titanic* to the ship of state, Ryan described the disaster as "typical" of the needless waste of life under the rule of men. "The need of women in all departments of human life to conserve life itself is pitiful. More than anything else in the world the Votes for Women movement seeks to bring humaneness, the valuation of human life, into the commerce and transportation and business of the world and establish things on a new basis, a basis in which the unit of measurement is life, nothing but life!" A member of the Women's Trade Union League (WTUL) rebuked male politicians for their "medieval minds" and their failure to recognize that "times have changed since the Knights of the Round Table rode out to protect the ladies fair." The "chivalry of today," she said, "will have to change its method if it is to do 'substantial justice' to women." Men who believed that their chivalry was sufficient in the modern world did "not know that women must protect themselves if they are to be protected adequately." The "new chivalry of this new day" would be "men and women working together for the good of humanity."[13]

Beginning by paying tribute to the *Titanic*'s heroes, feminists turned the chivalric myth against itself. Male chivalry was exceptional and inadequate. To make care and protection the rule required an active role for women in public life. Deference to men may have saved some lives on the *Titanic*, but only empowered women could initiate the real work of life-saving. In this version of the disaster, the emphasis on gender difference served radical ends. Women's special qualities—described here as more cultural than biological—justified participation rather than paternalism.

Dorr and Blackwell invoked chivalry only to note its limitations. Other feminists praised the *Titanic* heroes and then suggested alternative models of conduct. "Chivalry, no doubt, has its attractive, romantic side," admitted the *Progressive Woman*, "but just plain common sense would serve social progress so much better!" Charlotte Perkins Gilman offered an anthropological—and racist—interpretation of "the splendid record of human heroism" displayed on the *Titanic*. Chivalry was traditional among "the Teutonic and Scandinavian stocks," she explained, because these civilizations had never passed through a phase of polygamy and female slavery; from an early "matriarchal state" they had moved directly into a period of women's dependence on male providers through monogamous marriage. Lesser races, according to Gilman's evolutionary scheme, hadn't yet reached the chivalric stage, while Anglo-Saxon civilization was ready to advance beyond it. Elsewhere, Gilman described women at this stage as "parasitic"—confined to roles that overstressed the "feminine" qualities of weakness and passivity. In her take on the *Titanic*, she was milder than usual. "The courageous and self-sacrificing men who gave up their lives to save women are to be honored truly," she wrote. But Gilman also demanded that "we honor the women who waive this sex advantage and choose to die like brave and conscientious human beings, rather than live on a wholly feminine basis."[14]

The most common response of feminists to the disaster was to accept the conventional narrative's version of events while redirecting it to an alternative set of conclusions. A few, however, rejected the narrative outright by debunking the chivalric myth. Letting women and children into the lifeboats was the least the men could have done. "After all, the women on the boat were not responsible for the disaster," and it would have been "gross injustice to decree that the women, who have no voice in making and enforcing law on land or sea, should be left aboard a sinking ship, victims of man's cupidity." A woman who called herself "Daughter of Eve" announced in the *Baltimore Sun* that she would "have nothing to say" about "how much of this heroism was due to the belief in the unsinkable qualities of the ship, or what part pistols played in converting cowards into brave men." Perhaps the most subversive opinion of all was that of a Maryland suffragist who questioned the entire premise of extracting lessons from the tragedy. It was, she wrote, "a desecration to inject the question of woman suffrage into the *Titanic* disaster."[15] This was asking the impossible—for the public to express sorrow and grief alone, without looking for political and social implications. Feminists knew that political battles extended into the cultural realm. They knew, too, that to acquiesce in the disaster's lessons about eternal gender roles would be to concede a defeat at the height of their struggle.

Henry Louis Gates Sr. knew illiterate black soldiers in World War II who could reel off fifty verses of a poem—a "toast"—about the *Titanic* disaster. His son, the future literary critic, encountered a *Titanic* toast in 1956, when a teacher in a newly integrated West Virginia classroom asked the African-American students if they could recite any poetry. One of Gates's classmates stood up and began to narrate the story of Shine, a black stoker on the *Titanic*. The teacher, appalled by the poem's explicit language, cut him off. Gates calls the *Titanic* toasts "the most popular poem[s] in the black vernacular."[16]

At the time of the disaster, however, African Americans were as likely to greet the "Greatest of All News Stories" with silence as with eloquence.[17] In most of the African-American press, the *Titanic* wasn't news. Readers knew about the disaster; occasional editorials discussed it without elaborate explanation. It is possible that given the massive coverage in the commercial press, black newspapers decided that carrying the story would be redundant. It is equally possible that for many African Americans, there was no immediacy to the disaster. The black press continued to focus on matters that directly touched its constituency: the presidential campaign, state and local elections, Booker T. Washington, lynchings, church and lodge news, the International Negro Conference, the NAACP convention. What deeply engaged white Americans did not affect black Americans in the same way; what seemed universal to some—"*Titanic* Disaster Hits Home of the Entire Nation" read a typical headline—was actually a matter of perspective.[18]

Among those black editorialists who addressed the subject of the disaster, some made universalist claims of their own about what the *Indianapolis Freeman* called the "catastrophe of the day, if not of all time," and they too were capable of embracing the chivalric myth. "The world of civilized peoples was profoundly shocked. It has in various ways showed grief on account of the lamentable happening, and respect and admiration for those—the men especially—who knew how to die when necessity presented." At a time when whites used "civilized" as a term of exclusion, testaments to shared shock, grief, respect, and admiration represented a desire or demand for inclusion. In this limited way, perhaps, black writers consciously or unconsciously shipped subversive messages into conventional eulogies. The *Chicago Defender* celebrated "the splendid lesson of self-sacrifice of those men who waved their last farewell to their loved ones upon that night of horror" as "a lesson in the equality of man, as Prince and Peasant alike met death dealt from the hand of Nature." The *Indianapolis World* observed hopefully that "the disaster has done much to enforce the lesson of universal brotherhood and the duty of love and sympathy and helpfulness for all mankind."[19] In the black press, such lessons were assertions rather than descriptions. While the language was conventional, blacks may well have drawn lessons in equality different from those of class harmony. The disaster illuminated an ideal of universal brotherhood far removed from the realities of African-American lives.

Where the *Titanic* resonated with blacks, it did so primarily in religious terms. Though the denominations were segregated, African Americans shared the language of Protestantism with whites, and it is not surprising that their interpretations of the disaster overlapped. Black sermons focussed on an inscrutable God who worked through "great horrors as well as in the wonderful birth of the tiny flowers about us on every hand." At the Bethel A.M.E. church in Pittsburgh, the Reverend P. A. Scott took as his subject "Ye Know Not What I Shall Do Now, But in a Little While," and the congregation followed with the hymn "God Moves in a Mysterious Way, His Wonders to Perform." Mattye E. Anderson's poem "The *Titanic*" noted the bravery of the men who "lingered with pride" but then described their "Poor souls so desolate / Great wealth, the powerful and the strong, / Cruelly death sweeps them all along; / To a sorrowful fate." Lucian B. Watkins's "O Sea! A dirge; the tragedy of the *Titanic*, memorable of 1912" sounded the theme of redemption—"Dear hearts there to baptism did repair / In this soul's triumphant hour of prayer, / In true nobility"—but ended on the note that "All was but vanity!"[20]

The empty pride of power and wealth, the illusion of security, and the deflation of pretensions were messages black readers and congregations could readily accept. God had taught the rich and powerful a lesson in humility. "He is not interested in the increase of millionaires," said the *Richmond Planet*, "so much as He is in the increase of righteousness and the well being of the poor of the earth, equally the objects of His love as are the 'rich.'" While the *Afro-American Ledger* advised its readers that "nothing but profound sorrow should energize the breasts of mankind the world over in view of this awful calamity," it also declared that "the Almighty is not mocked."[21] Couched in general terms of man's pride and God's majesty, many sermons and editorials indirectly but perceptibly addressed issues of race, class, and power. Despite the *Ledger*'s advice, more than sorrow energized the breasts of black Americans.

Nowhere is this more evident than in the many African-American folk songs about the disaster. The black press—middle-class, literate, self-consciously literary, and dominated by Booker T. Washington's "Tuskegee machine"—tended toward conservatism. Folk songs, by contrast, were largely working-class, oral, and collective forms of expression. In a few of these songs, the possibility of redemption is left open. "De *Titanic*," which originated in Georgia and was sung by black troops bound for Europe in World War I, concludes with a standard image: "De people was thinkin' o' Jesus o' Nazaree, / While de band played 'Nearer My God to Thee!'" The version John Dos Passos heard in a New Jersey army barracks before shipping out to France includes the singing of the hymn but ends with a dismal scene of "de women and de children / a floating and a sinkin in de cold blue sea." Rabbit Brown's Louisiana ballad suggests that the passengers were unprepared—"Not thinking that death was looking, there upon that northern sea"—though it too concludes with "Nearer, My God, to Thee."

Other songs, however, cast doubt on redemption. In "The Great *Titanic*," from northwest Alabama, the passengers call out to God in the first verse: "People began to scream and cry, / Saying 'Lord, am I going to die?'" Following the chorus (which includes the famous camp song line "It was sad when that great ship went down"), the lyric speaks directly to class discrimination. The rich refuse to ride with the poor, "So they put the poor below, / They were the first to go." God then demonstrates his power by destroying the unsinkable ship and killing sixteen hundred people who "didn't know that the time had come." A Texas version of the ballad "God Moves on the Water" asserts that though "the peoples had to run and pray," the archetypal first-cabin passenger went down unredeemed. "Well, that Jacob Nash was a millionaire, / Lawd, he had plenty of money to spare; / When the great *Titanic* was sinkin' down, / Well, he could not pay his fare." With its doleful vocal, often accompanied by a wailing slide guitar, "God Moves" conveys genuine sorrow; lyrically, however, judgment and justice are the guiding themes. Jacob Nash—John Jacob Astor in some versions—was carrying too much baggage to get into heaven.[22]

Divine judgment was a common enough theme among African-American interpreters of the disaster to provoke an angry response from more conservative blacks. A follower of Booker T. Washington criticized the "hysterical denunciations" that charged "the destruction of life of God's desire to punish the 'wealthy sinners' on board." Attempts "to definitely fix the object of God's wrath" bordered on "sacrilege." Was it God's wrath when a black church was struck by lightning? When a black hospital burned down? When the Mississippi flooded and killed 500 blacks? The prevalence of religious interpretations of any kind disturbed and even embarrassed those who equated racial advancement with secularization. A chagrined writer for the *Pittsburgh Courier* mistakenly observed a "striking difference between the white press and the negro press" coverage of the *Titanic*. "Colored writers invariably infer or pre-suppose it to have been the work of God, or at least that God had some purpose in bringing it about. The white man discusses the matter with no such inference or prepossession." As long as the black man clung to "the silly belief that his misfortunes, defeats, reverses and tragedies were sent upon him by some God or Devil," progress was impossible.[23]

The central matter of interest and concern in black responses to the disaster was whether there were any African Americans on board the ship. (There were not, it turned out. Only recently have historians discovered that a Haitian family traveled on the *Titanic* in the second class.) Demanding inclusion even in disaster, some insisted that "the Afro-American must have been represented, as he generally is in everything in this country." While the conventional narrative had made heroism a matter of racial exclusiveness, black writers tried to broaden the chivalric honor roll. The "whole world" was quite properly "lauding the men on the ship for their heroism in their 'Women and children first' martyrdom," said the *St. Paul Appeal*, but "we can claim a few of the heroes" too. Though the "daily press has made no special mention of him, we know he was there, and that he died like the other men. And we shed tears to his memory as well as to the men of other nationalities who died with him." Like many suffragists, middle-class blacks accepted the Christian-chivalric myth only to expand it and, in their case, purge it of its racist connotations. "And when in the last day the sea gives up its dead," predicted the *New York Age*, the black hero, "like the others, will come into his crown of glory."[24]

The silence of the dailies on this heroic presence came as no surprise; white newspapers rarely reported on blacks except as criminals, which prompted a wry comment about the coverage of the disaster from the black press. "There may have been a negro in the sinking of the great steamship *Titanic* off the Newfoundland coast last week, but the newspapers have not as yet discovered the fact. It is rather remarkable that there could be so great a tragedy without a negro somewhere concealed or exposed in it." When the apocryphal story surfaced of the black stoker who was "shot because he was about to stab a wireless operator," it conformed to the pattern in which blacks were either absent as heroes or present as villains in narratives of tragedy or disaster. As the *Philadelphia Tribune* sarcastically observed, "We thought it would be strange if there were no colored persons aboard the fated ship. Of course, he had to be made to appear in the light of a dastard."[25]

Celebrations of the absence of blacks spurred a debate over what the proper African-American response should be. The staid *Chicago Defender* chastised the *Louisville News* for its opinion that the disaster "is a grim incident upon which to levy recompenses from the inexorable law of compensation, but there is cause for racial congratulation that there were no Negroes aboard the ill-fated *Titanic* when she dived to her doom." As Americans, the *Defender* declared, "we feel the loss as keenly as our white brother. We do not want to adjust our differences in such a matter. The Union soldier helped the Confederate soldier bury his dead. Are we less gallant?" A Philadelphia paper similarly spoke the language of brotherhood. While it appeared that no blacks had died on the *Titanic*, "nevertheless 'one touch of nature makes the whole world kin,' and our sympathy goes out to the bereaved friends and relatives of the unfortunates who went to meet their Maker so suddenly and unexpectedly." Yet not even the sober *Pittsburgh Courier* could forgo an ironic comment: "The Negroes who consider their poverty a curse may find consolation in the fact that they were not wealthy enough to take passage on the *Titanic*. Every adversity has its virtue."[26] Perhaps this wasn't divine justice, but it was a kind of coincidental redress.

In more subversive ways, absence and presence served as the themes of the two most remarkable black folk versions of the disaster: Huddie Ledbetter's blues ballad "*Titanic*" and the various *Titanic* toasts. Boasting about being nowhere near the scene of a disaster was a tradition of sorts in black folk songs. A lyric transcribed in Mississippi in 1909 asks "O where were you when the steamer when down, Captain?" and answers "I was with my honey in the heart of town." The *Titanic* replaced the riverboat after 1912 in places as far apart as Mt. Airy, North Carolina and central Alabama: "O, what were you singing / When the *Titanic* went down? / Sitting on a mule's back, / Singing 'Alabama Bound.'" But Leadbelly's song, which he began performing with Blind Lemon Jefferson in Dallas in 1912, names the absent person and specifies the reason for his absence: the heavyweight champion Jack Johnson and racism. "Jack Johnson want to get on board, / Captain said, 'I ain't haulin' no coal.'" While the lyrics do not say that the *Titanic* went down *because* the captain denied Johnson passage, they revel in the irony that discrimination saved the black hero from death. The exclusion of Johnson, as Lawrence Levine has noted, makes the disaster "an all-white affair" and thus a source of "pleasure" and relief rather than grief and loss. The song ends with rejoicing: "When he heard about that mighty shock, / Might o' seen a man doin' the Eagle Rock." In one version, Leadbelly not only describes a celebration, he demands it. "Black man oughta shout for joy, / Never lost a girl or either a boy."[27]

The precise origins of the *Titanic* toasts—which made such a strong impression on Henry Louis Gates Sr. during World War II—are uncertain; some were collected in Louisiana and Mississippi in the 1930s, others in such diverse locations as Texas, Missouri, and New York in the 1960s, but there is evidence that they date back closer to the time of the disaster itself. Toasts were a "social genre," narrative poems performed in all kinds of settings. In the adventures of Shine, the themes of presence and absence merge; Shine is on board when the ship hits the iceberg and long gone by the time it sinks. His story, through all its retellings and variations, manages to subvert nearly every feature of the conventional narrative. A worker from "down below," Shine is the first person to alert the captain to the magnitude of the accident. His reward for vigilance is a rebuke: "Go on back and start stackin' sacks, / we got nine pumps to keep the water back." After another attempt at warning the captain and another rebuke, Shine refuses to obey the order to return below deck. "Your shittin' is good and your shittin' is fine, /" he tells the captain, "but there's one time you white folks ain't gonna shit on Shine." (In some versions, Shine responds derisively to the captain's faith in the *Titanic*'s unsinkability: "I don't like chicken and I don't like ham— / And I don't believe your pumps is worth a damn!"; "Captain, captain, can't you see, / this ain't no time to bullshit me"; "Well, that seems damned funny, it may be damned fine, / but I'm gonna try to save this black ass of mine.") Realism and common sense reside in the black laborer, not in the white officer. The captain is a martinet—complacent and ignorant—a far cry from the newspaper hero who went down telling his crew to "Be British!" A "thousand millionaires" stare as Shine jumps ship and begins to swim. All they do is watch; Shine, not Butt or Astor, is the visible actor.

The conventional heroes are passive and impotent, and their women appeal to Shine to save them. The disaster, however, destroys the façade of Victorian respectability and all illusions of strong white manhood and pure white womanhood. First-cabin women, whether a "[r]ich man's daughter" or the "Captain's daughter," need Shine rather than the "protection" of their husbands and fathers; they explicitly offer him sexual favors for his help, which he refuses. "Shine say, 'One thing about you white folks I couldn't understand: / you all wouldn't offer me that pussy when we was all on land.'" He also refuses money. The captain, realizing his earlier mistake, pleads, "Shine, Shine, save poor me, / I'll make you richer than old John D," but Shine knows that money is worthless in these circumstances: "Shine turned around and took another notion, / say 'Captain, your money's counterfeit in this big-assed ocean." Shine's code is anything but chivalric. He understands that the first-cabin passengers would do nothing to save him, and he cuts through the hypocrisy of their sudden kindness and generosity by demanding that they live out their selfishness to the end. "A nickel is a nickel, a dime is a dime, / get your motherfucken [*sic*] ass over the side and swim like mine." In this Darwinian struggle, however, Shine is clearly superior; he has both the physical strength and the cunning to survive. He skillfully evades a shark attack and swims until he arrives safely in America (in Los Angeles when the *Titanic* begins to sink and New York by the time it disappears, on "Main Street," in Harlem or Jacksonville, depending on the version). When he is present at the disaster, Shine is heroic: strong, shrewd, courageous, willing to resist white authority and its bribes. Once he is on shore, he celebrates his triumph and his absence by going to a whorehouse and getting drunk.[28]

The presence of the *Titanic* in folk songs and toasts indicates both the depth of its resonance and the diversity of its meanings. It also suggests something about cultural categories. For many years, folklorists tried to preserve a rigid distinction between folk culture and popular culture. Folk expression was supposed to be local, organic, participatory, and pure, while popular culture was national, standardized, commercialized, and inauthentic.[29] Yet the *Titanic* was a national—in fact, international—event that entered "folk" consciousness, directly or indirectly, through the standardized media of a modern industrial society. However obscure the origins of the *Titanic* folk songs and toasts may be, one thing is certain: they did not grow organically out of the pure southern soil. "Folklorists might have been purists," Lawrence Levine writes, but "the folk rarely were." They didn't insist on local subject matter, and they didn't object to making money from their songs. Charles Haffer of

Clarksdale, Mississippi, who described himself as a "Noted Gospel Song Writer and Bible Lecturer," claimed that he wrote the first *Titanic* ballad and sold two or three thousand copies across the Delta. Singers like Leadbelly and Blind Willie Johnson, who didn't literally write their songs, made money by performing them in public places.[30]

All news of the disaster came first through the wire services and the commercial press. What various audiences—including the "folk"—did with that news is another story. Though white and black performers and audiences interpreted them differently, songs like "The Great *Titanic*" often crossed racial boundaries and represented a regional and working-class alternative to the national consensus. White country singers like Roy Acuff and Loretta Lynn, rooted in "hillbilly" music, also sang of poor passengers being put below where they were the first to go. The sources, in other words, may have been standardized, but the responses were not. Some "consumers" of the conventional narrative became active producers of alternative narratives, defying its tone as well as its content. Some even made the disaster into a joke.[31]

Seven months after the *Titanic* disaster, Eugene V. Debs received almost a million votes as the Socialist Party's presidential candidate. The year 1912 was, in many ways, the golden day of American socialism and labor radicalism: the year of the Industrial Workers of the World's successful "Bread and Roses" strike in the textile city of Lawrence, Massachusetts (settled a month before the *Titanic* went down); the year in which 1,200 Socialists held elected offices, including 79 mayors in 24 states; the year in which Theodore Roosevelt and the Progressive Party incorporated socialist planks into their national platform, cut into Taft's vote, and put Woodrow Wilson into the White House. The lines dividing socialism from mainstream American politics were never more blurred, nor was it possible to draw sharp distinctions between socialism and feminism, socialism and progressive Christianity, socialism and the more militant brands of middle-class reform.[32]

The American labor movement, of course, was not synonymous with socialism; it could not agree about the *Titanic* any more than it could agree on other issues. For the most part, union leaders blamed the disaster on "modern business methods" and demanded new laws to protect passengers and crews in the future. They supported the Senate investigation and its recommendations for reform. The American Federation of Labor boasted that it had been pushing for years for legislation that would require adequate life-saving provisions on American vessels. Led by the International Seamen's Union, the labor movement denounced the lack of trained crew members on the *Titanic* and criticized ship owners for cutting costs and jeopardizing safety by using unskilled workers. As usual, it had required "some great disaster" to expose corporate "mismanagement and incompetency" and "to arouse the public conscience." The campaign for passage of the Seamen's Act, led by insurgent Senator Robert M. LaFollette of Wisconsin, was not above playing on the xenophobia that characterized large segments of organized labor, especially the conservative craft unions of the AFL. LaFollette described the horrific prospect of getting "into a lifeboat in the crew of which there is a Turk, a Chinese, a Jap, a Greek, a Negro from South Africa, a Hungarian, and an Arabian."[33]

Workers of many persuasions found common ground in the belief that the *Titanic* was not an anomaly. The *Railroad Trainman's Journal* noted, for example, that "a half million a year pay death or disability tribute to industry" but that the "great world" found it easier to focus on a single tragedy than on the "steady grind" that "day after day, week after week, month after month, year after year takes life and limb." Why do "equally horrible but much costlier disasters in terms of human life," like mine cave-ins and explosions, get only passing attention? asked a Finnish newspaper in Fitchburg, Massachusetts. Another labor publication listed "Things That Are Worse," including mine disasters, child labor, prostitution, train wrecks, tuberculosis, poverty, sweatshops, and tenements—all of which, like the *Titanic*, were attributable to a greed that "puts profit above human rights and human welfare." The *Titanic*, according to a Teamsters editorial, provided "another lesson in our every day existence where human lives were offered up as a sacrifice, and principally the lives of working people." "Speed and greed," summed up the *Blacksmiths Journal*, "demand a frightful toll."[34]

When the crew of the *Olympic*, the *Titanic*'s sister ship, went on strike for safer conditions, the AFL defended their action and urged workers on land to make similar demands: "No locked doors to factories. No doors opening inward. No two-foot wooden staircases. No heaping up of inflammable materials regardless of life." The United Mine Workers could sympathize with the *Olympic* seamen, who were "enclosed for days and nights in a stuffy, heated room some fifty feet beneath the water line" and whose experience in the event of a disaster would not be enviable "even if accompanied by the band playing 'Nearer, My God, to Thee.'" The disaster only confirmed the need for a strong labor movement to protect workers and consumers from greedy or negligent owners. Union publicists seized on the *Titanic* as a rallying cry for workers to organize.[35]

Conservative craft unionists, however, tended to focus on the specific problems revealed by the disaster, and they phrased their attacks on greed in ways that avoided class antagonism. They, too, saw the *Titanic* as a great "illustration of the democracy of the human race; the millionaire and the peasant, the educated and the ignorant, all standing upon the same footing; the owner of diamonds and the wearer of 'homespun' on an equality as the end approached." A member of the International Brotherhood of Maintenance of Way Employes [*sic*] offered a verse rendition of the conventional democracy of death motif that suggests the hazards of drawing rigid boundaries between secular and religious readings of the disaster. "Poverty and wealth went hand in hand; / Side by side they sank. / God showed no distinction / In station, creed or rank." Many labor poems and editorials concluded with the band playing "Nearer, My God, to Thee." While noting that heroism was "not confined to any class or race," conservative unionists joined in the celebration of the first-cabin men—occasionally at the risk of inconsistency. James E. Kinsella, the "Post Office Poet," sounded positively radical when he wrote, "There were no lifeboats left on deck to save the steerage crew, / The toilers penned in the hold below wiped out by the billowy blue; / This press agent guff, this savory stuff, of saving the rich and poor, / The steerage died, swept down by the tide, in Neptune's gripping lure." Two stanzas later, however, "The Chevalier Bayard Major Butt died as young Sidneys die, / 'Women and children first,' he said, his ringing soldier cry." The end brought redemption: "By dying game you shed all blame—death wiped your 'scutcheon clean." The *Locomotive Engineers' Monthly Journal* reproached workers who took "satisfaction in the thought that for once the magnates could not buy their way out." Labor took a more expansive view of *Titanic* chivalry, opening the pantheon of heroes to include "the toiler strong" without necessarily challenging the predominant myths.[36]

Socialists and other labor radicals, on the other hand, constructed their own response to the *Titanic*—perhaps the most consistently subversive of all the counternarratives. They spoke directly to the silences in the conventional narrative, the class bias in its roll call of heroes, the conservative "lessons" it drew from the disaster. Only a few dissenting editorialists in the commercial press joined Charlotte Perkins Gilman in noting and criticizing the namelessness of the steerage victims and survivors. "In all that pain and grief and courage one bit of snobbery stands out," Gilman wrote; "—among those saved from death we find Mrs. So and So 'and maid'! Had the 'maid' no name, no anxious relatives?" The Yiddish socialist poet Morris Rosenfeld inquired more generally into "the people without names who perished on the ship *Titanic*." While Gilman viewed this as an unfortunate omission, others argued that class determined the *Titanic*'s status as news; it was a disaster only because of the presence of the rich and powerful. "Had the *Titanic* been a mudscow with the same number of useful workingmen on board," the *Appeal to Reason* speculated, and had it "gone down while engaged in some useful social work[,] the whole country would not have gasped with horror, nor would all the capitalist papers have given pages for weeks to reciting the terrible details."[37] Consciousness of the *Titanic*, in other words, was itself the product of capitalism and its desire to legitimate itself.

Confronted with the myth of first-cabin heroism, radicals attempted to recast the disaster in terms that would undermine rather than bolster capitalism. Debunking was one strategy—asserting that "[m]ost of this 'hero' business is rubbish anyhow." The so-called "acts of heroism of the gilt rabble" were simply a "lie," declared a "revolutionary" Italian newspaper in Paterson, New Jersey. Its anarchist counterpart in Lynn, Massachusetts claimed that millionaires interceded to save their dogs ahead of "the plebeian rabble." Speaking to striking coal miners on the capitol steps in Charleston, West Virginia, radical labor activist Mother Jones posed a series of questions meant to expose first-cabin heroism as a transparent fraud.

> I have been reading of the Titanic when she went down. Did you read of her? The big guns wanted to save themselves, and the fellows that were guiding below took up a club and said we will save our people. And then the papers came out and said those millionaires tried to save the women. Oh, Lord, why don't they give up their millions if they want to save the women and children? Why do they rob them of home, why do they rob millions of women to fill the hell-holes of capitalism[?]

Jones then launched into an elaborate anecdote about what the "Guggenheims" and their "blood-hounds" had done during a union organization drive in Colorado—ridden men out of town, thrown "widows and orphans out on the highways in the snow," jailed Mother Jones in a "pest house" when she had smallpox. Was heroism, she asked, likely among such people?[38]

Jones's speech also provided an alternative version of events in which it was the "big guns" who displayed their characteristic selfishness and the "fellows" from "below" who acted heroically. Her counternarrative, whether intentionally or not, inverted the well-circulated story of Major Butt with his iron bar beating back the crazed steerage men. Here it was the millionaires who had to be kept at bay by workingmen trying to "save our people." While "the daily press has immortalized the multi-millionaires as men of heroic mould," remarked a writer for the radical Western Federation of Miners, it ignored "the common men who made up the crew of the *Titanic*, who with pistols in their hands kept back the patrician mob, who yearned to seek safety in the life boats." In this alternative scenario, the first-class men were the "mob," and Astor, begging to go with his wife, had to be waved back by the "heroic crew whose chivalry towards women and children in the hour of peril and death, will immortalize them as the bravest of the brave." The *Jewish Daily Forward* imagined a conversation among the *Titanic*'s dead in which an "aristocrat" boasts that "[t]he papers are full of our heroic deaths" and the poor deride him: "Oy, that aristocrat fought to get into a boat but was held back by pistols. Now the papers are filled with their heroism. We poor folk who died while stoking the fires in the engine room until the very last minute, we third-class passengers who truly showed heroism, about us they write nothing."[39]

Class shaped ethnic responses to the disaster, too. Much of the immigrant and foreign-language press simply translated wire service stories and offered the usual combination of paeans to first-cabin heroism and jeremiads about speed and luxury—with important additions and exceptions. Irish Americans, for example, brought nationalism as well as class into their readings of the *Titanic*, debunking "the fake stories of heroism displayed by certain individuals and legends of the 'Be British' order," praising their "fellow-countrymen" for their "noble" behavior, excoriating the British crew for "lack of discipline and of fitness for their

FIGURE 11.2. The Strauses, transformed into honorary Anglo-Saxons in mainstream versions of the disaster, are reclaimed as Jews on the cover of a Yiddish song. (*Library of Congress*)

work," and exposing "the whole story" as "a bit of blooming English blundering."[40] Italian Americans challenged the allegations that their countrymen were shot down trying to force their way into the boats.[41] Jewish Americans not only decried the "tendency to limit the courage to dominant races and a dominant faith," but remade the Strauses, Guggenheim, and Henry B. Harris—transformed into honorary Anglo-Saxons in the mainstream press—into Jewish heroes. The *Jewish Advocate* used the disaster to agitate against pending immigration restriction bills: "The same people who sentimentalized over the actual death of those who lost their lives in the *Titanic* are eager to kill off all opportunity for thousands who desire to come here."[42] Most significantly, in articles such as "Finnish Passengers on the *Titanic*," "Were There Czechs on the *Titanic*?" "Irish Victims on the *Titanic*," "Complete List of Shipwrecked Italians," and "Many Jews Were Passengers on Ill-Fated S.S. *Titanic*," the ethnic press constituted its readers as communities of mourning and gave identity and dignity to the nameless "foreigners" in the conventional narrative.[43]

Even where they did not specifically debunk first-cabin heroism, working-class advocates told a radically different story. Admitting that "what happened in the steerage quarters" was "clouded" by the fact that most of the testimony had been "gleaned" from first- and second-class survivors, the radical press insisted "that bravery and unselfish devotion was [sic] not confined to the staterooms and that most of the men in the steerage went down because they gave their wives and children the first chance to escape." The conventional narrative, with its biases and exclusions, had become the "truth" through sheer repetition. "We have been told a thousand times and with as many variations of the bravery of the rich and prominent men aboard, but very little has been heard about the bravery of *the men and women in the steerage*." The heroism of immigrants, "consigned to the bottom like bilge," was of "no consequence to the press," an Italian socialist complained. To compensate, the radical press interviewed survivors from the third cabin and celebrated "the heroes in the hold."[44]

This labor critique of the conventional narrative extended beyond the biases of the press into efforts to shape the historical memory of the disaster. At the intersection of socialism and feminism, the *Progressive Woman* condemned the Woman's Titanic Memorial Fund for trying to give permanent form to a distorted version of events.

There is a movement on foot to build at Washington a monument to the heroes of the Titanic disaster. Said heroes are Messrs. Astor, Guggenheim, Butt, etc.—first cabin guests who "stood aside" to let first cabin women take the lifeboats in the wreck. It has developed that those who "stood aside" were unaware of the danger that threatened and are therefore less heroic than was at first supposed. However, there were men—stokers, engineers, etc.—who knew the exact situation they and the Titanic were in, who yet stood at their posts till the ship went down, never to come up again. These are the real heroes of the Titanic. If there is a monument raised for Titanic heroes, it should be to these unknown, unsung toilers in the hold of that unfortunate ship.

A poem called "Fair Play" made the point more generally: "A monument for millionaires / A monument for snobs. / No marble shaft for the men on the craft, / Who simply did their jobs."[45] In the radical counternarrative, heroism either transcended class or, as in this case, belonged exclusively to the proletariat. Class still determined conduct, but here ignorance and confusion described the "first cabin guests," while knowledge and fortitude characterized the workers.

Socialists joined in the ubiquitous warnings about luxury and greed and in the chorus calling for reform, but they did so in their own, more radical terms. They did not qualify their critique with the theme of redemption, nor did they accept the progressive belief in the basic soundness of the system. One radical writer wondered whether in their last moments, in the desperate knowledge that they would not be saved (or redeemed), the multimillionaires had thought of "the countless human beings whom they had wrecked and ruined in their mad gallop for wealth." Far from being heroic, the first-cabin men were implicated in their own fate. "So much space had to be given to the private promenades, golf links, swimming pools for the plutocrats aboard that there was no space left for life-boats when the crash came. Could misdirected ingenuity, perverted taste and mental and moral insanity go farther?" The *Masses* decried the "insanity of luxury, of foolish display and self-pampering even to the point of wrecking the safety and health of the luxurious themselves." In Charles Edward Russell's view, "the true history of the *Titanic* disaster" resided in conspicuous consumption—"features that would attract wealthy persons willing to pay great prices" for "useless luxuries." The men of the first cabin were both perpetrators and victims, murderers and murdered, in this "true history." The *Daily People* wryly observed that while the capitalist contingent on board had at least been able to enjoy the ship's attractions in exchange for the added danger, for the proletarian majority "the increased risk of drowning was thrown in for good measure" and nothing more.[46]

For Americans of many political persuasions, the cause of the disaster was the greed of the White Star Line; for socialists, however, that greed represented systemic corruption rather than an isolated transgression. "Greed and speed are the characteristics of the capitalist system," proclaimed Victor Berger, the Socialist congressman from Wisconsin. "They caused the disaster and are causing disasters almost as appalling every day in the industrial world." A writer with the fitting name (pseudonym?) John M. Work, while sympathetic to "the suffering and heartache caused by the wreck of the *Titanic*," offered the opinion that it was "a very slight tragedy" compared with the "millions upon millions who are enduring a living death under capitalism." Blaming the disaster on sin generally was also "humbug," said a poet in the anticlerical Polish humor magazine *God's Whip*. The clergy who saw it as God's "punishment for human pride" rather than a crime of capitalism were "trying to befuddle" the masses.[47]

Socialists were willing to identify specific villains but only as representatives of an evil system. It seemed almost too fitting that "Money Baron" J. P. Morgan, with his "ghoulish grasp for dividends," controlled the White Star Line. "So the *Titanic* was driven on lest Morgan might have to economize in his fleet of private yachts." He "had fattened his pockets from the conditions that made inevitable this feast of death." J. Bruce Ismay, the White Star Line's chairman who ingloriously escaped the sinking ship in a lifeboat, elicited some wishful thinking on the part of socialists and the syndicalists of the IWW. "Years ago, Ismay would have been painted a hero. Now even capitalism finds it hard to stomach him. There's a reason: capitalism is reaching a stage where its shortcomings are literally killing off and hurting its best supporters, à la the Astors and Strauses. Let the good work go on!" Others, however, refused to join in the "hounding" of Ismay on the grounds that fixing the guilt "upon some particular individual" diverted the "public wrath" from the real culprit: capitalism. Piecemeal reform and committee investigations were similarly diverting. "Any remedy will be absolutely futile no matter how ably applied so long as we retain the system," Russell argued. The time had come to move beyond "superficial thinking," "bromidic and tiresome reflections," to discover deeper causes and genuine solutions. Socialists were "out to abolish capitalism—and the necessity of investigating committees that land nowhere."[48]

In the conventional narrative, the story of the *Titanic* functioned as a parable of the natural goodness of class, racial, ethnic, and gender hierarchies. The Left, too, treated the *Titanic* as an object lesson, with the difference that the disaster was a metaphor for capitalism. "The tragedy of the month, the sinking of the *Titanic*," said the *Ladies' Garment Worker*, "is typical of the constant tragedies which occur in our industrial life." Like the ship of state, the *Titanic* sailed with "proud boasts" and illusions. On the upper deck, "comfort and luxury," "[f]easts, cards and gallantries" occupied the rich and beautiful. "Sounds of revelry" drowned out "the cry of the sick baby in the steerage," while "stokers far below in the stifling under-world" toiled and sweated "day and night." In the final moments, the first-cabin men awakened "from their orgies of self-indulgence" and realized "their manhood obligations," but their redemption was hollow—"too late for this life." As a visual metaphor for class hierarchy, the *Titanic* "illustrated in herself and in her destruction" the "contempt for human life which under capitalism inspired and presided over her creation." The *Masses* grieved over "Our 'Titanic' Civilization," while *Pravo*, a Czech socialist paper in Cleveland, observed how the ship and the disaster reflected "the attitude of the entire governing capitalist world of today. 'They' never fail to arrange for the most luxurious items . . . yet to take care of people's lives does not cross their minds." The "ship of life" would continue to "sink millions and millions of people," predicted the *Jewish Daily Forward*, as long as it was "commanded by the capitalist captains of industry."[49]

While the equation of the *Titanic* with capitalist society served as an indictment of the status quo, it also pointed hopefully toward the future. According to the metaphor, after all, capitalism was a sinking ship, and by extension, the proletariat was an iceberg. "The will of the vast working class is forming and hardening; obstructions to capitalism are cropping up in the most unexpected places; the collective mind of the working class may crystallize overnight, massive and unrelenting." (Neither icebergs nor class consciousness actually "crystallize overnight," of course. One thing radicals shared with their adversaries was inflated rhetoric.) In a different metaphor, "the iceberg of capitalist profit" floated "in the pathway of human progress, awaiting many more thousands of victims." The problem here was that icebergs are natural phenomena—hardly something the IWW would have wanted to say about capitalism; thus the metaphor shifted abruptly, to the "humane heart" mourning the tragedy while the "humane head" worked "to end human misery by ending capitalism." What confirmed the permanence of a certain vision of social order for conservatives represented the opposite to radicals. "Just as the *Titanic* went down in wreck and disaster so will capitalism which she so tragically typified also go down." Here, too, there would be casualties, "but it is to be hoped that when the crisis comes there may be life boats enough to carry humanity safely into the Socialist Republic."[50]

Paradoxically, visions of the classless future led some on the Left to embrace the myths they tried elsewhere to debunk. The *Appeal to Reason* described the steerage passengers as "penned in like cattle" and kept back "with loaded revolvers" so that "the rich passengers" could "make sure of their escape," yet somehow rich and poor alike had done the "fine thing" of observing the rule of the sea. Chivalric behavior, unfortunately, was the "extremely rare exception" rather than "the rule of life." By contrast, socialist society would be organized "on the basis of women and children first" and would prevent such tragedies from ever occurring. "Had the *Titanic* been constructed under social supervision and in social service, instead of being privately owned and launched and operated for private profit this appalling disaster would never have blackened the annals of humanity." Socialists and anarchists also redirected the "democracy of humanity" and "democracy of death" motifs to their own purposes. Images of "rich man and poor man, millionaire and stoker" standing together as "equals and brothers, without a barrier between them, going down to death together" did not suggest to the Left that the status quo was all brotherhood and harmony. But in a moment of crisis, they provided a glimpse of the classless future and confirmed "the faith of the Socialist, that all are children of the earth together, all members of one great family, all of a common origin, all sharing a common destiny, and all by every right entitled equally to light, happiness, opportunity and the bounty of the earth, our common mother!" In that moment, the artificial distinctions of the capitalist system were swept away, and Astor and the stokers *stood on one common basis of equality in the democracy of death.*"[51] Catastrophe exposed the socialism at the core of every human being—the "realities" beneath the capitalist façade.

By laying bare human nature, the *Titanic* demonstrated the viability of socialism. Critics who disparaged socialists for their utopianism—their naïve disregard for the fundamental selfishness of human beings—needed only to be reminded of the disaster. "For we might rest our whole cause upon what happened that night on the *Titanic*," beamed Charles Edward Russell. To those who insisted that socialism required "a change in human nature," we "point to that night on the *Titanic* and say that for human nature so noble and good to be perverted and dragged in the mire and slimed in the filth and hardened in the fires of Capitalism is the most unspeakable of crimes and that the race had never better friends than those that are trying to rid the earth of such a monster." The readiness with which even rich men sacrificed their lives for others showed that selfishness resided in the profit system, not in the human heart. Abraham Cahan declared that the disaster proved social Darwinism a lie: "Is this not the greatest evidence of the falsity of the claim that only the possibility of making money serves as an incentive for people, that that is human nature and cannot be altered?" Socialism, argued Jozef Sawicki in the *Polish Worker*, "will create conditions to obliterate the bad and nurture the good aspects of human character"—such as those revealed on board the sinking ship. Emma Goldman made the same case in a different way. Undercutting the myth of noblesse oblige, she envisioned the workers dying "for those far removed from us by a cold and cruel social and material gulf—for those who by their very position must needs be our enemies—for those who, a few moments before the disaster probably never gave a thought to the toilers and pariahs of the ship." Self-sacrifice of this kind was "so wonderful a feat of human nature as to silence forever the ridiculous argument" that the classless society was unnatural and therefore impossible.[52]

Human nature, in the context of the *Titanic* disaster, proved remarkably malleable. Americans across the political and social spectrum seemed actually to agree that the disaster carried lessons about what was and wasn't natural, but their agreement stopped there. When it came to the content of those lessons—was woman suffrage natural? feminism? racial equality? socialism?—consensus evaporated. As a social drama, as a public performance in which American culture thought out loud about itself, the *Titanic* disaster produced a cacophony of voices rather than a chorus. The conventional narrative tried to represent itself as common sense, to put itself beyond critical demystification, to treat the truths of the *Titanic* as self-evident, to allow for only one way of comprehending the event and its meanings. Yet dissenting voices responded to the conventional narrative, revised it, and in some cases overturned it completely. The insistence that a certain "picture invariably presents itself" failed to convince those who well understood the meanings such a picture conveyed. They preferred to draw their own.

The *Titanic* disaster was historically, not intrinsically meaningful. While we like to think that the disaster's resonance is timeless—that it has to do with universal themes of humans against nature, hubris, false confidence, the mystery of the sea, hydrophobia, heroism and cowardice—the *Titanic* seared itself into American memory not because it was timeless but because it was timely. Americans in 1912 made it speak to the concerns of contemporary politics, society, and culture. Though many of them claimed to have found transhistorical truths in the disaster, such claims were themselves historically grounded in their own contemporary circumstances and ideological purposes. The Titanic was no more inherently memorable than any other event. Making rather than finding its significance, people worked and fought to shape how the disaster would, they hoped, be remembered.

NOTES

1. Walter Lord, *A Night to Remember* (New York: Henry Holt, 1955), 139; Wyn Craig Wade, *The* Titanic: *End of a Dream* (New York: Rawson, Wade, 1979), 296; Charles Pellegrino, *Her Name,* Titanic: *The Untold Story of the Sinking and Finding of the Unsinkable Ship* (New York: McGraw-Hill, 1988), 32.

2. For a summary of the anthropological concept of social drama, see Chandra Mukerji and Michael Schudson, "Introduction: Rethinking Popular Culture," in *Rethinking Popular Culture: Contemporary Perspectives in Cultural Studies,* ed. Chandra Mukerji and Michael Schudson (Berkeley: University of California Press, 1991), 23. See also Victor Turner, "Liminality and the Performative Genres," in *Rite, Drama, Festival, Spectacle: Rehearsals Toward a Theory of Cultural Performance,* ed. John J. MacAloon (Philadelphia: Institute for the Study of Human Issues, 1984), 19-41.

3. Several recent studies of historical memory have shaped my own interpretive framework. John Bodnar, *Remaking America: Public Memory, Commemoration, and Patriotism in the Twentieth Century* (Princeton, N.J.: Princeton University Press, 1992); David Glassberg, *American Historical Pageantry: The Uses of Tradition in the Early Twentieth Century* (Chapel Hill: University of North Carolina Press, 1990); George Lipsitz, *Time Passages: Collective Memory and American Popular Culture* (Minneapolis: University of Minnesota Press, 1990); and David Thelen, ed.,

Memory and American History (Bloomington: Indiana University Press, 1990) all make use of the concept of "struggles" or "contestations over meaning."

4. See, for example, "*Titanic* Disaster Hits Home of Entire Nation," *San Francisco Examiner*, 17 April 1912, 2; "Heroic Acts on *Titanic* Never Surpassed in World's Annals," *Denver Post*, 17 April 1912, 2; "Saved from Wreck," *Chicago Tribune*, 17 April 1912, 1; "Waters of Atlantic Sound Requiem over Thousand Departed Souls," *Asheville Citizen*, 17 April 1912, 1; "Thousands Now Abandon All Hope for Loved Relatives on *Titanic*," *Charlotte Observer*, 17 April 1912, 1.

5. Eleanor Flexner, *Century of Struggle: The Woman's Rights Movement in the United States*, rev. ed. (Cambridge: Harvard University Press, 1975), 256, 263-68.

6. Aileen S. Kraditor, *The Ideas of the Woman Suffrage Movement, 1890–1920* (New York: Anchor, 1971), 38-39, 51, 52; Nancy F. Cott, *The Grounding of Modern Feminism* (New Haven, Conn.: Yale University Press, 1987), 29-30; Alan Dawley, *Struggles for Justice: Social Responsibility and the Liberal State* (Cambridge: Harvard University Press, 1991), 96.

7. Mrs. William M. Ellicott, quoted in "Women First, She Says," *Baltimore Sun*, 18 April 1912, 11.

8. Emma Goldman, "Suffrage Dealt Blow by Women of *Titanic*," *Denver Post*, 21 April 1912, sec. 1, 8.

9. Frances Wayne, "*Titanic* Disaster Furnishes No Proof that Women Are Unfit for Suffrage," *Denver Post*, 22 April 1912, 6; Helen Grenfell, Ben B. Lindsey, John T. Barnett, quoted in Wayne, "*Titanic* Disaster," 6.

10. Cott, Grounding of Modern Feminism, 3-5.

11. Rheta Childe Dorr, "'Women and Children First,'" *Woman's Journal*, 4 May 1912, 141; Alice Stone Blackwell, "The Lesson of the *Titanic*," *Woman's Journal*, 27 April 1912, 132; Milholland, quoted in "Women First Barbarous," *New York Tribune*, 19 April 1912, 16. See also Ann E. Larabee, "The American Hero and His Mechanical Bride: Gender Myths of the *Titanic* Disaster," *American Studies* 31, no. 1 (Spring 1990): 15-18.

12. "Masculine Chivalry," *Progressive Woman*, May 1912, 8; Alice Stone Blackwell, "Suffrage and Life-Saving," *Woman's Journal*, 27 April 1912, 132.

13. Agnes E. Ryan, "Lives Against Lives," *Woman's Journal*, 27 April 1912, 136; Blackwell, "Suffrage and Life-Saving," 132; Mary McDowell, "The New Chivalry and Industrial Life," *Life and Labor*, July 1913, 196, 198. McDowell's article was originally given as a speech at a WTUL meeting in St. Louis on June 2, 1912.

14. "Masculine Chivalry," 8; Charlotte Perkins Gilman, "The Saving of Women in Disaster," *Forerunner*, May 1912, 140. See also Gilman, *Women and Economics: A Study of the Economic Relation between Men and Women as a Factor in Social Evolution*, (New York: Harper & Row, 1966), 62 and passim.

15. "A Woman," Letter, *Baltimore Sun*, 22 April 1912, 6; Grace Guyton Kempter, Letter, *Baltimore Sun*, 25 April 1912, 6; "Daughter of Eve," Letter, *Bal-*

timore Sun, 1 May 1912, 6; Emma Maddox Funck, Letter, *Baltimore Sun*, 26 April 1912, 6.

16. Henry Louis Gates Jr., *Colored People: A Memoir* (New York: Alfred A. Knopf, 1994), 92-93; Henry Louis Gates Jr., "Sudden Def," *New Yorker*, 19 June 1995, 37.

17. The phrase was the title of an editorial in the *St. Louis Post-Dispatch*, 4 May 1912, 4.

18. "*Titanic* Disaster Hits Home," 2. Wyn Craig Wade notes the black press's lack of attention to the disaster in *The* Titanic: *End of a Dream*, 294. The *Cleveland Gazette, Richmond Planet, Savannah Tribune, St. Paul Appeal*, and *Washington Bee* printed some of the standard wire service material.

19. "The Lesson of the *Titanic*," *Indianapolis Freeman*, 27 April 1912, 4; "The Awakening," *Chicago Defender*, 20 April 1912, 4; "The Horror of the Sea," *Indianapolis World*, 27 April 1912, 4.

20. "The Awakening," 4; Mary D. Turner, "Bethel A.M.E. Church," *Pittsburgh Courier*, 27 April 1912, 6; Mrs. Mattye E. Anderson, "The *Titanic*," *Chicago Defender*, 20 April 1912, 4; Lucian B. Watkins, "O Sea! A Dirge; The Tragedy of the *Titanic*, Memorable of 1912," *Richmond Planet*, 25 May 1912, 4.

21. "Belshazzar's Feast," *Richmond Planet*, 20 April 1912, 4; "A Very Sad Affair with an Important Lesson," *Afro-American Ledger*, 20 April 1912, 4. See also, for example, "Sermon on the *Titanic* Disaster," *Afro-American Ledger*, 18 May 1912, 2.

22. Carl Sandburg, *The American Songbag* (New York: Harcourt, Brace, 1927), 254-56; Samuel B. Charters, *The Country Blues* (London: Michael Joseph, 1959), 62-63; Newman I. White, *American Negro Folk-Songs* (Cambridge: Harvard University Press, 1928), 347-48; Harold Courlander, *Negro Folk Music, U.S.A.* (New York: Columbia University Press, 1963), 76-77; John A. Lomax and Alan Lomax, *Our Singing Country: A Second Volume of American Ballads and Folk Songs* (New York: Macmillan, 1941), 26-27.

23. "The Horror of the Sea," 4; "Afro-American Cullings," *Pittsburgh Courier*, 7 June 1912, 8.

24. Editorial, *St. Paul Appeal*, 20 April 1912, 2; "Editorial Notes," *New York Age*, 25 April 1912, 4.

25. "Current Notes," *Savannah Tribune*, 25 May 1912, 3; Editorial, *Philadelphia Tribune*, 27 April 1912, 4.

26. *Louisville News*, quoted in *Chicago Defender*, 4 May 1912, 4; Editorial, *Chicago Defender*, 4 May 1912, 4; *Solid Rock Herald*, quoted in "Afro-American Press on *Titanic* Disaster," *Broad Ax*, 4 May 1912, 2; Editorial, *Pittsburgh Courier*, 27 April 1912.

27. White, *American Negro Folk-Songs*, 348-49; Charles Wolfe and Kip Lornell, *The Life and Legend of Leadbelly* (New York: HarperCollins, 1992), 44-45; Jerry Silverman, *Folk Blues* (New York: Macmillan, 1968), 149-50; Courlander, *Negro Folk Music*, 77-78; Lawrence W. Levine, *Black Culture and Black*

Consciousness: Afro-American Folk Thought from Slavery to Freedom (New York: Oxford University Press, 1977), 258.

28. Bruce Jackson, "The *Titanic* Toast," in *Veins of Humor*, Harvard English Studies 3, ed. Harry Levin (Cambridge: Harvard University Press, 1972), 205-23; Roger D. Abrahams, *Deep Down in the Jungle: Negro Narrative Folklore from the Streets of Philadelphia*, rev. ed. (Chicago: Aldine, 1970), 120-29; Levine, *Black Culture*, 428-29.

29. Robert L. Dorman, *Revolt of the Provinces: The Regionalist Movement in America, 1920-1945* (Chapel Hill: University of North Carolina Press, 1993), esp. chaps. 3-4; Lawrence W. Levine, "The Folklore of Industrial Society: Popular Culture and Its Audiences," *American Historical Review* 97, no. 5 (December 1992): 48-54.

30. Levine, "Folklore of Industrial Society," 1377 and passim; Alan Lomax, *The Land Where the Blues Began* (New York: Pantheon, 1993), 48-54.

31. The process at work in the African-American folk songs and toasts was the vernacular strategy of "signifyin(g)," which Gates defines as "a metaphor for textual revision"—the playing of language games—often "aimed at demystifying a subject." Henry Louis Gates Jr., *The Signifying Monkey: A Theory of African-American Literary Criticism* (New York: Oxford University Press, 1988), 88, 57, 52.

32. Ira Kipnis, *The American Socialist Movement, 1897-1912* (New York: Monthly Review Press, 1952), 35, 366-69; Melvyn Dubofsky, *We Shall Be All: A History of the Industrial Workers of the World* (Chicago: Quadrangle, 1969), chap. 10, esp. 253; James Weinstein, *The Decline of Socialism in America, 1912-1925*, 2d ed. (New Brunswick, N.J.: Rutgers University Press, 1984), 93-103; Dawley, *Struggles for Justice*, 136.

33. "The Great Catastrophe," *American Federation of Labor Weekly News Letter*, 20 April 1912, n.p.; "The *Titanic* Disaster—To Prevent Recurrence," *American Federationist*, July 1912, 545-48; "The *Titanic* Disaster," *Weekly Bulletin of the Clothing Trades*, 26 April 1912, 4; Editorial, *Glass Worker*, May 1912, 12; Editorial, *Mixer and Server*, May 1912, 46; "The *Titanic* Sea Horror Should Be a Lesson to the World," *Journal of the Switchmen's Union of North America*, May 1912, 8; "What Shall the Harvest Be?" *Coast Seaman's Journal*, 24 April 1912, 6; "Furnseth's Warning," *Shoe Workers' Journal*, June 1912, 11-12; "Remember!" *Railway Carmen's Journal*, June 1912, 413; Editorial, *Car Worker*, July 1912, 45-46; "Senator Smith's *Titanic* Speech," *Paper Makers' Journal*, June 1912, 4; "Another Sacrifice to the God of Speed," *Steam Shovel and Dredge*, May 1912, 403; LaFollette, quoted in Belle Case LaFollette and Fola LaFollette, *Robert M. LaFollette, June 14, 1855–June 18, 1925* (New York: Macmillan, 1953), 1: 528. The Seamen's Act was signed by Woodrow Wilson in March 1915.

34. "It Was Necessary to Kill Fifteen Hundred at a Time to Get Action," *Railroad Trainman*, June 1912, 535-36; Norm Cohen, *Long Steel Rail: The Railroad in American Folksong* (Urbana: University of Illinois Press, 1981), 171; "Mika Al-

heuttaa Titanic-Onnet-Tomuudessa Valtavan Huomion" [Why all the attention directed to the *Titanic* disaster?], *Raivaaja* [Pioneer], 18 April 1912, 7; Frank Durwood Adams, "S.O.S.—Save Our Souls," *Christian Socialist*, 25 April 1912, 2; George Emery, "Thoughts on the *Titanic* Disaster," *Metal Polishers, Buffers, Platers, Brass and Silver Workers Union of North America Journal*, May 1912, 6; Editorial, *Official Magazine of the International Brotherhood of Teamsters, Chauffeurs, Stablemen and Helpers of America*, May 1912, 10; "Man Is as Chaff Before the Breath of God," *Blacksmiths Journal*, May 1912, 41.

Most of the foreign-language press I cite can be found in the collections of the Immigration History Research Center at the University of Minnesota.

35. "At Work, with First Chance of Death," *American Federationist*, June 1912, 470; "First-Class Scabs," *United Mine Workers Journal*, 2 May 1912, 4.

36. George A. Hill, "The *Titanic*," *Advance Advocate*, June 1912, 458; "*Titanic* Disaster," *Railway Conductor*, May 1912, 391; "Aftermath," *Locomotive Firemen and Enginemen's Magazine*, June 1912, 838; William Havenstrite, "A Tragedy Glorified," *Elevator Constructor*, May 1912, 13; Thomas E. Burke, "Comment on Current Topics," *Plumbers', Gas and Steam fitters' Journal*, May 1912, 27; "Sublime!" *International Musician*, May 1912, 6; "The Flesh and the Spirit," *LW*, 27 April 1912, 4; "The *Titanic* Disaster," *Journal of the International Brotherhood of Boiler Makers, Iron Ship Builders and Helpers of America*, June 1912, 468; James E. Kinsella, "The Conquered Titan," *Union Postal Clerk*, July 1912, 11-12; "The Sinking of the *Titanic*," *Locomotive Engineers' Monthly Journal*, May 1912, 493-94.

37. Gilman, "The Saving of Women," 140; Morris Rosenfeld, "The People Without Names who Perished on the Ship *Titanic*," *Jewish Daily Forward*, 17 April 1912, 4; "The *Titanic* Tragedy," *Appeal to Reason*, 4 May 1912, 4.

38. "A Popular Scapegoat," *New York Call*, 23 April 1912, 6; "L'Immane Disastro del 'Titanic'" [The great *Titanic* disaster], *L'Era Nuova*, 27 April 1912, 1; Mother Jones, "Speech at a Public Meeting on the Steps of the Capitol, Charleston, West Virginia, 15 August 1912," in *The Speeches and Writings of Mother Jones*, ed. Edward M. Steel (Pittsburgh: University of Pittsburgh Press, 1988), 93-94.

39. "'There Are Others,'" *Miners Magazine*, 2 May 1912, 6; "The Proletariat," "The Floating Cemetery: A Conversation among the Drowned Ones of the *Titanic*," *Jewish Daily Forward*, 28 April 1912, 4.

40. "Flowers of British Chivalry," *Gaelic American*, 18 May 1912, 4; Robert Ellis Thompson, "The *Titanic* Disaster," *Irish World and American Industrial Liberator*, 27 April 1912, 5; "British Blundering," *Gaelic American*, 25 May 1912, 2.

41. "La Catastrofe del 'Titanic' Descritta dai Naufraghi Salvati" [The *Titanic* catastrophe described by shipwreck survivors], *L'Italia*, 27 April 1912, 7.

42. "A Quality of Courage," *Jewish Advocate*, 26 April 1912, 8; "A Fight for Freedom," *Jewish Advocate*, 10 May 1912, 8. The sheet music for Solomon Small's Yiddish song "The *Titanic* Disaster," for example, featured an illustration of the Strauses hovering in an embrace above the sinking ship, about to be crowned

by an angel. Solomon Small (Smulewitz) and H. A. Russotto, "The *Titanic* Disaster" (New York: Hebrew Publishing Co., 1912), Music Division, LC.

43. "'Titanicin' Suomalaiset Maikustajat" [Finnish passengers on the *Titanic*], *New York Uutiset*, 20 April 1912, 1; "Cesi Na 'Titanic'?" [Were there Czechs on the *Titanic*?], *Denni Hlasatel*, 17 April 1912, 1; "Irish Victims on *Titanic*," *Irish World and American Industrial Liberator*, 11 May 1912, 7; "Lista Completa dei Naufraghi Italiani" [Complete list of shipwrecked Italians], *L'Italia*, 4 May 1912, 1; "Many Jews Were Passengers on Ill-Fated S.S. *Titanic*," *Jewish Advocate*, 19 April 1912, 1.

44. "*Titanic* Passengers in Steerage Brave," *New York Call*, 25 April 1912, 2 [emphasis in original]; "*Titanic* Tragedy," 4; "Virtus," "*Titanic*—La Stampa—Eroismo dei Ricchi" [The *Titanic*—the press—the heroism of the rich], *La Fiaccola*, 4 May 1912, 1.

45. "Preventable Deaths of Workers," *Progressive Woman*, September 1912, 2; M. L. Clawson, "Fair Play," *Indianapolis World*, 18 May 1912, 1.

46. Editorial, *Miners Magazine*, 9 May 1912, 6; "*Titanic* Tragedy," 4; "Our 'Titanic' Civilization," *Masses*, June 1912, 3; Charles Edward Russell, "Murdered for Capitalism," *Coming Nation*, 27 April 1912, 3; "A *Titanic* Demonstration," *Daily People*, 18 April 1912, 2.

47. Berger, quoted in "Rich Men Not Only Heroes in Shipwreck," *Cleveland Press*, 24 April 1912, 11; John M. Work, "The Greater Tragedy," *New York Call*, 4 May 1912, 6 (also printed in *Bridgemen's Magazine*, May 1912, 343-44); Szczypawka, "Z Tygodniowych Refleksji" [From the weekly reflections], *Bicz Bozy*, 28 April 1912, 4.

48. "Titanicin Haaksirikko Ja Kapitalismi" [The *Titanic* disaster and capitalism], *Tyomies*, 21 April 1912, 2; A. M. Simons, "Dred that Dividends Might Grow," *Coming Nation*, 27 April 1912, 16; "*Titanic* Tragedy," 4; "News and Views," *Solidarity*, 4 May 1912, 2; "A Popular Scapegoat," 6; Russell, "Murdered for Capitalism," 4; Charles Edward Russell, "Inside of the *Titanic* Case," *Coming Nation*, 4 May 1912, 3; "Futile Questioning," *New York Call*, 22 April 1912, 6.

49. "Lessons from the *Titanic* Disaster," *Ladies' Garment Worker*, May 1912, 14; "*Titanic* Tragedy," 4; "Our 'Titanic' Civilization," esp. 3; Editorial, *Pravo*, 30 April 1912, 2; "Capitalistic Hurry-Up and the *Titanic* Disaster," *Jewish Daily Forward*, 18 April 1912, 4.

50. "Our 'Titanic' Civilization," 3; "News and Views," *Solidarity*, 27 April 1912, 2; "*Titanic* Tragedy," 4.

51. "*Titanic* Tragedy," 4 [emphasis in original]; Charles Edward Russell, "Realities," *Coming Nation*, 4 May 1912, 4.

52. Charles Edward Russell, "Human Nature," *Coming Nation*, 4 May 1912, 4; Victor A. Olander, "The *Titanic*," *Life and Labor*, June 1912, 180; "Human Nature as Evinced in the *Titanic* Disaster," *Jewish Daily Forward*, 20 April 1912, 4; Jozef Sawicki, "Z Powodu Wypadku Z Okretem Titanic" [On the occasion of the *Titanic* disaster], *Robotnik Polski*, 25 April 1912, 4; Goldman, quoted in "Suffrage Dealt Blow," *Denver Post*, 21 April 1912, sec. 1, 8.

12

"Piecing Together What History Has Broken to Bits"

Air Florida Flight 90 and the PATCO Disaster

Ralph James Savarese

History, wrote the German-Jewish critic Walter Benjamin in 1940, is "one single catastrophe which keeps piling wreckage upon wreckage." Inspired by Benjamin's hope of jolting history out of its catastrophic standstill, Ralph James Savarese seeks the utopian possibilities in the 1982 Air Florida crash in Washington, D.C.—in the heroism of the mysterious "man in the water" who came to the rescue of his fellow passengers and the convict–con artist who posed as a priest to comfort the bereaved families of the victims. Defying the formal conventions of traditional history and criticism, Savarese creates a "remembrance" of the disaster that is both imagistic and analytical. His essay juxtaposes scenes of the crash with descriptions of Ronald Reagan's ruthless suppression of the air traffic controllers' strike a few months earlier, discussions of the history of aviation, and illuminating references to Sigmund Freud, Herman Melville, Karl Marx, Walker Percy, and others who have ruminated on trauma and rescue.

Washington is a sad city. It is depressed. It is stunned and it is cold and its faith in the future is shaken. The economy is rotten and the federal government is cutting back and unemployment has spread to white-collar jobs and the Potomac River is a morgue for people who were heading for the sun. . . . There's been a plane crash, a train crash. A town that works for the federal government has been told over and over by its boss, the president of the United States, that it's the enemy. The belief that government can do good is out of style. The belief that government ought to at least try to do good is also out of style. This administration does not want to even try. . . . In Washington, poor women walk miles for some free American cheese. They stand for hours in numbing temperatures and then, after having done that, they have to produce documents to certify their poverty. A day later, the administration parties in honor of Lynn Nofziger. The party cost something like $30,000. The paper brings a daily outrage, another dollop of insensitivity from the White House. The ears of Mrs. William French Smith dangle earrings that cost more than a house.[1]

—Richard Cohen

GRAND SPOILER

JANUARY 1998. The House of Representatives is debating a bill that would rename Washington National Airport in honor of Ronald Reagan. Perhaps worried about his own future memorialization, President Clinton has expressed support for the bill, as have a host of other Democratic congressmen and senators. Describing something very much like the phenomenon of traumatic recall, German-Jewish critic Walter Benjamin writes in "Theses on the Philosophy of History," "To articulate the past historically does not mean to recognize it 'the way it really was' (Ranke). It means to seize hold of a memory as it flashes up at a moment of danger."[2]

INSTRUMENT PANEL/AIRSPEED DISPLAY

January 13, 1982. On its way to Tampa, Florida, a Boeing 737 takes off from Washington National Airport after sitting for fifty minutes on the runway in a snowstorm without being adequately de-iced. A minute later, it plows into the 14th Street Bridge, thoroughly pulverizing four cars, then "dives" (as the headline in the *Washington Post* will put it) into the Potomac River. For a brief moment, its badly fractured fuselage floats eerily on the surface. Six people in the tail have survived: five passengers and a flight attendant. The people in the four cars have been killed.[3]

FIGURE 12.1. Salvage crews hoist the tail section of shattered Air Florida Flight 90 from the ice-choked Potomac River. (UPI/Corbis-Bettmann)

The rescue is being caught on videotape—to be replayed ceaselessly this late January afternoon and evening. As an article in the *Post* (titled "Views from the Bridge—and of It on TV") will state, rather nonchalantly, "Without benefit of television, those on the bridge saw the tragedy only once."[4] Indeed, what television viewer won't remember that large, metallic bird hovering above the wreckage, that dazed woman floundering again and again in the icy water, too weak to grab hold of the Park Police helicopter's lifeline?

COACH SEAT: 15A

In her introduction to *Trauma: Explorations in Memory*, Cathy Caruth proposes that "to be traumatized is precisely to be possessed by an image," and she suggests that the "transformation of the trauma into a narrative memory that allows the story to be verbalized and communicated, to be integrated into one's own and others' knowledge of the past, may lose both the precision and the force that characterize traumatic recall." She worries, in other words (extrapolating from Freud), that the assimilation into consciousness of the disturbing event (image), the transformation of involuntary into voluntary memory, signals mastery, which ironically constitutes a kind of protective forgetting: prelude, perhaps, to a more literal or actual forgetting. As the epigraph for her book, Caruth presents a remark by an anonymous Vietnam veteran who, suffering from Post-Traumatic Stress Disorder, movingly laments, "I do not want to take drugs for my nightmares because I want to remain a memorial to my dead friends."[5]

SIDEWALL DECORATIVE PANEL

Walter Benjamin, writing in the 1940s, pays particular attention to what allowed Freud to theorize the problem of shell shock in World War I: namely, an observation concerning dreams "characteristic of [railroad] accident neuroses which reproduce the catastrophe in which the patient was involved" and the speculation that such dreams "endeavor to master" the traumatic event "retroactively." Put simply, in Freud's model, dreams serve a dual purpose: they strive for the neutralization of the traumatic memory even as they traumatize the dreamer.[6]

In his allegorical appropriation of this framework for the task of writing capitalist history (to him, an unending disaster), Benjamin imagines delaying recovery for as long as possible—indeed, until it coincides with revolution. If "all reification is a forgetting," as T. W. Adorno insists in a letter to Benjamin in 1940—if the oppressive social relations of commodity capitalism constitute an injury that "we" at best perpetually recover from and at worst never even acknowledge—then Benjamin sets out with a nearly apocalyptic "blasting" operation to arrest this "continuum," to reopen any number of specific wounds.[7]

INTERPHONE HANDSET

A waterlogged flight attendant? A fallen angel? A panicked altar girl for the once fussy (now dead) consumer? What is she doing there on the screen, cleaving mid-sentence the incredulous narratives of the afternoon soaps, appearing exaltedly—though, for a split second, unidentifiably—as the content of a *Special Report*?

HORIZONTAL STABILIZER

"History," Benjamin declares, *"breaks down* into images not into stories."[8] By "stories" he means both the conventional narrative of progress (the official record of capitalist consciousness, with its barbarous elisions and technological triumphalism) *and* traditional, demystifying critique (the record's familiar reprimand, with its haughty presumption of repair and jejune depiction of human suffering and utopian desire).

COACH SEAT: 16C

Shortly after the crash, a media critic will assert, "We go to our televisions now in times of tragedy the way our ancestors used to go to churches and town halls. We have to watch it over and over." He will not fully sense, however, the way this repetition actually presages the dissolution of the arresting spectacle or the way such images remain compelling only as long as they remain tantalizingly enigmatic.

"The images lost none of their power," he will argue, "and made sense of the disaster in the kind of terrible ceremony that repetition gave them." Implicitly acknowledging the collective stream of consciousness that makes up afternoon and evening TV and suggesting that the Air Florida disaster managed precisely to rupture this ho-hum procession of soap-opera entanglements, talk show guests, one-minute messages from Hamburger Helper, Clear-Stick Antiperspirant ("so that no one can see you sweat"), and "lemon-fresh" Joy (not to mention later, on the evening news, reports of a deepening recession, rising interest rates, further layoffs, drug-related inner-city murders, a bank hold-up, etc.), and even appealing instinctively to lyric poetry for an adequate model of catastrophic articulation and remembrance, he will conclude, "'After the first death,' as poet Dylan Thomas once wrote, 'there is no other.' And after the crash there was nothing else to watch or think about as long as television had us there."[9]

SINGLE SERVE MEAL CART

What of the incongruity and allegorical implications of this uniformed cherub flailing in the water? Has she no poise, no marketing savvy, no commitment to the flight attendant handbook? How might the flailing woman's forebear, Ellen Church, the very first stewardess, have responded to this unexpected, certainly unscheduled, touchdown?

OVERHEAD STOWAGE BIN

Recognizing, in the words of Caruth, that trauma's power derives precisely from "the truth of its incomprehensibility," "the force of its affront to understanding," Benjamin also recognizes that, left to its own devices, a traumatic memory might, as Adorno said of Benjamin's early plan for a fundamentally imagistic critique, be "consumed by its own aura." In other words, while such a memory might certainly command a form of compulsive and disturbing attention, it might also inhibit specific comprehension. And any project of historical remembrance without some "mastery" would hardly be remembrance at all. As the notion of a simultaneously traumatizing and re-cuperative dream should make clear, Benjamin is interested finally in a position somewhere between injury and recovery, between mem-ory and forgetting. After all, in "Theses on the Philosophy of His-tory," he states that "historical materialism wishes to *retain* that image of the past which unexpectedly appears to a man singled out by history at a moment of danger," thereby implying the inclusion of a good deal of fairly conventional mediation. It seeks to retain "that image" while moving toward analytical clarity.[10]

FLIGHT ATTENDANT JUMPSEAT

In the 1930s, as Carl Solberg explains in *Conquest of the Sky*, the stew-ardesses for United Airlines (the first carrier to employ such caregivers) were all undercover nurses and rugged air enthusiasts. In a letter to company executives proposing his idea, Steve Simpson, manager of the San Francisco office, had written,

> Of course it would be distinctly understood that there would be no reference to their hospital training or nursing experience, but it would be a mighty fine thing to have available, sub rosa, if neces-sary for airsickness. Imagine the psychology of having young women as regular members of the crew. Imagine the national pub-licity we could get from it, and the tremendous effect it would have on the traveling public. Also, imagine the value they would be to us not only in the neater and nicer method of serving food but looking out for the passenger's welfare.

Of course, Simpson had failed to say anything about the "welfare" of his prospective stewardesses. Certainly no second set had been envi-sioned to take care of the first in the event of a different kind of "air-sickness." Surveying the long history of "sky girl" unionization and pointing to the marketing that would sexually inflect these workers' economic objectification—in one ad from the late 1970s a female voice giddily exclaims, "We really move our tail for you!"—Georgia Nielsen cites a remark that perfectly captures the persistent attitude of airline management toward its ethereal employees: "Use them till their smiles wear out; then get a new bunch."[11]

ENGINE THRUST REVERSER

Joseph Corn reminds us in *The Winged Gospel: America's Romance with Aviation, 1900-1950* that the airplane was initially conceived as an instrument of social reform—though one abandoning the problems of capital, rising literally above them; an instrument "ending humanity's long and frustrating earthbound existence"; an instrument ushering in an "era beyond history when everything would be perfect, as in a utopia." Even more than the locomotive, it came cloaked in religious garb, what with the obvious, traditional association of flight with the divine and the irresistible (and updated) invitation to heavenly allegory: the pilgrim's *material* progress.[12]

OVERWING EMERGENCY EXIT

In an interview with Solberg, one of the original stewardesses for United speaks of planes frequently touching down in places unspecified by the official schedule. In one such landing in a wheatfield in Wyoming, "people," she says, "came in wagons and on horseback to see the plane. They'd never seen one before. They wanted to touch it and touch me."[13]

FUEL HOSE ASSEMBLY

A government employee on his way home from work stops his car and, seeing the woman, runs down to the river's edge. As scores merely look on passively at the drowning angel, the man jumps into the water and swims out to rescue her. "Her body just went limp," he will say. "I think she passed out. Her eyes rolled back and she started to go under. Something told me to go in after her." Later, this congressional budget office gopher and father of three, who makes $14,000 a year, will meet President Reagan at the White House and be proclaimed an American hero. In fact, two weeks after the crash, Reagan will again use the gopher as a potent symbol when, in another upgrade of sorts, he will be seated next to the First Lady during Reagan's high-flying State of the Union address. With the economy in recession, with the demise of all sorts of government aid programs, with homeless people camping out on the streets of Washington, with an additional 1.25 million industrial jobs to be eliminated by year's end—with critics, in short, calling the first twelve months of his presidential stewardship a veritable disaster— Reagan will point to a beaming Lennie Skutnick (and, in effect, to the sunken airliner being lifted from the frigid Potomac), saying, "Don't let anyone tell you that America's best days are behind her. We've seen it triumph too often in our lives to stop believing in it now."[14]

FIRST-CLASS SEAT: 3B

Nearly six months before the crash, a strike was called by the least likely of unions: in fact, by one of the few—the Professional Air Traffic Controllers Organization (PATCO)—that had voted for Reagan the previous year. PATCO had been demanding amelioration of a particularly debilitating commitment to "passenger welfare" that forced the average air traffic controller to retire as a result of stress-related disorders by the age of thirty-five.[15] A group of well-educated, relatively well-paid government employees had renounced their consumerist identities and reconceived of themselves as combatants in an old-fashioned labor struggle, and it had been met by a recalcitrant majority refusing to be inconvenienced and refusing to imagine any other social antagonists but the ones identified by the president. Those antagonists were, of course, communism abroad and greedy, self-interested labor unions at home.

At the very moment he was orchestrating massive government cuts, the president was branding the controllers, who were forbidden by law to strike, as neglecting their solemn governmental duty to serve the public and as jeopardizing the safety of "all Americans" (even, apparently, those who, by continuing to perform their jobs, would have been welcoming further psychological and bodily injury, and certainly those who, in their poverty, couldn't afford to fly). In what would become a recurring problem with memory, the Gipper had somehow forgotten that during the campaign he had explicitly promised to reform the FAA and, in doing so, to address the controllers' pressing concerns (including exactly the prospect of more aviation disasters). In the Cabinet Room, where a portrait of Calvin Coolidge hangs, Reagan spoke admiringly of Coolidge's brutal response to the Boston police strike of 1919, parroting his infamous remark: "There is no right to strike against the public any time, anywhere."[16]

PASSENGER BUSINESS CARD

Emphasizing the sheer potential of modern productive capabilities and, at the same time, the ceaseless assimilation of "the new" into the profit nexus, a younger Benjamin, in an earlier and less dire appropriation of Freud, described the goods of the nineteenth-century arcade, precursor to the shopping mall, as "wishful fantasies"—in effect, as the dozing century's utopian dreamwork. As images in a dream, the goods of the nineteenth-century arcade thus housed a distorted, even censored utopian wish. They actually reflected, Benjamin believed, a perverse awareness of the inequity and divisiveness of wage labor and capital accumulation and a desire for some truly collective alternative. Planning, in an early version of the *Arcades Project*, to mobilize a series of "found" dialectical images, Benjamin hoped to rescue the egalitarian promise of these once innovative commodities, which at the moment of their spectacular inception (that is, before they had become quotidian and, eventually, obsolete) had most clearly manifested the belief in a perfectible society and in the ability of industrial technology to bring it quickly about.[17]

Of course, an unconscious striving can be detected, as Benjamin himself implied, in almost any capitalist phenomenon, whether or not it is actually obsolete or even strictly a commodity: from the lipsticked pandering of lofty service workers to the agitated vigilance of air traffic controllers to, perhaps most compelling of all, the rapid transport innovations themselves. Nineteenth- and early twentieth-century transport innovations functioned, after all, as *the* referents of progress, especially, according to Susan Buck-Morss, "as spatial movement became so wedded to the concept of historical movement that these could no longer be distinguished."[18] Through the creation and provisioning of distant markets, these engines of capital made possible the enticing merchandise and hellish factories of a consumer society, and in their continuous movement they majestically enacted, Benjamin would say, the paradox of an imperceptible historical standstill. They majestically enacted, that is, the energetic stasis—the parodic advancement—of commodity capitalism.

COACH SEAT: 26D

With the flailing woman rescued by the Congressional Budget Office gopher, the Park Police helicopter turns its attention to the passengers clinging to the plane's tail—the only part of the plane that is not completely submerged. (Upon being salvaged, the tail will quickly receive a splash of paint as part of a marketing strategy designed to hide the insignia of the airline and thus to prevent it, in future wreckage photographs, from being associated with disaster. By some reports, the accident will end up costing the airline nearly 100,000 reservations and, eventually, bankruptcy itself.[19]) The passengers seem confused. As the helicopter's paramedic will later report, "At first they didn't understand what to do with the rope. I guess they were in shock. They just wanted to hold on to it."[20]

AFT TRASH BIN

In "Paris, Capital of the Nineteenth Century," when the younger Benjamin asserted that "ambiguity is the pictorial image of dialectics, the law of dialectics seen at a standstill," he was alluding to the arresting tension between an object's utopian potential and its inglorious utilization. And he was alluding additionally to the general cycle of frenzied innovation and obsolescence that produced one technological marvel after another but that, in failing to produce an egalitarian society, contributed instead to "the sterile continuum of the always the same" (or, as a nearly disconsolate Benjamin would put it in 1940 just before his death—actually hoping for some final, demonstrative calamity—to the "one single catastrophe which keeps piling wreckage upon wreckage" at the feet of the Angel of History). Similarly, when Benjamin stated that "this standstill is utopia, and the dialectical image is therefore a dream image," he was boldly characterizing his project's intended effect: a jolting intimation of the century's reified longing and, hence, of the possibility of genuine historical movement or belated revolutionary consciousness.[21]

EMERGENCY FIRST AID EQUIPMENT

"You want to know what being an air traffic controller is like?" Tina Clark asks sardonically in an interview with Bob Reiss. "Imagine 200 blind two-year-olds wandering around on the interstate, and you're driving 100 miles an hour and trying not to hit them." Another controller, in an interview with James Kaplan, reports that there can be as many as 110 takeoffs and landings per hour at Kennedy Airport. "That's one every thirty seconds," he says, "and you have to make a couple of transmissions for each. Theoretically we are responsible in one hour for more lives than a doctor could be in his entire career, and billions of dollars in equipment."[22]

MAGAZINE RACK

The walkout received almost no support from the people whom the recession and, in particular, Reagan's policies were hurting the most. Like fish circling an outboard TV, they continued to swallow the culture's consumerist bait. Not only did they refuse to acknowledge the oppressive working conditions that undergirded air traffic control; they refused to distinguish at all between the material positions of the relatively well off (or middle-class) controllers and the material positions, for example, of the indisputably well off (or essentially upper-class) profiteers of Wall Street. Exhibiting an emblematically vicious and displaced resentment, Mary June, who at the time of the strike was earning $14,000 a year working with the mentally disabled and who would later become an air traffic controller at John F. Kennedy International, recollects with sublime incomprehension, "In 1981 I saw all this strike stuff about air traffic controllers on TV. And they were crying about making forty to fifty thousand a year. Soon as they all got fired, my husband went and got me an application." Robert Poli, President of PATCO, would struggle unsuccessfully to dispute this depiction of the controllers as "spoiled," at one point writing in a letter to the editor of the *Washington Post*, "In the past four years, nearly 90 percent of all controllers who have retired have not done so because they completed a long and rewarding career. Rather, they were forced from their profession because an FAA Flight Surgeon ruled that their health had deteriorated to the point that they could not be allowed to continue."[23]

COACH SEAT: 31C

After a while, amid the haze of falling snow and failing light, an elderly gentleman, a bald man whom *Time* magazine will dub "the man in the water," helps a woman to tie the rope around her body, then courteously passes it, after she is rescued, to his fellow survivors. This passenger, the pilot will contend, "seemed the most alert."[24]

ARM REST

The public's disdain for the strikers wasn't simply a function of its consistent failure to recognize consumer society, in Winifried Wolf's phrase, as a poor "substitute for democracy" or to understand how, according to David Gartman, consumer goods "unite classes not in reality, by narrowing the gap of economic and political power, but merely in appearance, by obscuring class differences behind a façade of mass consumption." It was also a function of the specific exigencies heaved up during the agonizing death throes of industrial Fordism—that shift to an economy characterized by heightened competition and correspondingly merciless "strategies of flexible accumulation." Frequently called the "golden age" of postwar capitalism, Fordism had been soothingly predicated on the notion of an expanding middle class and an uneasy but nevertheless lasting truce with labor: two things that had made possible, as never before, precisely the "façade of [truly] mass consumption."[25]

INTERIOR INSULATION

One by one, the helicopter lifts them from the frigid water. Time is of the essence, the TV anchorman remarks (a bit too enthusiastically), for, like the flailing woman, they are in danger of succumbing not to their broken limbs but to hypothermia.

PORTABLE CREW OXYGEN BOTTLE

As Evan Watkins argues in his book *Throwaways*, a majority of Americans had been led to believe, ironically, that "variables of conflict" such as income differentials—which had in the past given rise to unions and bigger, progressive government (and, in turn, to a larger middle class)—were, in the convulsions of a burgeoning global service economy, like manual typewriters and eight-track cassettes, now themselves obsolete.[26] And just as obsolete, then, was the tactical standstill of the strike—really any attempt, not least one by civil servants, to impede the furious circuits of the "free" market. In this way, the air traffic controllers, with their efforts to "shut down the skies," unwittingly performed Reagan's specter of obtrusive, crisis-producing unions and big government.

It didn't matter, in other words, that unions and the welfare state might have appeared more necessary than ever or that the narrative of obsolescence might have constituted, as Watkins argues, an ideological production in the present, designed to serve the needs of a corporate elite and its vision of a post-industrial economy with an increasing number of unavoidably dismal, low-paying jobs. (And in the end, it certainly didn't matter that the crash dramatized, in the figures of Skutnick and the Park Police helicopter, the crucial interventionary role of government, however inadequate and always after the fact, in responding to the inevitable injuries of capitalism.) What mattered was the mythic hold of freedom on the consumptive imagination, the disingenuous reinvigoration of "rising social expectations," as a function of individual lifestyle choices, in a paradoxically more competitive and less accommodating marketplace.[27]

CENTER FUEL TANK

Undeterred by past egalitarian failures, the Benjamin of 1935 still believed in the viability, we might say, of a conductive relationship with the masses—in the tellingly progressive figure of "calm and adventurous traveling," which he would employ the following year in "The Work of Art in the Age of Mechanical Reproduction" to evoke the egalitarian potential of the new image-making technologies. In "Paris, Capital of the Nineteenth Century," he confidently declared, "In the convulsions of the commodity economy we begin to recognize the monuments of the bourgeoisie as ruins even before they have crumbled"—or, as the case may be, *crashed*. It isn't difficult to see how, four years later, a much more pessimistic Benjamin preserves the notions of ambiguity, image, and stasis while recasting them as the essential components of involuntary or forcible remembrance. "The concept of progress should be based on catastrophe," he complains in "N [Theoretics of Knowledge; Theory of Progress]," referring, with great frustration, to the incorrigible vehicles of capitalist forgetfulness: department store, airplane, popular film—the endless stream of enticing novelties. "That things just keep going *is* the catastrophe. It isn't that which lies ahead but that which always is given." By 1939, phenomena must be "rescued by the *demonstration* of the fissure in them," he contends, everywhere emphasizing his own arresting antidote to reification. In "Theses on the Philosophy of History," he even makes the historical materialist out to be a kind of necessary terrorist, describing him as someone "man enough to blast open the continuum of history."[28]

LEFT RUDDER PEDAL SHAFT

It was precisely the expedited movement of the new steam-powered vehicles and its ostensible fulfillment of the Enlightenment ideal of "communication"—which had arisen, Armand Mattelart tells us, from the tradition of political anatomy and its conception of a vitally interconnected *body* politic—that had initially inspired, both in this country and abroad, so many instances of "the technological sublime" (Leo Marx's term for the rhetoric expressing a progressive faith in technology). In 1832, for example, the Saint Simonian Michael Chevalier ecstatically proclaimed,

> To better communications is therefore to work for real, positive, and practical freedom. . . . I would go farther, and say that it amounts to making equality and democracy. Perfected means of transportation have the effect of reducing the distance not only from one point to another, but also from one class to another.[29]

In 1851, a Manhattan minister similarly extolled the unifying virtues of the locomotive and steamboat, using a metaphor that reflected at once a utopian wish and a casual unfamiliarity with the oppressive working conditions of the average textile laborer:

> These pillars of cloud by day and of fire by night are heralding our modern civilization to conquests and results not possible before. The fast-flying shuttles are weaving nations inextricably together in bonds of mutual acquaintance, friendship, and commercial intercourse. They will soon make war impossible. . . . They will lift the masses. . . . They will make—are making—a highway for our God.[30]

Again and again, in the sort of cycle Benjamin described, transportation enthusiasts would celebrate some new vehicle—its increased velocity and interior "communicating" spatial features—as a critical agent of democratization, and all the while an older vehicle of capital would be undermining the values of republican America.[31] The automobile would save democracy as the locomotive had not, the plane would save democracy as the car had not, and so on. With the progress of industrialization and the advent of suburban living, mid-to-late nineteenth- and early twentieth-century Americans would express, as late twentieth-century Americans would not, unmistakable anxiety about social stratification, proposing all sorts of ways—including public transportation, parks, and libraries—of bringing the classes together. However disingenuous such projects might be, they stand in stark contrast to the utter lack of them under Reagan. One need only point, for example, to the proliferation of gated communities and, in contrast, to the abandonment of the public park as a place of homelessness and crime to get a sense of the fortieth president's brazenly anti-egalitarian agenda.

SPARE LIFE VEST

If, as Saint Simon insisted in the late eighteenth century, "money is to the body politic what the blood is to the human heart," then even in the best of times the patient, Washington, D.C., would be in trouble. "Any part where the blood ceases to circulate," he explained, "languishes and is not long in dying." Thus, even before the recession of the early 1980s, when unemployment among African Americans reached 17.5 percent, Southeast Washington, for example, was almost entirely neglected. Under Reagan, the trickle-down theory of circulation, the policy of a clever heart, would simply leave the foot with even less blood.[32]

COACH SEATS: 21A-C

With his loose association of recession, the president's attack on big government, the proverbial dreamed-of Florida vacation, and the crash of a commercial airliner and a rush-hour Metro, Richard Cohen will come very close in his column on the event to proclaiming capitalism—and Reaganism specifically—a communication disaster. He will struggle poetically to articulate a blow to the historical project of democracy and a turning point in the history of this particular republic. In fact, he will come close to depicting the capital itself as a traumatized passenger, enduring, first, the economy's gruesome (and continuing) plunge and, then, the chilly finality of the Great Communicator's *opposition* to "rescue." "Washington is a sad city," Cohen will report, personifying the capital, imagining some darkly communicating body. "It is depressed. It is in mourning. It is stunned and it is cold and its faith in the future is shaken." In his dreamlike reproduction of the catastrophe, even the weather will cooperate in providing the proper symbolic backdrop for the demise of a people who were "heading for the sun": that collective destination once unforgettably advertised by the country's founding travel agents but in the late twentieth century increasingly pitched as a balmy shopping mall or golf course, an individual's private, brand-name heaven. The image of the once revolutionary vehicle in ruins, ceaselessly reproduced in the city's suddenly collective head, signifies the acquisition of a kind of political insight: the apt condensation of a fundamental conflict between the needs of an ever faster capitalism and the requirements of democracy.

FLIGHT CONTROL CABLES

Writing in 1853, during a period of similarly monumental social and economic upheaval, Herman Melville more explicitly alludes to a communication disaster in his story "Cock-A-Doodle-Doo!" as he attempts to convey, with respect to the new industrial technologies, the moment of initial utopian shock and disappointment. In the story, he constellates a series of dispirited egalitarians, proposing that each is the equivalent of a locomotive or steamboat accident victim—capital's hurled passenger (or rail kill). And his figure for such an injury to equality (that incompletely realized ideal), for the backward movement (or standstill) paradoxically accomplished by modernity's unregulated velocity and power, is also something like trauma: what he calls a "knocking on the head" and what, for a time, doctors in the latter part of the nineteenth century evocatively called "Railway Brain."[33]

Melville's constellation includes the failed European revolutionaries of 1848; American railroad and steamboat enthusiasts, who were, for the first time, confronting not only the actual horrors of the ever-proliferating railroad and steamboat accidents themselves but the accident reports, which customarily cited gross negligence and indifference to passenger safety on the part of profit-hungry operators; and, finally, the story's impoverished, debt-ridden narrator, whose creditor (the narrator says) "seems to run on a railroad track, too." "In all parts of the world," the story begins, "many high-spirited revolts from rascally despotisms had of late been knocked on the head; many dreadful casualties, by locomotive and steamer, had likewise knocked hundreds of high-spirited travelers on the head (I lost a dear friend in one of them); my own private affairs were also full of despotisms, casualties and knockings on the head." Understanding expedited movement as the agent not only of a sometimes literal annihilation ("for two hundred and fifty miles that iron fiend goes yelling through the land, crying 'More! more! more!'"), and imagining in the future still faster and more efficient vehicles of exploitation, the narrator of Melville's story (like many a floundering present-day liberal) clings to the values of an imperfect past. "Who wants to travel so fast?" he asks. "My grandfather did not, and he was no fool."[34]

FORWARD LAVATORY

Suffering from peptic ulcers, severe indigestion, hypertension, exhaustion, and any number of other medical problems, the almost parodically caring and elevated controllers seem, at least with their bodies, to register the toll of capitalist progress—that frenzied, competitive movement whose signature is often debilitating stress. Indeed, we might contrast a portrait of the beleaguered PATCO workers with a portrait of those other "controllers" and industry captains in the months before the strike (Melville's "thousand villains and asses who have the management of the railroads and steamboats, and innumerable other vital things in this world"): in other words, administration officials pedaling supply-side economic policy; Federal Reserve Board members trying from the summit of Mount Abstraction to prevent an even harder "landing" for the U.S. economy; corporate executives making decisions about layoffs according to the dictates of profitability and corporate earnings.[35]

VERTICAL STABILIZER

In "The Communist Manifesto," Karl Marx speaks of "the icy water of egotistical calculation."[36]

COACH SEAT: 28B

After three of the five have been rescued (half-lifted from, half-pulled across the shattered ice), and after the helicopter has returned to the scene of the wreckage, the bald man points to a woman who has decided rather injudiciously and impatiently to swim away from the bobbing tail. The 'copter follows her and pulls her to safety as well. But when it is finally his turn to be extricated, the bald man has disappeared, perhaps slipping beneath the surface of the river. The pilot and paramedic—who will later swear, like the passengers they rescued, to the presence of such a man—search desperately, even compulsively for him, but to no avail. "We looked in the water," the paramedic will explain, "in the wreck, everywhere, but he was gone. You can't stay in the cold water for too long. Whoever he was the people who were saved owe their lives to him."[37]

STOWAGE UNIT

By actually embodying the historical standstill, the transportation disaster fortifies the lesson of jolting ambiguity, all but hanging a banner above itself that reads "Progress in Ruins." From this "demonstration" of ambiguity—what Benjamin calls "a messianic cessation of happening"—comes forth an irrepressible hint, in F. D. Reeve's phrase, of "the alternatives behind experience," alternatives both past and present. Said differently, if "the imperceptible tending of all things toward utopia" is the activity, according to Fredric Jameson, of a "type of unconscious . . . formed not by the past [as with the Oedipal Complex] but by the future," then the future waits, paradoxically, for an instant of collective utopian *remembrance*: not of what is, but of what could be and, even more important, of what (since modernity) could always have been.[38]

In this way—conceding the veritably unshakable persistence of the capitalist status quo and imagining exactly the kind of moment in which a man might give up his life for others while the spouse of the Attorney General flaunts her diamond lobes (and in which other women, within reach of a different kind of government helicopter, swim miles for free American cheese)—Benjamin proclaims in the notes for the *Arcades Project*, "The dialectical image is to be defined as the *memoire involuntaire* of a redeemed humanity."[39] The wordlessly didactic "man in the water" (who will as quickly return to the murk of our national unconscious as he has risen to its icy surface) suggests, in other words, an escaped intimation of both a future that hasn't arrived and a present, a catastrophe, that has. With his final conception of imagistic montage as anything but "calm and adventurous traveling," Benjamin seeks analogously to "demonstrate" capitalism's perpetual communication disaster. And yet precisely because an actual transportation accident's own "demonstration" doesn't come with such a banner, the historical materialist must provide his peculiar form of mediation: reactivating a specific injury and at once facilitating and sabotaging its second recovery.

FIRST-CLASS SILVERWARE

The Southern writer Walker Percy, in his 1975 book *Message in a Bottle*, succinctly captures this notion of a disaster's stubbornly ambiguous "demonstration," but instead of unearthing the actual utopian potential that inheres in commodity capitalism, he exhumes a lurking and neglected Judeo-Christian god. Like other dire religious critics of American consumerism, he believes that such "demonstrations" are, paradoxically, welcome events, disturbing the quotidian and pounding some sense into a spiritually bankrupt and death-denying culture. The public's morbid interest in disaster reflects a nagging, if unspecified, dissatisfaction with capitalism's material comforts and technological accomplishments. An intimation of the divine ripping through modernity's metallic hubris, exposing the failure of the relentlessly new to vanquish death, the moment of ineffable illumination waits, Percy implies, for those who imagine that the divine itself has been rendered obsolete. "Why," he asks, more than a bit rhetorically, "is the good life which men have achieved in the twentieth century so bad that only news of world catastrophes, assassinations, plane crashes, mass murders, can divert one from the sadness of ordinary mornings?" "Why did the young French couple," he continues, "driving through the countryside with their baby, having heard the news of a crash nearby of an airliner killing three hundred people and littering the forest with bits of flesh, speed frantically toward the scene, stop the car, and, carrying the baby, rush toward the dead, running through thickets to avoid police barricades? Did they have relatives on the plane?"[40]

FLIGHT ATTENDANT SHOE

Several weeks after the crash of Air Florida Flight 90 and the appearance of Cohen's column on the disaster, another writer will refer to the heroism the crash elicited in terms ironically similar to commercial aviation's original consumer fantasy: as a brief respite from "the meanness of everyday life"—the meanness, that is, of late-capitalist social relations. For a few hours, the city will have appeared startlingly magnanimous, following the advice of Alyosha in *The Brothers Karamazov*, who, having been sent out into the world by his spiritual elder and searching for a viable ethics of human interaction, remarks with some naïveté to the crippled Lise, "Perhaps we should treat people as if they were patients in a hospital." The entire city will have seemed to become an emergency room—with simple goodwill and triumphant professionalism abounding. The flailing woman, it will have turned out, was really a passenger and not a panicked flight attendant, as the media will have been reporting. Moreover, to everyone's great relief, an attendant who did survive the crash (one of Ellen Church's deregulated, no-frills, but, alas, non-nursing descendants) will have apparently managed to cling to her training—or, rather, to something suddenly emerging from that training—inflating the only available life preserver for another injured passenger even as she herself was in danger of drowning.[41]

(A sense of mystery, however, will linger concerning the flailing woman's identity, as the day after the crash the Congressional Budget Office gopher will have maintained that the flailing woman *was* indeed a flight attendant because the only surviving flight attendant's roommate in Florida, recognizing the flailing woman on TV, will have called to thank him for rescuing her. The airline, though, will have released a statement to the contrary, claiming that the flight attendant distinctly remembers being rescued by a helicopter and not a low-level government employee.)

LEADING EDGE FLAPS

In S. A. Howland's popular 1840 *Steamboat Disasters and Railroad Accidents in the United States*, one of the first collections of its kind, we can observe the American origin of this mysterious fascination with transportation disasters. The book's first chapter, titled "Wreck of the Steam Packet Home, *On her passage from New York to Charleston, Oct. 9, 1837, by which melancholy occurrence ninety-five persons perished*," begins like this: "An occurrence so awful as the loss of the STEAMBOAT HOME, excites in the mind of a civilized and humane community, the most intense and painful interest." In fact, Howland writes again and again of an "intense interest," "a tragic interest," of "satisfying public curiosity." And yet nowhere does he attempt really to explain the nature of this morbid attraction, except to appeal to a sense of general Christian charity that, by definition, purports to care about the fate of virtually anyone in distress. About the wreck of the *Lexington*, he remarks,

> Amid this raging destruction, the Christian stands as the sun among the flying clouds of heaven, calm and serene; one moment lost in the confusion, the next emerging from it to utter words of comfort, or raise a prayer to God for the pardon of the guilty and horror-stricken.[42]

As it turns out, this facile explanation does in fact flirt with an awareness of the sort of equation between capitalism and catastrophe that Benjamin provocatively sets forth. "The heart must be callous, indeed," Howland writes, vaguely alluding to some equivalent social disaster, "that turns not from scenes like these with awakened and better feelings, and, looking back on past sufferings as beyond the reach of help, extends not the hand of charity to relieve those of the present,—sufficient of which ever exist around us."[43] Whereas Percy looks to religion for a way of renouncing the blandishments of commodity capitalism, Howland looks to religion for affirmation of these very blandishments, even as he senses their lurking inadequacy. Even, we might say, as he delights in their (and their consumers') horrific dismemberment and, in his melancholy, simultaneously holds out for the possibility of rescue.

FORWARD PRESSURE BULKHEAD

The media will not let go of "the man in the water," luxuriating in the idea of a supremely Good Samaritan. "That guy is amazing," the paper will report, quoting the paramedic. "All I can tell you is I've never seen that kind of guts. It seemed to me like he decided that the women, the men who were bleeding, needed to get out before him, and even as he was going under he stuck to his decision and helped them get out. Man that was bravery."[44] Unable to resist the temptation of Christian parable and allegory, the city's pastors will similarly cling to "the man in the water," so moved will they be by the man's nearly incomprehensible act of self-sacrifice—the mystery of his identity (and of his very existence) only adding to the act's tantalizing richness. Based on a rough description of the Samaritan, a grieving family will proudly claim him as their husband and father, though even they will not be entirely sure that the description fits their loved one.

LEFT WING

In speaking of "present [sufferings],—sufficient of which ever exist around us," Howland seems inescapably to be referring to America's growing poor, large numbers of whom were the victims of industrial forces that by 1840 had already been set in motion, though, of course, he doesn't actually mention these wage laborers or their oppressor—industrial capital—by name. Or, perhaps we should say that at least in *this* context he doesn't mention the latter by name. In "thrilling narrative" after narrative, however, he directly addresses the catastrophe that results when profits are chased with wild abandon. Concluding his narration of the wreck of the steamboat *New England*, Howland complains, "This running of machinery as long as it will last, and discovering its weakness and inefficiency but at the expense of the lives of scores of human beings, is not only recklessly heartless, but in the highest degree criminal, and should be frowned down by an indignant community, and rendered severely punishable by the laws of the land."[45] Though such an indictment would apply quite nicely to the treatment, say, of mill workers, Howland doesn't speak directly of *their* condition.

CENTER FUSELAGE

George Landow recalls how Friedrich Engels represents capitalist industrialization as an unacknowledged shipwreck in his 1844 *Condition of the Working Classes in England*. Engels, Landow says, "frequently emphasizes that 'nobody troubles about the poor as they struggle helplessly in the whirlpool of modern industrial life.' The worker 'sinks' into degradation 'owing to the introduction of steam power,' and once 'engulfed' by his surroundings, he soon perishes. No matter how hard he works, no matter how virtuously he lives, the worker may perish 'through no fault of his own and despite all his efforts to keep his head above water.'"[46] But whereas Engels uses the popular figure of shipwreck to proclaim a social disaster that no one sees, apparently unaware of having chosen a vehicle of comparison that customarily garnered all sorts of public interest and sympathy, Rebecca Harding Davis in her 1861 short story "Life in the Iron Mills" uses the figure very nearly to suggest that the public *does* "trouble" about the poor—only in displaced and condensed form.

An aspiring artist, Harding Davis's protagonist, Wolfe, dreams of a life beyond the factory. Then he becomes implicated in the robbery of his employer, is sent to jail, and, shortly thereafter, kills himself. Instructively linking Wolfe's debilitating employment making the materials needed for America's railroads and steamboats with the reading public's persistent, melodramatic fascination with transportation disasters and its habit of sentimental, Christian moralizing, Harding Davis's narrator bitterly asks,

> You wish to make a tragic story out of it? Why, in the police-reports of the morning paper you can find a dozen such tragedies: hints of shipwreck unlike any that ever befell on the high seas; hints that there a power was lost to heaven,—that there a soul went down where no tide can ebb or flow. Commonplace enough the hints are,—jocose, sometimes, done up in rhyme.[47]

Seventy years later, the German Marxist Ernst Bloch also hypothesizes a drama of apt condensation and displacement in his account of the nearly hysterical attention the nineteenth-century transportation disaster regularly commanded. Alluding to Marx's understanding of economic crisis (as Wolfgang Schivelbusch concisely puts it, "the disruption of the uncertain balance between buying and selling in the circulation of goods" and the fevered incorporation of technological innovation for competitive advantage), Bloch cleverly couples the capitalist economy with the locomotive disaster, referring to each as "the crisis of the uncontrolled thing." In fact, he provocatively suggests that we might read "the crash of collision, the roar of explosion, the cries of maimed people" as standing in for the pernicious effects of an economic downturn and, thus, as conveying for the bourgeoisie their own otherwise unarticulable objections to such well-dressed Christian barbarism.[48]

WING SLATS

In their coordinating function, air traffic controllers intimate not so much the need for a welfare state as the need for a radical alternative to the "free" market itself. Picture the controllers as trying to minimize "the uninterrupted disturbance, everlasting uncertainty and agitation" that Marx insisted characterized capitalism. In the summer of 1981, however, such a thoroughgoing and undiscriminating commitment to human life ("You worked traffic, you stayed cool, and you puked your guts out in the bathroom afterwards") found fuller expression, ironically, in a criminal act: a renunciation of duty that had potentially deadly consequences.[49]

We might regard the PATCO strikers, in some important respect, as having done their jobs most faithfully not in their towers in front of screens filled with moving blips but out on the picket line attempting to prevent the continuation—in fact, the worsening—of an undeclared disaster. Placards bobbing like signals just above their heads, they were trying, however consciously, to talk down a different kind of jet, a different kind of future. While the motivation for the strike had begun as a series of relatively narrow demands about better wages and working conditions, it culminated in a more "high-spirited" response to Reagan's bullying and in a fleeting glimmer of the lift of a genuine and, possibly one day, broader collectivity. "We knew the strike was inevitable," one controller remarked, "and we *really* got an emotional high out of it. Shift work had kept us from ever getting more than two-thirds of us together, but we got 89 percent to go out! The mood was *very* positive, and when all of us were together, we were *high*—only later when we were apart from each other, some began to doubt, and some began to have reservations."[50]

FLIGHT SPOILERS

"Identity of Plane Crash Hero Remains a Mystery," a headline in the *Washington Post* will exclaim a few days after the disaster.[51] Despite the mystery, a medal will be proposed for this passenger who gave up his life so that others might be saved. What is more, talk of glorious, triumphant altruism will continue to abound—exactly as some of the fired air traffic controllers will beg to have their old jobs back and as the murder rate in Southeast Washington will continue to climb. Still later, after more than half of the wreckage and bodies have been recovered and after the requisite autopsies have been performed, serious doubt will be cast on the existence of such a man. The D.C. medical examiner will have just reported that, of the fifty passengers so far examined, only one passenger, a bank examiner from Atlanta, died of anything other than blunt force trauma—in other words, that only one passenger died from drowning. And this person was not, the Park Police helicopter pilot and paramedic will stress again and again, the man seen passing the lifeline. That man did not have a beard. Now, like a politician switching parties to win an election, or merely to be on the side of the majority, the media will pursue the subtle disparagement of the celebrated ideal, luxuriating in its newly revealed phantom improbability. (Eventually, other bodies with water in their lungs, twenty-five of them, will be retrieved, and a conceivable hero will be selected.)

CARGO LINER

In *The Political Unconscious,* Jameson describes "a process whereby otherwise dangerous and protopolitical impulses are 'managed' and defused, rechanneled and offered spurious objects." Even—or, rather, especially—those commentators who will vigorously contest the cynical depreciation of "the man in the water" will end up working, like a toxic cleanup crew, to contain the threat implicit in his impractical heroics. Without a hint of resignation, Roger Rosenblatt, essayist for *Time* magazine and the man responsible for the Samaritan's resonant epithet, will champion him as "the best we can do." Finally no different from Reagan's panegyric, Rosenblatt's will allow the gesture to float free of the many laid-off workers, homeless people, and other floundering victims of Reaganism just on shore. By refusing, in other words, to make of the gesture a specific reprimand of late-capitalist social relations, he will efface the larger social arena to which the gesture might point and from which an alternative politics might emerge. Sentimental to the core, such approbation will isolate the gesture in a realm that requires absolutely nothing of the reader—nothing perhaps but an inspired gift of unwanted clothing to the local homeless shelter at Christmas time.[52]

Appearing amid the controversy, an editorial in the *Post* will reject what Paul Ricoeur has called a "hermeneutics of suspicion," intuitively understanding how the impulse to demystify can do away with utopian possibilities altogether. At the same time, it will reflect the clever alternative of merely incarcerating the desire for a better world, retaining it as a malnourished ideal that exerts only a limited influence on earthly (that is, capital's) affairs. The editorial will proceed,

> It never seems more than a few days before the contention, the bickering, the tugging at the idol begins. And now, right on schedule, it is here: was there really a heroic "man in the water" who gave his own life in the course of helping other Air Florida Flight 90 victims to live? Maybe it was more than one. Maybe it was no one. Maybe the whole thing was a misperception. . . . One gets an intimation from all this that even if and when the existence and identity of the man in question is established it will only be a matter of time before some researcher somewhere is quoted as saying that the poor fellow, suffering from hypothermia, probably didn't even know what he was doing.
>
> Our feeling is that very little of this argument matters. . . . The act itself has been memorialized already in the emotions of those countless Americans who heard of it, who gave it full range in their imaginations, who felt their own humanity honored and enlarged because of it. . . . The anonymity, so far, of the hero does no more to diminish the grandeur of his act than such anonymity does, say, to diminish the sacrifice made by the unknown soldier. On the contrary, in a strange way it merely universalizes it.

In vigorously defending the possibility of such altruism against the scrutiny of the academic researcher, the editorial will nevertheless fail to establish a link between the ennobling gesture and the arena in which it appeared. Indeed, by arguing for the gesture's "universality," it will occlude important differences between social actors—between the president, say, and the fired air traffic controllers. The editorial's treatment of the "man in the water" will thus manifest (like the early work of Benjamin) the need for a hermeneutics that is neither deflationary in its rational mastery nor exculpatory in its slavish veneration of ambiguity.[53]

COACH SEATS: 13A-C

At the center of this frantic management of protopolitical impulses will be the actual salvage operation itself. In the days following the crash, one won't be able to help being impressed by all of the sophisticated equipment, mobilized as in some sort of underwater ER to bring about the patient's dramatic, because improbable, recovery. With what compulsiveness will the patient's many parts (and patrons) be retrieved, this medico-religious ritual enacted. How remarkable the many elaborate, even bureaucratic, procedures. Disaster *does* have a schedule, the TV will exclaim! Civilization *can* conquer the uncivilized, which is to say the terrifyingly immobile and unshapely. One won't be able to help feeling better, though clearly feeling better will be a part of feeling bad—nonetheless an important step on the road to renewed faith. Technology, alas, can both take life and give it back; it can participate in its own watery recuperation.

The newspaper will keep meticulous track of the divers' progress. In one article, the names, ages, and former residences of the dead will appear as part of a chart whose headings proclaim (as if with joy, as if with New Testament jubilation), "Recovered Wednesday," "Recovered Thursday," "Recovered Friday," "Recovered Saturday."[54] Like Jesus reproaching the incredulous relatives of a naturally refrigerated (and, thus, not, as the Bible would have it, already decaying) Lazarus, the pun will attempt to wheedle the unconscious. And yet, what will be salvaged, of course, are not the lives of the passengers of Air Florida but the myth of progress and the urgent conflation of capitalist technology with religious promise.

FLIGHT DATA RECORDER

If "technology is theology modernized and made aesthetic," as Geoffrey Hartman claims—made actual or literal, he might have said—then the sudden, massive failure of a commercial airliner provokes a dark night of the machine, a reexamination of technological materialism and indeed an anxious, if for most people entirely implausible, glancing back at religion.[55] For there is nothing like a commercial aviation disaster and its obliterating dismemberment to reintroduce the obsolete (because immaterial) god, from whom aviation borrowed so much of its mythic packaging. Not only does an airliner invade the space formerly reserved for the divine, but the very language of commercial aviation is itself redolent of religion. Think of terms, to name just a few, like "pilot," a religious leader or guide; "souls," passengers on board; and "stick-shaker," a cockpit warning device designed to inform a pilot that his church—his holy "sky mall"—is about to fall due to loss of lift. The device owes its name to the hymn Protestant children used to be taught to sing each morning when they awoke; its refrain, "shake the devil stick," was said to dispel the devil.

It's the sort of alarm that sounds, for example when an inappropriately genuflecting 737 encounters wind shear, and it almost always receives a bit part in the postmodern morality play that is the battered black box recording. "Sound of stickshaker," a doomed recording will advise just before its standard closing line, which is "Sound of Impact." (The black box, it should be pointed out, is really a rather fearful yellow.) "Who will go with me into the ground?" might be the uncaptured refrain of Everyperson the Consumer. To my great distress, I've never heard of a pilot who implored his faithful to consume more enthusiastically or less perfunctorily, though the conditions have at times clearly demanded it: "Shop till you suddenly drop 14,000 feet!" Once, however, a remark like this did slip out while a plane I was on encountered severe turbulence during its Final Approach. The head flight attendant had just instructed us, her demanding brood, to return our seatbacks and tray-tables "to their fully *uptight* and locked positions." Then, after having remarked, with all of the sincerity that an intercom and a uniform can muster, "It's been a pleasure serving you," she said, "We'll be *in* the ground shortly."

Fractured for a moment beyond repair, commodity capitalism's vaguely salvific narrative, whose initial, explicit, nineteenth-century impulse was to understand technological innovation as the vehicle of *earthly* egalitarian transformation (clothed in familiar religious garb), thus nervously turns with the demise of an airliner to the spectacle of a massive, many-pronged assault on death. What the Park Police helicopters (and, later, the various commentators and clergy) can't accomplish, the floating cranes and divers will! Of course, the progressive narrative achieves its nearly imperceptible deflation when, for example, a given plane lands successfully in Toledo or Dallas, not heaven—when the last are again last: last off the plane or never on it.

INFLATABLE SLIDE

The night of the crash, a priest will appear with Ted Koppel on *Nightline*. He will have spent the evening consoling the relatives of the victims who have gathered at the Crystal City Marriott Hotel not far from the airport. Interviews with these relatives will confirm that the priest has been an enormous help. The priest himself will talk convincingly about the management of loss and the infinite refuge of God's love. Several days later, the public will learn that the priest was really a convict who had escaped from a federal penitentiary in Danbury, Connecticut. Missing since December 16 of the previous year, he will have at some point driven down to Washington, purchased his costume, and arrived at the Marriot in time to begin comforting the relatives of the victims of Air Florida Flight 90. Apparently, no one will have checked his credentials. Policewoman Rosiland Parker will be quoted in the paper as saying that the convict "has a history of showing up at disaster scenes. He gains the confidence of the relatives and later burglarizes their houses."[56] A police officer in Trenton, New Jersey will have been watching *Nightline* and will have recognized the priest as someone who did a number of jobs in his area. As a result, the convict will have been quickly reapprehended.

FIRST-CLASS COAT COMPARTMENT

In addition to an extraordinary fear of death, Don DeLillo, like Walker Percy, posits an ardent, masochistic wish for it. In fact, in the novel *White Noise*, DeLillo presents two pilots who seem to be reveling not just in death but in the prospect of complete, and therefore somehow redemptive, annihilation:

> The plane had lost power in all three engines, dropped from thirty-four thousand feet to twelve thousand feet. . . . Almost immediately a voice from the flight deck was heard on the intercom: "We're falling out of the sky! We're going down! We're a silver gleaming death machine!" This outburst struck the passengers as an all but total breakdown of authority, competence and command presence and it brought on a round of fresh and desperate wailing. . . . Then there was a second male voice from the flight deck, this one remarkably calm and precise,

making the passengers believe there was someone in charge after all, an element of hope: "This is American two-one-three to the cockpit voice recorder. Now we know what it's like. It is worse than we'd ever imagined. They didn't prepare us for this at the death simulator in Denver. Our fear is pure, so totally stripped of distractions and pressures as to be a form of transcendental meditation. In less than three minutes we will touch down, so to speak. They will find our bodies in some smoking field, strewn about in the grisly attitudes of death."[57]

It is precisely the disparity between the apparent seamlessness of corporate culture's slick negotiation of death, symbolized impressively by the plane's shiny skin and the crew's "command presence," and the rupturing return-of-the-repressed without a moment's notice that arouses such paradoxically welcome anxiety. Only the force of a crash, DeLillo implies, can shake the false utopia of the commodity. (Obviously, this sort of humor, proverbially linked to the gallows, can itself be a kind of skillful negotiation of death: deflection disguised as a spurious frontal assault. Shock jock Howard Stern will first make a name for himself in the days after the Washington crash by calling up Air Florida and asking, on air, to purchase a ticket to the 14th Street Bridge.)

SAFETY INSTRUCTION CARDS

Not surprisingly, the media will fail to draw a connection between the mysterious man in the water and the fraudulent priest, though both hint at a kind of alternative theology: one in which the promise of immortality might be discredited but not the promise of the collectively human—the promise, as Adorno characterizes it, of death's "epic unity with a full life," "what was once said to make death bearable." "As subjects live less," Adorno writes in *Negative Dialectics*, exposing the alienating and certainly undemocratic achievement of commodity worship, "death grows more precipitous, more terrifying. The fact that it literally turns them into things makes them aware of reification, their permanent death and the form of relations that is partly their fault."[58]

Surely, both the "man in the water" and the convict-priest point to something other than a reservation for Tampa's sunny, time-shared afterlife or an advertisement, near the barf bag in the in-flight magazine, for the new Mercedes. The convict-priest begs to be understood as mischievously separating the bereaved from their beguiling valuables—in a sense, as underscoring, along with the shock of disingenuous religion, the inadequacy of these two historically linked bulwarks against death. (The figure of the convict-priest thus only gives more resonance to Marx's disparaging description of commodity fetishism as a "theological caper."[59]) Death comes to represent for Adorno something like a final but terribly costly victory: an unbearably ironic life preserver, preserving not life itself but the space in which collective life might have been lived. We fear death, he suggests, precisely because we understand how well we forget and know that like the congealed labor in a set of tires, like the tires themselves once they have been discarded, we, too, will be quickly forgotten.

FIRST-CLASS SEATS: 3A-B

"None of these people will ever be permitted to come back. We don't want these people back. . . . It's taken 200 years for this democracy to develop as a system of law, and we just can't see that deteriorate based on a few people that just want to make more money. . . . As far as we are concerned, this is a nonstrike situation, and we're rebuilding the system. . . . It's over with"—the words of Drew Lewis, Secretary of Transportation, upon executing the president's order to terminate the striking controllers.[60]

CAPTAIN'S SEAT

Rolf Tiedemann refers to "dialectics at a standstill," Benjamin's term for the materialist practice of imagistic montage, as "piecing together what history has broken to bits." The Frankfurt School philosopher as National Transportation Safety Board (NTSB) investigator, member of a historical "go team"? Benjamin imagines producing an accident report that carries the force of the event it strives to explain, which is to say a report that is in some way profoundly inconclusive (and thus a plane, on which that report is based, that is far from completely put back together). The last thing Benjamin wants is a lesson learned—or, as Richard Wolin puts it, for "redemption [to have to] preserve itself in a small crack in the continuum of catastrophe," a small crack in the continuum of the essay or consciousness itself. Hope should not consist merely of the possibility of another devastating "demonstration," another instance of critical utopian me(n)tal fatigue. Refusing to put the plane back together as it was, Benjamin asks us instead to make out a vague, still-to-be-clarified figure on a hangar floor and then to project it piecemeal onto some barely discernible horizon. In this way, as an allegory of reactivated and unresolved trauma, dialectics at a standstill suggests not one but a series of occupations for the historical materialist: terrorist, diver, recalcitrant reassembler or utopian engineer—each the servant of potentially revolutionary remembrance.[61]

In a sense, Benjamin expresses his fidelity to the past by imagining that the past might still be up for grabs, so convincingly (if elusively) would a given catastrophe be "reproduced" by the "blasting" historical materialist. So distressingly vital are the Pullman strikers, for example, milling about at the bottom of our collective Lethe. Picture Benjamin's reader as having just crashed the past's clandestine meeting, a reader who, as one witness will describe the passengers of Air Florida Flight 90, is "looking straight ahead" and is "still in [her] seatbelt" behind the window of a once airborne vehicle.[62] The voices of capital's recent and long-ago aggrieved growing ever louder, now organizing, now resolving to act. . . . Benjamin thus conspires to redeem the countless missed opportunities for revolutionary change by having the reader travel traumatically to these opportunities, by having her relive or experience them as if they weren't over, weren't beyond caring about *or even transforming*.

AFT TOILET SEAT

Just after the hard landing of Air Florida Flight 90, as if in accordance with some sort of secret catastrophe time table, a crowded Metro derails near the Federal Triangle Station in downtown Washington, killing three and injuring more than twenty. Both disasters occur at the worst possible moment: as federal workers attempt to flee the city in advance of rush hour and the worsening storm. Mysteriously, five and a half months after PATCO went out on strike and Reagan quickly (and permanently) fired some eleven thousand of its members, dismantling the union and forcing it into bankruptcy as a result of more than $150 million in fines, the weather suddenly decides to express its pro-union sympathies. It suddenly decides, let us say, to act. As if to the tune of an old Joe hill song—

> *If we workers take a notion,*
> *we can stop all speeding trains;*
> *every ship upon the ocean*
> *we can tie with mighty chains;*
> *every wheel in the creation,*
> *every mine and every mill,*
> *fleets and armies of all nations*
> *will at our command stand still—*

the organized and conspiring snowflakes fall.[63] The planes that were supposed to have been "silent," as the strikers' handheld signs predicted in early August, are in fact (at least in the nation's capital) now temporarily "silent." (The military controllers, the "scabs" brought in to replace their union counterparts, stand idly—or, rather, less busily—in their tower.) In fact, virtually all of the ascendant vehicles of capitalism are "silent" but for the jittery police car and ambulance, themselves stuck in traffic and whining almost pointlessly. The entire city has come to a standstill in the snow.

CABIN WINDOW

When Benjamin asserts that "a historical materialist cannot do without the notion of a present which is not a transition, but in which time stands still and has come to a stop" and that "this notion defines the present in which he himself is writing history," he should be understood as trying to embody the predicament—indeed, the compulsive and compulsory retrospection—of the transportation accident victim or shell-shocked veteran. Such figures, Caruth suggests, "carry an impossible history within them" or are "themselves the symptom of a history that they cannot entirely possess"; she might have said, that they cannot (or should not) *entirely* understand.[64]

Accordingly, the historian practicing conventional demystifying critique might be thought of as unwittingly contributing, in the capacity of therapist, to what can only be called a presumptuous recovery: in fact, a smug accommodation to an unacceptable historical failure. Twelve years after the collapse of Communism, when even the hope for different social relations lies in ruins, the operation of critique now eerily confirms the speculation of the Right: that History itself has been demystified, that the century has finally worked through the trauma of *utopia* and its murderously unrealistic alternatives, arriving at a definitive and triumphantly gleeful clarity.[65] On the level of form, it suggests that it, too, has gotten over somebody else's injury.

ALUMINUM FLOORING

We might say that, for a period, there is, in the words of Marx, no "driv[ing] beyond every spatial barrier" by capital, no "annihilation of space by time" (though plenty of annihilation), no "locational movement . . . [which is] the necessary condition . . . of the transformation of [an] object *into a commodity*." Call the afternoon of January 13 a revolution (and, simultaneously, a performance of depression). At the decisive moment, these engines of capital, discovering their bondage, quickly change sides. The plane, for instance, refusing to go to Tampa, shucks off its corporate obedience and smarmy, mechanical alacrity, pursuing instead something akin to social seriousness or *gravity*. (As John McCole writes of commodity capitalism, "No limits are set to this unrelenting drive to violate the dignity of objects.")[66]

And so, the snowstorm clogs the central arteries into and out of the city; the Air Florida jet shuts down the sky and, in the process, tries to take out the 14th Street Bridge (that example of what Marx, and really any nineteenth-century student of the capitalist economy and its technologically generated utopian possibilities, would call "improved communications"); and, finally, the committed Metro renders the Orange and Blue line essentially useless. Only the collective vehicles of our nation's capital can be counted on, let us imagine, for real historical awareness and political resolve. Believing technological innovation to be the tool ultimately of the proletariat, Marx averred, "Revolutions are the locomotives of world history." Sadly echoing this fond hope, we might say, as Paul Virilio says in *Speed and Politics* of capitalism generally, that what the city witnesses is *literally* "a revolution in transportation, not in happiness."[67]

LOWER NOSE COMPARTMENT ACCESS

Famously, "The Communist Manifesto" takes solace in the fact that "man is at last compelled to face with sober senses, his real conditions of life, and his relations with his kind."[68] And yet, at this particular moment, such an awakening, such sobriety, plays into a sense of inexorably diminished expectations: a kind of "been there, done that" approach not only to unions and big government (and certainly to communism) but to human suffering and social injustice themselves. It is an approach in which the Left's voluntary memory turns out to be worse perhaps than no conscious memory at all. Now more than ever, reason itself functions as a kind of beefed-up stimulus shield and not as an expression of the still unsettled claim of utopia, a claim that can only be filed by an impractical imagination, an explosive or wily unconscious (which, perpetually reapprehended by the authorities, is forced to plot its next unauthorized parole). Benjamin envisions a future that might be properly disenchanted: when the movement of anything (whether reopened airport or reconstructed essay) won't signify resumptive forgetting and, hence, a much less anxious endorsement of the status quo.

LANDING GEAR

At the meeting honoring the Congressional Budget Office gopher, Reagan will be badgered about the PATCO strike and its possible involvement in the crash. The Soviets will already have commented unofficially on the disaster, suggesting that there is indeed a relationship between the oppression of the working man and the fate of Air Florida. As the *Washington Post* will have reported, a bit prosaically, "*Trud*, the Soviet labor union newspaper, said the replacement of the dismissed air traffic controllers by inexperienced 'scab' labor may have been 'fatal' for the Boeing 737. The newspaper *Sovietskaya Rossiya* published a similar account asserting that the administration was trying to avoid responsibility for the catastrophe by insisting that there were no reasons to believe that it may have been caused by a mistake by air traffic controllers."[69] Much later, at a moment of equivalent social meanness—indeed, of danger—the former president, his faculties all but gone, will himself be honored with the renaming of National Airport, despite his having crushed the PATCO strike and, in general, done more damage to the causes of government and labor than perhaps any president in the twentieth century.

FORWARD ENTRY

Resisting the move to rename all of Washington National Airport, a group of Democrats will have proposed a provocative, though unsuccessful compromise: that merely a particular *terminal* be named after the former president. And yet, with Democratic support for welfare reform, with a widening chasm between rich and poor, with more than 35 million people living in poverty during the biggest economic boom since the 1920s, with the absence of any discussion whatsoever of alternatives to the free market or of an inherent conflict between capital accumulation and the values of democracy, such resistance to wholehearted memorialization might, in the end, have done more damage than good. It might have indicated a considerable difference between the two parties' agendas, instead of just some awful nostalgia (or guilt) on the part of the Democrats about their progressive past. More important, it would still have failed to acknowledge the general calamity of the Reagan-Bush-Clinton era and the specific calamity of the PATCO defeat, which, as Arthur Shostak notes, left the labor movement "weaker and more vulnerable in the aftermath."[70]

"An appreciation or apology," writes Benjamin, "seeks to cover up the revolutionary moments in the course of history. It misses the points at which the transmission breaks down, and thus misses the roughness and jaggedness that offer a hold to someone wishing to get beyond those points"—like the very survivors of Air Florida Flight 90 who, knocked unconscious by the collision with the water, their legs broken, awoke suddenly, and, as one will have put it, "saw a hole in the plane two rows up" and "pulled up there somehow." Or indeed like those now struggling to get beyond the cynical repudiation of the welfare state and even the contradictory "apology" of liberalism itself.[71]

STICKSHAKER

Nearly a month after the crash, before the final recovery of the insurance settlements and the release of the official NTSB report (citing both inadequate de-icing procedures and insufficient thrust due to a faulty indicator), the cockpit voice recordings will appear toward the back of the first section of the *Washington Post*, under the faintly religious headline "Transcript of the Last Words" and adjacent to a large jewelry advertisement whose text will read, in giant print, "ASSISTANT BUYER'S SALE." At once an attempt to "stop up" and preserve "the last holes left open by the world of merchandise"—or, as Adorno might also describe it, our "constant panic in view of death"—the page will labor to produce, with its own form of montage, an allegory of astonishingly belated recognition.

The struggle by the pilot, copilot, and "speaker undetermined" (an off-duty pilot, it will have turned out, was sitting in the cockpit at the time of the crash) to convince themselves that everything was as it should be, though their gauges told them otherwise; the copilot's moving direct address ("Larry, we're going down, Larry") and the pilot's simple acknowledgment ("I know it") at the end; and, in the background, the irrefutable admonition of the throbbing stickshaker ("Pull up!" "Pull up!")—all of these will appear in the context of the equally beseeching ad. All of these will appear, more broadly, in the context of the Great Communicator's boundless optimism: engine of a jeweled assault on the very dream of equality. The president's problems with memory, both in and out of office, will speak for a people wanting a more perfect oblivion—reaching, that is, for each other only in death.

(1600:00) COPILOT: God, look at that thing.

(1600:02) COPILOT: That don't seem right, does it?

(1600:05) COPILOT: Ah, that's not right.

(1600:07) COPILOT: Well.

(1600:09) PILOT: Yes it is, there's eighty [apparent reference to airspeed of 80 knots].

(1600:10) COPILOT: Naw, I don't think that's right.

(1600:19) COPILOT: Ah, maybe it is.

(1600:21) PILOT: Hundred and twenty.

(1600:23) COPILOT: I don't know.

(1600:31) PILOT: Vee one [go or no go speed].

(1600:33) PILOT: Easy.

(1600:37) PILOT: Vee two [120 percent of normal stall speed].

(1600:39) Sound of Stickshaker [starts and continues until impact].

(1600:45) PILOT: Forward, forward.

(1600:47) SPEAKER UNDETERMINED: Easy.

(1600:48) PILOT: We only want five hundred.

(1600:50) PILOT: Come on, forward.

(1600:53) PILOT: Forward.

(1600:55) PILOT: Just barely climb.

(1600:59) SPEAKER UNDETERMINED: We're falling.

(1601:00) COPILOT: Larry, we're going down, Larry.

(1601:01) PILOT: I know it.

(1601:02) Sound of Impact.[72]

NOTES

1. Richard Cohen, "Depression," *Washington Post*, 17 January 1982, B1. *Washington Post* hereafter cited as *WP*.

2. Walter Benjamin, "Theses on the Philosophy of History," in *Illuminations* (New York: Harcourt Brace Jovanovich, Inc., 1968), 255.

3. Lawrence Meyer and Howie Kurtz, "71 Feared Dead as Jet Hits Bridge, Dives into Potomac," *WP*, 14 January 1982, A6; Macarthur Job, *Air Disaster*, vol. 2 (Fyshwick, Australia: Aerospace Publications, 1996), 88.

4. Michael McQueen and Mary Battiata, "Views from the Bridge—and of It on TV," *WP*, 16 January 1982, A10.

5. Cathy Caruth, *Trauma: Explorations in Memory* (Baltimore, Md.: Johns Hopkins University Press, 1995), 4-5, 153, vii.

6. Walter Benjamin, "On Some Motifs in Baudelaire," in *Illuminations*, 161.

7. T. W. Adorno, quoted in Wolfgang Schivelbusch, *The Railway Journey* (Berkeley: University of California Press, 1986), 163; Benjamin, "Theses," 253-64. Words such as "blasting" and "continuum" appear throughout Benjamin's writings but attain a nearly cataclysmic urgency in this final work from 1940.

About halfway through a much more extensive project on commercial aviation disasters, I came across Hillary Jewett's unpublished dissertation, *At the Scene of the Accident in the Nineteenth Century*, in which she rather offhandedly suggests that Benjamin's later work could be used to illuminate the phenomenon of the locomotive disaster.

8. Walter Benjamin, "N [Theoretics of Knowledge; Theory of Progress]," *The Philosophical Forum* 15, nos. 1-2 (fall-winter 1983-1984): 25.

9. Henry Allen, "TV's Images of Tragedy," *WP*, 14 January 1982, C1.

10. Caruth, *Trauma*, 153, 154; T. W. Adorno, "Letters to Walter Benjamin," in *Aesthetics and Politics*, ed. Ronald Taylor (London: NBL, 1979), 127; Benjamin, "Theses," 255.

11. Carl Solberg, *Conquest of the Skies* (Boston: Little, Brown and Co., 1979), 246; Georgia Nielsen, *From Sky Girl to Flight Attendant* (Ithaca, N.Y.: Industrial Labor Relations Press, 1982), 117, 81.

12. Joseph Corn, *The Winged Gospel* (New York: Oxford University Press, 1983), 31-32, 31.

13. Solberg, *Conquest*, 214.

14. Job, *Air Disaster*, 86; Lou Cannon, "A Promise to Stick with the Basic Script," *WP*, 27 January 1982, A14.

15. In the early 1970s, the newly created American Academy of Air Control Medicine reported that peptic or gastric ulcers were found in 36 of 111 air traffic controllers who said they felt ill during a one-year period. In fact, A. A. Hoehling reports that "on a given day fourteen controllers at Chicago's large flight operations center, not far from O'Hare International, were off duty with ulcers." See A. A. Hoehling, *Disaster: Major American Catastrophes* (New York: Hawthorne Books, Inc., 1973), 193.

16. Warren Brown and Laura Kiernan, "Reagan Threatens to Fire Striking Controllers," *WP*, 4 August 1981, A7.

17. Walter Benjamin, "Paris, Capital of the Nineteenth Century," in *Reflections* (New York: Harcourt Brace Jovanovich, Inc., 1978), 148.

18. Susan Buck-Morss, *The Dialectics of Seeing* (Cambridge, Mass.: MIT Press, 1993), 91.

19. Kevin McKean, "Anatomy of an Air Crash," *Discover Magazine*, April 1982, 20.

20. Juan Williams, "Passenger Aids Others, then Dies," *WP*, 14 January 1982, A7.

21. Benjamin, "Paris," 157. The phrase "the sterile continuum of the always the same" is Richard Wolin's. See Richard Wolin, *Walter Benjamin: An Aesthetic of Redemption* (Berkeley: University of California Press, 1994), 123; Benjamin, "Theses," 257.

22. Bob Reiss, *Frequent Flier* (New York: Simon & Schuster, 1994), 193; James Kaplan, *The Airport* (New York: William Morrow, 1994), 182.

23. Kaplan, *Airport*, 182; Robert Poli, "The Air Traffic Controllers Reply," *WP*, 7 August 1981, A14.

24. Williams, "Passenger Aids Others," A1.

25. Winifried Wolf, *Car Mania* (Chicago: Pluto Press, 1996), 72; David Gartman, *Auto Opium* (New York: Routledge, 1994), 15; David Harvey, *The Condition of Postmodernity* (Cambridge: Blackwell, 1993), 141. A good deal of Harvey's book elucidates precisely this shift to a post-industrial economy.

26. Evan Watkins, *Throwaways: Work Culture and Consumer Education* (Stanford, Calif.: Stanford University Press, 1993), 49. Watkins usefully explains the president's perplexing appeal in terms of an adept "capitalization" of massive economic change. This capitalization involved, in his

words, "a discursive restructuring of [social] expectations as a matter of free-dom from constraints" (171). By "constraints" Watkins means, of course, Reagan's sense of the "imbalances by which government regulation, union power, and the 'welfare establishment' had undermined the potential pro-ductivity of American business" (179).

27. Watkins, *Throwaways*, 198.

28. Walter Benjamin, "The Work of Art in the Age of Mechanical Repro-duction," in *Illuminations*, 236; Benjamin, "Paris," 162; Benjamin, "N [Theoret-ics]," 21; Benjamin, "Theses," 262.

29. See Armand Mattelart, *The Invention of Communication* (Minneapolis: University of Minnesota Press, 1996) for a detailed discussion of political anatomy and, more generally, of what he calls "a history of utopias of commu-nication" (47); Leo Marx, *The Machine in the Garden* (New York: Oxford Univer-sity Press, 1976), 195; Michael Chevalier, quoted in Mattelart, *Invention of Com-munication*, 106.

30. Quoted in Edward Spann, *The New Metropolis: New York City, 1840-1857* (New York: Columbia University Press, 1981), 16.

31. See Glen Holt, "The Changing Perception of Urban Pathology: An Essay on the Development of Mass Transit in the United States," in *Cities in American History*, ed. Kenneth Jackson and Stanley Schultz (New York: Alfred A. Knopf, 1972), 326.

32. St. Simon, quoted in Mattelart, *Invention of Communication*, 89-90.

33. Herman Melville, "Cock-A-Doodle-Doo!" in *Billy Budd, Sailor and Other Stories* (New York: Penguin Books, 1976), 103; see Schivelbusch, *Railway Journey*, 134-49, for a discussion of "Railway Brain" and the history of traumatic neurosis.

34. Melville, "Cock-A-Doodle-Doo!" 105, 103.

35. Ibid., 105.

36. Karl Marx, "Manifesto of the Communist Party," in *The Marx-Engels Reader*, ed. Robert Tucker (New York: W. W. Norton, 1978), 475.

37. Williams, "Passenger Aids Others," A1.

38. Benjamin, "Theses," 263; F. D. Reeve, *The White Monk: An Essay on Dos-toevsky and Melville* (Nashville, Tenn.: Vanderbilt University Press, 1989), 123; Fredric Jameson, *Marxism and Form* (Princeton, N.J.: Princeton University Press, 1971), 121, 129.

39. Benjamin, quoted in Graeme Gilloch, *Myth and Metropolis: Walter Ben-jamin and the City* (Cambridge: Blackwell Publishers, 1996), 114.

40. Walker Percy, *The Message in the Bottle* (New York: Farrar, Straus and Giroux, 1982), 7, 6.

41. Blaine Harden, "The Impresario of Heroism: How Reagan Fulfills Our Desperate Need for Reflected Glory," *WP*, 7 February 1982, B1; Fyodor Dosto-evsky, *The Brothers Karamazov* (New York: Bantam Books, 1970), 260.

42. S. A. Howland, *Steamboat Disasters and Railroad Accidents in the United States* (Worcester, Mass.: Dorr and Howland, 1840), 13, 14, 201, 199, 205-6.

43. Ibid., vi.

44. Williams, "Passenger Aids Others," A1.

45. Howland, *Steamboat Disasters*, 138.

46. George Landow, *Images of Crisis: Literary Iconology, 1750 to the Present* (Boston: Routledge & Kegan Paul, 1982), 110.

47. Rebecca Harding Davis, *Life in the Iron-Mills*, ed. Cecelia Tichi (New York: Bedford Books, 1998), 65.

48. Schivelbusch, *Railway Journey*, 132; Bloch, quoted in Schivelbusch, 129, 131.

49. Marx, "Communist Manifesto," 476; Arthur Shostak, *The Air Controllers' Controversy: Lessons from the PATCO Strike* (New York: Human Sciences Press, 1986), 22.

50. Shostak, *Air Controllers' Controversy*, 248.

51. Kenneth Bredemeier, "Identity of Plane Crash Hero Remains a Mystery," *WP*, 20 January 1982, A1.

52. Fredric Jameson, *The Political Unconscious* (Ithaca, N.Y.: Cornell University Press, 1981), 287; Roger Rosenblatt, "The Man in the Water," *Time Magazine*, 25 January 1982, 86.

53. See Paul Ricoeur, *De l'Interpretation* (Paris: Seuil, 1965), 33-44; Editorial, "The Unknown Hero," *WP*, 21 January 1982, A18.

54. "List of Air Crash Victims Identified to Date," *WP*, 17 January 1982, A10.

55. Geoffrey Hartman, *Criticism in the Wilderness* (New Haven, Conn.: Yale University Press, 1980), 83.

56. Mike Sager and Sandra Boodman, "Priest at Crash Scene is Held as Fugitive," *WP*, 17 January 1982, A10.

57. Don DeLillo, *White Noise* (New York: Penguin Books, 1985), 90.

58. T. W. Adorno, *Negative Dialectics* (New York: Continuum, 1973), 369, 370.

59. Marx, quoted in Buck-Morss, *Dialectics of Seeing*, 120. Buck-Morss's translation captures both the tone and the content of Marx's argument in the famous "fetishism of commodities" section of *Capital*.

60. Shostak, *Air Controllers' Controversy*, 123.

61. Rolf Tiedemann, "Dialectics at a Standstill," in *On Walter Benjamin: Critical Essays and Reflections* (Cambridge: MIT Press, 1991), 286; Wolin, *Walter Benjamin*, 130.

62. McQueen and Battiata, "Views from the Bridge," A10.

63. Joe Hill, "Workers of the World, Awaken," in *Rebel Voices: An I.W.W. Anthology*, ed. Joyce Kornbluh (Ann Arbor: University of Michigan Press, 1964), 143. Reprinted by permission of Industrial Workers of the World, 103 West Michigan Avenue, Ypsilanti, Mich., 48197.

64. Benjamin, "Theses," 262; Caruth, *Trauma*, 5.

65. I have in mind the work of someone like Francis Fukuyama. See Francis Fukuyama, *The End of History and the Last Man* (New York: Free Press, 1992).

66. Karl Marx, *Grundrisse* (New York: Vintage Books, 1973), 524, 534; John McCole, *Walter Benjamin and the Antinomies of Tradition* (Ithaca, N.Y.: Cornell University Press, 1993), 146.

67. Marx, *Grundrisse*, 542; Paul Virilio, *Speed and Politics* (New York: Semiotext[e], 1986), 29.

68. Marx, "Communist Manifesto," 476.

69. Dusko Doder, "Soviets Hint Air Controller Firings Caused Crash," *WP*, 17 January 1982, A10.

70. Shostak, *Air Controllers' Controversy*, 183.

71. Benjamin, "N [Theoretics]," 22; Mary Battiata and Jura Koncius, "A Survivor: 'We Weren't Going to Make It'," *WP*, 14 January 1982, A6.

72. The official report didn't entirely exonerate the air traffic controllers; it wondered why the airport had remained open during such a storm. Though the pilot in command was ultimately responsible for deciding whether or not to take off, a controller first had to clear him to do so. Adorno, *Negative Dialectics*, 370, 371; "Transcript of the Last Words," *WP*, 5 February 1982, A10.

13

The *Exxon Valdez* and Alaska in the American Imagination

Thomas A. Birkland and Regina G. Lawrence

The grounding of the Exxon Valdez *in 1989 resulted in the largest oil spill in United States history. While its sheer size alone made it a media event, the disaster gained far more coverage—in both volume and intensity—than any previous oil spill. Thomas A. Birkland and Regina G. Lawrence argue that the* Exxon Valdez *oil spill received so much attention because of its symbolic richness. The spill occurred in what many considered to be the last "unspoiled" area of the world, and its most important symbolic features were the images of Alaska itself. In the contest for public opinion between corporate interests and environmentalists, these images proved extraordinarily powerful. Where Duane A. Gill and J. Steven Picou's essay on the spill addresses the disaster's devastating impact on local culture, Birkland and Lawrence's contribution considers its broader political and cultural resonance.*[1]

> We go eastward to realize history and study the works of art and literature, retracing the steps of the race; we go westward as into the future, with a spirit of enterprise and adventure. . . . The West of which I speak is but another name for the Wild; and what I have been preparing to say is, that in Wildness is the preservation of the world.
>
> —Henry David Thoreau

INTRODUCTION

ON MARCH 24, 1989, the supertanker *Exxon Valdez* ran aground on Bligh Reef in Prince William Sound, Alaska, spilling eleven million gallons of crude oil into the waters of the sound and south central Alaska.[2] Almost immediately the news media converged on the site of the spill, beaming pictures of oiled shorelines, birds, and sea otters to a shocked and angry public.[3] The public reaction ranged from sorrow to outrage, reactions more intense than had been expressed in response to similar accidents.

The *Exxon Valdez* spill broke a fourteen-year congressional legislative deadlock, triggering passage of the federal Oil Pollution Act of 1990 and illustrating how "focusing events" can overcome impasses and spur policy change.[4] The spill became an integral part of the public imagination and of the history of the environmental movement. Clearly, the sheer size of the spill made the event important in and of itself; but the *setting* of the oil spill in Alaska added enormously to its social and political significance.

The spill's setting provided concrete story cues for journalists and evoked powerful imagery of Alaska as wilderness. The physical damage to this "unspoiled" and "pristine" setting vividly illustrated key elements of environmentalist thought and boosted, temporarily at least, environmentalists' access to the news media and, by extension, to the public. Thus, the *Valdez* spill became a key event in the history of the American environmental movement and in shaping public thinking about environmental problems, in no small part because it crystallized already simmering conflicts around a particularly dramatic event.

THE *EXXON VALDEZ* IN THE NATIONAL NEWS

At about 10:30 P.M. Alaska time on March 23, 1989, the *Exxon Valdez*, laden with 1.2 million barrels of North Slope crude oil, put out from Port Valdez bound for Long Beach, California. While departing Prince William Sound, Captain Joseph Hazelwood ordered the ship to turn left, out of the outbound shipping lane and into the inbound lanes, to avoid ice that was calving from nearby Columbia Glacier. Captain Hazelwood then retired to his cabin after ordering the uncertified third

FIGURES 13.1. and 13.2. Oiled wildlife in the *Exxon Valdez* spill. (Photo by Bob Hallinen/*Anchorage Daily News*)

mate to command the ship. Through a series of human and, possibly, mechanical errors, the ship failed to turn back toward the outbound shipping lanes, instead veering far to the left in a maneuver that carried it into the well-marked reef. The crew sensed something amiss minutes before the grounding of the ship and attempted to turn away from danger, but the ship did not respond. (Tankers take many miles to turn in the best conditions.) The ship scraped Bligh reef once and continued onward until, in Captain Hazelwood's words, it "fetched up hard aground" on the reef just after midnight on March 24. Several holes, some as large as twenty-five feet long, were opened in the ship's hull, resulting in the largest oil spill in U.S. history and the first major spill in Alaskan waters since the Trans-Alaska pipeline opened in 1977.

In the immediate aftermath of the spill, a flurry of attempts to clean up the oil and rehabilitate oiled wildlife, particularly seabirds and otters, preoccupied everyone involved. The official response of the federal government, of Exxon, and of the Alyeska Pipeline Service Company (the owner of the Trans-Alaska Pipeline) was fumbling, confused, and inadequate.⁵ Exxon was ill-equipped to handle the spill, while Alyeska claimed the spill was Exxon's problem and did little or nothing to aid in its containment. Nor did the federal government offer much help. It was not until three weeks after the spill that the White House federalized the cleanup effort, but by then the oil spilled from the *Exxon Valdez* had fouled nearly 1,600 square miles of water and 800 miles of shoreline in and around Prince William Sound—an area the size of Rhode Island. As the spill spread, a flurry of finger-pointing and blame-fixing followed in its wake. In the end, most responsible and dispassionate opinion concluded that the spill could have been prevented, that the response was inadequate, and that the promises made by the oil industry and by the state and federal governments to run an environmentally sound pipeline had not been fulfilled.

The *Valdez* spill generated intense media coverage. It was mentioned in 577 news stories in the major national print media between March and May 1989. The spill was also the subject of twenty-two network evening news stories between March 27 and March 31 alone, and of an additional seventy stories in April and May 1989. And the spill continued to generate coverage long after the broken ship had finally been towed to dry dock: nearly 1,000 print news stories and sixty-nine network news stories discussed the *Valdez* spill between June 1989 and the one-year anniversary in March 1990.

Not surprisingly, given this level of media coverage, the *Valdez* captured the public's attention. A 1997 Pew Center study found that the spill ranked among the top twenty news stories in terms of public attention in the previous *decade*. Compared with an average of 25 percent for most major news stories, 52 percent of respondents reported having followed the *Exxon Valdez* story "very closely."⁶

This degree of public attention reflects journalists' perceptions of the spill's newsworthiness. As news media from around the world converged on Valdez, reporters found irresistible story opportunities. The spill was a highly distressing event with a clear, visible, and extensive impact on its setting. It offered compelling visuals and sympathetic local victims. In addition, it immediately offered at least one villain, Captain Joseph Hazelwood, who was found to have been legally drunk at the time of the grounding and who had handed control of the ship over to his less qualified third mate before the ship ran aground. After the grounding of his ship, Hazelwood evaded authorities and initially refused to turn himself in. Within weeks, Hazelwood became an infamous household name, signified by one of David Letterman's "Top Ten Excuses for the *Exxon Valdez* Spill": "I was just trying to scrape some ice off the reef for my margarita."[7]

Yet the substantive and often complex policy issues related to the spill were not well covered by the news media, particularly television. Some outlets, to their credit (in particular, the *New York Times*), did discuss the policy implications of the spill in detail, but the primary story themes for most media were the volume and geographic extent of the spill, the mess the oil made along beaches, and the impact of the spill on the Alaskan environment and its people, particularly natives and fishers. This environment was more valued, at least in the news depictions, because the land was virgin, wild, rugged, trackless, and all the other adjectives that had been applied to the state.

In nearly every story about the *Exxon Valdez* in the first week, the on-scene reporter (that is, on scene in Valdez, where the networks set up shop, some 25 miles from the actual spill) introduced the story standing before a background of trees, water, and snowy mountains. The visuals chosen by the news editors highlighted the impact of the spill on wildlife and on fishermen, primarily in Valdez. (Cordova, the major fishing port on Prince William Sound, was mentioned much less often.)

The wildlife pictures were remarkably consistent in the first week, largely because the networks used footage provided by the Alaska Division of Fish and Wildlife. Thus, on March 31, all three networks showed—often without attribution—the same pictures of dead and dying birds (various ducks and cormorants, in particular) and dead and dying otters. Later stories showed the growing slick in Prince William Sound and the Gulf of Alaska, and efforts to clean the beaches with heavy machinery, dozens of workers, hoses, and what appear to be paper towels or rags. In such depictions, the long shots show the surrounding terrain, perhaps to reveal the scale of the slick, but also subtly to remind the viewer that this is *Alaska* in the pictures.

The nature, intensity, and drama of news coverage of the *Valdez* spill owed much to its setting. The stunning setting of Prince William Sound transformed an industrial accident into a highly compelling news story and an icon of the American environmental movement. While there are undoubtedly several reasons for the tremendous public interest in the *Exxon Valdez*, one of the more compelling is the place of Alaska in the American imagination as the last great American wilderness, the last western frontier.

ALASKA IN THE NATIONAL IMAGINATION

The mythology of Alaska's unspoiled, wild frontier, reflected in the state's slogan, "The Last Frontier,"[8] made the *Exxon Valdez* spill particularly troubling to many people in America and around the world.

The Alaskan wilderness has been suffused in the American imagination with what Roderick Nash describes as "the oldest American ambivalence"—our profoundly divided feelings regarding the West.[9] On one hand, Alaska represents what the West has symbolized for Americans since the days of Daniel Boone: a place of adventure and scenic beauty where one can pursue dreams of "a love of nature, of perfect freedom, and of the adventurous life in the woods," as Boone once wrote. Yet the Alaskan wilderness also represents the final chapter of Manifest Destiny, the final stage of the American westward movement, driven by an "antithesis between nature and civilization, between freedom and law."[10]

Beneath this antithesis is a deep ambivalence regarding two competing sets of values: the protection of nature for its own sake versus economic development of the West's abundant natural resources. This longstanding American tension is particularly stark in Alaska, whose residents enjoy the state's pristine, scenic wonders while profiting from the economic exploitation of its resources,[11] particularly oil. The Alaska Native Claims Settlement Act of 1971 has enmeshed Native Alaskans in the same ambivalence: some wish to log and mine the land for revenue, while others seek to preserve its core environmental and renewable resource values.[12]

Thus, Alaska—as both a physical and a psychic space—is among the most important battlefields on which the nature-versus-development conflict is fought. It also occupies a special place in the iconography of American environmental politics because, unlike similar struggles played out in many other western locales, the Alaskan wilderness became threatened with large-scale economic development at precisely the time that a well-developed philosophy of wilderness protection reached full flower in American culture. In the environmentalist heyday of the 1960s and 1970s, Alaska became "a celebrated cause, an opportunity to make up, if only symbolically, for the near-total elimination of wilderness in the rest of the nation."[13] By the late 1980s, Alaska's image as America's last wilderness frontier was deeply ingrained in the American mind, even as development of its resources had surged ahead. The *Exxon Valdez* represented not the beginning but a reanimation of the struggle for Alaska's future, and it cast new light on long-standing questions about our "last frontier."

THE SETTING: PRINCE WILLIAM SOUND

Prince William Sound is a particularly majestic setting, rich in scenery and wildlife. The oil quickly coated that scene and its inhabitants, and these visual images of the breathtaking beauty of the Sound covered with brown, gooey oil are what many people vividly remember about the spill.

Indeed, the setting of Prince William Sound—and its location in Alaska more generally—offered the news media a readymade narrative frame that juxtaposed the dirty oil with the previously unspoiled surroundings. The lead paragraph of one *Newsweek* story illustrates how the setting was used to frame the story of the spill:

> The worst oil disaster in North American waters, now in its second week, dumped 240,000 barrels of oil from the *Exxon Valdez*, one-fifth of its cargo [in] a pristine land of such surpassing majesty that the mountains seem to be painted by the brush of an artist rather than shaped by the brute forces of geology.[14]

But the setting of Prince William Sound did not merely provide a scenic backdrop for the news. It also shaped the telling of the *Valdez* story in very concrete ways. First, the sheltered setting of the Sound created more visible effects than if the spill had occurred in the open ocean. With nowhere else to go, the oil washed onto hundreds of miles of beaches rather than breaking up and sinking or evaporating far out of sight of reporters and TV cameras. The confined spill meant that plants and animals found escape difficult, if not impossible. Indeed, in the early days after the spill, one scientist reported, "the slick covers 100 percent of the affected area."[15] These conditions created a longer-lasting spill with longer-lasting visible effects than is true of many oil spills, providing the media with particularly compelling images and vivid evidence of environmental damage.

The most important element of the setting, however, was Prince William Sound's abundant wildlife. The Sound is home to the world's largest annual migration of marine birds (approximately 10 million) and the largest populations of bald eagles and sea otters in North America. It is the site of one of the world's largest salmon fisheries, and the spill occurred just before the annual release of salmon fry from the hatcheries and the annual harvest of herring roe. Salmon and the fishing industry thus became the major measurable indicators of the economic toll of the spill, with fishers among its most visible victims. But the abundance of animal victims at least equaled and possibly exceeded the direct human costs of the spill. This was especially true because the spill occurred in the early spring, when large numbers of whales, dolphins, seals, and sea lions migrate to the Sound.

Within a week of the spill, scientists began discovering large numbers of animals killed by crude oil. These discoveries quickly transformed the wildlife of Prince William Sound into compelling indicators of the spill's toll on the environment. It was soon estimated that hundreds, even thousands, of otters, birds, and other wildlife had died. The exact number killed was impossible to ascertain, since an unknown number died from drowning or sank after dying. After passions had cooled and scientific efforts could be undertaken, the extent of the damage done by the spill became even more ambiguous.[16]

The immediate perception of widespread damage was more important in media framing of the spill, however, than was the actual long-term effect of the spill. As the oil engulfed the Sound, its birds, sea otters, and other wildlife became the unlucky stars of the news. Indeed, oiled sea otters became particularly evocative symbols of the damage wrought by the *Valdez* spill. Otters appeal to people because they are what conservation biologists call a "charismatic species"[17]; they capture human imagination and sympathy because of their appearance and behavior. Otters are known for their playfulness and are among the most popular animals at zoos and aquariums. They eat shellfish by lying on their backs and opening the shells with rocks, and their faces seem very expressive to humans, with big eyes and cat-like whiskers. The damage to otters in particular provoked considerable post-spill outrage. Even today, otters remain an important symbol of the spill.

Some news organizations kept a running body count of animals killed, much like the human body count in typical news reporting of human disasters like earthquakes. For example, *Time* magazine reported:

At least 82 sea otters have been brought to a makeshift field hospital in Valdez. They were nearly frozen because a coat of oil had destroyed the insulating ability of their fur; 42 have died. Animals dead on arrival steadily filled up a white refrigerated truck trailer parked nearby. A black-tailed Sitka deer carcass stuck out of a 32-gal. garbage can, and dozens of otters lay in a pile, covered with plastic. Uncounted other victims will never be retrieved. A preliminary beach survey indicated an average of 80 oil-coated ducks and other kinds of birds per 100 meters. Bald eagles have been scavenging the contaminated birds, and the sound's population of 3,000 eagles may therefore be at risk.[18]

This is not the tone and style of coverage reserved for routine events in routine places. Clearly, journalists covering the *Exxon Valdez* did not simply report the bare facts of the spill; they focused concern on the spill's wild victims and dramatic natural setting.

THE STRUGGLE TO DEFINE THE *EXXON VALDEZ* IN THE NEWS

We focus here on the imagery and meaning of the *Exxon Valdez* as portrayed in the news because the news is the main symbolic arena in which "various social groups, institutions, and ideologies struggle over the definition and construction of social reality."[19] That is to say, the news is a product of the social negotiation of meaning, and it reflects the power of those who struggle to shape it.[20] Similarly, students of public policy making are increasingly recognizing that the public problems defined in the news and in other arenas are *social constructions* rather than just simple, factual depictions of problems with a rationally developed set of solutions: "problems" don't exist objectively as much as they exist in perception. What qualifies as a "problem" for any given society on any given day has little to do with its objective features (actual or potential future harms, for example) and much more to do with the things people notice, their widely shared perceptions of issues, and the competing claims about reality made by various groups.

The power to define meaning is closely related to the ability of groups to influence the issues that come to the attention of mass publics and policy makers[21] in a process called "agenda setting." The result of these efforts to raise or suppress issues on the agenda, and to create meaning after dramatic events, is often a broad consensus on the causes, meanings, and responsibilities for events that dominate *public* discourse, not merely elite conflict. This consensus is the product of journalistic routines and the efforts of affected groups to influence news coverage. It follows that what becomes understood as a *problem*—a societal condition that people believe is unacceptable and should be ameliorated by public policy[22]—can depend in large part upon whose perspectives are highlighted in the news.

Dramatic news events can play a vital role in the social construction of public problems.[23] Journalists do not simply report events, they imbue them with meaning in the process of converting them into news.[24] Especially important are "accidental" news events[25] like the *Exxon Valdez* spill.[26]

Routine news events generally dominate the news. These are news events that are preplanned by politicians and other officials to manage the news and communicate with the public. The nominating convention, the Rose Garden bill signing, and the summit meeting are all routine news events staged by officials largely to build and perpetuate particular public images.[27] Some news events, however, are unintentional or unplanned. They run the gamut from natural disasters, such as tornadoes and earthquakes, to humanly caused disasters, like space shuttle explosions or terrorist attacks, to events officials engage in but do not intend as news, such as presidential gaffes or sexual scandals. These "accidental" events can create pivotal moments in the news—moments when standard perspectives on social issues can be challenged.

What is particularly intriguing about accidental events is that they are not predefined for journalists in the way that routine events are. Consequently, as different groups vie to define them, accidental events can become the centerpieces of struggles to designate and define public problems. Focused through the lens of a dramatic news event, a new problem can gain currency or a recurring problem can resurface with new urgency in the news. Accidental events thus often become important and contested symbols used to construct public problems.

The *Exxon Valdez* and other disasters,[28] unlike routine events, tend to generate sustained, intense media coverage and thus are particularly likely to be used to define public problems. When all the elements of the story—the setting (Prince William Sound and Alaska), the most commonly depicted victims (animals, fishers, Native Alaskans), and the competing definitions of the problem (dependence on oil, greedy oil companies, or the drunk captain, for example)—converge, a highly dramatic news story becomes infused with multiple compelling meanings. Moreover, these events resonate with journalists and the public because, as Lance Bennett and Regina Lawrence[29] argue, they crystallize deep political and cultural tensions. Such events can become "news icons," which dominate the news and become a sort of shorthand reference not only to the event itself, but to the panoply of issues raised by the event as well.

For example, while Captain Hazelwood's culpability for the spill (due to his alleged drunkenness) seemed clear (even though, in the end, it was not), the oil industry's responsibility for the spill—and, in particular, its failed response to the spill—became the subject of intense controversy. Many local residents held Hazelwood less liable than either the company that employed him or the industry that had repeatedly promised that no spill of this magnitude was possible—and then had proved unable to contain it. Environmental activists quickly joined the fray, spearheading efforts to boycott Exxon, to raise public consciousness about oil consumption, and to arrest further oil development in the wilderness of Alaska. In this way, the *Exxon Valdez* came to represent more than one ship, one captain, or one oil spill. At a minimum, the *Exxon Valdez* stood for the range of opinion and controversy that had dogged oil production in Alaska since before statehood.

Before the spill, the oil industry's claims about the safety of oil drilling and oil transportation in Alaska and about its own competence to protect the environment from harm held sway. Since the first day of the pipeline's operation in 1977, there had been no major spill, and any issues about Alaskan oil were low among most Americans' concerns. After the spill, the balance of rhetorical power shifted. The imagery of the *Valdez* spill lent itself to the claims of environmentalists more readily than to the claims of the oil industry and other pro-development forces. Environmentalists highlighted the costs of the spill beyond the immediate human and economic impact; even if human lives were not lost, they argued, livelihoods, natural resources, and the sense of Alaska as "unspoiled" or "pristine" were equally valuable and had been damaged, perhaps irreparably. As Jay Hair of the National Wildlife Federation told *Newsweek*, "The American public has paid dearly for Exxon's incompetence."[30] "There's no doubt in my mind," he claimed, "that the long-term environmental consequences of the Prince William Sound oil spill will far exceed those of Chernobyl or Bhopal. It's probably fair to say that in our lifetime we will never see the sound the way it was on March 23, 1989."[31]

The symbolism of the *Valdez* spill encouraged grassroots activists and national leaders to define broader environmental problems that ranged beyond the immediate impact of the *Valdez* spill. For opponents of the now-decommissioned Shoreham nuclear power plant in Long Island, for example, the spill illustrated that even highly unlikely accidents can happen. Then-Senator Albert Gore Jr. observed: "This may be one of those defining moments that we have heard about. . . . A huge spill like this focuses media coverage and political attention, not only on the environment itself, but also on the larger problems for which it is a metaphor: we are spilling chemicals in massive quantities into our ground water, surface water, atmosphere and stratosphere."[32]

Exxon's claims—and those of the oil industry at large—faltered against the spill's imagery and news value. Environmental groups could use the symbols of oiled sea otters, dead birds, and workers wiping oiled rocks with towels to illustrate their argument that the spill was an act of needless and possibly irreversible human destruction of the environment. These images trumped the oil industry's symbol-poor arguments that the spill was not serious and should not be seen as an indicator of any need for greater environmental regulation. After all, it was quite difficult for the oil industry to capture, in one image or symbol, years of reasonably safe operation of the pipeline and the tankers, but it was quite easy to show oil company failure with images of oiled beaches and wildlife from a single spill.

Perhaps because environmentalists' claims fit so well with the symbolism of the spill, print news organizations treated them as key sources in their stories about the spill. (Television network news appeared more "balanced" but was much less likely to delve as deeply into these issues.) Though outgunned by oil industry sources,[33] who possessed more resources and greater experience in working with and managing media coverage, environmentalists often competed successfully with pro-development forces for news coverage and, most important, for their desired spin on the news. Indeed, in all the lead paragraphs of *Valdez* stories in the *New York Times*, *Los Angeles Times*, *Time*, and *Newsweek*, the oil industry rarely succeeded in setting the tone and substance of a news story with its arguments.

When the oil industry appeared as the leading voice in the debate, it was nearly always in the role of a foil for other, more critical perspectives. The opening paragraphs of an April 1989 *Time* article offer one example:

> By midweek Exxon, owner of the wounded tanker, admitted that the largest oil spill in U.S. history was spreading out of control; by week's end the slick covered almost 900 sq. mi. southwest of Valdez, Alaska, posing a deadly danger to the marine and bird life that teems in Prince William Sound. The story, a tale of unrelieved gloom with no heroes, resembled a Greek tragedy updated by Murphy's Law. Everything that could go wrong did; everyone involved, including the Alaska state government and the U.S. Coast Guard, made damaging errors; hubris in the form of complacency (it has never happened, so it won't) took a heavy toll; and events marched relentlessly from bad to worse toward the worst possible.[34]

Environmentalists or an environmentalist perspective also occasionally got the last word at the expense of the oil industry, as in the closing paragraph of a May 1989 *Newsweek* article (note the reporter's tongue-in-cheek tone in describing Exxon's position):

> Exxon chairman Lawrence G. Rawl was taking none of the blame last week. Facing hundreds of protesters outside Exxon's annual meeting in Parsippany, N.J.—and a relative handful of unhappy shareowners within—he brushed aside requests for his resignation, or establishment of a billion-dollar cleanup fund sought by environmentalists. "The worst thing we can do is divert attention from the cleanup," he said virtuously. As of last week, 12.5 of the 728 miles of coastline affected by the spill had been partially cleaned.[35]

Similarly, a *Time* magazine article concluded by describing the significance of the *Exxon Valdez*:

> Finding more oil is not the answer to [the nation's] energy needs; a coherent policy encouraging fuel conservation is. . . . Thus the time has come to get tough about conservation. . . . If Americans can abandon wasteful habits, Alaska will be under much less pressure to squander its precious wilderness.[36]

THE *VALDEZ* AS A CRYSTALLIZATION OF POLITICAL AND CULTURAL CONFLICTS

As the *Valdez* spill became a vehicle for environmentalist groups and their ideas to enter the news with new force, it illustrated several key tenets of environmentalist thought and highlighted central ideas at stake in political struggles over environmental protection. First, the spill underlined the difficulty of preserving wild areas against development pressures. Oiled wildlife and soiled beaches aptly represented the fragility of the wild environment and the ease with which it can be harmed by human activity. The sheer numbers of otters, birds, and other creatures injured or killed by the oil vividly symbolized the notion that human arrogance had recklessly endangered other species. As Connecticut Senator Joseph Lieberman observed, the spill "illustrates in a devastating way how delicate the environment of Alaska can be and how impotent we are to protect it from our own mistakes."[37]

Second, images of oil-covered beaches contrasted the relative ease of inflicting environmental damage with the difficulty of undoing it. Cleanup workers found the oil-slicked beaches virtually impossible to walk across, let alone clean. As the volatile components in the oil evaporated, the remaining compound thickened into a sludge resistant even to chemical dispersants. The oil quickly seeped between rocks to coat and penetrate the ground underneath. Television, newspapers, and newsmagazines carried haunting pictures of workers dressed from head to toe in orange rubber suits, wandering a moonscape of oil-soaked beaches with hoses spewing high-pressure hot water and futilely wiping down individual rocks with paper towels or rags.

Most broadly, the spill highlighted deep conflicts in American politics and culture over America's use of Alaskan resources. Many Americans tend to picture Alaska in a primitive state, yet Alaska also hosts a cyclical but dynamic and growing resource-extraction economy. The extraction activity often takes place in remote and challenging areas and is supported by organizations with regional offices in urban Anchorage. Anchorage, while promoting its location in *Alaska* (both as a location and as a symbol) to those who value Alaska in all its meanings, is also a modern American city of about 200,000 people, complete with malls, tract housing, and freeways; it is in many ways indistinguishable from most small- to medium-size cities in North America.

The *Valdez* spill was shocking to many people because they did not realize how far development had already proceeded on the "last frontier," whether that development was symbolized by the Anchorage skyline or the tanker traffic at Port Valdez or the continued exploration for oil in northern Alaska. The shock also reflected a cultural divide between most Alaskans, who favor more economic development, and the environmental movement. Blessed with a far cleaner and more beautiful natural environment and more abundant natural resources than most other states, Alaska vividly dramatizes the larger American struggle to strike a balance between development and protection of the environment.

Despite many Alaskans' concern about the environmental costs, support for the resource-extraction economy remains a powerful force in Alaska state politics, especially given the annual Permanent Fund Dividend Alaskans receive from oil revenues.[38] As a result, the State of Alaska and its citizens often clash with the federal government and its goals for preservation of an Alaskan environment that most non-Alaskans will never see but that many non-Alaskans value for its wilderness.[39] These conflicts have fueled continuous, heated political battles for years. The conflict came to a head in 1980, when the Alaska National Interest Lands Conservation Act established federal protection for 28 percent of the state's lands (an area larger than California). The Arctic National Wildlife Refuge, which has long been coveted by development interests who hope to tap into large oil reserves underneath it, has been determinedly defended by environmentalists as part of a unique and fragile ecosystem and as a *national* environmental asset. Its opening to oil exploration was and remains stalled by the *Exxon Valdez* spill, and it appears unlikely that this will change; the George W. Bush administration's efforts to open the area to development have run into fierce opposition. The most important political battle may have been the Trans-Alaska Pipeline Authorization Act of 1973, which was a major victory for the oil industry over many Alaskans and "outside" environmentalists. In spite of congressional authorization to build the pipeline (and to waive environmental laws to do so), environmentalists and fishers both in and outside Alaska continued to fear the pipeline's impact on a broad swath of the state, from its origin in Prudhoe Bay to its terminus in Prince William Sound.

The *Valdez* spill captured in dramatic images and a compelling news narrative this deep and ongoing conflict in American and Alaskan

FIGURE I3.3. The *Exxon Valdez* remains an evocative symbol, more than ten years later. (Courtesy Schwinn Bicycle and Fitness, Inc.)

politics between the symbolism of the Last Frontier and the reality of Alaskan economic development. The oil industry's traditional public relations response to this conflict has been repeatedly to assure the public that oil drilling and oil transportation will not harm the scenery and wildlife of Alaska. In fact, oil industry advertisements of the 1970s and 1980s emphasized the compatibility of development and the natural environment. One picture in an eight-page advertising spread in national newsmagazines, for example, showed caribou walking peacefully among the Alaskan oil fields.[40] Presidential candidate George Bush echoed these arguments in the 1988 campaign, when he said of the Alaskan pipeline, "The caribou love it. They rub up against it, and they have babies. There are more caribou in Alaska than you can shake a stick at."[41]

The pictures generated by the *Valdez* spill could not have challenged the oil industry's imagery more directly. While the *Valdez* spill starkly illustrated this conflict felt so keenly by many Alaskans, it illustrated for many other Americans a broader, more general conflict between the environment and the exigencies of continued economic growth. Because of *Valdez*,

> Legislators and regulators are asking tough questions: Should oil exploration in Alaska be drastically curtailed, or even stopped? Should larger areas of the state be put under federal protection from development? If the U.S. holds back the pumping of Alaskan oil, how will the country satisfy its hunger for energy? . . . Until the Exxon Valdez hit a reef, these questions did not seem quite so urgent.

CONCLUSION

Many environmental events punctuated the late 1980s. The wanderings of the infamous garbage barge *Mobro*, the Atlantic beaches soiled with medical wastes and syringes, and the drought, heat wave, and Yellowstone fires of 1988 brought increased public attention to the problems of the environment. At the end of the 1980s, the *Exxon Valdez* oil spill illustrated in particularly dramatic fashion the growing tensions between interests advocating development of natural resources and environmentalists who sought to preserve the health and beauty of the environment. As Alaska Governor Steve Cowper said of his constituents, "There's going to be a permanent change in the political chemistry of Alaska as a result of this tragedy. Most Alaskans are going to reassess their attitude toward oil and development in this state."[42] Senator Joseph Lieberman observed that the *Valdez* spill had shifted the political terrain around a variety of environmental conflicts, such as oil drilling in the Arctic National Wildlife Refuge. "The train was moving pretty rapidly out of the station," said Lieberman. "Now they've put the brakes on it and put it into reverse."[43]

As images of oil-soaked otters flooded television screens (and adorned the advertisements and mass mailings of environmental groups), oil spills gained a prominent place on the media and governmental agendas, and environmentalists won a seat at the policy-making table that had previously been denied them. In this event-driven context, the problems of existing oil-spill liability policy were highlighted, and the seeds of the Oil Pollution Act of 1990 were sown in congressional committees, as was a renewed commitment to protect the Arctic National Wildlife Reserve.[44] Given the vast distance between the site of the spill and policy makers in Washington, D.C., it is clear that this mobilization and issue expansion would not have been possible without the intense media coverage that shaped how the story of the spill was told.

The *Exxon Valdez* spill reveals how dramatic accidental events can act as vehicles to provide relatively marginalized ideas new access and legitimacy in the news,[45] and how the symbolic dimensions of such events can propel them into national consciousness. The imagery arising out of the spill—gushing black oil, fouled beaches, oiled and drowning otters, angry local fisherman, and the backdrop of Prince William Sound—made the story irresistible to journalists and provocative to the public. Ultimately, the *Exxon Valdez* oil spill's power to focus media and public attention on environmentalists' claims owed much to its setting in Alaska, the great symbol of America's last western frontier.

NOTES

1. The authors thank Jennifer Krausnick and Lanethea Mathews for their research and editorial assistance. Earlier and somewhat different versions of this article were presented at the 1997 meeting of the American Studies Association, the 1999 meeting of the Western Political Science Association, and the 1999 meeting of the International Communications Association.

2. The formal, legal name of the ship was the *Exxon Valdez*. For convenience, we sometimes shorten that name to simply "the *Valdez*." The ship grounded off the coast of the town of Valdez, Alaska, and so Valdez often stands for both the site of the spill and the ship. It is also worth noting that the town and ship are pronounced "val-DEEZ."

3. Art Davidson, *In the Wake of the* Exxon Valdez (San Francisco: Sierra Club Books, 1990); John Keeble, *Out of the Channel* (New York: HarperCollins, 1994); Jeff Wheelwright, *Degrees of Disaster: Prince William Sound: How Nature Reels and Rebounds* (New York: Simon and Schuster, 1994).

4. John Kingdon, *Agendas, Alternatives and Public Policies,* 2d ed. (New York: HarperCollins); Thomas Birkland, *After Disaster: Agenda Setting, Public Policy, and Focusing Events* (Washington, D.C.: Georgetown University Press, 1997).

5. Alaska Department of Environmental Conservation, *The* Exxon Valdez *Oil Spill: Final Report, State of Alaska Response* (Anchorage: Alaska Department of Environmental Conservation, 1993).

6. Kimberly Parker and Claudia Deane, "Ten Years of the Pew News Interest Index," Pew Research Center for the People and the Press, http://www.people-press.org, 1997.

7. Richard Behar, "Joe's Bad Trip," *Time,* 24 July 1989, 42.

8. Roderick Nash, *Wilderness and the American Mind,* 3d ed. (New Haven, Conn.: Yale University Press, 1982); Orlando Miller, *The Frontier in Alaska and the Matanuska Colony* (New Haven, Conn.: Yale University Press, 1975); John A. McPhee, *Coming Into the Country* (New York: Farrar, Straus and Giroux, 1977).

9. Nash, *Wilderness and the American Mind,* 314.

10. Henry Nash Smith, *Virgin Land* (Cambridge: Harvard University Press, 1970), 60.

11. Miller, *The Frontier in Alaska.*

12. See, for example, John G. Mitchell, "In the Wake of the Spill: Ten Years after the *Exxon Valdez*," *National Geographic* 195 (March 1999): 96-117.

13. Nash, *Wilderness and the American Mind,* 278-79.

14. Sharon Begley, Lisa Drew, and Mary Hager, "Smothering the Waters," *Newsweek,* 10 April 1989, 54.

15. Malcolm W. Browne, "Oil on Surface Covers Deeper Threat," *New York Times,* 31 March 1989, A12.

16. John A. Weins, "Oil, Seabirds, and Science," *BioScience* 46, no. 8 (1996): 587-93; Wheelwright, *Degrees of Disaster.*

17. Jim Wilson, "Charisma! " *International Wildlife* 26 (January 1996): 20-40.

18. Michael D. Lemonick, "The Two Alaskas," *Time,* 17 April 1989, 56-65.

19. Michael Gurevitch and Mark R. Levy, "Preface," in *Mass Communication Review Yearbook 5,* ed. Michael Gurevitch and Mark R. Levy (Beverly Hills, Calif.: Sage, 1985).

20. Robert M. Entman, "Framing: Toward Clarification of a Fractured Paradigm," *Journal of Communication* 43, no. 4 (1993): 51-59; Philip Schlesinger, "Rethinking the Sociology of Journalism: Source Strategies and the Limits of Media-Centrism," in *Public Communication: The New Imperatives*, ed. Marjorie Ferguson (London: Sage, 1990), 61-85; Gadi Wolfsfeld, *Media and Political Conflict: News from the Middle East* (Cambridge: Cambridge University Press, 1997).

21. E. E. Schattschneider, *The Semisovereign People* (New York: Holt, Rinehart, and Winston, 1960).

22. Kingdon, *Agendas*, 90-115.

23. Judith A. Aks, William Haltom, and Michael McCann, "The Political Kidnapping of Stella Liebeck: A Case Study of Media Coverage of Punitive Damages," paper presented at the annual meeting of the Western Political Science Association, Tucson, Arizona, March 13-15, 1997; Joel Best, *Images of Issues* (New York: Aldine de Gruyter, 1998); Stephen Hilgartner and Charles L. Bosk, "The Rise and Fall of Social Problems: A Public Arenas Model," *American Journal of Sociology* 94, no. 1 (1988): 53-78; Regina Lawrence, *The Politics of Force: The Media, Policy Discourse, and the Construction of Police Brutality* (Berkeley: University of California Press, 2000).

24. S. Hall, C. Critcher, T. Jefferson, J. Clarke, and B. Roberts, *Policing the Crisis: Mugging, the State, and Law and Order* (London: Macmillan, 1978).

25. Harvey Molotch and Marilyn Lester, "Accidental News: The Great Oil Spill as Local Occurrence and National Event," *American Journal of Sociology* 81, no. 2 (1974): 235-61.

26. For the sake of simplicity, we fold together under the term "accidental event" two kinds of events that Molotch and Lester distinguish: "scandals" and "accidents." Scandals, in their formulation, are public events arising out of activities purposely undertaken but not intended for public consumption. Thus, even events that are privately intentional, such as the official who sexually harasses a coworker, may not be intended as public events. In our formulation, the term "accidental" refers less to the particular characteristics of an occurrence than to its status as a public event; accidental events are neither intended occurrences nor meant to be communicated to a public audience.

27. See, for example, Daniel Boorstin, *The Image: A Guide to Pseudo-Events in America* (New York: Vintage, 1992).

28. In this case, we use the term "disaster" advisedly. Environmental accidents such as oil spills, refinery and chemical plant fires and explosions, and the like are sometimes difficult to depict as "disasters" because they sometimes fail to kill anyone or do property damage beyond the immediate area of the accident. Of course, the *Exxon Valdez*'s effects extended beyond the ship, but the scope and nature of those ill effects are still a topic of considerable debate; thus there can not as yet be any consensus that the spill was a "disaster." As one Alaska state senator told us, in so many words, the spill was not a disaster because no one was killed.

29. W. Lance Bennett and Regina G. Lawrence, "News Icons and the Main-streaming of Social Change," *Journal of Communication* 45 (1995): 20-39.

30. George Hackett, "Environmental Politics," *Newsweek*, 17 April 1989, 18.

31. Geoffrey Cowley and Lynda Wright, "Dead Otters, Silent Ducks," *Newsweek*, 24 April 1989, 70.

32. E. J. Dionne Jr., "Big Oil Spill Leaves Its Mark on Politics of Environment," *New York Times*, 3 April 1989, A1.

33. Conrad Smith, "News Sources and Power Elites in Newspaper Coverage of the *Exxon Valdez* Oil Spill," paper presented to the Association for Education in Journalism and Mass Communication, Boston, 1991. See also Conrad Smith, *Media and Apocalypse: News Coverage of the Yellowstone Forest Fires,* Exxon Valdez *Oil Spill, and Loma Prieta Earthquake* (Westport, Conn.: Greenwood Press, 1992).

34. George J. Church, "The Big Spill," *Time,* 10 April 1989, 38.

35. Jerry Adler and Lynda Wright, "One Way to End a Career," *Newsweek*, 29 May 1989, 52.

36. Lemonick, "The Two Alaskas."

37. Church, "The Big Spill."

38. The Permanent Fund is a fund into which oil royalties are deposited. Because of oil royalties and handsome investment profits, the fund's value is about $20 billion. A portion of the earnings on this fund is paid to Alaska residents each year—the 1998 dividend was about $1,500. The dividend program was designed to give Alaskans a stake in the fund so that it would not become a source of excess funds for extravagant state spending during the flush years of the oil boom. Indeed, the dividend has recently pumped money into a stagnant Alaska economy that has been severely damaged by depressed oil prices. The connection between the dividend and oil revenues is strong in Alaskans' minds, and reinforces widely held beliefs there of the dependence of Alaska on the oil industry. Revenue from oil also accounts for about 85 percent of Alaska's state budget, and Alaskans pay no state sales tax and no state income tax.

39. See, for example, John H. Cushman Jr., "Alaska Delegation Pushes Agenda of Development," *New York Times*, 13 September 1998, 46.

40. Nash, *Wilderness and the American Mind*, 299.

41. Dionne, "Big Oil Leaves Its Mark."

42. Lemonick, "The Two Alaskas."

43. Hackett, "Environmental Politics."

44. Thomas Birkland, "Focusing Events, Mobilization, and Agenda Setting," *Journal of Public Policy* 18, no. 3 (1998): 53-74.

45. Molotch and Lester, "Accidental News"; Bennett and Lawrence, "News Icons"; Lawrence, *Politics of Force.*

Contributors

STEVEN BIEL is Director of Studies and Lecturer in History and Literature at Harvard University. He is the author of *Down with the Old Canoe: A Cultural History of the* Titanic *Disaster* (W. W. Norton, 1996) and *Independent Intellectuals in the United States, 1910-1945* (New York University Press, 1992), and the editor of *Titanica: The Disaster of the Century in Poetry, Song, and Prose* (W. W. Norton, 1998).

THOMAS A. BIRKLAND is an associate professor of political science and public administration and policy in the Nelson A. Rockefeller College of Public Affairs and Policy at the State University of New York at Albany. He lived in Anchorage from 1970 to 1980, and part-time from 1981 to 1984. His book, *After Disaster: Agenda Setting, Public Policy, and Focusing Events*, was published in 1997 by Georgetown University Press.

PATRICIA BELLIS BIXEL is an assistant professor of history at Maine Maritime Academy. She is co-author of *Galveston and the 1900 Storm: Catastrophe and Catalyst* (University of Texas Press, 2000).

DUANE A. GILL is a professor of sociology in the Social Science Research Center and Department of Sociology, Anthropology and Social Work at Mississippi State University. He is co-editor of *The* Exxon Valdez *Disaster: Readings on a Modern Social Problem* (Kendall/Hunt, 1997). He currently serves on the Minerals Management Service Outer Continental Shelf Scientific Committee and the Gulf of Mexico Fisheries Management Council Social and Economic Panel.

ANDREW HAZUCHA is an assistant professor of English at Carson-Newman College, where he teaches courses in eighteenth- and nineteenth-century British literature. He is currently working on a study of William Wordsworth's environmental prose writings.

SHEILA HONES is an associate professor in the Department of Area Studies in the Graduate School of Arts and Sciences at the University of Tokyo. Her main field is North American Studies, particularly American literature and cultural geography. She has published two other essays on *The Atlantic Monthly*.

ANN LARABEE, an associate professor of American Thought and Language at Michigan State University, is the author of *Decade of Disaster* (University of Illinois Press, 2000), as well as numerous articles on technological disaster. Her work on the *Challenger* explosion was awarded *Postmodern Culture Journal*'s Electronic Text Award.

REGINA G. LAWRENCE is an assistant professor in the Division of Political Science at Portland State University in Portland, Oregon. Her research interests are in political communication, and particularly in the role of dramatic events in news coverage of public policy issues. Her book, *The Politics of Force: The Media, Policy Discourse, and the Construction of Police Brutality*, was published by the University of California Press in 2000.

MATTHEW MULCAHY is an assistant professor of history at Loyola College in Baltimore. He received his Ph.D. from the University of Minnesota and is working on a book titled *Melancholy and Fatal Calamities: Natural Disasters and Colonial Society in the English Greater Caribbean, 1607–1786*.

J. STEVEN PICOU is professor of sociology and Chair of the Department of Sociology and Anthropology at the University of South Alabama. He is the co-author of *American Sociology: Theoretical and Methodological Structure* (University Press of America, 1981), co-editor of *The Exxon Valdez Disaster: Readings on a Modern Social Problem* (Kendall/ Hunt, 1997), and author of numerous articles. He currently serves on a National Academy of Sciences Committee to review the Gulf of Alaska Ecosystem Monitoring Program.

KEVIN ROZARIO is an assistant professor in the American Studies program at Smith College. He earned his Ph.D. in history from Yale University and has previously taught at Oberlin and Wellesley colleges. He is currently working on a book called *Nature's Evil Dreams: Disaster and the Making of Modern America*.

RALPH JAMES SAVARESE is an assistant professor of American literature and creative writing at Grinnell College. He is at work on a book entitled *We'll Be In the Ground Shortly: Commercial Aviation Disasters and Commodity Culture*.

CARL SMITH is Franklyn Bliss Snyder Professor of American Studies and English, and professor of history, at Northwestern University. He is the author of *Urban Disorder and the Shape of Belief: The Great Chicago Fire, the Haymarket Bomb, and the Model Town of Pullman* (University of Chicago Press, 1995) and *Chicago and the American Literary Imagination, 1880-1920* (University of Chicago Press, 1984). He is the curator of the online historical exhibitions, *The Great Chicago Fire and the Web of Memory* (http://www.chicagohistory.org/fire) and *The Dramas of Haymarket* (http://www.chicagohistory.org/dramas), which were produced in 1996 and 2000 by the Chicago Historical Society and Academic Technologies at Northwestern University.

TED STEINBERG is professor of history and law at Case Western Reserve University in Cleveland, Ohio. He is the author of *Acts of God: The Unnatural History of Natural Disaster in America* (New York: Oxford University Press, 2000) and *Down to Earth: Nature's Role in American History* (Oxford University Press, forthcoming).

ALAN TAYLOR teaches the history of early America and the American West at the University of California at Davis. He is the author of *Liberty Men and Great Proprietors: The Revolutionary Settlement on the Maine Frontier, 1760-1820* (University of North Carolina Press, 1990) and *William Cooper's Town: Power and Persuasion on the Frontier of the Early American Republic* (Alfred A. Knopf, 1995), which was awarded the New York State Historical Association Manuscript Award, the Bancroft Prize, and the Pulitzer Prize in history.

Permissions

We gratefully acknowledge those who have given us permission to reprint the following:

Steven Biel, "'Unknown and Unsung': Feminist, African American, and Radical Responses to the *Titanic* Disaster," from Steven Biel, *Down with the Old Canoe: A Cultural History of the* Titanic *Disaster* (New York: W. W. Norton, 1996). Copyright 1996 by Steven Biel. Used by permission of W. W. Norton & Company, Inc.

Patricia Bellis Bixel and Elizabeth Hayes Turner, "Everything that Mortal Men Can Do: Protecting Galveston Island," from Patricia Bellis Bixel and Elizabeth Hayes Turner, *Galveston and the 1900 Storm: Catastrophe and Catalyst* (Austin: University of Texas Press, 2000). Copyright 2000. By permission of the University of Texas Press.

Lawrence Ferlinghetti, "Reading Yeats I Do Not Think," from *Pictures of the Gone World*. Used by permission of City Lights Books.

Joe Hill, "Workers of the World, Awaken," from *The I.W.W. Songbook*. Used by permission of Industrial Workers of the World, 103 W. Michigan Avenue, Ypsilanti, Michigan 48197.

Ann Larabee, "Lifeboat Ethics," from Ann Larabee, *Decade of Disaster* (Champaign: University of Illinois Press, 2000). Copyright 2000 by the Board of Trustees of the University of Illinois. Used by permission of the University of Illinois Press.

J. Steven Picou and Duane A. Gill, "The Day the Water Died: The *Exxon Valdez* Disaster and Indigenous Culture," from J. Steven Picou, Duane A. Gill, and Maurie J. Cohen, *The* Exxon Valdez *Disaster: Readings on a*

Modern Social Problem (Dubuque, Iowa: Kendall/Hunt Publishing Company, 1999). Copyright 1999. Used by permission.

Carl Smith, "Trial by Fire," from Carl Smith, *Urban Disorder and the Shape of Belief: The Great Chicago Fire, the Haymarket Bomb, and the Model Town of Pullman* (Chicago: University of Chicago Press, 1995). Copyright 1995 by Carl Smith.

Ted Steinberg, "Smoke and Mirrors: The San Francisco Earthquake and Seismic Denial," from Theodore Steinburg, *Acts of God: The Unnatural History of Natural Disaster in America* (New York: Oxford University Press, 2000). Copyright 2000 by Theodore Steinberg. Used by permission of Oxford University Press, Inc.

Alan Taylor, "'The Hungry Year': 1789 on the Northern Border of Revolutionary America," from *Dreadful Visitations*, ed. Alessa Johns (New York: Routledge, 1999). Copyright 1999 from *Dreadful Visitations* by Alessa Johns. Reproduced by permission of Taylor & Francis, Inc./ Routledge, Inc., http://www.routledge-ny.com.

Index